NGOs and Human Rights

Pennsylvania Studies in Human Rights

Bert B. Lockwood, Jr., Series Editor

A complete list of books in the series
is available from the publisher.

NGOs and Human Rights

Promise and Performance

Edited by
CLAUDE E. WELCH, JR.

PENN

University of Pennsylvania Press

Philadelphia

10 9 8 7 6 5 4 3 2 1

Published by
University of Pennsylvania Press
Philadelphia, Pennsylvania 19104-4011

Library of Congress Cataloging-in-Publication Data
NGOs and human rights : promise and performance /
edited by Claude E. Welch, Jr.
p.   cm. — (Pennsylvania studies in human rights)
Includes bibliographical references and index.
ISBN 0-8122-3569-X (cloth : alk. paper)
1. Human rights.   2. Non-governmental organizations.
I. Welch, Claude Emerson.   II. Series.
JC571 .N485   2000
323—dc21   00-033798

Contents

List of Acronyms   vii

Introduction
Claude E. Welch, Jr.   1

Part I. Civil and Political Rights: The "Classic" Northern Paradigm

1. Assessing the Effectiveness of International Human Rights NGOs: Amnesty International
Morton E. Winston   25

2. "A Calendar of Abuses": Amnesty International's Campaign on Guatemala
Ann Marie Clark   55

3. Human Rights Watch: An Overview
Widney Brown   72

4. Amnesty International and Human Rights Watch: A Comparison
Claude E. Welch, Jr.   85

5. The Role of the International Commission of Jurists
Nathalie Prouvez and Nicolas M. L. Bovay   119

6. The International Human Rights Law Group: Human Rights and Access to Justice in Postconflict Environments
Mark K. Bromley   141

7. Human Rights International NGOs: A Critical Evaluation
Makau Mutua   151

Part II. Economic, Social, and Cultural Rights: An Increasingly Significant Emphasis

8. FoodFirst Information and Action Network
Brigitte Hamm   167

9. Action for Development in Uganda
Susan Dicklitch   182

10. Evaluating Development-Oriented NGOs
T. Jeffrey Scott   204

Part III. Analyzing and Enhancing Effectiveness

11. Measuring the Impact of Human Rights Organizations
David L. Cingranelli and David L. Richards   225

12. The Internet: One More Tool in the Struggle for Human Rights
Laurie S. Wiseberg   238

13. The Role of the Ford Foundation
William D. Carmichael   248

Conclusion
Claude E. Welch, Jr.   261

List of Contributors   281

Index   283

Acknowledgments   291

Acronyms

ACFODE	Action for Development (Uganda)
ACHPR	African Commission on Human and Peoples' Rights
ACLU	American Civil Liberties Union (United States)
ACTV	African Center for Rehabilitation and Treatment of Torture Victims (Uganda)
ADB	African Development Bank
AGM	Annual General Meeting (Amnesty International)
AI	Amnesty International
AIUSA	Amnesty International United States of America
ANC	African National Congress (South Africa)
APC	Association of Progressive Communicators
CALDH	Centro de Acción Legal y Derechos Humanos (Center for Legal and Human Rights Action, Guatemala)
CALS	Centre for Applied Legal Studies (South Africa)
CDDH	Steering Committee on Human Rights (Council of Europe)
CEDAW	Convention on the Elimination of All Forms of Discrimination Against Women
CEH	Comisión para el Esclarecemiento Histórico (Commission for Historical Clarification, Guatemala)
CERJ	Consejo de Comunidades Étnicas "Runujel Junam" (Council of Ethnic Communities "We Are All Equal," Guatemala)
CESCR	Committee on Economic, Social, and Cultural Rights
CIA	Central Intelligence Agency (United States)
CIJL	Centre for the Independence of Judges and Lawyers
CONAVIGUA	Coordinadora Nacional de Viudas de Guatemala (National Coordinating Committee of Guatemalan Widows, Guatemala)
DANIDA	Danish International Development Agency (Denmark)
DED	Deutsche Entwicklungsdienst (German Development Service, Germany)

DENIVA	Development Network of Indigenous Voluntary Associations (Uganda)
DFID	Department for International Development (Great Britain)
DH-DEV	Committee of Experts on Developments in Human Rights (Council of Europe)
ECHR	European Convention on Human Rights
ECOSOC	Economic and Social Council (United Nations)
EKD	Evangelische Kirche Deutschlands (German Evangelical Church)
ESC	European Social Charter
EU	European Union
FAD	Foundation for African Development
FAO	Food and Agriculture Organization (United Nations)
FAWE	Forum for Women Educationalists (Uganda)
FGM	female genital mutilation
FHRI	Foundation for Human Rights Initiative (Uganda)
FIAN	FoodFirst Information and Action Network (Germany)
FIDA	Federación Internationale des Abogadas (Association of Women Lawyers)
FIDH	Fédération internationale des droits de l'homme (International Federation of Human Rights, France)
FOPROMU	Forum for Promotion of Movement Politics in Uganda
GAM	Grupo Apoyo Mutual (Mutual Support Group for Relatives of the Disappeared, Guatemala)
GATT	General Agreement on Trade and Tariffs
GONGO	government-organized non-governmental organization
HIVOS	Humanist Institute for Co-operation with Development (Uganda)
HRI	Human Rights Internet (Canada)
HRW	Human Rights Watch (United States)
HURINET	Human Rights Network (Uganda)
IACHR	Inter-American Commission on Human Rights
IC	International Council (FIAN)
ICC	International Criminal Court
ICCPR	International Covenant on Civil and Political Rights
ICESCR	International Covenant on Economic, Social, and Cultural Rights
ICJ	International Commission of Jurists
ICRC	International Committee of the Red Cross
ICM	International Council Meeting (Amnesty International)
IDA	international development agency
IEC	International Executive Committee (Amnesty International, FIAN International)
IFAD	International Fund for Agricultural Development
IFI	international financial institution

IGC	International Global Communications
IGO	intergovernmental organization
IHRLG	International Human Rights Law Group (United States)
IHRNGO	international human rights nongovernmental organization
ILHR	International League for Human Rights (United States)
ILO	International Labor Organization
IMF	International Monetary Fund
INGO	international nongovernmental organization
IS	International Secretariat (Amnesty International, FIAN International)
KAF	Konrad Adenauer Foundation (Germany)
LC	Local Council (Uganda)
LCHR	Lawyers Committee for Human Rights (United States)
LDF	Legal Defense and Educational Fund (United States)
LRA	Lord's Resistance Army (Uganda)
LRT	Legal Resources Trust (South Africa)
MSA	Mokken scale analysis
MAI	Multilateral Agreement on Investment
NAACP	National Association for the Advancement of Colored People (United States)
NAFTA	North American Free Trade Agreement
NATO	North Atlantic Treaty Organization
NAWOU	National Association of Women's Organizations of Uganda
NED	National Endowment for Democracy (United States)
NGO	nongovernmental organization
NOCEM	National Organization for Civic Education and Election Monitoring (Uganda)
NOVIB	Nederlandse Organisatie Voor Internationale Ontwikkelingssamenwerking (Dutch Organization for International Development Cooperation, Netherlands)
NURRU	Network of Ugandan Researchers and Research Users
OAS	Organization of American States
OAU	Organization of African Unity
ODHAG	Oficina de Derechos Humanos del Arzobispado de Guatemala (Human Rights Office of the Archbishop of Guatemala, Guatemala)
ODS	Optical Disk System (United Nations)
OECD	Organization for Economic Cooperation and Development
POC	prisoner of conscience (Amnesty International)
PSA	public service announcement
PTS	Political Terror Scale
QUANGO	quasi-NGO
SIDA	Swedish International Development Agency

TASO	The AIDS Service Organization (Uganda)
TNC	transnational corporation
UDHR	Universal Declaration of Human Rights
UHRA	Uganda Human Rights Activists (Uganda)
UHRC	Uganda Human Rights Commission (Uganda)
UNESCO	United Nations Educational, Scientific, and Cultural Organization
UNGA	United Nations General Assembly
UNHCHR	United Nations High Commissioner for Human Rights
UNHCR	United Nations High Commission for Refugees
UNIFEM	United Nations Development Fund for Women
UPAF	Uganda Prisoners' Aid Foundation
URDT	Rural Development and Training Program (Uganda)
USAID	United States Agency for International Development
UWFCT	Uganda Women's Finance and Credit Trust
VDPA	Vienna Declaration and Programme of Action
VVAF	Vietnam Veterans of America Foundation
WESHR	Women's Economic and Social Human Rights Index
WFP	World Food Programme
WOLA	Washington Office on Latin America (United States)
WTO	World Trade Organization

Introduction

Claude E. Welch, Jr.

Five Issues for NGO Strategists

The proliferation of nongovernmental organizations is one the most striking features of the contemporary world. The nongovernmental sector has exploded since World War II, its curve of growth seemingly exponential. According to the Union of International Associations, the number of "conventional" NGOs stood at 973 in 1956, a figure that more than doubled in 1968 to 1,899, doubled again by 1981 to 4,265, and by 1996 had reached 5,471.[1]

This historical dimension is important. Nonstate actors tiptoed onto the international stage a century ago, playing small roles, their asides to the audience of world public opinion having limited impact on the major actors, which were governments. The NGOs, as bit players, were rarely written into the scripts of global and domestic politics, with the major exception of the International Committee of the Red Cross. But by the start of the twenty-first century, nongovernmental organizations were definitely part of the entire production. They distributed disaster relief and development aid, consulted openly with governments about the wording of international treaties, increasingly monitored governments' performance, and received increasing academic study.

It is time for careful assessment of their success. How well have human rights NGOs performed the tasks they have established for themselves?

NGOs and Human Rights: Promise and Performance seeks to answer five simple—or perhaps not so simple—questions:

What are the chief goals of human rights NGOs?
Who sets these goals, and how?
What strategies are utilized to achieve these goals?
What resources are necessary to implement these strategies successfully?
How is "success" or "effectiveness" defined and determined by the NGOs, their funders, and their critics?

Each of these questions can be broken down, in turn, into more discrete issues.

Chief goals. Does a particular NGO have a clear, single, overarching purpose or goal, or does it pursue several loosely linked objectives? Are the major goals explicit in the NGO's mandate or constitution, or implicit in the ways in which it operates? Are these objectives relatively rigid, requiring a complex process of adoption or amendment, or are they relatively fungible, readily and rapidly adapted to changing circumstances? In a related fashion, are the goals broadly or narrowly stated?

Establishing and revising goals. In the words of a classic political question, who rules? Does the NGO set its own objectives internally, or are these in effect dictated externally? Who among the internal decision makers are most important in establishing goals: the founder(s), the top-ranking staff, the board of directors, or the members? Which among the external influences may be most significant in determining objectives: the major funder(s), the persons being served, the government under whose aegis the NGO operates, or another? If the organization is not adequately pursuing goals desired by a significant segment, do these persons create a new organization, or are they more likely to work within the existing framework, despite its inadequacies?

Strategies. How does the NGO translate relatively broad goals or objectives into specific campaigns and actions? Who carries out this translation, and with what types of information? Given the alternative frameworks suggested by scholars of NGOs, which formulation best captures the reality of the NGO world?

Resources. Broadly speaking, do actually or potentially available funds determine the organization's strategies, or are these strategies shaped prior to seeking specific resources? If the NGO relies heavily on a single major source of funds, how do the leaders cope with the possible loss of these funds? If there are many competitors for recognition and resources, how does the NGO establish what in the commercial world would be called product recognition? From the side of the donor(s), who gives and why? And how much is necessary for the organization to be truly effective?

Assessing effectiveness. What correlation is there between claimed and "real" effectiveness? Is it possible to compare an organization's strategic plan—what it claims it would do, given specific resources—with actual results? Given the multicausality of political events, what effects have human rights NGOs actually had when (say) a widely publicized prisoner of conscience is released, when a government ratifies an international human rights convention, or when abusive police behavior toward members of a particular group diminishes? Ultimately, should we be more persuaded by the successes that NGOs have claimed, or did they contribute only marginally to changes that would have occurred "naturally"? Even if NGOs have succeeded in reaching their goals, have they achieved their ultimately intended effects?

Questions of this sort confront all advocacy organizations. For organizations in the private sector, the metrics of success seem clear: profitability, rate of growth, product innovation, market share, and the like. For organizations in the public sector, however, calculations about desired outcomes are both more complex and less clear. Claims of success cannot readily be verified. Governments may be unlikely to attribute policy change to NGO pressure; few sovereign entities willingly admit that a small domestic group of citizens, or even a large external group of noncitizens, has succeeded with its pressure. At the same time, however, NGOs must claim that diminished human rights abuses have resulted from their actions, in order to justify their value to members and supporters. Official denials of NGOs' impact by some governments go hand in hand with NGOs' claims of effectiveness. Yet other governments work closely with human rights groups in setting agendas and standards, as well as in monitoring states' performance. Only by looking directly at the goals and actions of NGOs can their success be determined.

What Human Rights NGOs Are Supposed to Do

As advocacy organizations, human rights NGOs have traditionally concentrated their efforts on a few crucial areas: working with (or against) governments in developing agendas for action; in standard setting (that is, establishing international norms for state behavior, set forth in legally binding treaties that have been negotiated and ratified by governments); in preparing and providing information about abuses based on research; in lobbying officials and media; and in providing direct assistance to victims of human rights abuses. Each of these objectives merits a few sentences, looking selectively at recent publications.

Standard Setting

The first crucial area of NGO activity has been standard setting for human rights, an area that, in traditional terms of sovereignty, belongs exclusively to governments. There are some historical precedents for involving nonstate actors in helping devise treaties. In the main, however, human rights NGOs remained on the sidelines until after World War II, and in crucial respects until the 1980s, when the diminution of Cold War tensions and the decline of bureaucratic-authoritarian governments opened additional political space for NGOs. A few highlights must be mentioned.

In the closing days of World War II, several American NGOs persuaded the U.S. delegation to refer explicitly to human rights in the Charter of the United Nations, which was then being drafted.[2]

The landmark 1948 Universal Declaration of Human Rights also benefited from NGO involvement. In the words of former secretary-general U Thant of the UN, "during 1947 and 1948, non-governmental organizations participated at every stage in the strenuous process of preparing the [UDHR]."[3]

Thanks to its influential Campaign for the Abolition of Torture, Amnesty International (AI) figured prominently during the early 1970s in building global understanding of torture. The Declaration on the Protection of All Persons from Being Subjected to Torture and Other Cruel, Inhuman or Degrading Treatment or Punishment, unanimously adopted by the UN General Assembly in 1975, bore many hallmarks of AI's involvement.[4]

In the late 1970s, organizations concerned with children worked closely with sympathetic governments in transforming a nonbinding declaration into the legally binding Convention on the Rights of the Child. Much of the treaty's language came directly from a coalition of NGOs led by Defence of Children International.[5]

In 1992, the Rio treaty established a Council on Sustainable Development, in which NGOs would sit on an equal basis with governments, having previously recommended substantial parts of the biodiversity treaty.[6]

The International Campaign to Ban Landmines, winner of the 1998 Nobel Peace Prize, not only persuaded governments to lead the struggle against antagonistic major powers, but also gained the support of more than 1,200 NGOs in pressing for the Convention on the Prohibition, Stockpiling, Production and Transfer of Anti-Personnel Mines and on Their Destruction (the Ottawa Convention).[7]

An increasing number of scholars have examined this accelerating rate of NGO involvement in standard setting. They show how human rights groups worked with sympathetic governments to bring effective texts to drafting conferences. This task is particularly difficult, since treaty drafting is based on achieving consensus. International negotiations involve give-and-take, compromises over wording that will satisfy an incredible variety of states. NGOs have provided legal or other technical expertise, in addition to mobilizing public opinion.

Ethan Nadelmann concentrated on the evolution of norms, with specific attention to "global prohibition regimes," and with valuable details from the pre–World War II period.[8] His survey—utilizing piracy and privateering, slavery and the slave trade, fugitives beyond borders, international drug trafficking, prostitution, and the killing of whales and elephants—showed an intermingling of actions by states with pressures by citizen organizations. The five successive stages are as follows:

The targeted activity is considered entirely legitimate under certain conditions and with respect to certain groups of people; states are often the principal protagonists.

"Moral entrepreneurs" (including international legal scholars, religious groups, and others) seek to redefine the activity as both a problem and an evil.

Proponents of global bans start to press for the suppression and criminalization of the particular activity, with the eventual drafting of international conventions.

A global prohibition regime comes into existence, while, nationally, the activity becomes the subject of criminal laws and police action throughout much of the world.

Finally—and in the cases studied by Nadelmann, only from the nineteenth century on —the scope of the proscribed activity is greatly reduced, since states have largely "eliminated or neutralized the effective vacuums of sovereign authority, both on land and sea, on which regime dissenters depended for their freedom and sanctuary."

Ann Marie Clark, a contributor to this volume, focused on Amnesty International's role in helping bring torture, disappearances, and extrajudicial execution to global attention.[9] As a pioneering organization, AI took a role in drafting legally binding treaties. It developed many techniques now widely employed by human rights NGOs, such as utilizing direct letter-writing campaigns. From its outset, Clark emphasized, Amnesty International stressed principles, political impartiality, and attention to facts. "Principled norms" emerge as a result of the pressure from human rights NGOs on governments. Thus, nongovernmental organizations now participate in an area which states have long held as centrally important to their sovereign nature, namely the establishment of binding agreements.

Cynthia Price Cohen—herself a major contributor to the Convention on the Rights of the Child—analyzed how a coalition of NGOs, headed by Defence of Children International, substantially influenced the language of the 1989 convention.[10] In a similar fashion, NGOs worked with sympathetic governments and mobilized international public opinion effectively, leading in a surprisingly brief time to significant new restrictions on landmines.[11]

In conclusion, to the extent NGOs participated in drafting new standards for states' actions, they did so initially largely as experts, treating issues as technical rather than political. This role increased and became more political as NGOs gained legitimacy, shaped international public opinion, and formed coalitions with sympathetic governments. Through increased cooperation, rights-protective language could be introduced and adopted at the conferences drafting new international treaties.

Providing Information

Scholars concur that information gathering, verification, and dissemination is one goal —and perhaps the central one—of human rights NGOs.

William Korey's recent massive book includes numerous examples of, and quotations about, crucial NGO information-gathering efforts.[12] For example, "without [the flow of information, documentation, and data from] NGOs, the entire human rights implementation system at the UN would come to a halt."[13] NGOs "performed the critical function of the mechanism [UN working groups or special rapporteurs]—acquiring and verifying information on human rights abridgements . . . the overwhelming bulk of the 'credible and reliable' information has been and is provided by NGOs."[14] These citations are typical. Later chapters in this book provide ample additional evidence of this NGO goal, demonstrating the adage about the pen being mightier than the sword.

Lobbying

NGOs have consistently worked both with and against governments. Cooperation comes in large part through treaty drafting, as already noted. But to get to that stage, NGOs must lobby, in order to build coalitions of support with fellow NGOs and with sympathetic states. They lobby for ratification, then monitor performance—both items to which I shall return shortly.

To reach this point, nongovernment organizations engage in campaigns of public information. Take, as examples, efforts to condemn apartheid, to publicize limits on freedom of expression in Eastern Europe, to demonstrate the prevalence of torture, or to show the bloody civilian casualty consequences of landmines. All were the subjects of major international campaigns led by NGOs. They lobbied to show how governments' actions within their own boundaries—where they supposedly exercised sovereign control—posed threats internationally and internally. The information NGOs so sedulously gather, verify, and disseminate is their major weapon in lobbying governments to change policies.

Providing Assistance

Publicizing abuses of human rights does not go far enough; the victims deserve help. The searchlight of publicity Amnesty International could focus on prisoners of conscience was complemented by a fund to assist victims. Scores of human rights NGOs have offered legal assistance to the poor or oppressed. And, on a far larger scale, NGOs focused on relief and development have increasingly recognized that simple provision of emergency assistance should be complemented by concerted efforts to change governments' rights-abusive policies. The result has been greater cooperation between NGOs concerned with humanitarian assistance and human rights NGOs, a theme explored in preliminary fashion later in this book.

How NGOs Operate

I turn in this section, more briefly, to how NGOs review and revise their goals, what strategies they follow, how they obtain resources, and how they define and measure success.

Goal Setting

As I have already noted, human rights NGOs pursue a wide variety of goals. But how are these established and revised?

For some of these organizations, the equivalent of institutional biographies have been published. Anyone interested in the International Commission of Jurists[15] or Amnesty International can consult full-length books. Korey's well-informed, fact-laden book should be read by any person concerned with human rights.[16] Although his emphasis rests heavily on U.S.-based human rights NGOs (with the exceptions of Amnesty International and the International Commission of Jurists),[17] Korey has provided a valuable reference. Especially useful are his insights into the leadership of Amnesty International and Human Rights Watch, the two best funded and most influential among contemporary human rights NGOs.

Institutional biographies help us understand who sets the goals, how these goals are revised, what resources are obtained and how, and how "success" is defined and measured. They differ from the self-congratulatory spiels NGOs put on their Web sites or publish in their campaign and fund-raising literature. Institutional biographies take us inside specific organizations, answering crucial questions about leadership in dispassionate, analytical terms. Alas, such studies seem out of fashion, despite their value. For example, some U.S.-based private foundations received critical attention in the 1970s and early 1980s, notably in relation to American foreign policy; there were also analyses in the early 1990s of CARE and Oxfam, two organizations examined in a later chapter.[18] It is time to revitalize the genre. Foundations now disburse hundreds of millions of dollars more in grants than a few decades back. The choices their leaders make and their interactions with human rights NGOs remain stories largely untold. For it is in the interaction of goals, leadership, and resources that strategies are developed, implemented, and assessed.

Strategies

NGOs and Human Rights: Promise and Performance deals with issues at the forefront of much contemporary social science. We live in a world in which governments' once sovereign powers have been challenged increasingly by NGOs, multinational corporations, emerging international public opinion, international financial institutions, and many others. Globalization is a fact of twenty-first-century life, with immense implications for all types of groups. And, for human rights organizations, networks of issues and electronic connections provide crucial links. The strategies NGOs adopt are not isolated but interactive.

Take, for example, links among public interest groups in order to change state behavior and popular attitudes. Margaret Keck and Kathryn Sikkink emphasize the significance of transnational advocacy networks, a complex minuet of governments and NGOs that, over time, have transformed public opinion and created at least the rudiments of international promotion and protection systems for human rights.[19] The four campaigns they summarize in *Activists Beyond Borders: Advocacy Networks in International Politics* provide interesting historical examples. Each started "with an idea that was almost unimaginable, even by its early proponents."[20] These cases include

- International pressures for the abolition of slavery in the United States, 1833–65, a movement that was a "notable success,"[21] in which transnational linkage politics proved valuable.

- The international movement for woman suffrage, which led to "surprisingly rapid results."[22]
- The campaign against foot-binding in China from 1874 to 1911, which similarly showed "very rapid progress" as well as "a pattern characteristic of modern networks, where both foreign and domestic actors were crucial to the success of the campaign."[23]
- Far less successful, the campaign against female circumcision in Kenya from 1923 to 1941, in which this form of violence against women (to use the contemporary term) became associated with Kikuyu nationalism. The campaign to abolish female circumcision "became a symbol for colonial attempts to impose outside values and rules upon the population."[24]

Keck and Sikkink carry their comparisons into three contemporary international networks as well: human rights, environmentalism, and women's issues. Here the authors provide numerous insights on the interaction of NGOs and governments, drawn from interviews and wide reading. Among their observations that are highly relevant to this chapter and book:

NGOs provide 85 percent of the information provided to the UN Centre for Human Rights, according to former director Theo Van Boven.[25]

Field officers of major foundations came into conflict with their headquarters in urging support for human rights NGOs, "since human rights work was often viewed as attacking the state rather than strengthening it."[26]

Indirect pressure can be directed against repressive governments by NGOs' providing information about abuses directly to human rights officers in U.S. embassies.[27]

In Argentina and Mexico, "foreign governments placed pressure on human rights violators only *after* nongovernmental actors had identified, documented, and denounced human rights violations."[28]

Keck and Sikkink also distinguish among four types of political action NGOs pursue. Their delineation of "information politics," "symbolic politics," "linkage politics," and "accountability politics" has, I believe, extraordinary explanatory power. Later chapters in this book, particularly that on Amnesty International by Morton E. Winston, draw upon the valuable framework of *Activists Beyond Borders*.

In his institutional biography of the International Commission of Jurists (ICJ), one of the very few book-length studies of an NGO, Howard Tolley traced a fascinating history.[29] The ICJ has functioned like other human rights NGOs in serving as "an opinion tribunal that induces compliance by shaming the guilty."[30] Nongovernmental organizations cannot enforce human rights; states are responsible. Yet, Tolley observes that NGOs "contribute significantly to the rudimentary implementation and enforcement of international human rights law."[31] The ICJ's casework for individual victims (nearly six hundred interventions in more than a hundred countries), its publicity about gross violations (reports on about ten governments per year through its *Review*, and more than twenty mission reports in the 1970–90 period), and its efforts to activate United Nations action in areas related to the rule of law, are all significant. Tolley concludes that NGOs "do not pose a serious threat to state sovereignty, but their activities have affected world politics. . . . The ICJ has become as important to world politics and international law as domestic interest groups are to the U.S. legislature, judiciary and executive."[32] Rule of law programs developed by the International Commission of Jurists are examined in Chapter 5.

In an earlier work, focused on locally based human rights organizations in sub-Saharan Africa,[33] I hypothesized that NGO performance was affected by four variables: financial resources, popular backing/membership, societal diversity, and political space available to NGOs. This volume was organized mnemonically in terms of six different strategies pursued by NGOs, which I deemed the three Es (education, enforcement, and empowerment) and the three Ds (documentation, democratization, and development). My emphasis lay on sub-Saharan Africa, with attention given primarily to Ethiopia, Namibia, Nigeria, and Senegal. I gave little attention to the large, mostly Western-based international human rights NGOs, such as Amnesty International or Human Rights Watch, that have absorbed far more scholarly attention,[34] preferring instead to concentrate on the far less known and studied indigenous organizations.[35] The six strategies seem widely applicable. On the other hand, the four variables now appear limited. Quality of leadership, albeit difficult to define and very complex to measure save with twenty-twenty hindsight, affects how well NGOs achieve their goals.

Since their founding, Amnesty International, Human Rights Watch, and other significant human rights groups have stressed research. Careful, clear, and convincing documentation of abuses establishes their credibility. What government officials deny, NGOs can demonstrate. The "official story" has its counterpart in unofficial fact, as uncovered and confirmed by organizations. If knowledge is power, human rights NGOs have some claim. Almost without exception, they lack the financial and political resources of their target governments, and certainly none has any coercive capacity. But they do play crucial roles in documentation.

Laurie Wiseberg, the doyenne of human rights NGO analysis, has given decades of her life to understanding their operations. She and her late husband Harry Scoble established Human Rights Internet (HRI), adopting this term long before computer buffs. They examined how Amnesty International launched its noted antitorture campaign.[36] Growing from this, Scoble identified six key functions for NGOs: information gathering, evaluation, and dissemination; advocacy; humanitarian relief and/or legal aid to victims and families; building solidarity among the oppressed, and internationalizing and legitimating local concerns; moral condemnation and praise; and lobbying national and intergovernmental authorities.[37] Wiseberg recently stressed two "absolutely indispensable functions," namely information gathering, evaluation, and dissemination; and keeping the political process open or creating political space for democratic forces.[38] Neither mentioned norm creation and standard setting directly, perhaps indicating that success in this area has been relatively recent.

Research by itself accomplishes little in terms of direct impact on victims of abuses or on abusive situations themselves, unless it is accompanied by direct or indirect assistance to victims and changes in conditions. Study precedes action, but does not substitute for it. The steps that human rights NGOs tend to take are relatively weak, in the eyes of some critics. They have long relied on the power of publicity per se. Faith in the efficacy of the published report, as Stanley Cohen has aptly pointed out, is a cardinal characteristic of international human rights NGOs.[39] The number of studies carried out by major international human rights NGOs (INGOs) runs into the hundreds each year. Without the information provided by NGOs, effective oversight by UN and regional human rights treaty bodies would sink into terminal torpor.

But are reports enough? Research is an instrument, not an end in itself. As will be shown in later chapters, the two best-known human rights NGOs, Amnesty International and Human Rights Watch, have increasingly emphasized advocacy. Careful investigation remains a bedrock for leading human rights NGOs, with changes in government actions, public outlooks, and basic conditions the desired result. Research must be linked to improved conditions, to campaigns of advocacy, and to support from appropriate resources. Amnesty International in the 1970s adopted approximately 45,000 prisoners of conscience and justifiably crowed when nearly half of them were released; research on their imprisonment led to pressure from AI chapters and to thousands of successful outcomes.

The increased recognition of NGOs is thus a fact of contemporary political life—as can be seen as a result, in large part, of their central role in gathering and disseminating information. It is also the result of advocacy. For many the tasks of documentation—of careful checking and rechecking of facts—have far less allure than immediate action. Writing a report seems far less tangible than feeding starving refugees, treating a victim of physical abuse, or providing a haven for a persecuted political advocate. Providing direct assistance to victims is a praiseworthy task. As we shall see subsequently, most of the NGOs examined in this book concentrate on advocacy; direct action on behalf of victims is found more with development-oriented or humanitarian assistance NGOs. But the distinction between research- and advocacy-oriented NGOs and assistance-oriented NGOs is not a hard and fast one.

Resources

I wrote earlier of the value of institutional biographies. The authors of such studies must give careful attention to the resources NGOs utilize: who provides them, who decides how they are utilized?

NGOs cannot depend on taxes, as can governments; they cannot promise shares in potential profits for investors. Their budgets derive, to a substantial extent, from the largesse of foundations. The human rights groups that have mushroomed (particularly since the mid-1970s) testify to the significance of foundations. One stands out in particular. The Ford Foundation took the lead. It largely made possible the creation of Helsinki Watch, the first major unit of Human Rights Watch. Consider the following examples of the impact of the Ford Foundation drawn from Korey's recent book:[40]

The Southern Africa Project, linked to the Lawyers' Committee for Civil Rights under Law, helped in the legal defense of black activists, including many involved in the Black Consciousness Movement.[41]

Ford funded a series of studies on child labor in nine countries or colonies (Colombia, India, Portugal, and Hong Kong in 1978; Italy, Malaysia, South Africa, Spain, and Thailand in 1979), useful in preparing the way for the 1989 Convention on the Rights of the Child.[42]

The small but historically significant NGO Anti-Slavery International for the Protection of Human Rights received Ford support for projects in the 1980s, as the organization moved to broaden its outlook and change its name.[43] (Founded in 1839 in England as the Anti-Slavery Society, it has taken on issues that are, alas, still timely, such as debt bondage, serfdom, bride price, and child labor peonage.)

In 1976, the Ford Foundation announced it would allocate $500,000 that year to strengthen human rights NGOs,[44] a figure that was increased in later years, as William D. Carmichael, the foundation's former vice president, discusses in Chapter 13.

One of the first beneficiaries of Ford's new emphasis was the International League for Human Rights, able to hire new interns in 1976—just as Jimmy Carter and Andrei Sakharov were publicly exchanging thoughts on human rights.[45]

Helsinki Watch, the initial major unit of Human Rights Watch, received $400,000 from Ford for its establishment in 1978; Korey notes the important role of former Supreme Court justice Arthur Goldberg, then serving as U.S. ambassador to the first review conference for the Helsinki Final Act. Ford also assisted financially in establishing other Helsinki NGOs in Europe, starting in 1982.[46]

Ford funds underwrote the costs of the Management Assistance Group that, in the 1993–95 period, helped resolve major internal issues in Human Rights Watch.[47]

In dispensing millions of dollars to human rights groups, most notably since 1976, the Ford Foundation had an agenda in mind, but was open to how it might be best achieved. Its officers in the field and in New York City had broad goals, leaving the specific methodologies to leaders of the NGOs. Not all givers were as accommodating, however. "Strings" can be attached, compromising the independence from outside givers that human rights organizations claim they require. In particular, governments are suspect donors, since they account for a substantial share of abuses.[48]

Amnesty International stands at one pole, in terms of the NGOs covered in this book: it does not accept funds from governments, save under highly restricted circumstances; it is chary of foundation grants; and it relies on members' dues and contributions for much of its budget. Among major human rights organizations, the AI formula is unique. Its membership base provides a substantial portion of the annual budget. AI and Human Rights Watch (HRW) — indeed, most large human rights groups — derive their funds from sources in the industrialized North, AI significantly from the United States and members of the European Union, HRW almost exclusively from the United States. Over time, each organization has become solidly institutionalized: its existence is not severely jeopardized if a major donor reduces or ends its contributions. At the other pole of our imaginary spectrum of NGO resources, we could situate Action for Development (ACFODE), a Ugandan women's NGO examined in Chapter 9. More than 90 percent of its budget comes from foundations headquartered in industrialized states, or from agencies funded largely by the governments of these countries. Donors could exercise considerable leverage, should they choose, over the projects ACFODE undertakes — they are the pipers. And, since continued financial support is contingent on success, potentially in terms established more by the funder than by the NGO, the definition and evaluation of success take on critical importance.

"Success" and "Effectiveness"

"Success" and "effectiveness" mean, in simplest terms, achieving the maximum results from the resources invested. Success for a human rights NGO may be in the eye of the beholder — but does the most appropriate judgment come from the persons served, activists of the organization, providers of resources, disinterested outside observers, or others? Each has a valid perspective that must be drawn upon for full, accurate assessment; determination of success should ideally incorporate all these points of view. I shall reserve judgment of the effectiveness of NGOs discussed in this book until the conclusion.

Comparative evidence of success already exists. Looking at eleven countries with serious human rights violations, the authors of a recent study found "similar patterns and processes in very different settings."[49] In their assessment, such a state can become a target of internal and external pressure. A five-stage "spiral model" of change then seems to occur: (1) repression and activation of a network; (2) denial by the norm-violating state; (3) tactical concessions; (4) "prescriptive status," in which the various actors (states, NGOs, intergovernmental organizations) regularly refer to human rights norms; and (5) rule-consistent behavior.[50] And, to cut to the bottom line, "the transnational networks of human rights activists are indeed the single most important group of actors to put a norm-violating government on the international agenda through a process of moral consciousness-raising. . . . transnational human rights pressures and policies, including the activities of advocacy networks, have made a very significant difference in bringing about improvements in human rights practices in diverse countries around the world."[51] The evidence cited — from Kenya and Uganda; Tunisia and Morocco; Indonesia and the Philippines; Chile and Guatemala; Poland and Czechoslovakia; and South Africa—is convincing. The combination of internal and external pressures *does* make a difference. Success can be documented.

To conclude this section, agreement on what human rights NGOs do best remains an area of continuing scholarly debate. But there is a clear lesson. What NGOs are recognized as able to accomplish differs markedly in 2000 from 1980, from 1960, or indeed from any earlier period. As NGOs have grown in numbers, as I described at the outset, they have likewise expanded in functions. Transnational networks of organizations can exert significant pressure on states, resulting in improved protection of human rights. Significant evidence for these assertions comes from a variety of literature, and from the chapters which follow.

Preview of Topics Addressed

NGOs and Human Rights: Promise and Performance is, by necessity, selective. There are thousands of NGOs that claim to promote human rights; only a few are examined here (though the editor and authors have tried to be sensitive both to significance and to type of organization). The book is also deliberately somewhat eclectic. It lacks (with the notable exception of one chapter on a women's rights-oriented NGO in Uganda) details about the dynamics of Third World human rights organizations. Such groups merit far more analysis than they have received; detailed studies are few in number.[52] I hope this book helps spur the collection of more data, explicit attention to NGO goals and performance, and detailed comparison of the strategies by which human rights NGOs in a variety of settings seek to achieve their goals.

To give interested readers a summary of what they can expect in later pages, let me summarize the major assertions and conclusions of the following chapters. Note that almost all authors in this volume have coupled their research on human rights with individual activism. Many of the chapters benefit from the perspective of insiders, without being apologetic or unduly laudatory. Personal commitment to the cause of human rights does not override scholarly analysis of these rights.

The chapters in Part I examine some of the most significant human rights organizations concerned with civil and political rights. Amnesty International, Human Rights Watch, and the International Commission of Jurists, based respectively in London, New York, and Geneva, are "classic" organizations among the top INGOs. They are not the only ones, but certainly they have records of accomplishment worthy of close attention. How they determine and revise their goals, what strategies they employ, how they seek necessary resources, and how they assess their effectiveness can be answered with greater assurance as a result of analyses in Part I.

Reflecting its size, lengthy history, and undoubted influence, Amnesty International is the subject of several early chapters.

Since its creation in 1961, following publication of an appeal for the release of political prisoners, AI has grown spectacularly. Morton E. Winston, who is both a major scholar of human rights and a long-term activist for Amnesty International, sets the picture. He contrasts AI's undoubted success in many areas with issues in which the organization's complex means of decision making and strictly observed mandate impeded effective or timely action. Amnesty International did not adopt Nelson Mandela or other members of the African National Congress as prisoners of conscience (POCs), for example, since the ANC would not rule out possible use of violence in its campaign against apartheid, thus making its members ineligible for POC status. AI did not join the international campaign to ban the manufacture and deployment of land mines on the grounds that antipersonnel mines inflicted indiscriminate injury, while AI deplored violence specifically targeted against individuals. These perhaps-missed opportunities are far outweighed by what the organization has achieved, however. The release of close to 20,000 prisoners of conscience since 1961 testifies, at least in part, to AI's vigorous program of research, adoption, and campaigning. As a human rights advocacy organization, Amnesty International is unique in the number of its members (about one million), and distinctive in its commitment to educating them about new initiatives. Other NGOs may be more nimble and quick in adopting new goals, for decisions can be made by a small number of persons accountable essentially to themselves (and to their major funders). AI by contrast seeks to build consensus among its members, using a grassroots or populist approach rather than an elite approach. Activists trained by Amnesty have established other human rights NGOs. Its reach into secondary schools has sensitized new generations of activists. But the organization seems to have reached a plateau in membership during the 1990s, with implications for how it has carried out its mandate.

The second chapter devoted to Amnesty International takes a single case, one that helped force a reexamination of its methods. Ann Marie Clark focuses on AI's steps to uncover, publicize, and halt the Guatemalan government's murderous campaign of disappearances and extrajudicial executions in the 1970s and 1980s. AI's time-tested method, that of adopting prisoners of conscience, proved ill-adapted to the Guatemalan context. Quick action through appeals was essential to save the lives of the disappeared, with immediate appeals for release rather than lengthy processes of study and adoption necessary for success. The administration of General Efraín Ríos Montt proved obdurate in the face of NGO pressure. Measured against AI's classic means of operation, the Guatemalan campaign proved to be an exercise in frustration. Successive military leaders were reluctant to halt their murderous practices, even to admit such actions were occurring with official blessing. The severity of abuses in Guatemala and the seemingly minimal impact of human rights NGOs during more than a decade of major repression seem to underscore their limitations: nongovernmental organizations have generally proven far more effective in raising awareness about abuses than in directly solving them.

The limelight shifts then to Human Rights Watch, which has grown in more than twenty years to extraordinary prominence among NGOs, especially in the United States. Widney Brown writes from her vantage point as a staff member, following fifteen years of private legal practice. HRW has grown incrementally, adding geographic and thematic sections. It seeks to promote change by reporting facts and creating effective mechanisms to protect human rights. Brown provides several details about the organization's youngest division, devoted to women's rights. Her clear recounting of HRW's history and objectives sets the stage for other analyses of this important organization contained in *NGOs and Human Rights: Promise and Performance.*

In Chapter 4, I compare Amnesty International with its younger fellow organization Human Rights Watch. Though similar in their broad commitment to the promotion and protection of human rights, and in particular to rights of the person and civil and political rights, AI and HRW differ markedly in other respects. Amnesty International works within a relatively strict mandate, as discussed in detail by Winston; institutional adaptation to new opportunities has been slow, at least relative to Human Rights Watch. Neither organization accepts government funds, but their fund-raising strategies diverge in significant ways: Amnesty stresses members' contributions, while Human Rights Watch relies heavily on foundation grants and large donations from affluent individuals. HRW has, since its inception, focused much of its advocacy efforts on the American government and public, and increasingly on other governments, intergovernmental organizations (IGOs), and even corporations and international financial institutions. AI's work in advocacy has been less focused: while the organization has more than 4,300 local groups, and national sections in fifty-five countries,[53] some of them with 100,000 or more members, much advocacy is centralized in the London-based International Secretariat, making it somewhat more generic. HRW's reports provide recommendations for specific government actions, often in a more pointed fashion than AI's reports. Further, the media contacts Human Rights Watch enjoys help its overall publicity. (Indeed, citation in the *New York Times* or the *Washington Post* is counted as a success by Human Rights Watch, much as Amnesty International would trumpet the release of a prisoner of conscience.) AI cannot claim the access Human Rights Watch has been able to achieve in the United States, but does enjoy high credibility and good media coverage in many countries (never as much coverage, of course, as NGO leaders would desire).

The International Commission of Jurists (ICJ) occupies a position of honor among human rights organizations, due to its long history, commitment to the rule of law, and involvement in numerous networks. In the view of the International Commission of Jurists, without the rule of law and the independence of lawyers and judiciary, human rights would not be adequately protected. Since the adoption of the Bangalore Plan of Action in 1995, the ICJ has given equal priority to economic, social, and cultural rights. Two "insiders," Nicolas M. L. Bovay and Nathalie Prouvez, examine various roles the ICJ has played in recent years. Its record of success (marked, for example, by the drafting of the agreement establishing the International Criminal Court) seems significant, given the organization's structure: a self-perpetuating elite governing group; its small, Geneva-based staff; and its near total reliance on grants. The ICJ has sought to bridge North-South gaps. Adama Dieng, its Senegalese head, knows well the profound gaps in affluence and rights protection that exist in the third-millennium world. The growing number of poor in Africa, Asia, Latin America, and the Middle East may seem to gain little directly from the ICJ's standard activities as they were conceived early in the Cold War. Bovay and Prouvez show how the ICJ has reexamined its objectives, and how, as a rule-of-law organization, it gives more attention than do Amnesty International and Human Rights Watch to economic and social conditions. In its first four decades or so, the ICJ may have embodied the commitment to "conventional doctrinalism" criticized by Makau Mutua, but it has since sought ways to adjust its goals and reach success in a wider variety of areas.

The U.S.-based International Human Rights Law Group (or the Law Group, as it is generally called) has undertaken a variety of programs. Mark K. Bromley concentrates on its model for the rule of law within a human rights framework. Among the chief lessons he cites are the importance of supporting local NGOs, dynamic leaders, and professionals; of clarifying goals; of building an inclusive demand for the rule of law; and of enforcing rights-protective decisions. Success can only be measured, Bromley concludes, over the long term.

A critical view of the large, Western-based human rights INGOs comes in Chapter 7 from Makau Mutua. Part I, which started with tempered praise for these organizations, thus concludes with a pointed critique of them. Himself a Kenyan who combines personal involvement in human rights activism with extensive scholarship, Mutua argues that INGOs such as Amnesty International, Human Rights Watch, the International Commission of Jurists, or the International Human Rights Law Group have unduly privileged civil and political rights. Despite numerous reiterations of the "universal, indivisible and interdependent nature of human rights," to use the terminology of the 1993 Vienna World Conference on Human Rights, economic, social, and cultural rights receive far less attention from these organizations. Mutua finds the reasons often suggested for their neglect unpersuasive. "Conventional doctrinalists" in the leading international human rights NGOs promote certain basic Western liberal values. Why? This "ideological orientation" stems from their moral, financial, and social support. Although greater lip service is being given to the "indivisibility" of rights, partiality remains. INGOs have taken cover, Mutua observes, by stressing major human rights treaties ("instruments," in the parlance of international law). He concludes that leading human rights NGOs should abandon their facade of neutrality, since they advocate a clear political agenda.

Part II of the book looks at organizations that concentrate on economic, social, and cultural rights.

FIAN International (FoodFirst Information and Action Network) was created in 1986, primarily by members of the Austrian, Belgian, and German sections of Amnesty International who were dissatisfied with AI's indifference to issues of economic, social, and cultural rights at that time. FIAN International was one of the first INGOs to focus on the right to adequate food, which it monitors worldwide. Reinforcing a point made by Mutua, Brigitte Hamm notes that human rights NGOs place far less emphasis on economic, social, and cultural rights than on civil liberties and political rights. She also observes that many governments consider economic, social, and cultural rights as aspirational goals rather than justiciable rights. FIAN works to reframe this understanding of human rights by trying to achieve recognition of the right to food and of economic, social, and cultural rights in general, including their further strengthening and institutionalization. A major demand of FIAN is to establish an optional protocol to the International Covenant on Economic, Social, and Cultural Rights. The majority of FIAN's work is with concrete actions, linking the right to food to land rights and to agrarian reform in Third World countries. Working with eleven country sections and seven "coordinations" (sections that are being formed), FIAN engages in about fifty new actions annually. One of FIAN's major strategies is networking with domestic NGOs and small peasant organizations. Its lobbying has included areas such as cutbacks of social services in Germany, opposition to a proposed land lease law in Egypt, support for women in the Colombian flower industry, and land rights of indigenous people of the Philippines—in short, it has adopted a varied menu of activities.

Even more obscure than the European-based FIAN is the Ugandan NGO Action for Development (ACFODE). As explained by Susan Dicklitch, ACFODE concentrates on boosting the human rights of one of the most disadvantaged social groups in the world—rural African women. Based in Uganda and founded by women of relatively elite background (they were associated with Makerere University), ACFODE seeks through advocacy and education to increase women's participation in decision making; to improve and enforce women's rights; to portray women positively in all walks of life; and, most broadly, to create a rights-protective society in Uganda. Quite a set of tasks indeed for an organization based on volunteers and staff funded primarily from European and North American agencies.

ACFODE illustrates a problem typical of human rights NGOs in developing countries. The resources they need for effectiveness cannot be found domestically; they must be sought internationally, often on a project-by-project basis. Empowerment, development, education, and conscientization require years, perhaps decades. Long-term programs are needed, yet funding usually dribbles forth for short-term projects. The successes this small Ugandan organization has achieved are dwarfed by the enormity of the human rights challenges facing the entire society.

ACFODE operates on a shoestring compared with the two mammoth NGOs described by T. Jeffrey Scott. While ACFODE raised $16,000 from domestic sources and a few times that amount from international donors, Oxfam and CARE count their annual budgets in hundreds of millions of dollars per year. Both are long-standing, very large, complex international organizations; both were founded amidst the upheaval of World War II to deal, at least initially, with European starvation, and have long since shifted their focus to impoverished areas of the globe. While humanitarian assistance in emergency situations accounts for much of their activity, Oxfam and CARE alike demonstrate the adage that an ounce of prevention is worth a pound of cure. They are now largely development-oriented NGOs, each probably disbursing more dollars annually in projects and disaster relief than all nationally based human rights NGOs in Africa,

Asia, Latin America, and the Middle East raised and spent from domestic sources during the entire decade of the 1990s. The disparity in resources is enormous. But how does this affect their operations? Distance from governments may be relevant. CARE was conceived of as an adjunct to American foreign policy and continues to extensively utilize foods and funds under PL 480. Oxfam started as a small NGO at the height of World War II, and, through its eleven national sections, shows marked scope for policy innovation and critiques of governments' policies. Scott's chapter suggests a new direction for research. The indivisibility of rights and increasing recognition of economic and social rights expand the functions and strategies adopted by the organizations in Part I. Future studies of NGO actions should carefully examine areas of linkage or convergence between human rights organizations on the one hand, and humanitarian and/or development entities on the other.

Part III shifts attention from specific NGOs and INGOs to more general issues central to understanding how these organizations function. The case studies of the preceding chapters (the organizational minibiographies) lead into the generalizations of this section. How are human rights NGOs supported? How do they communicate with each other and with their publics? How can scholars best document their accomplishments?

David L. Cingranelli and David L. Richards express concern about the lack of comparative and quantitative analysis about NGOs' effectiveness. In their words, "No comparative, systematic, quantitative research has been conducted linking the activities of national or international non-governmental human rights organizations (NGOs and INGOs) to improvements in the human rights practices of governments." Note the important adjective "quantitative." Published studies have generally fallen into four types: case studies (as witness several chapters of this volume), comparative studies of select organizations, analyses of specific countries or regions, and studies of political processes surrounding human rights standard setting and enforcement. What steps can be taken for meaningful quantitative as contrasted with such qualitative research? Cingranelli and Richards delineate several necessary elements: separating the influences of NGOs on governments from other influences; utilizing information about governments' human rights practices over extended periods of time; avoiding biased sources; separating practices and conditions; and controlling for alternative explanations. These present serious challenges to the interested scholar, and account in many respects for the paucity of quantitative research on the impact of human rights NGOs. The authors conclude that any such rigorous assessment should focus on a single country, or compare a few countries, over an extended period of time.

The global revolution in communications has impacted sharply, and generally positively, on human rights NGOs. Fax machines and electronic mail permit immediate dissemination of information (assuming, of course, that the circuits and electric power are functioning). Handheld video cameras provide striking visual evidence of human rights abuses. Exploding opportunities for publication as authoritarian systems have been dismantled have bolstered human rights NGOs. The Internet and HTML have made it possible for human rights organizations to publicize their findings in immediate, graphic ways. Browsers and search engines enable those with Web access to point, click, and thereby enter a new era of information. Laurie S. Wiseberg and the organization she cofounded, Human Rights Internet, have provided a focus for NGOs for a quarter century. The conclusions of this highly respected participant-observer are important. Electronic mail has vastly accelerated the speed of communications, and dramatically cut their cost. The Internet has had a revolutionary impact on the dissemination of information, serving thus as both a publishing tool and an ever-growing basis for research. However, Wiseberg concludes, little systematic analysis has been prepared on the impact of the Internet, while access to it and training for it remain serious obstacles for human rights NGOs in parts of the developing world.

No survey of the activities of human rights INGOs and NGOs would be complete without attention to foundations, and in particular to the Ford Foundation. Since 1976, it has awarded some $100 million to human rights NGOs—most of which, in William D. Carmichael's words, are marked by "disturbingly fragile" financial underpinnings. Starting from a framework strongly influenced by the Cold War, the Ford Foundation focused on governments, and was chary about potentially offending public officials. Latin America in the 1960s and 1970s witnessed the establishment of several authoritarian governments; thus the need for support of NGOs grew. Some "impressive results" have been obtained, Carmichael comments, but the need for external financial support will continue.

To conclude the book, I summarize answers to the five questions posed in this introduction, and suggest strategies for enhancing NGO effectiveness. I observe that economic and social rights, while still subordinate to civil and political rights for most of the organizations examined, are receiving increased attention. NGOs have taken part in standard setting and direct protection of human rights, although promotion remains their central purpose. Although the founders cast long shadows over their organizations, all have adapted their goals and revised their strategies, lest the NGOs be relegated to the sidelines. Such changes have emanated almost entirely from leaders, not from members—and support from foundations has often made expansion possible. Local NGOs form increasingly important parts of networks. Forming coalitions with and building the capacity of these NGOs count among the most significant current strategies of the large, Western-based organizations. However, it remains difficult to determine the precise impact of specific organizations.

With this background now in mind, let us turn to the evidence.

Notes

1. Union of International Associations, *Yearbook of International Organizations 1996–97* (accessed through *http://www.uia/org/uiastats*, August 12, 1999).
2. William Korey, *NGOs and the Universal Declaration of Human Rights: "A Curious Grapevine"* (New York: St. Martin's Press, 1998), pp. 30–41.
3. Quoted in ibid., p. 45.
4. Virginia A. Leary, "A New Role for Non-Governmental Organizations in Human Rights: A

Case Study of Non-Governmental Participation in the Development of International Norms on Torture," in Antonio Cassese, ed., *U.N. Law/Fundamental Rights* (Alphen aan den Rijn: Sitjhoff and Noordhoff, 1979), pp. 197–210; Korey, *NGOs and the Universal Declaration of Human Rights*, pp. 170–75.

5. Cynthia Price Cohen, Stuart N. Hart, and Susan M. Kosloske, "The Role of Nongovernmental Organizations in the Drafting of the Convention on the Rights of the Child," *Human Rights Quarterly* 12, 1 (1990), pp. 137–47.

6. Julie Fisher, *The Road from Rio: Sustainable Development and the Nongovernmental Movement in the Third World* (Westport, Conn.: Praeger, 1993).

7. Maxwell A. Cameron, Robert J. Lawson, and Brian W. Tomlin, eds., *To Walk Without Fear: The Global Movement to Ban Landmines* (Toronto: Oxford University Press, 1998).

8. Ethan A. Nadelmann, "Global Prohibition Regimes: The Evolution of Norms in International Society," *International Organization* 44 (1990), pp. 479–526; quotations in this paragraph from p. 485.

9. Ann Marie Clark, *Strong Principles, Strengthening Practices: Amnesty International and Three Cases of Change in International Human Rights Standards* (Ph.D. dissertation, University of Minnesota, 1995).

10. Cohen, Hart, and Kosloske, "The Role of Nongovernmental Organizations."

11. Cameron, Lawson, and Tomlin, *To Walk Without Fear.*

12. Korey, *NGOs and the Universal Declaration of Human Rights.*

13. Ibid., p. 9.

14. Ibid., p. 259.

15. Howard B. Tolley, Jr., *The International Commission of Jurists: Global Advocates for Human Rights* (Philadelphia: University of Pennsylvania Press, 1994).

16. Korey, *NGOs and the Universal Declaration of Human Rights.*

17. For example, he mentions Defence of Children International (incorrectly termed "Defense for Children International" only once (p. 272), refers only twice to the Fédération internationale des droits de l'homme (International Federation of Human Rights) (pp. 53, 87), omits the World Council of Churches, and does not discuss in any depth the strong role of British NGOs in the global mobilization against apartheid. Korey's main thesis is that major advances in the promotion and protection of human rights require NGOs to work closely with major governments, and particularly with the American government. He makes a good case for this thesis, armed with impressive historic details and strengthened by his personal involvement in decades of effort. (Korey has worked with B'nai B'rith; two of his previous books dealt with anti-Semitism in Russia; he has also published numerous articles in influential journals such as *Foreign Affairs.*) Because of his strong interest in Eastern Europe, the fact that Korey mentions George Soros only twice may appear surprising, for Soros-funded human rights NGOs have sprung up throughout the former Soviet bloc. These organizations (including the Open Society Institute) are fascinating newcomers, whose impact hopefully will be traced by many scholars.

18. Edward H. Berman, *The Ideology of Philanthropy: The Influence of the Carnegie, Ford, and Rockefeller Foundations on American Foreign Policy* (Albany: State University of New York Press, 1983); Waldemar A. Neilsen, *The Big Foundations* (New York: Columbia University Press, a Twentieth Century Fund Study, 1972).

19. Margaret E. Keck and Kathryn Sikkink, *Activists Beyond Borders: Advocacy Networks in International Politics* (Ithaca, N.Y.: Cornell University Press, 1998).

20. Ibid., p. 40.

21. Ibid., p. 41.

22. Ibid., p. 58.

23. Ibid., pp. 64–65.

24. Ibid., p. 70.

25. Ibid., p. 96. According to Cook, "NGOs are by far the main providers of information to the UN human rights system. . . . if it had been dependent on governments, it would have ground to a halt long ago." Helena Cook, "Amnesty International at the United Nations," in Peter Willetts,

ed., *"The Conscience of the World": The Influence of Non-Governmental Organisations in the UN System* (Washington, D.C.: Brookings Institution, 1996), pp. 181–213; quote from p. 198.

26. Keck and Sikkink, *Activists Beyond Borders*, p. 98.

27. Ibid., p. 103.

28. Ibid., p. 117.

29. Tolley, *The International Commission of Jurists*.

30. Ibid., p. 213.

31. Ibid., p. 214.

32. Ibid., p. 281.

33. Claude E. Welch, Jr., *Protecting Human Rights in Africa: Roles and Strategies of Nongovernmental Organizations* (Philadelphia: University of Pennsylvania Press, 1995).

34. I did make one notable exception, commenting at length how the International Commission of Jurists has facilitated interactions of African NGOs with the African Commission on Human and Peoples' Rights. The Geneva-based Inter-African Committee on Traditional Practices that Affect the Health of Women and Children also received attention; however, most of its direct work with local groups is carried out by national affiliates, and the office near the Palais des Nations serves increasingly as a means of contact with the United Nations and other international NGOs, while the office in Addis Ababa takes on greater programmatic responsibility.

35. They were not, however, separate from the world of human rights INGOs and IGOs, given the need to pressure governments for more effective performance.

36. Harry M. Scoble and Laurie Wiseberg, "Human Rights NGOs: Notes Toward Comparative Analysis," *Human Rights* 9, 4 (1976), pp. 611–644.

37. Harry M. Scoble, "Human Rights Non-Governmental Organizations in Black Africa: Their Problems and Prospects in the Wake of the Banjul Charter," in Claude E. Welch, Jr., and Ronald I. Meltzer, eds., *Human Rights and Development in Africa* (Albany: State University of New York Press, 1984), p. 177.

38. Laurie S. Wiseberg, *Protecting Human Rights Defenders: The Importance of Freedom of Association for Human Rights NGOs* (Montreal: International Centre for Human Rights and Democratic Development, 1993), p. 4.

39. Stanley Cohen, *Denial and Acknowledgement: The Impact of Information About Human Rights Violations* (Jerusalem: Center for Human Rights, Hebrew University, 1995).

40. Korey, *NGOs and the Universal Declaration of Human Rights*.

41. Ibid., p. 115.

42. Ibid., p. 127.

43. Ibid., p. 133.

44. Ibid., p. 144.

45. Ibid., p. 154.

46. Ibid., pp. 237–38, 242.

47. Ibid., p. 348.

48. My cautious academic language is deliberate. Classic human rights NGOs have pursued objectives defined in the "international bill of rights," which, in the main, reflects distinctions between offenses in the public and the private realms. If a ratifying government (or its agent) breaches either of the International Covenants, it bears a higher degree of responsibility than for actions in (for example) family life. However, a state cannot escape responsibility for private abridgements of rights, since human rights treaties have increasingly established legal obligations outside the formal public realm of actions taken directly by governments. Two noteworthy examples are the Convention on the Elimination of All Forms of Discrimination Against Women (which has the dubious distinction of having more reservations than any other human rights treaty) and the Convention on the Rights of the Child (the most widely ratified of the UN-sponsored human rights treaties). The public/private distinction at this point has relevance primarily in ongoing debates about the appropriate scope of NGOs. As is argued particularly in the chapter by Mutua, NGOs centered on "first-generation" rights started with a nearly exclusive focus on the public realm. Narrow concentration on this does not, and has not, precluded

a gradual broadening by these NGOs. I present some evidence in Chapter 4 for Human Rights Watch, two of whose recent reports on India not only broke new ground organizationally, but also examined economic and social conditions.

49. Thomas Risse, Stephen C. Ropp, and Kathryn Sikkink, eds., *The Power of Human Rights: International Norms and Domestic Change* (Cambridge: Cambridge University Press, 1999), p. 3.

50. Ibid., pp. 22–32.

51. Ibid., pp. 242, 275.

52. Among the few exceptions is Welch, *Protecting Human Rights in Africa.*

53. *Amnesty International Report 1998* (London: Amnesty International, 1999), p. 377.

Part I
Civil and Political Rights
The "Classic" Northern Paradigm

Chapter 1
Assessing the Effectiveness of International Human Rights NGOs
Amnesty International

Morton E. Winston

It is better to light a candle than to curse the darkness.

Amnesty International (AI) is the world's preeminent human rights advocacy organization. Its logo, a candle wrapped in barbed wire, is instantly recognizable as a symbol of hope against the forces of oppression. AI has amassed a record of uncompromising defense of basic human rights that has won it the admiration and respect of the entire world. From AI's modest beginnings in a full-page advertisement in the London *Observer* of May 28, 1961, on eight "Forgotten Prisoners," taken out by its founder, the British lawyer Peter Benenson; to being awarded the Nobel Peace Prize in 1977 for its work in documenting the human rights abuses of Argentina's "dirty war"; to the remarkable international rock concert tour "Human Rights Now!" AI sponsored in 1988, and its tent sheltering His Holiness the Dalai Lama at the 1993 Vienna World Conference on Human Rights; and to AI members compiling more than 13 million signatures avowing the principles of the Universal Declaration of Human Rights and handing them over to United Nations Secretary-General Kofi Annan in Paris on the fiftieth anniversary of that document's passage on December 10, 1998, Amnesty International has often set the standard for other human rights organizations to follow.

AI has been called the "conscience of the world" for its tireless work in documenting and publicizing human rights violations, such as unfair trials for political prisoners, the imprisonment of prisoners of conscience (a term that Amnesty coined), executions (extrajudicial and judicial), disappearances, the practice of torture, judicial harassment of journalists and trade unionists, massacres of innocents, and instances of genocide, among others. Despite its somewhat misleading name (which has now become a valuable brand name rather like Kleenex or Xerox), Amnesty International has never been about forgetting the crimes of the past. AI was one of the main nongovernmental organizations (NGOs) that pushed for the establishment of the International Criminal Court (ICC) at the Rome Conference in 1998, and AI has consistently opposed granting blanket amnesties to members of former governments who may have been the perpetrators of human rights violations while they held office.

With such a high reputation for integrity, accuracy, credibility, and caring, an image that has been carefully nurtured by the organization over its history of nearly forty years, it is not an easy task to objectively assess AI's effectiveness as an organization. The standard view among traditional political realists has been that so-called nonstate actors (a broad category that includes nonprofit civil society organizations, businesses and corporations of all kinds, media outlets, and educational and religious institutions) have only a negligible effect on the behavior of states which act consistently only to advance their own national interests.[1] Viewed from this perspective, international human rights NGOs such as Amnesty, and its chief rival Human Rights Watch, are at best gadflies; while they may occasionally irritate states with stinging criticisms of their human rights practices, they can in fact do little to change their behavior or policies.

A revisionist view now fashionable among some political scientists is that globalization is bringing about the erosion of the power of the nation-state and that NGOs are rushing to fill the void by substituting "people power" for the more traditional forms of state action in the international arena. Jessica T. Mathews has dubbed this phenomenon a "power shift" that augurs the end of the Westphalian system of territorial states.[2] Aided by modern communications technologies such as the Internet, the more than 50,000 NGOs in the world today "are quicker than governments to respond to new demands and opportunities. . . . [and] when adequately funded, can outperform government in the delivery of many public services . . . and are better than governments at dealing with problems that grow slowly and effect society through the cumulative effect on individuals—the 'soft' threats of environmental degradation, denial of human rights, population growth, and lack of development that may already be causing more deaths than traditional acts of aggression."[3] On this view, NGOs are rapidly taking over many of the functions traditionally viewed as the responsibilities of governments, and are thus creating a new international system of governance that to a large extent bypasses the nation-state system. In particular, human rights NGOs have taken over from reluctant governments the function of documenting compliance with international human rights standards, and by documenting ongoing violations and abuses, provide the "moral spurs" that drive the community of nations toward the fuller realization of rights for all.

While moderately instructive, neither of these broad perspectives provides an adequate framework for assessing the effectiveness of a particular international human rights organization like Amnesty International. Just as there are different sorts of NGOs for different kinds of issues—refugee, relief, environmental, wildlife, developmental, religious, educational, health related, and community based, to name just a few of the main categories—even within the human rights field, there are also different sorts of

NGOs with quite distinct missions, techniques, and organizational forms. Even when we restrict our attention to the few truly international human rights NGOs, notably AI, HRW, the International Commission of Jurists, Physicians for Human Rights, and a few others, we see a significant diversity in goals, strategies, action techniques, and organizational forms. However, there is often also a significant area of overlap between the missions of various organizations around particular issues or countries, so that it is often difficult to disentangle their separate influences from their aggregate and cumulative influence on other political actors.

It is these common purposes among the major international human rights NGOs that lends credence to the rather celebratory view of human rights NGOs found in William Korey's meticulously researched work *NGOs and the Universal Declaration of Human Rights: "A Curious Grapevine,"* whose main burden is to argue that the NGO human rights movement, more than any other single force, has been responsible for implementing the promises made in the Universal Declaration of Human Rights. Korey suggests that besides functioning as Eleanor Roosevelt's "curious grapevine" that penetrates the darkest secrets of closed societies and shines the light of publicity on their human rights violations so they can be judged in the court of world public opinion, international human rights NGOs have also been largely responsible for placing the topic of human rights firmly in the center of the political agenda, creating new international legal standards, building international enforcement institutions, mobilizing public opinion to oppose violations, and even (he sometimes suggests) bringing about major historical changes, such as the collapse of the Soviet Union, the fall of the Berlin Wall, and the end of apartheid in South Africa.[4]

The problem with such claims, of course, is that history is not a controlled experiment, so that it is methodologically impossible to factor out the contributions of the various agents, forces, and influences that may have had some role in producing major historical changes such as those mentioned. But, the same is true even if we focus on more modest and discrete changes, such as the creation of the office of UN High Commissioner for Human Rights in 1995 or the International Criminal Court (ICC) in 1998. In both of these instances the work of Amnesty International undoubtedly had some significant influence. AI lobbied the UN and member states aggressively on creating a High Commissioner for Human Rights and collected over a million signatures on a petition. It was also very much "in the loop" concerning the creation of the ICC. But even in these instances, AI was not the only actor in the field at the time; several other international human rights NGOs were also "pushers" on these issues, as were the governments of several nations. Of course, AI and HRW and others worked hard to influence the U.S. government position, and even had some highly placed and influential human rights people with connections to these organizations in the U.S. delegation.[5] But then, how is it possible to measure influence? How is one to factor out the various contributing influences and give credit to one or two specific actors involved in a complex negotiating process?

The same sorts of caveats apply to other areas of human rights work. While Amnesty can give numbers as to how many of its adopted prisoners were eventually released (about 50 percent of the more than 45,000 prisoners it has adopted since 1961), it has been reluctant to claim credit for any particular victory of this kind.[6] Prisoners are rarely released immediately after AI takes action, and governments are for the most part eager to demonstrate that they when they do release prisoners they are not doing so because of "international pressure." But how does one calculate the number of persons who have not been unjustly imprisoned, tortured, or unfairly tried for political crimes because Amnesty and similar organizations have been around to call the governments on it should they engage in such practices? How does one quantify the number of prisoners and others who have been given that intangible quality of hope just by knowing that such organizations exist to stand up to repressive governments as their champions? How can one really objectively assess the effectiveness of a human rights organization such as Amnesty International?[7]

In order to get a handle on the question of the effectiveness of an organization, one must at least ask what its mission is, that is, what it is trying to accomplish. Unlike NGOs that provide direct services to beneficiaries, human rights NGOs like AI are primarily advocacy organizations. While one can count the number of meals served to homeless people, or the number of refugees housed in camps, or the number of students sent to university on scholarship, it is difficult, and perhaps impossible, to quantify the influence that advocacy organizations have on their intended targets. Amnesty's mission is defined in its statute, which functions as the organization's constitutional charter. In its first annual report, a document of sixteen pages, the "Objects of Amnesty" were identified as follows:

The principal object of AMNESTY is to mobilize public opinion in defence of those men and women who are imprisoned because their ideas are unacceptable to their governments. It has been formed so that there should be some central, international organization capable of concentrating efforts to secure the release of these "Prisoners of Conscience," and to secure world wide recognition of Articles 18 and 19 of the Universal Declaration of Human Rights. Essentially an impartial organization as regards religion and politics, it aims at uniting groups in different countries working towards the same end—the freedom and dignity of the human mind.[8]

This report goes on to describe the creation of the Amnesty library, the first missions that the organization undertook in early 1962 to Ghana, Czechoslovakia, Portugal, and East Germany, and the financial accounts for that year showing expenses of £7859.56.[9]

The most recent Amnesty International annual report provides the following description of its current mission:

1. The object of Amnesty International is to contribute to the observance throughout the world of human rights as set out in the Universal Declaration of Human Rights.
In pursuance of this object, and recognizing the obligation on each person to extend to others rights and freedoms equal to his or her own, Amnesty International adopts as its mandate:
• To promote awareness of and adherence to the Universal Declaration of Human Rights and

other internationally recognized human rights instruments, the values enshrined in them, and the indivisibility and interdependence of all human rights and freedoms;
• To oppose grave violations of the rights of every person freely to hold and to express his or her convictions and to be free from discrimination and of the right of every person to physical and mental integrity, and, in particular, to oppose by all appropriate means irrespective of political considerations:
a) the imprisonment, detention or other physical restrictions imposed on any person by reason of his or her political, religious or other conscientiously held beliefs or by reason of his or her ethnic origin, sex, colour, language, national or social origin, economic status, birth or other status, provided that he or she has not used or advocated violence (hereinafter referred to as "prisoners of conscience");
b) the detention of any political prisoner without fair trial within a reasonable time or any trial procedures relating to such prisoners that do not conform to internationally recognized norms;
c) the death penalty, and the torture or other cruel, inhuman or degrading treatment or punishment of prisoners or other detained or restricted persons, whether or not the persons affected have used or advocated violence;
d) the extrajudicial execution of persons whether or not imprisoned, detained or restricted, and "disappearances," whether or not the persons affected have used or advocated violence.[10]

Despite the obvious expansion in the kinds of human rights violations that Amnesty opposes, there is a significant continuity in its basic prisoner-oriented mission. The 1998 international budget was nearly £17 million.[11] There are currently 54 national sections of AI. AI sent out over 150 missions to around 100 countries in 1998, and it claimed to have more than one million members in nearly 150 countries.[12]

Given its expanding mission and its organizational growth over nearly forty years, how can one assess AI's effectiveness? The approach taken in this essay is that Amnesty's effectiveness is best understood not only in terms of its achieving its programmatic objectives for human rights observance, but also significantly in terms of what Amnesty has done to promote the idea of international human rights and in building the human rights movement as a whole. Amnesty International has functioned effectively as a training institute for human rights activists. Several million individuals have been or are currently members of AI; many others have first learned about human rights issues and concepts and engaged in human rights activism, that is, taken "Human Rights 101," through working for Amnesty. AI has become the world's leading human rights organization, in large part, because it serves this educational function more than any other international human rights NGO. This is AI's most significant contribution to the human rights movement and to the development of the global human rights culture.

AI as a Social Movement Organization

Amnesty International is a prototypical example of what Margaret Keck and Kathryn Sikkink call a "transnational advocacy network" or what some other theorists have referred to as a "social movement organization."[13] Keck and Sikkink argue for their terminology by noting that "Networks are forms of organization characterized by voluntary, reciprocal, and horizontal patterns of communication and exchange." They also note that, "Advocacy captures what is unique about these transnational networks: they are organized to promote causes, principled ideas, and norms, and they often involve individuals advocating policy changes that cannot be easily linked to a rationalist understanding of their 'interests'."[14] The term "public interest group" might also fit here, since, as David P. Forsythe notes, human rights organizations like AI advocate for interests other than their own, namely those of the victims and potential victims of human rights violations.[15] But since most of the members of AI are not themselves victims or potential victims, their motivation grows out of a sense of international social solidarity with the people for whom they work. So the term "solidarity organization" might also be useful.

However, by talking only about "networks" and "organizations" it is possible to miss a significant point, namely that formal organizations like AI grew out of a preexisting social movement within global civil society. International human rights NGOs like AI were created precisely in order to provide focus and organizational power for what began as an amorphous social movement of like-minded individuals—the human rights movement. The human rights movement is much older and much broader than AI or any other particular organization or network; like other human rights organizations, AI exists primarily to serve that movement. Once social movement organizations come into existence they do shape the further development of the social movements from which they sprang, and so one can speak of bidirectional causality. However, one should be clear that the egg (the social movement) came before the chicken (the social movement organization or transnational advocacy network).

Social movements can be characterized as "communities of belief." Religions are also communities of belief, as are political parties and scientific disciplines. While scientific groups embody "epistemic communities" that claim to possess some special knowledge about nature and the methods needed to discover more of it, the modern human rights movement can be understood as an "ethical community" whose primary function is to preserve, promote, and propagate a particular set of ethical norms and values, namely, the ideology of international human rights as that notion has been understood in the half century following World War II.[16] Thus if we understand transnational advocacy networks or social movement organizations like AI properly, we see them in the first instance as organizations whose main function is to propagate the ethical culture of the global human rights movement.

AI's organizational form—in particular, being first and foremost a membership organization—has enabled it to effectively propagate the human rights ethos within global civil society. AI's sheer number of members and sections sets it apart from other international human rights NGOs and gives it its distinctive identity as an organization of human rights activists, rather than just an elite human rights research institute. AI's basic message—that ordinary people, from every nation, and every walk of life, should and can do something to secure human rights for all—translates well into almost every language, and finds enthusiastic agreement among people nearly everywhere.

As a membership organization, AI has a strongly democratic organizational culture. This is one of the great strengths of the organization, and also one of its greatest weaknesses. One can see this clearly in its internal governance structure. AI is governed by a biannual congress, the International Council Meeting (ICM). Delegates to the ICM are elected by each national section of AI, usually by the section board, or directly by members at the Annual General Meeting (AGM) of the section. Section boards' own members are usually elected at AGMs, but are sometimes elected by a mail ballot sent to all registered members, as in the case of AIUSA. The ICM is similar to a mini–UN General Assembly. The delegates to ICMs debate and vote upon resolutions presented to the ICM by national sections dealing with various issues, such as the scope of AI's mission or "mandate," policies concerning research, campaigns and membership actions, organizational and financial matters. ICM delegates also elect members to an international governing board, the International Executive Committee (IEC), whose nine members steer the organization between ICMs, and are responsible for supervising the secretary-general of Amnesty International, who, in turn, is both the chief international spokesperson for AI and the top senior manager of the International Secretariat (IS) and its staff of more than three hundred.[17] AI thus has a structure similar to that of a transnational corporation with quasi-independent national subsidiaries, with the important exception that the national boards and the international executive board are elected by the members of the organization in their own countries rather than appointed by headquarters.[18] Other international human rights NGOs, for instance HRW, have self-perpetuating boards of directors, no members to speak of, and function more like privately owned not-for-profit corporations run by small groups of individuals belonging to the human rights elite. This gives their boards decision-making agility as compared to AI's IEC, which must seek the approval of its worldwide membership before making any significant changes in the organization's policies or priorities.[19] This contrast between elitist and populist or grassroots organizational structures is key to any understanding of AI's effectiveness as a human rights advocacy organization.

In addition to its democratic character, AI has a distinctive ethical culture, whose main feature is, of course, an uncompromising defense of human rights. However, there is more to it than that. Perhaps the most important feature of AI's ethical culture is its commitment to international solidarity. AI members learn that they can and should work to advance the human rights of persons in distant lands who are suffering violations or abuses. For most of its history AI has maintained something called the "Work on Own Country Rule," which prohibits AI members from taking up efforts on individual prisoner appeal cases in their own countries, and which also prohibits AI national sections from undertaking research on their own governments' human rights practices. There have been various justifications offered for this policy: that it is needed to maintain political impartiality, that it helps to protect AI members from government harassment and repression, and that it helps to ensure AI's reputation for objectivity. But the basic reason for it is that it prevents AI members from doing nothing but a certain kind of "identity politics" around human rights concerns in their own countries, and reinforces the core ethic of international solidarity.

The Work on Own Country rule has been significantly modified in the past decade, making it possible for AI members to do more kinds of human rights campaigning and action on their own countries. However, the spirit of international solidarity is still the dominant ethic within AI and is one of its most significant contributions to the human rights movement. It is relatively easy for most people to identify with the suffering due to injustice visited upon their own people. If the international human rights movement relied wholly on this kind of identity politics, it could not sustain the claim that human rights are universal and belong equally to all persons. Instead, one would have the rights of the English, French, Americans, Poles, Russians, and so forth. By insisting that the human rights of Russians, Chinese, or Peruvians are also of concern to Americans, Spaniards, Danes, and the like, AI has underscored the international character of these rights and made work for their defense a responsibility of a new class of global citizens.

The Work on Own Country policy has also had a significant effect on AI's organizational development. It has led to the centralization of the research function in a single headquarters, the International Secretariat (IS) in London, and the specialization of national sections into primarily campaigning, fund-raising and membership development organizations. Had AI not had this rule from the beginning, one can imagine that there would now be a quite different organizational structure, one in which the research function was distributed internationally with national section offices functioning also as centers for human rights research and documentation in their own and neighboring countries. AI is now moving cautiously in this direction. For the past decade or so AI has been trying to decentralize some research functions while linking them more directly to membership development by establishing field offices on various continents. However, this process has been slow and has not succeeded in significantly altering the organization's fundamental division of labor between the IS (research) and the sections (campaigning, membership development, and fund-raising).

This organizational formula has made AI the world's leading human rights advocacy organization. However, several caveats are needed in order to qualify this broad claim. Although AI claims to have a million or more members in 150 countries and national sections in 54 countries, its presence in the South is still very thin. In many cases, sections in developing countries consist of only a few hundred members and a handful of local groups. AI has, for at least the past decade, been actively trying to develop its national sections and membership in the South, but these efforts have met with at best limited success. AI's strength, both in people and in finances, remains in the North, particularly in Western Europe and North America.

A second important caveat is that AI has been really effective only in propagating selected aspects of the human rights paradigm, namely the relatively narrow band of civil, political, and judicial rights that form the core of its so-called oppositional mandate. In 1991 AI changed its statute to place the promotion of all of the human rights enshrined in the Universal Declaration of Human Rights (UDHR) on equal footing with its opposition to the imprisonment of POCs, advocacy of fair trials, and its work against torture, disappearances, extrajudicial executions, and judicial executions. But this change is still being assimilated by the movement's membership. AI members tend to be uncomfortable talking about economic, social, and cultural rights since there still does not exist the kind of "thick" moral consensus about these categories of rights within the movement that is found for first-generation civil, political, and judicial rights. AI research and reporting now includes information about the economic and social conditions of a country as context for its reporting of traditional kinds of human rights violations, but it has not undertaken to actually oppose particular instances of the deprivation, denial, or infringement of economic rights.

The third caveat I should like to mention here is that, in recent years, Amnesty International has, in the view of many observers, lost its status as an opinion leader within the human rights movement, and has taken on more the role of follower or Johnny-come-lately. AI unquestionably had the status of organizational leadership of the global human rights movement through the 1970s, and in particular, AI's reporting on the dirty war in Argentina (which won it a Nobel Peace Prize in 1977) is still a paradigm of human rights work. It probably maintained its status as the opinion leader throughout the 1980s, with the notable exceptions of its work around the Helsinki Final Act and on South Africa. AI's main rival, Human Rights Watch, grew out of the Helsinki Watch Committee, formed in 1978, which was chaired by Robert Bernstein and directed by Jeri Laber. Helsinki Watch was created at the suggestion of former U.S. Supreme Court justice Arthur Goldberg who was dismayed at the poor press coverage in the United States of Soviet human rights violations.[20] While AI did, of course, also work on human rights violations within the Soviet Union, AI's role as the main NGO advocate on Eastern European human rights issues was gradually eclipsed by Helsinki Watch with its more specialized mission and more energetic work.

On South Africa, while AI produced a great deal of research on human rights violations under apartheid, and worked for the release of thousands of unjustly imprisoned persons, it also struggled with the question of whether or not to condemn and oppose apartheid per se, ultimately ending up with a decision that it could not condemn apartheid as such since it was construed to be a political ideology (rather than a system of political and economic oppression or a system of adverse discrimination based on race), and AI's traditional view was that it should remain neutral with respect to opposing political ideologies. AI also refused to add its weight to the sanctions and divestment movement, and instead adopted a policy under which it remained neutral on the questions of sanctions, divestment, and company boycotts. These were, in my view, serious conceptual and political mistakes for the organization, ones that put it at odds with the broader antiapartheid movement, the global human rights movement, and ultimately with the course of history.

In the 1990s, AI badly missed the boat on the International Campaign to Ban Landmines. When the campaign was launched in May 1993 by a coalition of six NGOs, including HRW and Physicians for Human Rights, as well as the initiating organization, the Vietnam Veterans of America Foundation (VVAF), several AI observers (including myself) were present at the campaign launch conference. I wrote a report that basically said: "This is a human rights issue for the 1990s. The campaign to ban landmines is going places, and AI had better join it." But another AI observer wrote a report arguing that, appealing as the goals of the land mine campaign were, they fell outside of AI's mandate because the killings involved were not "deliberate" or "targeted" in the way that extrajudicial executions and disappearances are, both of which were by then recognized as part of the core oppositional mandate. This other report carried the day until the December 1997 International Council Meeting at which the council finally decided to amend AI's policies to allow AI to oppose the deployment of "indiscriminate weapons," including antipersonnel land mines. This decision came less than a month after VVAF's Jody Williams and the International Campaign to Ban Landmines were awarded the 1997 Nobel Prize for Peace.

This case illustrates the problem with AI's culture of democratic decision making. While the more elitely governed human rights NGOs can seize opportunities and challenges that can serve to break new ground for the global human rights movement, AI, because of its cumbersome democratic decision-making processes, must wait, study the issue, and build consensus within its far-flung and diverse membership before it can make any major move. The organizational dialectic in these debates generally swings between "traditionalists" who want AI to stick with its original "focused prisoner-oriented mandate" and to utilize its resources to oppose the traditional categories of human rights violations against which the organization has worked in the past, versus the movement "progressives" who want AI to respond effectively to new issues and to the emerging concerns of the global human rights movement. While there are traditionalists and progressives both within AI's volunteer leadership and within the staff of the International Secretariat, the concentration of staff in London, combined with a slow rate of growth of organizational resources in the 1990s, make it difficult for movement progressives to enact rapid strategic changes in the organization's policies and priorities. There is also the factor of the graying of the membership, particularly in Western Europe, whose large established sections tend to be strongholds of traditionalism. AIUSA, the largest AI section both in terms of membership and budget, also has one of the largest youth movements, and is not surprisingly also regarded as one of the most progressive in terms of movement policies and priorities.[21]

But all parts of the movement value the fact that AI *is* so big, so international, so membership-based, and so democratic, and thus there is a strong tendency to avoid or finesse issues that would seriously divide the organization. The motto has long been "One movement, one message, many voices." This commitment forces AI to adopt a slow-moving process of consensus-based internal decision making before the organization makes any major changes in its policies or strategies. However, I do not wish to leave the impression that AI is completely out of step with the dynamics of the global human rights movement. Quite the contrary, precisely because AI is a democratic membership organization, it can, more than any other international human rights NGO, claim to represent the global human rights movement. AI did, in 1991, change its statute to allow its members to work on behalf of gay men and lesbians who have been imprisoned, tortured, or executed because of their sexual orientation. From the point of view of many activists in the gay/lesbian/bisexual human rights movement, AI's coming around to this position took too long. But, in order to adopt this position, AI had not only to convince a group of activists based in the United States and Western Europe, but also had to win the agreement of Latin American, African, Middle Eastern, and Asian members whose cultures and national laws are far less tolerant than those of the Western nations on this issue.[22] AI also came around quickly on women's rights issues such as female genital mutilation and on working against other abuses directed against women both by governments and nonstate actors. As was mentioned earlier, AI also changed its policy on indiscriminate weapons, including antipersonnel landmines, and has now joined the landmines campaign. AI does respond to the changing concerns of the contemporary human rights movement; it's just that AI is rarely the international human rights NGO that leads the way on cutting-edge issues these days, because it first has to bring everyone in the organization along.

Viewed from the vantage point of human rights training, this slowness may be a good thing. Because of its democratic character, AI must first educate its own members about human rights issues and concerns before it can make any significant changes in its policies and directions. This is a powerful way of renewing the culture of the organization and also a powerful way of propelling the human rights NGO movement forward in new directions. Many individuals have had careers of some length with AI, but then left it to start up their own human rights organizations, or to work with other NGOs. One of the main reasons why people leave AI is dissatisfaction with the organization's slow decision-making processes, and its consequent built-in organizational inertia. People who want to move more quickly into new areas of work, or who want to be able to do human rights work in new and creative ways, leave AI, often after serving a kind of apprenticeship. These "AI graduates" have provided the person power and much of the vitality for the dramatic growth of the global human rights movement in the past thirty-five years. The training and eventual graduation of these thousands of committed and talented human rights activists, is, in my view, AI's most important contribution to the global human rights movement. But it is, after all, only a collateral benefit to its real work of protecting and promoting human rights.

How Amnesty Works

AI's role in propagating the values of the human rights movement and in creating new active members of this movement represents only one facet of its effectiveness. The real test of an advocacy organization's effectiveness must be its power to influence and alter the behavior of other political actors. After all, AI does not have as its main goal just making people feel good about connecting people with similar values; its work is to influence political behavior of nation states with respect to human rights.

Keck and Sikkink provide a useful typology of the specific kinds of tactics that transnational advocacy networks use in their efforts to persuade, socialize, and pressure other political actors:

1. *information politics*, or the ability to quickly and credibly generate politically usable information and move it to where it will have the most impact;
2. *symbolic politics*, or the ability to call upon symbols, actions, stories that make sense of a situation for an audience that is frequently far away;
3. *leverage politics*, or the ability to call upon powerful actors to affect a situation where weaker members of a network are unlikely to have influence; and
4. *accountability politics*, or the effort to hold powerful actors to their previously stated policies or principles.[23]

AI performs all of these functions and employs all of these tactics, as well as some others, but with varying degrees of success. It is useful to use this schema for evaluating AI's programmatic effectiveness.

Information Politics

AI is primarily an information-gathering and information-disseminating organization. It gathers information about human rights violations from news sources, networks of informants, NGO contacts in countries around the world, and by means of research missions to particular countries. It analyzes, corroborates, and checks the information it receives, and then it decides whether and how to distribute it. AI has enjoyed a high reputation for the accuracy of the information it publishes, and by and large, this reputation is deserved. However, AI is not infallible, and has on occasion been misled or mistaken in what it reports. AI works hard to protect its reputation for accuracy and reliability, in part by trying to be balanced, impartial, objective, and nonpartisan in its reporting. There is, however, a trade-off between thoroughness in checking one's information and timeliness in reporting it. AI's reports, while generally accurate, are not always timely, nor do they always contain policy analyses that are useful to decision makers.

In fact, AI has far fewer resources for information gathering than the major news networks (Reuters, UPI, AP, etc.) and even major news organizations such as the *New York Times* or CNN. The difference is that AI has a constant focus on just one kind of news—human rights news—while these other organizations do not. Most journalists have ethical standards about checking their sources before they go to press, but the premium placed on timeliness by news organizations often forces them to put things out before they can be thoroughly verified. In this respect, international human rights

NGOs are more careful but less timely than news organizations in what they report. On the other hand, international human rights NGOs are less scrupulous than, say, prosecutors, who require a higher standard of evidence or proof of crimes before bringing charges. AI does not get into the business of "naming names" of suspected perpetrators for this reason.

One can say that, overall, AI has been quite effective in gathering human rights news and information. However, there are problems with the way in which AI and other human rights NGOs disseminate and distribute their information. There are two types of audiences for human rights news: an elite audience of opinion makers and persons of influence, and a mass audience of attentive citizens. In order to reach the latter audience, AI, like other human rights NGOs, must rely mainly on the mass media as conveyors of their information. It is necessary to pitch and sell human rights news to editors in the hope that they will report it in their newspapers, or on their television or radio programs, and so reach a mass audience that presumably includes the attentive citizens. This is harder to do than one might first imagine. In fact, very few of AI's press releases actually make it into the mainstream of news reporting, at least in the United States. The track record is better with the elite media and poorer with television and other popular entertainment media. But, in general, AI has a hard time getting its information out to a mass audience.

AI is somewhat more effective in distributing its information to the elite audience of opinion and decision makers. AIUSA, for instance, routinely sends new AI reports directly to State Department desk officers, members of Congress, and other Washington power brokers. AI sections in Western European countries are even more effective in getting the attention of parliamentarians and government officials in their respective countries and the European Union. However, in the United States (the country with which I am most familiar), AI's information is often disregarded by policy makers and opinion shapers. There are several reasons for this. First, AI's information is not always very timely. Second, the U.S. State Department has a much better and larger network for collecting and analyzing human rights news from virtually every country in the world with which the United States maintains diplomatic relations. The annual Department of State Report on Human Rights Practices is much more detailed, covers more kinds of rights issues, and in some cases, is more up-to-date than comparable AI annual reports. In the past, these State Department reports were frequently biased to suit current U.S. policy (e.g., in Central America during the 1980s), but in recent years this problem has largely been corrected.

But, there is another problem with AI reporting as compared, say, with HRW's. Most policy makers and members of the political elite *know* the facts already; what they want to know is what they should *do* about them. AI, because it addresses many governments, addresses none in particular, and as a result AI's reports are rather light on political analysis and recommended options for policy makers. HRW is more cunning than AI in this regard, but mainly because it addresses much of its reporting specifically to the U.S. government. HRW also enjoys better access to the elite media in the

United States, particularly in New York City, than does AIUSA, and this is due mainly to the personal connections of its founding chairman and to the work of a very effective media department. But, despite these differences, both AI and HRW have to work at getting their information out to their audiences, and this is often hard to do. It is hard because both of these organizations still rely mainly on the print media to disseminate their information. Stanley Cohen had it right when he wrote:

The notion of witnessing and telling the truth that informs the production of human rights information belongs to a simpler era. The task is now more complicated than our traditional methods of reporting allow. On the one hand, the increased awareness of human rights, the spread of new information technologies, and the globalization of the mass media mean that the sovereign state is being "watched" like never before. On the other hand, the profusion of so many images, the blurring of the lines between fiction and fact (reconstructions, factoids, and documentary dramas), and the relativist excesses of postmodernism and multiculturalism make the representation of old-fashioned human rights news more difficult than ever.[24]

The "CNN effect" is very real, but human rights NGOs are still, by and large, not gearing their information gathering to broadcast television news. Until quite recently AI did not take video cameras on research missions. One short video segment of, say, Rodney King's beating by Los Angeles police officers, or the "training video" showing prison guards in the Brazoria County, Texas, detention center making prisoners crawl on the floor while being bitten by dogs, or Abner Louima in his hospital bed after having been brutally assaulted by some of New York's finest, do more to make the subject of human rights violations in the United States salient to Americans than Amnesty's carefully researched and extensively documented 150-page report on American human rights violations in "Rights for All" (October 1998). The fact is that far fewer people will read this report in a year than, say, will read *People* magazine in a week. As a result, most Americans will end up knowing more about which celebrities' marriages are on the rocks than they do about police brutality and inhumane prison conditions in the United States. AI is getting more sophisticated about its media strategy and has recently launched media training activities in several of its developing sections. It is also now using digital technologies to film human rights violations and relay them to broadcasters using satellite telephones. But AI still has a way to go until it is fully functional in the world of electronic images and text.[25]

Symbolic Politics

The idea of the prisoner of conscience (POC) is one of AI's most important contributions to the human rights movement. The personification of the victims of patterns of human rights violations by means of the POC functions as a powerful moral symbol for activists. The POC combines the "justice and rights" or "masculine" ethical orientation with the "vulnerability and care" or "feminine" ethical orientation.[26] Groups which have "adopted" a POC develop a real emotional bond with the person for whom they are working, even though in most cases, all they know about that person is what is contained in their action file. The individual POC becomes a symbol of injustice in a particular country and also an object of care. By uniting these two kinds of ethical motives, the invention of the POC propelled AI's rise during its first two decades of its development.

However, things have changed. There is now a POC shortage in AI and there has been for several years, due largely to the end of the Cold War and apartheid, and to changing patterns of human rights violations in other countries and regions of the world. Repressive governments now often resort to more atrocious practices in dealing with dissidents than merely locking them up; such persons are now routinely murdered or disappeared instead of imprisoned. AI has tried to deal with this grim reality in various ways: it now issues action files on persons who are believed to be deceased. Local groups accept these cases, but frankly, the thrill is gone. It is not much fun to work for months or years on a disappearance case only to learn in the end that one's fears were correct and that the person in question is dead. Longtime traditional AI members have been mourning the "loss of the POC" for at least the past decade. What they are mourning is the loss of the personified symbol of human rights violations whom they can hope to set free by their work.

AI practices symbolic politics in other ways. The basic adoption tactic functions by making prisoners or potential victims of human rights violations so famous that the authorities will think twice before killing them. Occasionally, individual POCs become extremely famous and attain the status of human rights icons; individuals such as Václav Havel, Andrei Sakharov, Aung San Suu Kyi, Vera Chirwa, and others occupy or have occupied this status. Personages such as these play an important role in human rights education and advocacy work with AI's membership and in the wider human rights movement since they offer a potent symbolic representation of the plight of thousands of others who are suffering similar fates, but whose names are unknown.

Leverage Politics

Keck and Sikkink have a useful diagram showing how leverage politics are supposed to work (Figure 1). I have taken the liberty of modifying their diagram by adding two additional lines of influence. One is a direct line going from the NGO (or in AI's case INGO) directly to the target state's government, and a second line going through transnational corporations (TNCs) to the target state. I would also suggest that what they term "blockage" can be interpreted as repressive measures directed against indigenous groups or individuals by their governments, and that the information flow to the international human rights NGO comes from a variety of other sources in addition to local human rights NGOs. But the basic idea of the boomerang is right.

AI's basic action technique is to apply direct pressure on offending governments through its membership. The lever here resides in the notion that AI can mobilize world public opinion against human rights violations. AI's basic method of mobilizing this asset is through the use of country campaigns in which the worldwide membership is

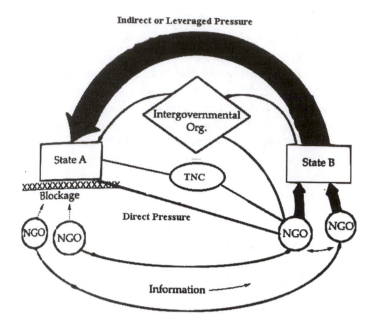

Figure 1. Boomerang Pattern. State A blocks redress to organizations within it; they activate network, whose members pressure their own states and (if relevant) a third-party organization, which in turn pressure State A. From Margaret E. Keck and Kathryn Sikkink, *Activists Beyond Borders: Advocacy Networks in International Politics* (Ithaca, N.Y.: Cornell University Press, 1998), p. 13.

focused on patterns of human rights violations found in particular countries. Over the years AI has organized and mounted scores of country campaigns. Its most recent (as of the time of this essay) is its most ambitious campaign to date—on human rights violations in the United States, launched on October 8, 1998. AI planned this campaign for more than two years. The centerpiece of the American campaign, like other AI campaigns, is a report documenting patterns of human rights violations of concern to AI in the country in question. Much of the information in this report will be repackaged by AIUSA and the secretariats of other national sections and disseminated to members and to the wider activist community in various more useable forms. There is also a carefully thought out media strategy associated with the campaign both for the American audience and for international audiences. AI members in other countries are asked to write letters to U.S. officials in Washington and in most state governments politely requesting them to "establish independent monitoring bodies to investigate allegations of police brutality and abuses in prisons and jails; ban the use of remote control electro-shock stun belts, hog-tying, and other dangerous restraint procedures; ratify without reservations the UN Convention on the Rights of the Child and also the Convention on the Elimination of All Forms of Discrimination Against Women; ensure that asylum-seekers are detained only as a last resort, and never in jails along with criminal defendants; ban the death penalty for juvenile offenders as a first step towards the abolition of the death penalty; and adopt and rigorously enforce a binding code of conduct, based on human rights, covering all transfers of military, security, and police equipment, services, and expertise."[27]

It remains to be seen how the federal, state, and municipal governments concerned will respond to this campaign. If Cohen's analysis is to be believed, the main reaction will be to deny all charges and accuse AI of biased or inaccurate reporting. It is also likely that AI's concerns will simply be ignored and its campaign press releases buried by the blizzard of meaningless information that is constantly emanating from our nation's media. However, the reception in other countries is likely to be quite different indeed. AI's report will confirm and deepen the beliefs about the United States already present in the human rights community abroad and provide a focus for action. It will also help to dispel the perception that AI only picks on small, developing countries in the South in its reports and that it is afraid to take on the world's only remaining superpower. But the unanswered question about this campaign is still, How effective will AI's strategy and tactics be in dealing with the world's most powerful nation?

My guess is that the answer will turn out to be modest in terms of basic programmatic goals, such as banning juvenile executions as a first step towards ending the death penalty in the United States. Imagine for a moment how George W. Bush, governor of Texas, must react to receiving hundreds of letters from Europeans telling him not to execute a prisoner on death row. The basic political reaction is to dismiss them because the authors of the letters are not constituents. For this campaign, then, AIUSA members, particularly those in states like Texas, must play a much more central role than in some other AI country campaigns, since only here are AI members also constituents. But even so, AI's political clout is tiny as compared to other U.S. NGOs. AIUSA has in total about 300,000 members. It is dwarfed in size, money, and political influence by the likes of the National Rifle Association and the Christian Coalition, so much so that American politicians reckon that they can safely ignore its concerns and write off the human rights vote.[28]

Aside from direct action on U.S. officials by members both here and abroad, AI will also ask members in other countries to raise their concerns about the United States with officials of their own governments. This is the basic type of leverage politics. But again, it remains to be seen how potent this will be with respect to the United States. When members of AIUSA raise concerns about, say, Nigeria with U.S. government officials, they get a respectful hearing, but usually not much action. If the U.S. government did act on AI's concerns and communicate them to the Nigerian authorities as concerns of the U.S. government (as sometimes happens), then AI's message would be powerfully leveraged. So much more so if other governments in Europe and Africa can also be persuaded to adopt AI's concerns and translate them into their own foreign policy goals. However, it remains to be seen how many foreign governments will be willing to do this with respect to the United States. Many will decline to do so because they may fear retribution. Others may decline because they believe that their voices will be ineffective. It is not at all a sure thing that the United States will respond to this kind of leveraged pressure from other governments; American exceptionalism with respect to human rights is deep seated in the American political culture, and as a result, many U.S. officials are ready to dismiss such "foreign influences" as political nonstarters.[29]

In the past few years, AI has been working on developing a third type of leverage politics, using multinational or transnational corporations as the medium of influence on governments. To tell the truth, there has not been much real action on human rights resulting from this approach; however, in theory at least, TNCs could be powerful levers. As part of the United States campaign, members in AI's German section will be writing letters to officials of BMW and Daimler-Chrysler, asking them to raise the issue of the death penalty with state officials in Georgia and North Carolina where they have plants. It will be interesting to see what, if anything, comes of this tactic.

In general, there is an inverse relationship between the power of the lever AI tries to use and the likelihood that it will deliver its message to the intended target. There is a high probability that AI members around the world will work as hard on this campaign as they do on others and send thousands of letters and cards carrying AI's messages to U.S. officials. However, the power that AI members have to influence the behavior of these same officials is minimal. On the obverse, foreign governments, intergovernmental organizations, and TNCs based elsewhere can potentially have a considerable influence on the U.S. government; however, it is not likely that they will use their influence to deliver AI's messages.

Taken severally, each of the lines of influence is unlikely to produce the intended results. However, the hope is that the aggregate effect of using all of these tactics in concert will produce some changes in U.S. policy and practice. It is by "joining the arms" of the various sectors and strategies that AI campaigning can make a difference.

Accountability Politics

AI bases all of its campaigns and actions on international human rights law. This has been the basic strategy of the human rights movement since the end of World War II. During the first phase of this period the main goal was one of "norm setting." This is the process of developing and legitimizing international human rights standards against which the performance of governments can be assessed. AI has played an important role in this process and can take a good deal of credit for the Convention Against Torture and Other Cruel, Inhuman, or Degrading Treatment or Punishment (1984) and several other human rights regimes that are now in force.

In the 1990s the human rights movement has realized that this work is largely (but not entirely) over and that it must now turn its attention to the enforcement and implementation of the existing body of norms. However, again, the actual results of this work are slight. AI together with HRW has been calling for the arrest of indicted war criminals from Bosnia for more than two years, but the main perpetrators are still at large. AI criticized the South African Truth and Reconciliation Commission for sacrificing justice in the quest for national reconciliation, but had little effect on changing the terms of their work. In other cases, such as Haiti, Guatemala, and El Salvador, no attempt has been made to punish the colonels who ran the death squads; rather, they were given deals by the U.S. government and now live in comfortable exile. In other words, impunity for massive human rights crimes is still the norm. Ending impunity by establishing a permanent ICC with broad prosecutorial powers is an important goal of the contemporary human rights movement, and Amnesty has been in step with this goal and has in fact played a leading role. However, we are, unfortunately, still at the threshold of this work and much remains to be done.

The framework developed by Keck and Sikkink provides a useful approach to assessing the effectiveness of AI's work, but before we leave this topic, we should look more carefully at its comprehensiveness. Harry Scoble and Laurie Wiseberg developed an analysis of the major functions of human rights NGOs which divides them as follows: (1) information gathering, evaluation, and dissemination; (2) advocacy; (3) developing human rights norms and lobbying; (4) legal aid and humanitarian relief; (5) building solidarity; and (6) moral condemnation and praise.[30] There is a good deal of overlap here with Keck and Sikkink's information, symbolic, leverage, and accountability politics, but, legal aid, relief, and solidarity are also identified as functions of human rights NGOs.

Amnesty International does address these functions. There has been for many years a little-known prisoner relief fund within AI and another separate fund, the Ivan Morris Fund within AIUSA, that provides small grants to former POCs and their families. On occasion these funds have also been used to help defray legal expenses and in others to allow former prisoners to receive medical treatment. These are tangible direct services that AI provides to some of its adopted POCs. Recently, AIUSA has helped to establish the Center for Justice and Accountability, an independent NGO that brings suits under the Alien Torts Claims Act on behalf of people who have been tortured now residing in the United States. In these and other respects, Amnesty International continues to be a vital and creative force within the global human rights movement while holding firm on its basic commitment to international solidarity in defense of basic human rights.

Globalization and the Future of the Human Rights Movement

AI was founded at the height of the Cold War, and its early structure and mission were framed in the terms of assumptions of that period. The first Amnesty groups were assigned three prisoner cases: one from the East, one from the West, and one from a nonaligned nation, in order to emphasize the political and ideological impartiality of the organization. All that is now history. The end of the Cold War heralded what many in the human rights community believed would be a great opportunity to advance the cause of international human rights. And so it has in some cases: in South Africa the long struggle against apartheid was finally won, and in Eastern Europe and the republics of the former Soviet Union citizens gained new political rights and civil liberties and have overcome decades of human rights violations.[31]

But the decade of the 1990s has also brought with it new human rights problems and challenges: genocide and ethnic cleansing, widespread deprivation of economic rights, and a more complex geopolitical environment. Fareed Zakaria has noted that the end of the Cold War brought with it a rise in the number of "illiberal democracies," but no coincident increase in respect for and observance of traditional civil and political rights, let alone economic, social, and cultural rights.[32] Indeed, there is no necessary progression from economic liberalization to genuine participatory democracy to the observance of human rights. The phenomenon of economic globalization is being driven by forces other than the global human rights movement—mainly, of course, by the interests of global capital, transnational corporations, and their political allies—and to suggest, as some have, that economic development will automatically yield dividends in terms of better adherence to human rights is a crude oversimplification, and perhaps even a gross distortion. However, globalization, for better or worse, is here to stay. As Amnesty International moves forward into the next century it must adapt to these political and economic realities. In particular, it must respond effectively to the opportunities and challenges created by a rapidly globalizing multipolar world.

Among the obvious opportunities is the fact that electronic media, such as the Internet and global communications satellites, are shrinking the world in a way that tends to make national borders more permeable to information flows, thus allowing the electronic media to give human rights news and information a greater immediacy and impact. Electronic communications also enable far-flung organizations like AI to manage their internal affairs and decision making much more rapidly and efficiently than relying on the Royal Mail or the U.S. Postal Service. Because AI already has an international infrastructure with established sections in all of the developed and many developing countries, it is well positioned to take advantage of these technological advances and to make itself into a truly global information-gathering and information-disseminating human rights organization. Modern communications also allow for more rapid mobilization of AI activists around the world on breaking issues, campaigns, and actions designed to protect or promote human rights. AI has been moving rapidly and determinedly into the information age with Web sites, e-mail networks, listservs, and a Lotus-notes-based international consultation system. During the past year, AI has installed e-mail capability along with requisite training and support in a half dozen or more of its developing sections. This aspect of globalization, information globalization, has not passed the organization by.

However, globalization in its other forms—economic, financial, legal, and political—is also presenting challenges for AI and the global human rights movement. In this concluding section I want to identify and briefly discuss five of these challenges: (1) the dramatic increase in the number of small, domestic human rights NGOs; (2) the growing political and economic importance of nonstate actors, in particular, transnational corporations; (3) the incomplete absorption of economic, social, and cultural rights into AI's mission; (4) the unresolved debate over the universality of human rights against charges of Western cultural bias; and (5) the issue of how to respond to massive violations of human rights such as ethnic cleansing and genocide. Each of these matters presents opportunities as well as challenges to AI concerning its traditional policies and modes of operation. How AI responds to these issues will determine how the organization will fare in the coming years.

1. In 1993 the UN estimated that there were 29,000 nongovernmental organizations in existence.[33] Many of these, of course, have missions that are quite distinct from Amnesty's, but many are human rights organizations that focus on particular matters or on particular countries. AI has, since its inception, tried to cover all countries, but has limited its mission by means of a rather restrictive mandate dealing only with serious violations of several of the most important security and liberty rights. Over the years, there has been constant pressure to expand and enlarge the mandate to allow AI members to work on different kinds of issues: discrimination against gays and lesbians, domestic violence against women, land rights of indigenous peoples, asylum claims of political refugees, arms trade issues, and others. Often it is the newer NGOs that will focus on these emerging issues. Amnesty has taken on some of these emerging areas of work; however, it often lacks the resources and capacity to take on new areas of work in a serious way, and so human rights activists who are particularly interested in these emerging areas of human rights work are deterred from working on them through Amnesty and join or start other organizations which have a sharper focus on the issues that matter to them the most. In one sense, this is a good thing, since, as was mentioned earlier, AI graduates provide much of the talent and drive in the newer human rights NGOs and thereby enrich and expand the human rights movement as a whole. On the other hand, for AI, it means that many talented human rights activists become alienated or drift away from the organization. This, I believe, explains in part why membership growth in AI has remained essentially flat during most of the decade while the human rights movement as a whole has been growing rapidly.

Amnesty cannot possibly hope to do all of the kinds of human rights work that the thousands of new human rights NGOs are doing. But neither can it afford to ignore the changing priorities of the global human rights movement. The challenge for AI is to allow its members to work in partnerships and coalitions with like-minded human rights NGOs on issues of common concern without losing their own identities as members of Amnesty. AI has traditionally been viewed as somewhat standoffish in its dealings with other organizations, often refusing to join NGO coalitions because of fears that their goals and methods depart from the AI mandate. This is changing, but needs to change even more. Several years ago AI revised its policies on working with other NGOs, making it easier for national sections and local groups to work collaboratively. Relations between Amnesty researchers in London and contacts and informants in the countries they research have become more collegial and cooperative. Many AI sections now have regular collaborative relationships with other NGOs. In this new NGO environment, AI structures must learn to be good partners to smaller, domestic NGOs with which Amnesty shares common interests.

2. One of the most significant challenges facing AI is the erosion of the power of the nation-state and the consequent need to refocus AI's traditional state-centered approach to human rights enforcement. According to the conventional division of moral labor implicit in the post–World War II UN human rights framework, the task of securing human rights is the primary responsibility of national governments. Governments which are signatories of international human rights covenants and conventions are obliged by the current system of international human rights laws to establish institutions operating within their own borders designed to effectively guarantee the enjoyment of human rights to their own citizens. This scheme is essentially national self-help supplemented in some cases by voluntary agencies and bilateral aid programs.

AI has traditionally addressed its concerns to national governments on the assumption that officials of governments are those who are accountable for implementing and enforcing human rights standards within their own countries. This "state-centric" approach, however, is limited in several respects: it does not work well in cases of civil war or domestic insurrections where often both the ruling government and the rebel forces are engaged in human rights violations, and it does not work at all in cases of collapsed states where there is in fact no central government to which AI can address its concerns.

Since 1991 AI has begun addressing various kinds of nonstate actors, in particular, armed opposition groups, paramilitary organizations, and even in some cases, political groups that are not ruling governments. There has been a lively debate within the organization about the need to find ways of addressing other categories of nonstate actors, in particular, transnational corporations. The problem here is that the international human rights law framework on which AI bases its work is designed by and for governments, and it does not at present include specific standards that apply to corporations under which they, or their officers, can be held strictly accountable for upholding human rights standards. Economic globalization has not been accompanied by legal globalization in this respect. However, it is clear to many observers that transnational corporations are very important players in international politics, and often exercise more influence over domestic authorities than do officials of other states. So, AI has joined the business social responsibility movement and has for the past several years been trying to engage corporations in dialogue and urge them to adopt company codes of conduct that recognize their obligations to uphold human rights within their own spheres of operation, and to join with others in promoting the observance of human rights within the countries in which they operate. These efforts have met with some success, but many activists remain quite skeptical about the real payoff of this kind of approach, and would prefer to see corporations made strictly accountable under new international laws.[34]

But the problem runs ever deeper, since, as Anthony McGrew has observed: "For many peoples in the South, economic globalization constitutes a fundamental constraint upon the substantive realization or implementation of economic and social rights."[35] Structural adjustment programs, the lowering of barriers to international trade and investment, and other aspects of neoliberal economic globalization policies have undermined the principle that the state should be the guarantor of the economic rights of its citizens. If rich and economically stable nations such as the United States have turned away from the idea that every society owes its citizens "a standard of living adequate for the health and well-being of himself and his family, including food, clothing, housing, and medical care and necessary social services" (UDHR Art. 25), what is one to expect of much poorer, lesser-developed nations whose economies are vulnerable to massive disruption at the whim of the "electronic herd" of international currency speculators? Is it, in fact, still even reasonable to assert such claims to economic security as "human rights"?

3. A third important challenge to AI and the human rights movement concerns the issue of relativism or selectivity of human rights, particularly as concerns economic, social, and cultural rights. AI has only recently begun talking about economic, social, and cultural rights, and has been often, and in my view rightly, criticized for this selectivity, as are many western governments. On the other hand, AI takes an absolutist position with respect to civil and political rights against countries like the People's Republic of China and Cuba, whose governments do recognize and uphold the importance of economic rights as well as the right to development. While AI now officially promotes the observance of all human rights, and AI spokespersons have been stressing the idea of the indivisibility of all human rights for the past few years, in fact the organization has yet to fully take economic, social, and cultural rights on board. Information about economic conditions now appears as background contextualization in recent Amnesty country reports, but the organization does not directly research or document violations or deprivations of economic rights.

This reluctance to take economic rights seriously is explicable in a number of different ways: first, there has traditionally been a "thinner" moral consensus about these rights, particularly in the West, than about first-generation civil and political rights; second, the existing standards are often vague and there are competing interpretations of what constitutes violations; and third, it would require a massive infusion of new resources and expertise for AI, or any other major human rights NGO, to research and document economic rights violations at the same level of quality as they now research and document violations of core rights to security and liberty. However, the fact remains that when AI and other major Western-based human rights NGOs systematically ignore economic rights, they inevitably give the impression that they regard violations of these rights as less grave than violations of the civil and political rights that have been the focus of AI's work.

The organization's position on economic, social, and cultural rights has long been an issue of contention within AI. At present it appears to this observer that AI is gradually moving towards an "umbrella" mandate that will replace the old "limited mandate" that the organization has upheld since its creation. Under the concept of an umbrella mandate, AI will, as an organization, work to secure the observance throughout the world of all of the human rights recognized under international human rights law. This would, of course, include the kinds of rights violations that AI has traditionally opposed, but an umbrella mandate would also enable AI members and structures to address human rights issues that are currently outside the mandate, in particular, violations of economic, social, and cultural rights. The major problem standing in the way of this change is a lack of capacity within the International Secretariat to effectively research violations of these kinds. Even with greater research capacity, however, it will still be necessary to steward resources and to set research priorities. This prioritization process will take the place of the rigid limits of AI's traditional mandate, while allowing the organization to plow new ground in human rights reporting by bringing to light patterns of human rights violations that involve systematic deprivation of economic, social, and cultural rights, as well as the traditional civil and political ones. AI's research and campaigning will, of necessity, be selective in the sense that it is not capable of providing truly universal coverage of all categories of human rights violations in all countries. However, if this change is made, it will no longer be selective in the really pernicious sense of valuing some kinds of human rights more than others.

4. The 1993 Vienna World Conference on Human Rights witnessed the most serious challenge to the principle of the universality of human rights norms and standards since the end of World War II. Many of the major human rights NGOs, including Amnesty, were alarmed by some language included in the Bangkok Preparatory Conference report at the urging of several East Asian governments which said that, "while human rights are universal in nature, they must be considered in the context of a dynamic and evolving process of international norm-setting, bearing in mind the significance of national and religious particularities and various historical, cultural and religious backgrounds."[36] Although from some vantage points this is an innocuous statement, Amnesty viewed it as the thin edge of a wedge leading to the denial of the bedrock principle of universality on which it bases its work—that the same human rights standards apply equally to all societies. To counter this suggestion, at the urging of Amnesty and some other human rights NGOs and some Western governments, the final draft of the Vienna Declaration and Programme of Action contained the statement, "The universal nature of these rights and freedoms is beyond question."[37]

This declaration at Vienna, however, did little to end the debate about the universality of human rights; in fact it merely papered over it. As Philip Alston acutely observed:

While it is desirable to acknowledge the relevance of different cultural, philosophical, social, and religious factors in relation to the application and interpretation of human rights norms, many are reluctant to do so for fear that this would undermine the fundamental principle of universality. As a result, the quest for a glib formula which will dispose of the issue in a manner that is deemed acceptable to the principal geopolitical actors assumes overriding importance. Thus the outcome achieved at Vienna is considered highly satisfactory, despite the extent to which it glosses over the debate that is desperately needed if the human rights movement is to move to a more sophisticated plane.[38]

This is sage advice. AI, along with other actors within the human rights movement, must begin to construct a more cosmopolitan conception of human rights, one which is enriched by cultural, religious, and historical differences among nations and peoples, and which leads to an unforced consensus about human rights values and human rights norms, rather than simply relying on the ideology of the European Enlightenment and the legal conventions established when the United Nations was founded in the shadow of World War II. As Charles Taylor describes it, such a new "cosmopolitan" consensus would be one in which "different groups, countries, religious communities, and civilizations, although holding incompatible fundamental views on theology, metaphysics, human nature, and so on, would come to an agreement on certain norms that ought to govern human behavior. Each would have its own way of justifying this from out of its profound background conception."[39] Amnesty has shown little interest in moving toward this more sophisticated, albeit still speculative, plane, preferring to base its judgments and critical pronouncements on the standard Western liberal view of individual human rights. AI seeks to apply this single standard of human rights to all nations; but, of course, the question is "Whose standard is it?" For many, the standard liberal theory of rights is seen as a cultural imposition of peculiarly Western norms and values on other cultures with their own great moral traditions. Glossing over this problem ignores the fact that there are different meanings of "universality," and as Iris Marion Young has argued, sometimes "universality of citizenship in the sense of the inclusion and participation of everyone in public life and democratic processes . . . today is impeded rather than furthered by the commonly held conviction that when they exercise their citizenship, persons should adopt a universal point of view and leave behind the perceptions that they derive from their particular experience and social position."[40] At the international level a parallel claim has been advanced by some East Asian and Islamic states as a statement about their view of the proper basis for their participation in the global human rights culture. It is a serious point that should not be dismissed as merely special pleading or a "gift to tyrants." At some point Amnesty International is going to have to face up to this challenge, or be left behind as a new conception of human rights is being forged by others.[41]

   5. The final challenge to the human rights movement and AI concerns the question of how to respond to systematic and massive human rights violations. At the beginning of the modern human rights movement it may have appeared plausible to suppose that if only enough people knew about human rights violations taking place in distant lands, they would cease. Documenting and publicizing human rights violations has been Amnesty's main mission since it was founded. However, we now know that bad publicity is often not enough to bring about changes in the behavior of abusive governments. Nowadays government officials and concerned citizens generally understand what sorts of violations and abuses are taking place in which countries. There is

plenty of human rights news and information. What people want to know is what they can do about it.

The weakness of the present system of human rights enforcement is illustrated by means of several recent examples of the failure of the international community to respond to situations in which national governments failed to honor these obligations and pursued policies which led to massive human rights violations, for example, in ethnic cleansing in Bosnia, genocide in Rwanda, and most recently, the crisis in Kosovo. Humanitarian interventions designed to protect people whose human rights are being grievously violated by their own governments conflict with the doctrine of state sovereignty which is the foundation of the present United Nations system for the maintenance of peace and the international protection of human rights. The problem is complicated by the fact that within the present system it is unclear who, if anyone, has the right and the responsibility to intervene to prevent and/or suppress massive human rights violations. As a result of these problems we experience repeated failures of the UN and of the community of nations to respond adequately to violations taking place within the borders of sovereign states.[42]

Amnesty's role in these crises has been to document abuses and in some cases to mount letter-writing or petition campaigns, but it has stopped short of endorsing economic sanctions to punish abusive governments and from calling for forceful military interventions to suppress grave and massive violations. While not a pacifist organization, AI has since the early 1980s saddled itself with a policy under which it "takes no position" on the advisability of armed interventions in such cases. AI has a similar "no position" policy concerning the application of economic sanctions against governments that violate human rights and consumer boycotts against companies designed to induce them to change their human rights policies and practices. Basically, AI uses adverse publicity and its technique of moral shaming to try to alter the behavior of governments and other political actors, but refuses to take any stand on the use of more coercive measures. These policies are cautious and intentionally inoffensive, but they also leave AI consistently on the sidelines in the great debates of the day. As the Kosovo case seems to demonstrate, the community of nations is moving gradually towards the recognition of a "soft law" principle under which humanitarian interventions within the borders of sovereign states can be accepted as customary practice under international law.[43] If so, Amnesty International is following rather than leading the movement towards establishing this principle.

To be fair, AI has in recent years taken a more proactive position regarding countries that have the potential to explode into ethnopolitical violence, and has joined with several other NGOs in developing an early warning system for such conflicts. It has also begun addressing its concerns and issuing recommendations to intergovernmental organizations such as the United Nations and NATO concerning their peacekeeping and enforcement activities. But until the organization comes to grips with the basic issues concerning the use of economic sanctions and the acceptability of humanitarian invention, it will remain a minor player in these debates.

How AI faces these various challenges and dilemmas will determine whether or not it continues to lead the global human rights movement, or whether it falls behind while other smaller and more agile organizations pick up the baton. Amnesty International does not have the resources to do everything well, and thus must choose its priorities and directions carefully. But it does have thousands of committed volunteers and staff members around the world who in their daily lives act as global citizens spreading of the human rights ethos, standing in solidarity with victims, and building the human rights machinery that will be needed to advance the struggle for human rights and human dignity in the twenty-first century. AI has been and can continue to be an engine of growth for the global human rights movement, a movement whose vision AI has helped to shape. Moral progress towards realizing this vision, although clearly discernable over the past several centuries, is often maddeningly slow. Until the human rights vision is realized, there will still be a place for an organization such as Amnesty International to act as the "conscience of the world," shining a bright light of hope into those dark places where people still suffer from oppression.

Notes

The author wishes to thank Hervé Berger, Mary Gray, Bill Schulz, Susan Waltz, and Claude Welch for their helpful comments on earlier drafts of this chapter. The views expressed here, however, are solely those of the author in his personal capacity as a private scholar, and do not represent the official positions of Amnesty International or Amnesty International USA.

1. William Korey has pointed out that Hans Morgenthau's *Politics Among Nations*, first published in 1948 and often regarded as the bible of political realism, did not even mention human rights until its sixth edition published in 1986. William Korey, *NGOs and the Universal Declaration of Human Rights: "A Curious Grapevine"* (New York: St. Martin's Press, 1998), p. 3. Susan Waltz has noted that discussion of human rights did not start showing up regularly in any introductory International Relations texts until the late 1980s, as the critique of structural realism began to percolate through the discipline (personal communication).

2. Jessica T. Mathews, "Power Shift," *Foreign Affairs*. (Jan.-Feb. 1997), reprinted in *Is Global Capitalism Working? A Foreign Affairs Reader* (Washington, D.C.: Council on Foreign Relations, 1998), pp. 55–71.

3. Ibid. p. 68.

4. A couple of years ago while in Berlin for an AI meeting, I went to see if I could find some remnants of the Berlin Wall. All that is left of it now is a few pieces near the Potsdamer Platz, site of the new capitol complex for the united Germany. One of these fragments stands behind a refreshment stand under the Infobox, and on the top of that fragment are written the words "Trophy of Human Rights." Portions of the wall are now being rebuilt as a memorial.

5. In this case, however, the U.S. delegation did not conform its behavior to the wishes of the human rights NGOs, and instead tried to act as a "spoiler" at the ICC treaty conference and nearly succeeded in derailing it.

6. *Amnesty International Review*, 1998.

7. Social constructivists, of course, would object that one can't objectively assess anything, since every assessor has some social point of view. For the record, my own point of view is that of a longtime participant-observer of Amnesty International, who despite being an "insider" also has cultivated a critical distance from the organization, its processes and policies. My attitude toward AI is rather like that of a loyal spouse of many years: I've lived with AI for a long time, and I know all of its faults and shortcomings; yet I stay with AI and love it nonetheless. Many others have had relationships with AI that ended in divorce. Theirs would be a different point of view. From

my point of view, many of those who passed through AI and went on to found or work for other human rights organizations have "graduated." I am, as it were, still in school.

8. Amnesty: (International Movement for freedom of opinion and religion). First Annual Report (1961–62), 1 Mitre Court Building, Temple, London EC4.

9. For more on the early history of Amnesty International see Egon Larsen, *A Flame in Barbed Wire: The Story of Amnesty International* (New York: W. W. Norton, 1979).

10. Statute of Amnesty International as amended by the decision of the 1997 ICM, Capetown, South Africa, Dec. 14–20, 1997, AI Index POL 20/01/97.

11. By the international budget I am referring only to the fiscal year budget of the International Secretariat. Each of AI's national sections have its own budget. The budget of the International Secretariat represents only about 20 percent of the total budget available to all AI structures internationally. I am indebted to Mary Gray for this clarification.

12. *Amnesty International Review*, 1998.

13. Margaret E. Keck and Kathryn Sikkink, *Activists Beyond Borders: Advocacy Networks in International Politics* (Ithaca, N.Y.: Cornell University Press, 1998). Saul Mendlovitz has employed the alternative term "social movement organization" in some of his writings.

14. Keck and Sikkink, *Activists Beyond Borders*, pp. 8–9.

15. David P. Forsythe, *Human Rights in International Relations: Liberalism in a Realist World* (Cambridge: Cambridge University Press, 2000), chapter 7.

16. I do not wish to suggest that the human rights movement began only after World War II. In fact, its roots in the philosophical doctrine of natural law are ancient, and, of course, the core ideals of liberty, equality, solidarity, and freedom from oppression are ones associated with the Enlightenment and the French and American revolutions. In the nineteenth century, the anti-slavery movement and the women's suffrage movement were expressions of the human rights ethos. The Paris-based International Federation of Human Rights was founded in the 1920s, forty years before Amnesty International. For a masterful account of the historical origins and development of the modern human rights movement, see Paul Gordon Lauren, *The Evolution of International Human Rights: Visions Seen* (Philadelphia: University of Pennsylvania Press, 1998).

17. The current secretary-general of Amnesty International is Pierre Sané.

18. Like transnational corporations, however, the subsidiaries of AI—its sections—provide financial support to the parent concern, in this case the International Secretariat housed in London. Until quite recently all fund-raising was done in the sections, each of which then paid an annual assessment, on a graduated scale based on section income, to support the work of the IS. Sections raise funds for the organization in a variety of ways, ranging from community bake sales to sophisticated, professionally run direct mail programs. Most of the donations to Amnesty are small and come from individuals. Corporate and foundation support is limited, and the organization has a policy of refusing to accept funds from governments. Most other IHRNGOs depend largely on grants from private foundations and gifts from wealthy individuals for their support. While several AI sections do enjoy some income from foundations and wealthy individuals, the international movement also functions as an internal grant-making body through its Section Development Committee, which provides funding for operational expenses of many smaller and developing AI sections.

19. A recent internal working paper on AI's decision-making processes concluded that it takes approximately three years for a decision affecting the entire organization to be raised, studied, consulted upon, and voted upon. It takes additional time for decisions to be implemented, of course, making AI very slow to respond to changes in the geopolitical environment compared to other IHRNGOs.

20. Korey, *NGOs and the Universal Declaration of Human Rights*, pp. 237 ff.

21. Susan Waltz has pointed out to me that the division between "traditionalists" and "progressives" somewhat oversimplifies the complex internal politics of AI. It is not meant to suggest that different AI sections can be classified as one or the other, since each section has its own internal political dynamics, as does the international level of decision making. For instance, at recent ICMs it was the Africans who most strenuously objected to expanding the mandate on homosexuality, and it was also the Africans who were the most impassioned supporters of AI taking up

work on female genital mutilation. Japan has been strongly opposed to taking up work against indiscriminate weapons, including landmines, but Japan has also argued that the ultimate indiscriminate weapon is the nuclear bomb. Different national AI sections approach the array of possible work for AI out of their own national experience and the positions they take at international meetings are largely a product of their internal national dialogues about the directions the organization should take.

22. The need to gather wide consensus is reinforced by the rules of the ICM under which each section has one vote in working parties. This means that the larger, northern sections, which enjoy voting rights proportional to the size of their memberships in the resolutions plenaries, must court the support and votes of the smaller sections, usually from the South, in the working parties, if there is to be any hope of having their issues considered by the plenary.

23. Keck and Sikkink, *Activists Beyond Borders*, p. 16.

24. Stanley Cohen, "Government Responses to Human Rights Reports: Claims, Denials, and Counterclaims," *Human Rights Quarterly* 18, no. 3 (August 1996), p. 542. See also his book *Denial and Acknowledgment: The Impact of Information about Human Rights Violations* (Jerusalem: Center for Human Rights, Hebrew University, 1995).

25. However, it is important to remember that allegations of human rights misconduct come under intense scrutiny by the authorities of the governments being shamed, consequently AI must also be prepared to defend its claims by means of scrupulous research methods and careful documentation. Dramatic video clips can never replace AI's traditional reports, but can amplify their impact on a mass audience.

26. For those unfamiliar with this concept see Carol Gilligan, *In a Different Voice: Psychological Theory and Women's Development* (Cambridge, Mass.: Harvard University Press, 1982).

27. *USA Human Rights Practices Under Scrutiny: Amnesty International Launches USA Campaign.* Executive Summary, Recommendations (October 6, 1998).

28. There have, in fact, been a number of victories that can be credited to the USA campaign. The Detroit City Council, thanks to Amnesty's testimony, passed a resolution calling on the State of Michigan to end all prison practices that allow, promote, or enforce violence against women in Michigan prisons. Bills criminalizing sexual contact between male guards and female prisoners were passed in Virginia, West Virginia, Washington, Montana, and Nebraska. The Illinois Department of Corrections changed its policies concerning the use of restraints on pregnant inmates in transit to hospitals. A California federal judge banned the use of stun belts in Los Angeles County courts, and the New York Department of Correction cancelled its order for stun belts. AI's campaign helped to contribute to an unprecedented interest in police brutality, racial profiling, and the treatment of juvenile offenders. In March 1999 President Clinton gave a radio address on "Strengthening Police Integrity" that urged Congress to approve an additional $20 million in federal funding for police ethics and integrity training, and in June of that year the Justice Department held a national summit on police brutality. The State of Montana abolished the use of the death penalty for juvenile defendants, and in several other states juvenile offenders received stays of execution or commutations. The issue of the death penalty has gained greater salience in national political debate, partly as a result of AI's campaign. The USA campaign also elicited a very energetic response from AI activists in sections around the world, and many articles about the issues raised by the campaign appeared in the world media. The human rights record of the U.S. was challenged at the OSCE meetings in Warsaw, in the UN Commission on Human Rights, and at the African-American summit in Accra, Ghana. In general, the campaign succeeded in its main objective—to raise national and international awareness about the human rights record of the world's most powerful nation. See Amnesty International USA Campaign, *Rights for All*, Campaign Bulletin number 3 (December 1999), AI Index AMR 51/185/99.

29. For a useful detailed analysis of American exceptionalism, see Johan D. van der Vyver, "Universality and Relativity of Human Rights: American Relativism," *Buffalo Human Rights Law Review* 4 (1998), pp. 43–78.

30. See the discussion of this scheme in Richard Pierre Claude and Burns H. Weston, eds., *Human Rights in the World Community: Issues and Action*, 2nd ed. (Philadelphia: University of Pennsylvania Press, 1992), pp. 364–70.

31. I do not wish to suggest that in either of these examples the countries mentioned are now free of serious human rights problems. They aren't, but the problems have changed.

32. Fareed Zakaria, "The Rise of Illiberal Democracy," *Foreign Affairs* 76, no. 6 (Nov.-Dec. 1997), p. 23.

33. Cited in Anthony G. McGrew, "Human Rights in a Global Age: Coming to Terms with Globalization," in Tony Evans, ed., *Human Rights Fifty Years On: A Reappraisal* (Manchester: Manchester University Press, 1998), p. 190.

34. For a useful overview of this field of emerging human rights activism see *Multinational Enterprises and Human Rights: A Report by the Dutch Section of Amnesty International and Pax Christi International* (Utrecht, 1998). Available from AI-Dutch Section, Keizersgracht 620, NK-1017 ER Amsterdam, The Netherlands.

35. McGrew, "Human Rights in a Global Age," p. 204.

36. *The Bangkok Declaration*, April 2, 1993, Art. 8.

37. *Vienna Declaration and Programme of Action*, June 25, 1993, part II, paragraph 1.

38. Philip Alston, "The UN's Human Rights Record: From San Francisco to Vienna and Beyond," *Human Rights Quarterly* 16, no. 2 (May 1994), pp. 380–81.

39. Charles Taylor, "Conditions of an Unforced Consensus on Human Rights," in Joanne R. Bauer and Daniel A. Bell, eds., *The East Asian Challenge for Human Rights* (Cambridge: Cambridge University Press, 1999), p. 124.

40. Iris Marion Young, "Polity and Group Difference: A Critique of the Ideal of Universal Citizenship," *Ethics* 99 (1989), p. 274.

41. The issue of universality is complex and difficult in more ways than I can indicate in this brief discussion. There are, of course, significant risks of retrogression if the foundational question of the universality of human rights norms were to be reopened in the way that Taylor and Young, among others, have suggested. It is also easier for academics to take radical philosophical positions on such matters than it is for human rights activists who document human rights violations. For the latter, the legal standard provided by the UDHR and other international human rights law is indispensable.

42. The Kosovo case, perhaps, represents a turning point in the recent history of these failures since NATO's bombing campaign was intended to serve humanitarian ends. However, it is too early to draw any conclusions about this case at the time of writing (June 1999).

43. For a discussion of this matter, see Bruno Simma, "NATO, the UN and the Use of Force: Legal Aspects," and the reply by Antonio Cassese, "Ex iniuria ius oritur: Are We Moving Towards International Legitimation of Forcible Humanitarian Countermeasures in the World Community?" *European Journal of International Law* 10 (spring 1999). Accessed on May 3, 1999: *http://www.ejil.org/journal/Vol10/No1/ab1.html.*

Chapter 2
"A Calendar of Abuses"
Amnesty International's Campaign on Guatemala

Ann Marie Clark

Nongovernmental human rights advocacy groups use an array of tactics to try to persuade or pressure offending governments to stop human rights abuses. Their efforts may range from private diplomatic-style approaches, to lobbying within international organizations, to highly organized publicity and letter-writing campaigns that directly involve the international public. The human rights organization Amnesty International (AI) has relied mainly on public initiatives—international lobbying and public campaigning—to apply pressure for human rights reform in particular countries. While anecdotal evidence suggests that such campaigns matter to the countries involved, the campaigns' specific effects are often hard to discern.

This chapter is a study of Amnesty International's work on Guatemala during a particularly difficult period for human rights in that country. I examine AI's impact at three points in recent Guatemalan history before 1985, the year in which a democratic government took power. Amnesty International became an increasingly effective reporter of human rights violations during this period, which increased international regard for AI as an information source, but it achieved only limited direct influence on Guatemalan human rights policies themselves.

Amnesty International: Background and Approach

As indicated in the Introduction and Chapter 1, Amnesty International was founded in London in 1961 to free nonviolent political prisoners around the world who were imprisoned for their beliefs. The founders coined the name "prisoners of conscience" to refer to those whose cases were assigned for "adoption" to groups of AI members meeting in their local communities.[1] AI has always stressed ideological nonpartisanship as well as direct, cordial communication between its members and government authorities.

Some AI members still work on behalf of prisoners of conscience, but AI's purview has broadened considerably over its nearly four decades. Beginning with the global

Campaign for the Abolition of Torture in the early 1970s, the organization has supplemented its work for individuals with efforts to address human rights violations in thematic fashion. Its initiatives have included the development and promotion of international legal norms, as well as direct efforts to stop human rights abuses.[2] From the original mandate as champion for prisoners of conscience, AI's active concerns broadened to work against torture, extrajudicial killings, disappearances, and the death penalty, and for free and fair trials for all.[3] AI has been criticized in the past for too narrow a focus on civil and political rights and rights to personal integrity, but maintains as a matter of principle that human rights are "indivisible and interdependent." Especially in recent years as it has been joined on the global scene by other prominent rights groups with slightly different foci, such as Human Rights Watch, AI has often worked jointly with other organizations to accomplish human rights-related goals.

Three factors characterize AI's distinctive approach to campaigning for human rights improvement.[4] First, AI expands the scope of conflict from the domestic to the international arena[5] — one way to tip the balance of power toward the victims of human rights abuses. By involving a wider international audience through its reports and public campaigning, governments' records of human rights abuse are transformed from private matters for sovereign states to matters for international concern. In bringing about the transformation, AI also transposes the target government's actions into a forum where international norms and human rights agreements may more easily be invoked.

Second, AI employs symbols with few legitimate opposites in the public eye to mobilize individuals to act on behalf of the victims of human rights abuses. The idea of human rights has a powerful symbolic force that inspires members' loyalty and draws in onlookers. The organization's hierarchical organizational structure, with its International Secretariat providing carefully researched information, analysis, and strategies to national sections with local members, enables AI to direct transnational public pressure against the target government and to learn from the experiences of its members.

Third, AI makes pragmatic yet principled demands for action of target governments. For example, AI may request the release of named prisoners, the investigation of cases of disappearance, or the honoring of pertinent domestic and international legal safeguards for detained persons. The direct invocation of principle in specific cases links concrete requests with compelling symbolism.

The three features reinforce one another: the organization raises the stakes of the conflict by publicizing human rights violations at an international level, but at the same time the issues are carefully framed and demands are focused in order to gain leverage against the target government. Difficult cases put these techniques to the test.

Challenges for Human Rights NGOs

In their attempts to document and intervene against life-shattering, society-rending violence by governmental or paragovernmental authorities against individuals and groups, international monitoring and activist groups face several challenges. First, such groups have "little or no legal, economic, or physical force to wield against sovereign states."[6] They may possess some form of consultative status with regional or global intergovernmental organizations, but nongovernmental organizations (NGOs) rarely have standing equal to states in such venues. Second, there are challenges related to the nature of the human rights violations that NGOs confront. Governments often try to keep such violations secret, blocking monitoring efforts. Human rights violations may take place in the chaotic context of internal war, which complicates the ability of outside monitors to verify abuses and attribute responsibility. International NGOs can augment the efforts of domestic groups to end human rights abuses, but human rights violations terrorize populations, suppress protest by their very nature, and often vitiate existing organizations of civil society within a country, thus limiting the capacity for internal-external linkages. And finally, governmental elites often portray repressive policies as counterinsurgency measures to protect national security, inherently placing human rights values below civil order or economic well-being.

Guatemala presented all of the above challenges and more for Amnesty International in the time period examined here, 1966–83. Changes in the nature of repression made it difficult for AI to focus demands for action. At times, the U.S. government contravened AI's efforts, mitigating the impact of AI's criticism. The assumption underlying this study is that very difficult cases can be as instructive as successes. For human rights advocacy, as for other nonmilitary attempts at international influence, success must be understood as a matter of degree.[7]

The Guatemalan Case

Political violence in Guatemala has been widespread and relatively continuous since the democratically elected Arbenz regime was overthrown, with CIA help, in 1954. Indeed, the term "disappearance," meaning the practice of abducting suspected opponents of a political regime, was coined in Guatemala. An estimated 38,000 Guatemalans were lost to disappearances between 1966 and 1986, representing 39 percent of the total number of disappeared in Latin America.[8] While it has been a relative constant in recent Guatemalan life, the nature of repression has varied from city to countryside and from urban death squad killings to disappearances, peasant massacres, and forced relocation.

The history of the Guatemalan case exhibits how new forms of human rights abuse have challenged AI's techniques. In its well-honed adoption process, AI investigates a prisoner's case to confirm that he or she qualifies as a prisoner of conscience: one who has not advocated or used violence and has been imprisoned for political reasons.[9] The prisoner is then assigned to a local AI group, which takes on the work of drawing attention to the case and petitioning the authorities for release. Disappearances, short-term detention, and torture thwart adoption, because there is not enough time to fully investigate the case and mobilize an adoption group. When a person "disappears," there often is no knowing where he or she is being held or even whether the victim is alive.

Amnesty International had to develop new techniques to cope with such changes, which have occurred worldwide.

There was little human rights organizing within Guatemala in the period under study. The extent of Guatemalan repression meant that the wide range of groups usually to be found in civil society had been repressed, eliminated, or prevented from forming for much of the time that AI has actively concerned itself with Guatemala. Thus, AI had to rely almost exclusively on external international pressure and work in international organizations. For the analyst, therefore, Guatemala presents a set of circumstances in which international action could not, in general, occur in tandem with domestic pressure groups. This contrasts with high-profile cases like Chile, Argentina, or South Africa, where prominent opposition organizations did act from within those countries during periods of repression. The analytical advantages deriving from this last point should not be overstated, but we may assume that in the Guatemalan case international influence attempts upon the human rights situation in Guatemala occurred in relative isolation from internal pressure attempts. It should also be added that, while Amnesty was not the only external nongovernmental organization active on Guatemala in this period, it was the largest and the most prominent. Americas Watch was not formed until 1981.

The case study is divided into three periods. It begins with 1966–78, which saw the resurgence of Guatemalan terror in response to renewed guerrilla activity, and initial attempts by AI to address the human rights abuses there. The study focuses in detail on 1979, when AI initiated its first full-scale, public campaign targeting Guatemala. That year saw increased guerrilla activity and intensified government-sponsored repression in Guatemala, but because of AI's campaign, information on Guatemalan human rights violations and responses to AI activity were meticulously publicized. The last part of the case study focuses on 1982–83, when Guatemala was ruled by General Efraín Ríos Montt. This was one of the worst periods of repression in Guatemalan history, and it also marked a shift from urban to rural violence against the predominantly indigenous peasantry. Support from the United States bolstered the Guatemalan regime against human rights monitoring and pressure attempts by outside groups.

AI and the Resurgence of Guatemalan Terror, 1966–78

During this period, AI's technique of prisoner adoption, the basic mechanism of AI's pragmatic, principled approach to governments, became almost obsolete for Guatemala. AI was forced to innovate in order to deal with the increasing problem of disappearances.

While factions of the Guatemalan military vied with one another for power in the early 1960s, a "small yet troublesome guerrilla campaign" arose in the rural areas, intensifying anticommunist fears among the right-wing military.[10] The army employed a counterinsurgency strategy of disappearances and political killings as a response.[11] AI later noted that although the government's actions began in the name of "counterinsurgency, 'pacification,' and anti-communism," killings and disappearances "continued unchecked and actually widened following the virtual elimination of the organized rural guerrillas by 1968."[12] Guerrilla activity arose again around 1978, but according to the 1999 report of Guatemala's Commission for Historical Clarification (Comisión para el Esclarecemiento Histórico [CEH]) covering the period since 1962, acts by the government accounted for 93 percent of all human rights violations registered by the CEH, while just 3 percent were attributable to the guerrilla opposition.[13]

As the Guatemalan government began the use of increasingly systematic counter-insurgency practices, Amnesty International was just beginning to turn toward Latin America. AI's 1969 annual report announced a "new programme of work" on Latin America, but made no mention of Guatemala.[14] AI was recovering from a 1967 leadership crisis at its international headquarters, and was rebuilding and professionalizing its staff. The organization itself clearly viewed its overall efficacy as on the rise, noting a 1968–69 worldwide "increase in the number of cases where it is clear that Amnesty was partly, if not wholly, responsible for the release of a prisoner."[15] At that time, AI chose to emphasize prisoner case adoption rather than reports on countries or prison conditions on pragmatic grounds, because "unfortunately reports do not release prisoners while pressure and adoption may."[16]

Despite some resource-related delays at Amnesty headquarters,[17] Guatemala emerged as a major concern for AI in the early 1970s. AI first mentioned Guatemala in its 1971 annual report as one of several countries under a state of emergency.[18] Although AI's 1972–73 annual report stated that AI knew "little" about Guatemalan political prisoners themselves, it called the Guatemalan situation "tragic," and noted "the high incidence of disappearances of Guatemalan citizens" as a continuing problem.[19] AI actions in this year included a letter to the minister of the interior "to inquire about the fate of eight abducted trade unionists and members of the Communist party," and the involvement of AI local groups in a special project to inquire about "some 65 cases of disappearances."[20] AI also appointed a Latin America field secretary in 1974–75 to build membership in Latin America, make contacts with sympathetic organizations in the region, and develop Spanish-language publications, although finances were still tight.[21]

In 1975, prisoner adoption was "still the heart of AI's work," despite the fact that it was beginning to address other human rights themes, particularly torture.[22] A year later, AI's deputy secretary-general asserted that "Amnesty International's role has become more and more important and has expanded considerably, without losing its distinct mark of specific concern for Prisoners of Conscience." He noted that "the original forgotten prisoner has become something of a rarity today, happily, and largely because of AI and the media."[23] The comments signal a transition from the simplicity of AI's earlier mission.

Despite the organization's continued focus on prisoner cases, the 1966–78 period saw the diversification of AI techniques against human rights violations in Guatemala. New methods included the Urgent Action network (a continuing quick notification service, begun in the mid-1970s, that prompts individual AI members to write letters of concern about actual or threatened arbitrary detentions, torture, disappearances, or extrajudicial executions), more contacts with international organizations, including the United Nations and the Inter-American Commission on Human Rights (IACHR) of the Organization of American States (OAS), and more efforts to publicize the problem of disappearances.

Publicity was not the only channel of communication that AI could use. AI also sent letters directly to government elites. Secretary-General Martin Ennals wrote directly to President Kjell Laugerud in May 1975. The letter welcomed actions by the Guatemalan government that might serve to enhance human rights, reminded the president of human rights violations that AI had learned of, and inquired about certain individual cases. AI's 1975 letter forwarded a list, taken from a Guatemala City newspaper, of 135 people reported killed or found dead. Laugerud did not respond directly to the letter, and the dossier of disappearances was submitted to the IACHR in 1976.[24] The IACHR informed AI that the Guatemalan government claimed to have carried out investigations that disproved AI's allegations. AI responded to the commission that, if so, it should be noted that Guatemala had "failed to offer any facts concerning the names of individuals."[25]

During the latter half of the 1970s, AI's prisoner adoption diminished to almost nil in Guatemala, because there were no longer any reported cases of long-term imprisonment in Guatemala, although "hundreds [were] held, interrogated, tortured and eventually murdered."[26] Thus, AI had to operate without its most unique and well-honed tactic. The organization made active attempts to acquire prisoner adoption cases: eight new investigation cases, "most of them disappearances," were added in 1974–75 to the disappearance cases already being investigated by eleven of AI's local groups.[27] However, the 1975 report contains the last mention of assigning of individual Guatemalan detention cases to local groups. From July 1977 to June 1978 there were no Guatemalan prisoners of conscience adopted, although more than 300 disappearances were recorded.[28] By the end of the 1970s, AI had switched to the increased use of Urgent Action bulletins, continued heavy cooperation with the IACHR, and intensified research and publication of information about Guatemalan violations. AI issued its first four Guatemala-related Urgent Action bulletins in 1976 (out of 148 in total for all countries), of which three alerted members to disappearances and one publicized a legal concern and fear of torture.[29]

In the late 1960s and early 1970s, new forms of repression in Guatemala and elsewhere challenged AI's proven pressure techniques. AI maintained a commitment to action for prisoners of conscience rather than to information for its own sake. However, on the strength of its reporting, by the end of the 1970s AI found that its authoritative reports were actively awaited by the world community. AI became an increasingly busy monitor of human rights in Latin America; for example, it made submissions to the IACHR in every year of the 1970s. The organization received the Nobel Peace Prize in 1977, which did much to raise its global public profile. AI's increasing renown heightened its potential to influence popular opinion, even though its techniques were deeply challenged by the situation in Guatemala.

The 1979 Country Campaign on Guatemala

In 1979, Amnesty International initiated an intensified, country-level campaign against human rights violations in Guatemala. The "country campaign" is AI's term for a limited period of intense publicity and action by its membership, directed at "countries whose records on human rights [warrant] full publicity."[30] Campaign participants receive mailings from the AI staff before and during a campaign, informing them about the subject of the campaign and suggesting recommended actions. Country campaigns are designed to focus attention on persistent, systematic human rights violations. They are often accompanied by a special report aimed at the wider public.

The 1979 Guatemala campaign was organized around symbolically meaningful dates for Guatemala and the international community. It commenced on September 15, 1979, Guatemala's Independence Day, and lasted five months. The year 1978 had been designated UN Human Rights Year, and AI's initial campaign publicity revolved around a newsprint leaflet entitled *The Human Rights Year in Guatemala: A Calendar of Abuses.* The calendar chronicled 365 days' worth of human rights violations in Guatemala, beginning with the massacre of over one hundred indigenous people in the town of Panzós on May 29, 1978. At approximately the midpoint of the campaign, a special letter-writing action to express concern to Guatemalan officials was organized for December 10, which was International Human Rights Day and the thirtieth anniversary of the Universal Declaration of Human Rights.

The ironic contrast between symbols of human rights and the graphic violations present in Guatemala, exemplified in the *Calendar of Abuses,* emphasized the urgency of the situation. The symbolic dates chosen for the inception of the campaign and the letter-writing action provided a publicity device: a convenient introduction to the story for the news media; insurance for AI that stories would get attention on certain days; and entry points for public pressure on the offending government.

At the time of the campaign, President Fernando Romeo Lucas García had been in office just over a year. His rule had brought a large-scale reactivation of counterinsurgency activity, beginning with "massive, selective repression" in urban areas.[31] An AI mission to Guatemala in August 1979, just prior to the campaign, found that "victims in this new wave of violence have been primarily trade unionists, campesinos, and political opposition."[32] AI reported in its 1979 testimony to the OAS that a new counterinsurgency group, Ejército Secreto Anticomunista (Secret Anticommunist Army), had formed as an "umbrella group" of security forces and others, with the objective of "solv[ing] problems related to land titles, union organizing drives or economic development projects by killing or intimidating those they oppose."[33]

Resistance to the regime was also increasing, with a renewal of guerrilla activity, although it was not as organized as in the previous decade. The Washington Office on

Latin America reported in December 1979 that the "atmosphere of continuing repression" was forcing peasants toward violence, and to look "increasingly [toward] . . . the small armed bands of leftists for support."[34] The increased revolutionary activity gave government forces further pretext to target peasants for violent repression. A flagrant incident of human rights violations occurred on January 31, 1980, during the last month of AI's campaign, when thirty-nine peasants who had occupied the Spanish embassy in Guatemala City to protest army atrocities in their villages were killed in a police attack on the embassy.[35]

During the campaign, AI quoted Guatemalan journalist Saul David Oliva as saying that 1978 was the most violent year in Guatemala's history.[36] Although AI avoids public comparisons of separate countries, its level of concern about Guatemala was indicated in the comment of an AI staffer, who privately opined at the time that the Lucas García regime, with Idi Amin's Uganda, was one of the worst violators of human rights in the world.[37] Although the U.S. Congress had withdrawn U.S. foreign military credit sales to Guatemala based on human rights concerns in 1977, Guatemala continued to receive military assistance from the United States during the new wave of violence, through circumvention of U.S. legislative provisions.[38]

Initially, the negative international publicity seems to have caused the Guatemalan government to close ranks, a reaction that has also been observed when governments face external pressure from economic sanctions.[39] There were hostile attacks on AI in the domestic press at the outset of the campaign, calling AI an organization "without any moral authority" and "ignorant of our situation."[40] In December 1979, AI published a memorandum that outlined government abuses and called for an OAS investigation. AI had submitted the memo directly to Lucas García a month earlier. After the memo became public, AI noted that authorities took further measures to control the press, which included limiting accounts of killings and mutilated bodies to reports authorized by the police.[41]

In other press accounts and paid advertisements, some of which AI reported during the campaign, representatives of the government argued, for example, that AI had slandered Guatemala, that AI had no authority to pass judgment on Guatemala's internal affairs, and that many of AI's letters come from "well-meaning ladies who . . . believe the fabulous tales about Guatemala which the so-called Amnesty International is distributing."[42] Lucas García himself charged AI with trying to damage Guatemala's tourist trade. At a press conference, the president repudiated reports of violence in Guatemala and denied the existence of social divisions or "guerrilla organizations able to upset internal order."[43] Some officials also took the trouble to correspond directly with some AI members. One government minister acknowledged the deaths of neutral civilians but attributed the violence to "marxist-leninist guerrillas, who paradoxically murder with one hand while the other hoists the flag of human rights."[44]

AI did have at least one ally within the Guatemalan government. The vice-president, Francisco Villagrán Kramer, was a political liberal who had hoped to change things from within.[45] As part of its campaign, Amnesty International called on Guatemala to permit an IACHR investigation, and Villagrán Kramer threatened to resign if the government failed to respond. Guatemala finally invited the IACHR to visit, but after several attempts by the IACHR to set a date, the government stopped answering its communications. The IACHR at last concluded that Guatemala did not intend to host a visit.[46] Villagrán Kramer did resign on September 1, 1980, and went into exile in the United States. His resignation statement cited government persecution of trade unionists, political leaders, students, and indigenous groups, "serious differences" with President Lucas, and "the lack of any institutional forums to debate the grave national problems which affect Guatemala."[47]

The campaign publicity expanded the international audience and mobilized compelling symbols. Given the presence of renewed internal resistance and some dissent at high levels of the government, the campaign held some promise for sowing seeds of influence on Guatemalan human rights. However, it appears that the government became even less receptive to international calls for accountability. AI's campaign could not build the kinds of links with groups within Guatemala that might have added to coordinated internal and external political pressure on the regime, because domestic civil society was decimated by the enduring government-sponsored violence.[48]

Amnesty did not stop reporting on Guatemala after the 1979 campaign ended, and there is evidence that the cumulative reports of human rights violations contributed to the U.S. Congress's unwillingness to grant further aid to Guatemala, at the same time that it caused Lucas García to stand fast. Ronald Reagan's presidential administration in the United States, which began in 1981 to try to bolster Lucas García in the wake of the Sandinista revolution in Nicaragua, was unable to gain even "minor concessions [from Lucas García] that would mollify Congress" enough to widen channels of aid.[49] According to one analyst, the Reagan administration's "campaign had just begun to unfold when Amnesty International released the most incriminating report it had ever published on Guatemala. By documenting conclusively . . . that 'tortures and murders are part of a deliberate and long-standing program of the Guatemalan government,' Amnesty struck an untimely blow to Washington's emerging argument that right-wing terror was independent of government responsibility."[50]

Publicity over Guatemala's continued human rights violations damaged the government's international reputation, bringing significant political and economic consequences. Guatemala's "loss of prestige," coupled with widespread corruption under Lucas García and the continued presence of guerrillas in the countryside, hindered Guatemala's ability to get economic and development loans.[51] Together, these factors contributed to malaise among the Guatemalan military officers who backed a coup against Lucas García in 1982. However, the terror continued.

International Interference Under Ríos Montt, 1982–83

If any regime could make Lucas García's human rights record look better by comparison, it was that of his successor, General Efraín Ríos Montt. Ríos Montt led a military triumvirate that seized power on March 23, 1982. On June 6, he dissolved the triumvirate and assumed sole power. Then came the "bloodiest period of rural repression in the twentieth century."[52] The locus of violence moved from the city to the countryside, and the primary target shifted from urban professionals, trade unionists, and students to the predominantly indigenous peasants. Because Lucas García had more or less eliminated organized urban resistance, the next remaining targets were indigenous civilians—held suspect by virtue of proximity to rural-based guerrillas, according to the doctrine of counterinsurgency.[53] The character of the violence changed from disappearances perpetrated by death squads to "massive assassinations of peasants and indians [sic] with guns, machetes, or knives; the bombing and machine gunning of villages by land and air; the burning of houses, churches and communal houses as well as crops."[54] The rural violence, perpetrated by the army or by civil patrol groups overseen by the army, became increasingly systematic.[55]

During this period the battle over rhetorical interpretations of the Guatemalan violence continued. In 1979 AI had been able to use publicity to muster international attention that begged for a response or accounting by the regime, but by the 1982 Guatemala was enjoying rhetorical and material support from the Reagan administration. While continuing its direct and public criticism of human rights in Guatemala, Amnesty found that, on occasion, its allegations were now being denied not just by Guatemala, but by the U.S. State Department.

Five days after Ríos Montt assumed sole power in Guatemala, AI's secretary-general, Thomas Hammarberg, sent him a letter outlining the organization's human rights concerns. Hammarberg called for impartial investigations into deaths and disappearances, ratification of specified, relevant instruments of international law, and regularized legal procedures for dealing with detainees. He also offered assistance in consulting the IACHR and the UN Working Group on Enforced or Involuntary Disappearances, which had just been established the year before to investigate such violations. AI received no response to the letter, wrote again in August 1982 and April 1983, and again received no reply.[56]

In July 1982, AI published *Massive Extrajudicial Executions in Rural Areas under the Government of General Efraín Ríos Montt.* The report estimated that 2,600 were dead in rural massacres: a "conservative and responsible" estimate, according to AI's sister organization, Americas Watch.[57] The Guatemalan government replied that the report was "a horror story conceived by an insane writer."[58] AI said that Guatemala had "informed the . . . news media that Amnesty International was engaged in a campaign of defamation."[59]

As established above, it was typical for a target government to respond to AI reports with epithets rather than considered acknowledgment. This time, however, the United States began a defamation campaign of its own—against a collection of human rights groups critical of the Guatemalan regime, and especially against AI. Assistant Secretary of State Thomas Enders wrote a five-page letter to AI "disputing its conclusions and accusing it of lacking professionalism and relying on biased sources."[60] The

Reagan administration continued through the remainder of 1982 to insist, against the evidence being offered by AI and other human rights groups, that the human rights situation in Guatemala had improved. The U.S. government response to more damning allegations from AI in late 1982 came out even before Guatemala's response.[61] AI's 1983 report summarized AI's findings that under Ríos Montt, there had been "many thousands" of victims of extrajudicial executions, disappearances, and torture, with most abuses committed by security forces under government control.[62] The United States stuck with its claim that the killing was being done by guerrillas, and questioned AI's sources because they differed from the State Department's. A contemporaneous report sardonically observed that the discrepancy was "not surprising since, as the State Department explained, its sources are the local press (censored by the military . . .), the army, the police," and U.S. intelligence.[63] A scholarly comparison of the claims concluded that "the evidence . . . placed responsibility on the government," a conclusion confirmed in the comprehensive 1999 report by Guatemala's Commission for Historical Clarification.[64] Still, after the State Department's attacks, AI privately went "back to the drawing board" to verify and reevaluate its evidence and information sources within Guatemala. The introspection delayed its Guatemala work during late 1982 and early 1983.

In tandem with the Reagan administration's charges against AI, the United States also leveled a series of political accusations in the United Nations. The U.S. ambassador to the UN, Jeane Kirkpatrick, charged in 1981 that the UN itself was involved in a politicized condemnation of Guatemala.[65] The UN was actually relatively inattentive to Guatemala's human rights problems. After four years with no investigation into Guatemalan human rights, in 1983 the UN appointed a Special Rapporteur for Guatemala. Operating as independent experts rather than as representatives of any country, UN Special Rapporteurs are sometimes able to do constructive fact-finding. However, the UN's appointee, Mark Colville, proved surprisingly uncritical of violations in Guatemala. One account suggests that Colville, a British lawyer, was looking for "facts that would stand up in court," which from the outset made it difficult for him to credit any of the evidence that could be gathered concerning disappearances.[66] To the consternation of human rights groups, after Ríos Montt was pushed out of office in an August 1983 coup, Colville refrained from publishing critical findings about that regime, its predecessor, or its successor.[67]

The turn of events at the UN effectively shielded the Guatemalan government from the potential force of international official fact-finding and criticism. While an unbiased UN investigation might have corroborated the claims of AI and other nongovernmental human rights groups, Colville's work was at odds with them. More publicly confrontive than AI on this issue, Americas Watch, by this time engaged in an active program of work on Latin America, pointedly "challenged all attempts to downplay violations" involving it in "a furious argument with the U.S. State Department in late 1982" and in a dispute with Colville.[68]

Ríos Montt was ousted by his defense minister, General Oscar Mejía Victores. Although loss of prestige due to human rights violations was probably a factor in the downfall of Lucas García, the coup against Ríos Montt was due mainly to internal divisions, precipitated by his effort to impose a sales tax in July 1983.[69] Violence and human rights abuses continued under Mejía Victores, and even after Guatemala's transition to civilian rule in 1985.

Conclusion

Guatemala presented a worst-case challenge for Amnesty International's human rights advocacy. As violence intensified in the late 1970s and early 1980s, both the Guatemalan government and other powerful actors in the international system repudiated or ignored calls for human rights improvement. Guatemala returned to a democratically elected government in 1985, but not until the end of 1996 was a UN-sponsored peace agreement concluded between the government and the Guatemalan armed opposition. The agreement also brought into effect a Global Human Rights Accord for Guatemala, which had been drawn up in 1994 as part of the peace process. The agreements have not put a complete stop to disappearances and other serious human rights violations, but the scale is far below that of the past.[70]

Neither the past failures to stop the terrible political violence nor the recent, incremental improvements should be fully attributed to any single actor. But, although AI's direct effectiveness at influencing and ameliorating human rights policies was limited, there are questions one might ask to judge the results of AI's international activity for human rights in Guatemala. The first is whether AI succeeded, for Guatemala, in the things it is generally good at, including creating a broader audience, invoking compelling symbols, and making principled yet pragmatic demands. The second, indirect indicator of the long-term potential for human rights protection in Guatemala—to which there would necessarily be many contributors in addition to AI—is the presence or absence of a culture of human rights within Guatemala that incorporates links between domestic organizations and external supporters of Guatemalan human rights.

AI's Activity

Amnesty International successfully generated an expanded international audience for Guatemalan human rights issues during the worst periods of violence. However, in the periods under study, AI was not always able to control how the expanded conflict over Guatemala was interpreted. Given the countervailing pressure from the United States and a noncommittal UN, internationalized debate over human rights norms could not jell into consensus to do something for the victims of human rights abuse in Guatemala. In the decade 1968–78, AI generated publicity about human rights in Guatemala, but detainees were becoming disappeared with increasing frequency, which precluded prisoner adoption. The 1979 country campaign and AI's continuing publicity and use of symbols was able to influence Guatemala's external, international environment enough to put pressure on the government to respond somehow or risk loss of prestige. However, that became less true in the early 1980s, once Guatemala had the backing of the U.S. presidential administration. Thus, even AI's strong suit is open to deliberate interference by powerful state and intergovernmental actors, at least in the short term.

AI's efforts to reach inside Guatemala and influence the regime through direct appeals also appeared, during the early 1980s, to have been stymied. To make direct demands on the government, AI depends on effective communication with the target government, and on creating a climate that at a minimum does not reward refusal to comply with human rights norms, and in more successful cases, tips the balance in favor of continued improvement. Creating the conditions for compliance also depends on communicating information to the international community and creating a consensus about what must be done. Despite deliberate changes in specific AI techniques over the years, there is little evidence of direct impact upon internal Guatemalan human rights policies themselves in the period under study. However, we do not know what might have happened in Guatemala in the absence of the activity of AI and other international human rights groups.

A Culture of Human Rights?

On reflection, the story traced above is discouraging. It seems to be a tale of decreasing effectiveness and decreased control over outcomes for human rights activists. But nonmilitary influence attempts are "low-profile, continuous" processes.[71] In each of the three periods examined above, organized internal pressure for human rights was virtually absent in Guatemala. Further, each period saw military rule. When a target government lacks organized internal pressure for human rights and a tradition of accountability to the populace, the possibilities for extending the effectiveness of a group like AI plummet.

Both of those factors have changed, albeit slowly and incrementally, in intervening years. Democracy has permitted a wider opening for fledgling internal human rights organizations, which have been able to develop links with existing transnational activist networks.[72] Even though the first president under democracy, Vinicio Cerezo, was criticized for continued human rights violations under his government, he did establish closer contact with the OAS and nongovernmental human rights groups than his predecessors, and created a national attorney general for human rights, the Procurador de los Derechos Humanos.

The number of civil society organizations concerned with human rights within Guatemala has expanded dramatically under democracy. The Grupo Apoyo Mutual (GAM, Mutual Support Group for Relatives of the Disappeared) was formed in 1984, just before the transition to democracy. Other important grassroots groups include the Coordinadora Nacional de Viudas de Guatemala (CONAVIGUA, National Coordinating Committee of Guatemalan Widows), formed in 1988, and the Consejo de Comunidades Étnicas "Runujel Junam" (CERJ, Council of Ethnic Communities "We Are

All Equal"). A new organization, Alianza Contra la Impunidad (Alliance Against Impunity), was established in mid-1996 as a coalition of numerous smaller groups.

Legal initiatives at the level of civil society have also been taken. In 1990 the Roman Catholic Church created the Oficina de Derechos Humanos del Arzobispado de Guatemala (ODHAG, Human Rights Office of the Archbishop of Guatemala), which began providing independent human rights education, documentation, and legal assistance for victims. That same year, the Centro de Acción Legal y Derechos Humanos (CALDH, Center for Legal and Human Rights Action) was formed in Washington, D.C., to facilitate links between Guatemalan domestic groups and international governmental and nongovernmental organizations.[73] CALDH established an active office in Guatemala as well. These organizations maintain contact with AI and other NGOs and international governmental human rights bodies.

For many reasons, international links with domestic organizations enable faster and better informed international responses to human rights abuses.[74] The need for international links as a protective measure is emphasized by the fact that domestic activism still carries risk in Guatemala. In April 1991, Americas Watch published a memo indicating that Guatemalan human rights activists were coming under attack.[75] A 1997 Amnesty report raised the same concern again.[76] Indeed, the founder and head of ODHAG, Bishop Juán Gerardi, was assassinated on April 26, 1998, only days after his office released a report containing thousands of Guatemalans' testimony on human rights violations. Since then, human rights workers, including Gerardi's successor, have continued to be threatened.[77] In May 1998, AI issued a press release asking, "Is Guatemala falling back to its tragic past?"[78] Amnesty International has continued to condemn new violations and the lack of accountability for old ones in Guatemala; the challenge there is to fulfill the political agreements and to deal with the past. External pressure has a place in creating incentives for elites to improve their image, in providing whatever safety third-party observers can issue when domestic activists speak out, and in furnishing accurate information about violations and relative deterioration or improvement, both for the international public and international organizations. Because prevention of new violations depends on increasing respect for human rights in a sometimes troublesome domestic and international context, the establishment of human rights still looks to be a difficult challenge for Guatemala and international actors seeking to support and hasten the process.

Notes

For access to documents, thanks are due to David Weissbrodt and the University of Minnesota Human Rights Library.

   1. Edy Kaufman, "Prisoners of Conscience: The Shaping of a New Human Rights Concept," *Human Rights Quarterly* 13 (1991), pp. 339–67.

   2. On AI and human rights norms, see Ann Marie Clark, *Diplomacy of Conscience: Amnesty International and Changing Human Rights Norms* (Princeton: Princeton University Press, forthcoming).

   3. Amnesty International, *Amnesty International Report 1998* (London: Amnesty International

Publications, 1998), frontispiece. For an analysis, see Peter R. Baehr, "Amnesty International and Its Self-Imposed Limited Mandate," *Netherlands Quarterly of Human Rights* 12, no. 1 (1994), pp. 5–21.

4. Ann Marie Clark and James A. McCann, "Enforcing International Standards of Justice: Amnesty International's Constructive Conflict Expansion," *Peace and Change* 16, no. 4 (October 1991), pp. 379–99.

5. The concept of expanding the scope of conflict is borrowed from a classic treatment of U.S. politics, E. E. Schattsneider, *The Semisovereign People* (Hinsdale, Ill.: Dryden Press, 1972).

6. Clark and McCann, "Enforcing International Standards," p. 381.

7. David Baldwin, *Economic Statecraft* (Princeton: Princeton University Press, 1985), p. 148.

8. Americas Watch (citing Guatemala Human Rights Commission statistics), *Civil Patrols in Guatemala* (New York: Americas Watch, August 1986), p. 3.

9. In an early annual report Amnesty International described its work simply as a "three-phase program: detection, investigation, and adoption." Amnesty International, *Annual Report, 1 June 1966–31 May 1967* (London: International Secretariat, Amnesty International, 1967).

10. Jim Handy, *Gift of the Devil: A History of Guatemala* (Toronto: Between the Lines, 1984).

11. Amnesty International, *Guatemala: Amnesty International Briefing Paper No. 8* (London: Amnesty International Publications, December 1976), p. 1.

12. Ibid.

13. Commission for Historical Clarification, *Guatemala: Memory of Silence* (Guatemala City: CEH, 1999), Conclusions, part 2, para. 128. Authorized posting on-line by the American Association for the Advancement of Science, at *http://hrdata.aaas.org/ceh*. The CEH found that 23,671 people were victims of arbitrary execution, and 6,159 were victims of forced disappearance, and estimated based on its own and other studies that about 200,000 people were killed or disappeared in the violence. Ibid., Conclusions, part 1, paras. 1–2.

14. Amnesty International, *Amnesty International Annual Report 1968–69* (London: Amnesty International Publications, 1969), p. 3.

15. Ibid., p. 6, referring to letters of thanks from released prisoners.

16. Martin Ennals, "Introduction," in Amnesty International, *Amnesty International Annual Report 1969–70* (London: Amnesty International Publications, 1970), p. 2.

17. "Staff shortages" in 1971–72 delayed AI's initiatives in Latin America. Amnesty International, *Amnesty International Annual Report, 1971–72* (London: Amnesty International Publications, 1972), p. 45.

18. Ibid., p. 61.

19. Amnesty International, *Amnesty International Annual Report 1972–73* (London: Amnesty International Publications, 1973), p. 6.

20. Ibid., p. 49.

21. Amnesty International, *Amnesty International Annual Report 1974–75* (London: Amnesty International Publications, 1975), pp. 13, 34.

22. Dirk Boerner, "Preface," in ibid., p. 6.

23. Hans Ehrenstrale, "Introduction," in Amnesty International, *Amnesty International Report 1975–76* (London: Amnesty International Publications, 1976), p. 9.

24. Amnesty International, *Annual Report 1975–76*, p. 100.

25. AI then responded to the commission: "Amnesty International's response of 17 September 1976 to the Commission noted this omission." Martin Ennals, "Introduction," in Amnesty International, *Amnesty International Report 1977* (London: Amnesty International Publications, 1977), pp. 26–27.

26. Amnesty International, *Amnesty International Report 1980* (London: Amnesty International Publications, 1980), p. 139.

27. Amnesty International, *Annual Report 1974–75*, p. 72. Although most research was carried out by staff at AI's London headquarters, groups were sometimes assigned cases and asked to express concern to authorities on an "investigatory" basis when AI was unsure whether the case met its prisoner adoption criteria. This was done for some early disappearance cases when the victim's status was unclear.

28. Amnesty International, *Amnesty International Report 1978* (London: Amnesty International Publications, 1978), p. 123.

29. For this information, I thank Scott Harrison and Ellen Moore of Amnesty International's Urgent Action Office in Nederland, Colorado.

30. Amnesty International, *Amnesty International Report 1980*, p. 16.

31. Jean-Marie Simon, *Guatemala: Eternal Spring, Eternal Tyranny* (New York: Norton, 1987), p. 72; Amnesty International, *Guatemala: The Human Rights Record* (London: Amnesty International Publications, 1987), p. 6.

32. Amnesty International, "Guatemala Campaign: OAS Testimony: Disappearances and Political Killings in Guatemala" (Amnesty International Document AMR/34/48/79), p. 5.

33. Ibid., p. 3.

34. Washington Office on Latin America, *Latin America Update*, November-December 1979, p. 2.

35. "Guatemalan massacre points to growing peasant resistance," *Latin America Regional Reports (Mexico and Central America)*, February 15, 1980, RM-80-02, p. 1.

36. Amnesty International, *Guatemala Campaign Circular No. 8*, July 10, 1979, p. 2; Amnesty International, *Amnesty International Report 1979* (London: Amnesty International Publications, 1979), p. 63.

37. Simon, *Guatemala*, p. 72.

38. For details, see Paul Albert, "The Undermining of the Legal Standards for Human Rights Violations in United States Foreign Policy: The Case of 'Improvement' in Guatemala," *Columbia Human Rights Law Journal* 14 (1982–83), pp. 231–74.

39. James M. Lindsay, "Trade Sanctions as Policy Instruments: A Re-examination," *International Studies Quarterly* 30 (1986), p. 170.

40. Typical was "Ninguna importancia da el gobierno a campaña de 'Amnesty International' [Government grants no importance to 'Amnesty International' campaign]," *El Gráfico* (Guatemala), September 13, 1979, p. 4. Author's translation.

41. Amnesty International, *Guatemala Campaign: Statements by Guatemalan Authorities on the Amnesty International Campaign*, January 24, 1980 (Amnesty International Index AMR 34/07/80), p. 2.

42. Remarks attributed to Minister of the Interior Donaldo Alvarez Ruiz, by the Guatemalan newspaper *El Gráfico*. The examples in this paragraph are drawn from Amnesty International, *Guatemala Campaign: Statements by Guatemalan Authorities*, pp. 3–6.

43. Ibid.; reports in the Times (London) and Interpress (London).

44. Ibid.; remarks by Minister of Defense Otto Spiegeler Noriega in a letter to a Swiss AI member.

45. Simon, *Guatemala*, p. 71.

46. Thomas Buergenthal, Robert Norris, and Dinah Shelton, *Protecting Human Rights in the Americas* (Strasbourg: International Institute of Human Rights, 1986), pp. 161–62.

47. Washington Office on Latin America, "Two Resignations of Guatemalans," *Latin America Update* 5, no. 5 (September-October 1980), p. 7. (Elias Barahona y Barahona, press secretary to Guatemala's Interior Ministry, made the second resignation.)

48. Lisa L. Martin and Kathryn Sikkink, "U.S. Policy and Human Rights in Argentina and Guatemala, 1973–1980," in Peter B. Evans, Harold K. Jacobson, and Robert D. Putnam, eds., *Double-Edged Diplomacy: International Bargaining and Domestic Politics* (Berkeley: University of California Press, 1993), p. 345.

49. Piero Gleijeses, "Guatemala: Crisis and Response," in Johns Hopkins University Study Group on United States–Guatemalan Relations, *Report on Guatemala: Findings of the Study Group on United States–Guatemalan Relations* (Boulder, Colo.: Westview, 1985), p. 60.

50. Ibid. The report Gleijeses refers to is probably Amnesty International, *Guatemala: A Government Program of Political Murder* (London: Amnesty International Publications, 1981).

51. Albert, "The Undermining of the Legal Standards for Human Rights Violations," p. 256.

52. Simon, *Guatemala*, p. 108.

53. Albert, "The Undermining of the Legal Standards for Human Rights Violations," pp. 254, 259–60.

54. Organization of American States, *Report on the Situation of Human Rights in the Republic of Guatemala* (Washington, D.C.: OAS, 1983; OEA/Ser.L/V/II.61), p. 61.

55. George Black, *Garrison Guatemala* (New York: Monthly Review Press, 1984), pp. 134–35; "Ríos Montt faces problems on the right . . . but has some successes against the left," *Latin America Regional Reports (Mexico and Central America)* September 24, 1982, RM-82-08, p. 6.

56. Amnesty International, *Amnesty International Report 1983* (London: Amnesty International Publications, 1983), p. 140; Amnesty International, *Amnesty International Report 1984* (London: Amnesty International Publications, 1984), p. 158.

57. Black, *Garrison Guatemala*, p. 136, n. 55.

58. Ibid., p. 158.

59. Amnesty International, *Amnesty International Report 1983*, p. 141.

60. Black, *Garrison Guatemala*, p. 159.

61. "Army discontent threatens Ríos Montt," *Latin America Regional Report (LARR)*, October 29, 1982, RM-82-09, p. 3.

62. Amnesty International, *Amnesty International Report 1983*, p. 139.

63. "Army discontent threatens Ríos Montt," *LARR*, 3.

64. Albert, "The Undermining of the Legal Standards for Human Rights Violations," p. 261; Commission for Historical Clarification, *Guatemala: Memory of Silence*.

65. Iain Guest, *Behind the Disappearances: Argentina's Dirty War against Human Rights and the United Nations* (Philadelphia: University of Pennsylvania Press, 1990), p. 314.

66. Ibid., p. 368.

67. Ibid., p. 370.

68. Ibid., p. 548, n. 8.

69. Simon, *Guatemala*, p. 121.

70. Amnesty International, "Guatemala: Appeals Against Impunity" (London: Amnesty International Publications, April 1997), accessible on-line at *http://www.amnesty.org/ailib/aipub/1997/AMR/23400397*.

71. Baldwin, *Economic Statecraft*, pp. 148–49.

72. See Susan Burgerman, "Mobilizing Principles: The Role of Transnational Activists in Promoting Human Rights Principles," *Human Rights Quarterly* 20 (1998), pp. 905–23.

73. Ibid., p. 912.

74. Ibid., p. 916; Ann Marie Clark, "The Contribution of NGOs to International Society," *Journal of International Affairs* 48, no. 2 (1995), p. 524.

75. Americas Watch, *Guatemala: Slaying of Rights Activists, Impunity Prevail Under New Government* (New York: Americas Watch, April 14, 1991).

76. Amnesty International, "Guatemala: Appeals Against Impunity."

77. Human Rights Watch, "Guatemala: Raid on Rights Defender's Home Condemned," press release, April 16, 1999.

78. Amnesty International, "Is Guatemala Falling Back to Its Tragic Past?" news release, May 13, 1998.

Chapter 3
Human Rights Watch
An Overview

Widney Brown

Human Rights Watch was founded in 1978 as Helsinki Watch when a group of activists, led by Robert Bernstein and Aryeh Neier, began monitoring compliance of the signatory countries with the Helsinki Accords. From 1973 to 1975, the United States, the USSR, Canada, and every European country except Albania negotiated and eventually signed the Helsinki Accords at the Conference on Security and Cooperation in Europe. The Helsinki Accords were widely perceived to have been a success for the USSR, because the accords endorsed the inviolability of Europe's borders as demarcated at the end of World War II. However, the Helsinki Accords contained a third "basket" of rights, largely ignored by the press and commentators, which included a commitment from the participating states to respect human rights and fundamental freedoms. This had the effect of explicitly introducing human rights into bilateral United States–USSR relations and provided an opening for nongovernmental actors to lobby the U.S. government to push the Soviet Union to uphold those rights. Equally important, the Helsinki Accords called on citizens to monitor their own governments' compliance. From this rather narrow beginning rooted in the Cold War, Human Rights Watch has evolved into an international human rights organization of significant scope and influence.

Human Rights Watch (HRW) is currently composed of five regional divisions: Africa (1987), Americas (1981), Asia (1985), Europe and Central Asia (originally Helsinki Watch, 1978), and Middle East and North Africa (1989); and three thematic divisions: arms, children's rights, and women's rights. It also focuses on several special issues, including academic freedom, corporations and human rights, drugs and human rights, labor rights, prisons, refugees, international justice, and the International Criminal Court. Human Rights Watch is now committed to monitoring over seventy countries for violations of civil and political rights and, to a lesser extent, economic rights. Although not obvious from the institutional structure, Human Rights Watch increasingly reports on human rights violations within the United States. HRW's first report on the United States was a 1982 analysis of U.S. compliance with the Helsinki Accords. In 1989, Human Rights Watch published a report on violations of the right to free expression through the imposition of censorship on school newspapers. In the last three years, Human Rights Watch has published two reports on sexual abuse of women in U.S. prisons, a report of police abuse, a report on felony disenfranchisement, two reports on supermaximum prisons, a report on detention of asylum seekers in U.S. jails, and two reports on human rights violations in juvenile detention facilities.

Since its inception, Human Rights Watch has placed particular emphasis on influencing U.S. government policies. Originally, the focus was on U.S. foreign policy, but increasingly, the United States' own human rights record has come under scrutiny, in large part because the United States has been slow to ratify international human rights treaties and has been resistant to the concept that the American government was as equally bound by international human rights standards as other sovereign nations. Although the U.S. government remains one of Human Rights Watch's primary advocacy targets, it has grown to do extensive advocacy with numerous governments, the European Union, the United Nations and its associated organizations and programs, the World Bank, the International Monetary Fund, and multinational corporations.

The Women's Rights Division

The Women's Rights Project, now a division, was established in 1990 to research and document the ways in which women experience human rights violations. The decision to create the division arose from the recognition within HRW that its ongoing work failed to address pervasive but largely ignored human rights violations suffered by women. These include violations which have been traditionally recognized, such as torture, disappearances, and denial of the rights of free association, as well as violations which are gender based or gender specific, such as sexual violence, trafficking, and gender-based discrimination. The Women's Rights Division documents state complicity in violence and legalized and de facto discrimination, as well as the failure of states to respond to and redress gender-based violence and discrimination. The division has conducted research and published reports on a wide range of issues including police abuse in Brazil, virginity testing in Turkey, sexual abuse against women incarcerated in U.S. state prisons, trafficking of women in a variety of countries, pregnancy testing of women working in the maquiladora sector in Mexico, rape of women in detention by police in Pakistan, and violence against women in refugee camps.

At its inception, the staff consisted of founder Dorothy Q. Thomas, an associate and fellow. Over time it has grown to include researchers with expertise not just in women's human rights, but also in each of the regional areas covered by Human Rights Watch. The project received an initial start-up grant and the director was responsible for raising the funds to continue the project's research and advocacy. Human Rights Watch signaled its permanent commitment to the project by integrating it into the overall operating budget and making it a division. The ground-breaking research done by the Women's Rights Division significantly raised its profile and led to its rapid growth from a small project to a full division between 1990 and 1998.

Thomas had worked on southern and South Africa, prior to joining Human Rights Watch, as the project coordinator for the Namibia Project of the Lawyers' Committee for Civil Rights Under Law. She left Human Rights Watch in 1998, after nurturing the project through its infancy into full divisional status. Shortly after leaving Human Rights Watch, Thomas received a MacArthur "genius" grant in recognition of her work promoting women's human rights. The new executive director is Regan E. Ralph, who has expertise in the Middle East as well as experience working on domestic civil rights and economic justice issues and was one of the first researchers to join the project. The current staff brings diverse work and educational experience to the division.

Major Goals of Human Rights Watch

One of Human Rights Watch's main goals is to promote changes which increase recognition and protection of human rights. Its main tool for achieving these changes is through reporting facts. Human Rights Watch investigates allegations of human rights violations, publishes reports documenting abuse, and uses the extensively researched fact-based reports as tools for change. This requires careful and thorough documentation of alleged abuses; the ability to demonstrate accountability for those abuses by the state or other entity in charge, through acts of either commission or omission, under international law; and the ability to disseminate the information at both the national and international level. Although the U.S. government remains a central target of Human Rights Watch's advocacy work, reports contain recommendations targeted at the offending government, intergovernmental organizations, and the international community, particularly donor countries, and are intended as advocacy tools for national human rights organizations.

Early in Human Rights Watch's history, when the organization added Americas Watch to the existing Helsinki Watch, the value of promoting change through reporting facts was convincingly demonstrated. In 1985, Human Rights Watch opened an office in El Salvador and began publicizing abuses by the Salvadoran forces and their allies. Its findings posed an enormous problem for the U.S. government, which was vigorously defending the Salvadoran regime and supporting the military with technical assistance, arms, and money. For three years the Reagan administration continuously challenged the accuracy of Human Rights Watch reports and denied the government's participation in human rights violations in El Salvador. This battle, largely played out in the press, eventually tilted toward Human Rights Watch when the United States Congress, responding to pressure from constituents and convinced, in part, by Human Rights Watch's accurate reporting, cut off military aid to the Salvadoran government.

Another significant Human Rights Watch goal is to support the creation of effective mechanisms to promote and protect human rights around the world and to end impunity for violators of human rights. Examples of this work, some of which I will describe in detail later in this chapter, include advocating for the creation of special mechanisms within the United Nations; pushing the UN Security Council to set up two ad hoc criminal tribunals for the former Yugoslavia and for Rwanda; spearheading the International Campaign to Ban Landmines; and continuing work on the creation of a permanent international criminal court.

The Women's Rights Division shares the institution's goals, but also has additional goals which relate directly to the challenges of promoting women's human rights, namely, compelling governments, traditional human rights organizations, and scholars to recognize gender-specific violations of human rights and gender-based obstacles to the enjoyment of rights. In June 1993, the women's human rights community presented a petition signed by 240,000 people from 120 countries to the United Nations Conference on Human Rights in Vienna, forcing a belated recognition by the international community that "women's rights are human rights." Notwithstanding the increased visibility of gender-based human rights violations, the willingness of the international community to hold violators accountable is shaky at best. For example, at the Rome Treaty Conference for the creation of an international criminal court in July 1998, most countries remained passive in the face of a systematic attack by a small group of reactionary countries on the proposed elements of the treaty aimed at ensuring that gender-based crimes and crimes of sexual violence would be vigorously and effectively prosecuted.

Members of the Clinton administration, unlike members of past U.S. administrations, have spoken out in defense of women's human rights. Secretary of State Madeleine Albright has repeatedly attacked cultural defenses or justifications for violations of women's human rights, arguing, for example, that domestic violence "is criminal, not cultural." Nonetheless, the U.S. government continues to be reluctant to address such human rights violations as foreign policy issues. Furthermore, when the Women's Rights Division has repeatedly challenged the federal and state governments to "bring human rights home," for example, with regard to ending sexual violence against incarcerated women in U.S. prisons, the Women's Rights Division staff finds itself facing a double denial: human rights aren't violated in the United States, and what the women are experiencing is insignificant or even a result of their provocative actions.

Another Women's Rights Division goal is to strengthen the understanding of the interrelatedness of violations which women experience, in particular the relationship between gender-based discrimination and violence against women. Women's second-class status in the world make them particularly vulnerable to gender-based violence and unable to access the criminal justice system in an attempt to end the violence. For example, a woman who is denied access to education, the right to own property, access to credit, the right to enter into a contract, and the right to travel freely, would find it difficult to leave an abusive relationship even if the criminal justice system recognized domestic violence as a crime. Her lack of education would probably create a barrier to accessing and understanding the criminal justice system; her inability to own property, enter into contracts, and get credit would mean that she would probably be financially dependent on her abusive partner; and her inability to travel freely might prevent her from leaving the abusive situation, even temporarily.

Finally, the Women's Rights Division is committed to working with women's organizations throughout the world to make the connections between "women's issues" and women's human rights, to build capacity and to help strengthen their work by contextualizing it within a human rights framework. For this reason, the Women's Rights Division coauthored *Women's Human Rights, Step by Step*, a practical guide to understanding the human rights framework, the United Nations, advocacy, and documentation. The Women's Rights Division staff is also actively involved in capacity building, conducting training with nongovernmental organizations interested in learning from Human Rights Watch's experiences documenting human rights abuses and conducting advocacy on women's human rights issues. The Women's Rights Division has benefited from this capacity-building work, as it helps establish ongoing relationships with local nongovernmental organizations, which then facilitate the division's work in the area. Most recently, the division's researcher documenting human rights violations that occurred during the Kosovo conflict provided technical support to women's rights organizations in Albania and was able to get pertinent information on the situation of women in the refugee camps in there.

The Women's Rights Division also has an important role within Human Rights Watch. The goal of the division is not just to conduct its own research and advocacy, but also to facilitate the integration of documentation and advocacy on women's rights issues within the other divisions and projects. This cross-fertilization requires the institutional recognition that researchers within the division have an expertise and understanding of women's human rights violations that are outside traditionally recognized models, for example, state accountability for private crimes ignored by the state such as domestic violence. It also requires Human Rights Watch to recognize that women's rights are human rights, that is, that the work of the Women's Rights Division is not peripheral to the mandate of the organization. It has also given the Women's Rights Division insight into the challenges and complexities of truly accomplishing the widely articulated but seldom realized goal of "gender mainstreaming." (Gender mainstreaming is the process of analyzing how the United Nations and governments address both substantive and procedural issues, in order to determine the extent to which these issues are addressed in a manner that ignores the experiences and needs of women.)

How Goals Are Set and Expanded

As noted above, Human Rights Watch began by monitoring compliance of the signatory countries to the Helsinki Accords drafted at the Conference on Security and Cooperation in Europe. The Helsinki Accords enumerated specific rights, including civil, cultural, economic, political, and social rights. However, the U.S. government focused most of its attention on what U.S. president Gerald Ford called "the most fundamental human rights—liberty of thought, conscience, and faith; the exercise of civil and political rights; the rights of minorities." As Helsinki Watch advocated that the U.S. government push for these rights in bilateral negotiations with the USSR and other "iron curtain" countries, economic rights fell off the radar screen.

As Human Rights Watch began reporting on other regions of the world, the focus remained on violations of civil and political rights. Human Rights Watch made this decision based on the belief that given limited resources, the institution could be more effective in addressing these rights violations, and because in many countries in which Human Rights Watch was working, the clear priority was addressing egregious violations of political and civil rights. This has led to criticism, echoed in Chapter 7 by Makau Mutua, that Human Rights Watch, like many Western human rights organizations, has contributed to the privileging of civil and political rights over economic and social rights. The end of the Cold War has allowed activists more room to challenge the arguments privileging civil and political rights or differentiating them from economic rights. In the post–Cold War era, nearly all states proclaim their commitment to human rights and recognize that if they commit or allow gross violations of traditionally recognized civil and political rights, the very legitimacy of their governments will be challenged. However, the international community seems less willing to challenge violations of economic rights, although the decision of UN High Commissioner Mary Robinson to make promotion of the right to development a central part of her mandate may force the international community to take economic rights seriously.

In keeping with these post–Cold War changes, in the mid-1990s, Human Rights Watch initiated internal discussions on expanding its mandate to cover violations of economic rights. Urged on by strong support from the staff, the board adopted a policy that includes documenting economic rights violations that are caused in part by violations of a civil or political right. Labor rights is the most obvious area for researching this intersection of rights violations. In 1998, Human Rights Watch began a labor rights project, building on work done by the various divisions on forced labor and child labor practices. Other economic rights violations which Human Rights Watch is exploring include violations of the rights to health and education. The board recently renewed its commitment to this work and acknowledged that it will take time for researchers within Human Rights Watch to develop the expertise to assess and document economic rights violations. The Women's Rights Division was a strong supporter of this change in mandate, because, as noted above, women rarely experience isolated violations of their rights and, because of their second class status in many countries, they are particularly vulnerable both to violations of their economic rights and their civil and political rights.

Internal Governance and Financing

Human Rights Watch is governed by a board of directors with thirty-three members. From its founding in 1978 to 1997, cofounder Robert Bernstein served as chair of the board. In 1998, Jonathan Fanton became chair. The original board was composed of many members of the Fund for Free Expression, a group of writers and publishers who advocated the release of writers imprisoned for their writing and political activities throughout the world. The board has evolved into a more traditional model in which members bring particular expertise in institution building to the organization, not the least of which is fund-raising. Each division has an advisory committee. Usually, members of the board of directors serve on one divisional advisory committee with the balance of members being composed of people with either the appropriate regional or thematic expertise. The sizes of the advisory committees vary from division to division but typically number around twenty-five.

Within the Women's Rights Division, the advisory committee serves many functions: it participates in critical policy discussions, provides expertise in a wide range of areas, promotes the work of the division, and raises funds. Some members have also participated in either research or advocacy missions. Typically, advisory committees meet three or four times a year and interact freely with the staff.

The structure of Human Rights Watch has changed significantly in the past several years. For more than a decade, each of the regional divisions enjoyed near total autonomy in both their day-to-day functioning and their substantive work. Helsinki Watch, as the original "watch" group, had a very high profile, enjoyed widespread respect in the international human rights movement, and had a long history of documenting human rights abuses in Europe, Turkey, and the former Soviet Union. In the mid-1990s, Helsinki Watch and the other regional and thematic divisions made the difficult decision to merge into a single identifiable entity, Human Rights Watch. In making this decision, the better-known and established divisions gave up their name recognition in order to create an organization which would be able, in the long run, to leverage the influence of each of its parts into a greater whole.

Human Rights Watch has a core executive staff responsible for overseeing operations and coordinating the work of the entire organization. The staff includes an executive director, associate director, development director, communications director, advocacy director, program director, general counsel, finance director, and human resources director. Each division is composed of an executive director, deputy director, advocacy director, and several researchers and support staff. The organization strives to balance the independence of the divisions with the need to work cooperatively, both to give coherence to the larger body of work and to increase the institution's ability to advocate successfully the adoption of policies which incorporate a human rights analysis by both governments and other institutions. This balancing of divisional autonomy with institutional coherence must take into account that people from different regions of the world may be confronting very different human rights struggles.

Human Rights Watch is funded in large part by U.S.-based foundations such as the Ford Foundation, the John D. and Catherine T. MacArthur Foundation, and the Open Society Institute. Human Rights Watch also relies upon a significant number of major individual supporters. It has an absolute prohibition on accepting funds either directly or indirectly from governments. This prohibition is aimed at avoiding even the appearance of undue government influence on any choices or investigations made by Human Rights Watch and to avoid the inference that the organization is implicitly endorsing a government as not being a human rights violator. A more complex funding issue confronting Human Rights Watch is support from business entities. As Human Rights Watch begins exploring economic rights violations and continues its work on human rights and corporations, potential funding from business entities raises similar questions of conflict of interest. To date, Human Rights Watch has made decisions about such funding on a case-by-case basis.

In 1998, Human Rights Watch launched an endowment campaign in the hopes of creating a source of general support funds to give the organization a measure of financial security. Human Rights Watch sponsors a film festival program which is primarily designed as an education project but which also raises money for the organization through festivals held in several cities. The final source of income is an annual dinner at which Human Rights Watch honors the work of several human rights defenders. Human Rights Watch invites human rights defenders from around the world to visit the United States, meet with nongovernmental and governmental organizations and share their experiences and expertise with the staff and other constituencies in the United States.

Preferred Type of Output

Human Rights Watch has long sought an effective balance between research and advocacy. In the early years, Human Rights Watch relied almost exclusively on high-level advocacy aimed at the U.S. government's foreign policy makers, who could be persuaded to take action or adopt policies based on Human Rights Watch's research and analysis of human rights abuses by specific governments. Researchers, schooled in human rights documentation, would identify a right, investigate allegations of violations of that right, document and describe the details of the specific violations, and publish this information along with recommendations for the U.S. government's foreign policy response to these violations. Researchers would push for hearings before the Foreign Relations Committee or some other appropriate congressional entity, would meet with policy makers at the State Department, and would seek media coverage of the issue.

Over time, Human Rights Watch's advocacy tactics have had to evolve to reflect changes in the balance of power in the world, most notably the disintegration of the USSR and the transition of many governments from military dictatorships to democracies. Advocacy strategies also had to incorporate the growth of Human Rights Watch's work to include women's rights and children's rights. To address how global relationships have changed, Human Rights Watch began examining other means of holding governments and quasi-governmental actors accountable for violations. Increasingly Human Rights Watch has turned to the European Union, the Organization for Security and Cooperation in Europe, and other intergovernmental organizations to put pressure on offending governments to end human rights abuses. Human Rights Watch also is cultivating ongoing dialogues directly with many governments, as evidenced by the presence of the organization in Moscow, Hong Kong, Rio de Janeiro, Tashkent, Dushanbe, and Tbilisi. In the mid 1990s, Human Rights Watch also began doing extensive advocacy with and monitoring of the United Nations and its related programs and agencies, including creating the position of a UN representative. In 1998, Human Rights Watch added the position of global advocacy director with the aim of coordinating the advocacy being conducted by the various divisions and projects. Despite this increased profile for advocacy within Human Rights Watch, a central principle guiding its work is that research remains the sine qua non of its mandate.

The Women's Rights Division in particular has found that traditional advocacy strategies are often unavailing. Only rarely do abuses of women's human rights generate significant or sustained interests among major players in shaping foreign policy. There is almost always some crisis situation which will absorb governmental attention and resources and take precedence over addressing women's human rights. Although many governments pay lip service to the concept of women's human rights, most governments continue to address widespread violations with token gestures. Yet, within the women's human rights movement there is the understanding that women will never be able to enjoy the full range of human rights without a radical shift in women's status from marginalized to fully equal. Such a transformation requires not only restructuring existing systems and comprehensive statutory reform, but also requires examining assumptions about women in every realm. Thus, the Women's Rights Division recognizes the importance of establishing ongoing working relationships with domestic women's rights organizations and traditional human rights organizations and of coordinating advocacy so that governments are pressured by the international community as well as a wide range of national or regional nongovernmental organizations. Only when sustained and multilevel pressure is brought to bear will governments take the steps necessary to promote women's human rights.

Increasingly, Human Rights Watch uses the Internet and its Web site to disseminate reports and press releases, to update readers on government responses to reports of human rights violations, to educate the public on human rights issues, to suggest actions to take on particular issues, and to focus attention on Human Rights Watch's campaigns. The Human Rights Watch Web site (*http://www.hrw.org*) is accessible in English, Spanish, French, Arabic, Russian, Chinese, and Portuguese. A recent example of increased use of Human Rights Watch's Internet and Web site occurred during the recent crisis in Kosovo. Human Rights Watch researchers working in the refugee camps in Albania and Macedonia were able to send the results of their interviews with the refugees fleeing Kosovo directly to the Human Rights Watch staff in New York, who in turn issued Kosovo updates through a listserv and posted them to the Human Rights Watch Web site. When NATO troops entered Kosovo, Human Rights Watch researchers accompanied the press corps and again were able to send information and download pictures which were then posted to the Web, giving activists, scholars, and the press access to the latest Human Rights Watch findings.

Types of Policy Input Sought and by Whom

Each division and project within Human Rights Watch consults with a variety of people with expertise in related fields. For example, the advisory committee for the Women's Rights Division includes lawyers, professors, activists, and researchers with expertise in areas ranging from international human rights law, health and human rights, maternal mortality, gender, and the criminal justice system, to reproductive health and rights. The Women's Rights Division advisory committee serves as both a source of expertise as well as a sounding board for the division as it examines new areas in which to document violations, shapes specific recommendations and advocacy plans. The advisory committee also strives to think strategically about the work being done by the division, its relationship to the larger institution, and its relationship to work being done by other organizations.

As the division takes on new issues and/or begins work in a country for the first time, the staff relies on consultation with local activists, regional activists, and people with expertise or experience which helps them understand the context in which they are working. For example, the Women's Rights Division conducted work on sexual and domestic violence against Burundian women in Tanzanian refugee camps. An integral part of the research included conversations with Tanzanian lawyers who explained how domestic law did or did not address sexual and domestic violence; interviews with field staff of the United Nations High Commissioner for Refugees (UNHCR) in Tanzania as well as policy makers in Geneva; and interviews with a wide range of UNHCR's partners, who were able to tell the researchers what obstacles they faced in implementing policies on a day-to-day basis in the camps and how the administration of the Tanzanian camp differed from other camps. Additional interviews were conducted with refugees, camp staff, refugee governing committees, UNHCR officials, and government officials in Tanzania. As a result of this process, the Women's Rights Division was able to contextualize its findings within a broad understanding of the challenges facing host governments and the UNHCR in protecting women refugees, and to tailor its recommendations to address both larger policy challenges and specific challenges facing the refugees in Tanzania.

Assessment of Goals and Activities

Each division and project within Human Rights Watch is responsible for assessing the effectiveness of its reporting and advocacy and adjusting its work plans accordingly. However, since the unification of Human Rights Watch, each division and project is also responsible for doing work that reflects the scope of the institution's mandate. The program director facilitates coordination between the divisions and projects to ensure that, as new issues arise from the research, the institution's response is consistent both with its mandate and from division to division.

In the mid-1990s, in light of the rapid growth of Human Rights Watch, the Ford

Foundation proposed that it fund a strategic review of the institution. This entailed interviewing a wide range of actors from human rights organizations throughout the world. Virtually everyone interviewed noted the importance of Human Rights Watch's research and its potential as an advocacy tool. Some interviewees expressed concern that Human Rights Watch did not sufficiently maintain a connection with domestic non-governmental organizations, which is critical given the rapidity with which situations can change. Still other questioned Human Rights Watch's continued exclusive focus on civil and political rights. Based on this critique, Human Rights Watch staff and board members conducted a reevaluation of its work. As a result, Human Rights Watch, recognizing its unique niche, reaffirmed the importance of targeting U.S. foreign policy makers. However, responding to the criticism with regard to its relationship with domestic human rights organizations, Human Rights Watch has sought to improve those relations. Two divisions, Asia and Africa, have nongovernmental liaisons who maintain relationships with domestic human rights organizations and to a lesser extent engage in capacity building. In the other divisions, the advocacy directors are primarily responsible for building and maintaining relationships with domestic and regional NGOs. As noted above, Human Rights Watch also made the decision to begin documenting violations of economic rights.

Coping with Change

As Human Rights Watch has grown, the biggest challenges are maintaining the most effective balance between research and advocacy, allowing the various parts of the organization independence without sacrificing internal cogency, leveraging its influence, and determining which advocacy projects make the best use of institutional resources. As Human Rights Watch's advocacy goals become more sophisticated, the balance between research and publishing, on the one hand, and advocacy, on the other hand, becomes more challenging, particularly since the balancing entails financial resources, time, and energy and has no guaranteed outcome. For example, in 1992, Human Rights Watch became one of the founding members of the International Campaign to Ban Landmines. It is currently a member of the campaign's coordinating committee and serves as coordinator of the new landmine monitor initiative of the campaign. Not surprisingly, Human Rights Watch became involved in the campaign while researching a comprehensive report documenting the death and destruction caused by landmines. The campaign was launched in 1992 and the report, *Landmines: A Deadly Legacy*, was published in October 1993. Having made the decision to be involved with the campaign, the Arms Division of Human Rights Watch continued to research and report on landmines, publishing five reports and four fact sheets over a six-year period. However, in addition to the time spent conducting further research, the division also dedicated one person full-time to support the campaign. After intense frustration with the failure of the United Nations to move forward on the issue, the campaign bore fruit. With the support of the Canadian government and a significant number of small and medium-sized governments, a group of 122 countries gathered in Ottawa in December 1997 to sign a treaty that bans the use, production, stockpiling, and transfer of antipersonnel mines. The treaty went into effect on March 1, 1999. Although this particular advocacy project has been quite successful and even garnered a Nobel Peace Prize for the International Campaign to Ban Landmines and its coordinator, Jody Williams, the success came after years of frustration and is still muted by the failure of the U.S. government to support the ban and ratify the treaty. Although many aspects of the campaign are unlikely to be replicated in other situations, it may serve as a model on how to make significant progress in addressing a human rights issue without the support of either the United Nations or the United States.

In contrast to Human Rights Watch's work on the International Campaign to Ban Landmines, which has an impact in virtually every country in the world, an ongoing recent campaign on Dalit (or "Untouchable") human rights has focused on an issue that affects people primarily in one country, India. The work by the Asia Division is an example of close collaboration with domestic nongovernmental organizations, and it demonstrates the impact of framing an issue in human rights terms and integrating a gender perspective into a human rights report. In both the land mine and the Dalit rights campaigns the challenge is to ascertain the potential impact of the advocacy work, the uniqueness of Human Rights Watch's contribution, and the place of the work within the institution's mandate. Although the campaigns are very different, both are examples of Human Rights Watch's increased commitment to long-term advocacy planning.

Evidence of Governmental Change in Response to Human Rights Watch

It is rare that any person or organization doing advocacy work can point to a specific act of advocacy and a specific outcome and claim a cause and effect relationship between the two events. Human Rights Watch does not work on promoting and protecting human rights in a vacuum, but rather is part of a large assortment of organizations working on the issues. In particular areas, Human Rights Watch's expertise or long-term commitment to an issue may have been a significant contributing factor to change, but again, nongovernmental actors are just one of many factors. Nonetheless, it is important to acknowledge that Human Rights Watch has been part of a movement that has introduced the language of human rights into mainstream press coverage of national and international political reporting in the United States. Human Rights Watch has sought to build effective mechanisms to promote human rights, for example, with its vigorous participation in the creation of the International Criminal Court. It has raised public awareness in the United States of the connection between U.S. foreign policies and accountability for human rights violations and has been outspoken in exposing the double standard of the U.S. government in criticizing human rights violations abroad while denying the existence and seriousness of human rights violations at home. Human Rights Watch was also an important voice in arguing that, under existing international humanitarian law, rape is a war crime.

In one of its more sustained advocacy efforts, the Women's Rights Division has been working since 1994 on ending human rights abuses of women incarcerated in U.S. prisons. It is clear that this work, done in close collaboration with state and national nongovernmental organizations and activists, has been instrumental in changing the dialogue from that of protecting "prisoners' rights," a difficult proposition in the current political and social climate, to one of ending human rights violations. However, Human Rights Watch's work in this area would have been futile if not for the ongoing sustained work of many organizations which worked to end abuses against incarcerated women, even when no press or politicians were watching. Human Rights Watch and other international organizations must identify, support, and work with individuals and organizations who, regardless of their characterization of the work, have been struggling to end human rights abuses, and whose work will continue long after Human Rights Watch or other international NGOs have moved on to the next project. Human Rights Watch's international profile creates a space in which domestic organizations and activists can do their work, and also makes it difficult for governments to summarily dismiss the work of these organizations and activists.

As the centrality of human rights grows in importance within the international community, the less likely it is that Human Rights Watch or any other international nongovernmental organization will be able to take credit for specific improvements in human rights. However, the very increased prominence of human rights points to the importance of having domestic, regional, and international nongovernmental organizations working together to compel all countries to promote and respect human rights.

As Human Rights Watch grows, the institution faces many significant challenges. First, Human Rights Watch, despite the diversity of its staff and the scope of its research, has not achieved its goal of internationalizing its staff, board, and advisory committees. Second, as states increasingly accept the human rights paradigm, particularly regarding civil and political rights, the role of Human Rights Watch's work in promoting and protecting these rights will become less important than addressing failures of implementation and compliance. This will require a type of research and advocacy which recognizes that the genuine adoption of human rights policies is but a first step in protecting and promoting human rights. Finally, as global politics evolve and the global economy exerts unprecedented influence over both internal and foreign policy, Human Rights Watch will be faced with choosing the best ways to address the promotion and protection of economic and social rights in a world where a vast number of people struggle merely to survive.

Chapter 4
Amnesty International and Human Rights Watch
A Comparison

Claude E. Welch, Jr.

A Framework for Analysis

All organizations confront classic issues about their roles—the long-standing questions of who gets what, why, and how. If you will pardon the play on words, I shall concentrate on ROLES as an acronym—*resources, organization, leadership, execution* of objectives, and choice of *strategy*. Each of these aspects is critical to the entity. What budget can it utilize to work toward its objectives? How does the organization establish its lines of communication, set forth its goals, or conform with legal strictures on its structure? In what ways are leaders selected, trained, advanced (or retrenched), and evaluated? What strategy and tactics are adopted, given the organization's resources, objectives, leadership, and previous implementation? Given that NGOs rely heavily on volunteers, what balance should be achieved between professionals and supporters? These are weighty matters, examined to date primarily in articles or chapters about single organizations, rarely in comparative frameworks as in this volume as a whole.

In formal terms, NGOs have a limited place in the structure of intergovernmental organizations (IGOs), including the various human rights treaty regimes. The post–World War II international human rights edifice has been built on the classic foundation of states, notably through the UN and through regional IGOs such as the Council of Europe or the Organization of American States. Although numerous citizen organizations, largely from the United States, commented on drafts and participated in the San Francisco conference,[1] the United Nations was a creation of the victorious allied governments. References in its charter to other entities (as in its opening capitalized words, "WE THE PEOPLES OF THE UNITED NATIONS . . .", or the noble purpose "to develop friendly relations among nations based on respect for the principle of equal rights and self-determination of peoples . . .") have never masked the reality of governmental power. Member countries pledged in the charter to "promot[e] and encourag[e] respect for human rights and for fundamental freedoms for all without distinction as to race, sex, language, or religion." Even though American NGOs were largely responsible for introducing human rights into the preamble and into the principles and purposes of the UN charter, as noted in the Introduction, their roles were clearly subordinate to those of governments.

States establish the framework for international supervision of human rights (standard setting) and play the paramount role in the protection of human rights (enforcement). The overwhelming majority of UN member states voted in favor of the (nonbinding) Universal Declaration of Human Rights (UDHR) in 1948, and several even have explicitly incorporated references to the UDHR in their constitutions. Six major UN treaties, and further conventions at regional levels, have spelled out specific obligations for the states that have ratified them, and established specific regimes for monitoring performance. Other international obligations have grown during these decades. Global responsibility for human rights performance now seems well established. Pre–World War II assertions about legal positivism and domestic sovereignty, and the postwar fact of Article 2 (7) of the UN Charter must be tested against contemporary realities. No state can claim to stand apart from global human rights expectations—some based in customary international law, some based on treaty law, and some based on popular expectations expressed in part through NGOs. Gossamer webs of obligation with respect to states' international accountability for internal actions have developed.

Central to these webs of obligation—this "curious grapevine," in Eleanor Roosevelt's phrase—have been nongovernmental organizations. Recalling the points raised earlier in the Introduction and in the preceding chapters, we can confidently accept the following points:

- Although NGOs cannot expect to rival states in terms of their direct impact upon all citizens of specific countries, they influence government actions with respect to some areas.
- NGOs pursue a variety of strategies, shifting goals on occasion and tactics more frequently.
- Provision of information is central to NGO effectiveness.
- Networking among public interest groups has proven essential, particularly in terms of standard setting in human rights.

Amnesty International

Since its founding, Amnesty International (AI) has grown into the world's largest and possibly most effective human rights organization. In terms of budget, staff, global reach, apparent impact, and related criteria, AI towers above others.[2] Its history and impact have been chronicled by many and are summarized by other authors in this section; hence, I will remark only on strategic choices relevant to its success.[3]

Let us start with the observations of former AI secretary-general Martin Ennals[4] made in the early 1980s when the organization was, in his words, a "small body [that] has grown amazingly."[5] Its power—the only power it could "hope to exercise"—is publicity, or the threat of using it.[6] "Slow and systematic methods of persistence, reasonableness, courtesy, challenges at the international level or publication" constitute Amnesty's major weapons.[7] Impartiality in publicity and accuracy in research remain essential. With its structure financed heavily by members' contributions, AI carries no taint of governmental involvement. National sections are autonomous (though with initial approval of their statute and structure coming from the International Executive Committee). As Ennals aptly noted, "AI is above all therefore an international movement with national foundations, but with international policies based on restricted objectives universally applied."[8]

The organization had yet to recognize the importance of its extraordinarily important campaign against torture, or to have drawn major lessons from its mixed experience in Guatemala, when Ennals wrote. At that time, and to a significant extent today, "AI is essentially a case-work organization."[9] However, the organization had by the early 1980s grasped the importance of documenting situations that (in the words of noted ECOSOC resolution 1503) reveal "a consistent pattern of gross violations of human rights." AI has supplemented its initial focus on prisoners of conscience (POCs) with attention to campaigns on particular issues or countries. To quote Morton E. Winston, the former chair of the United States section of Amnesty International and contributor to this volume, "While it has not entirely abandoned its prisoner orientation, AI's working methods in recent years have tended to focus more on 'situations' and 'patterns of violations' using individual cases as illustrations."[10]

Keck and Sikkink[11] specify several reasons for Amnesty's success. AI has chosen to focus on specific individuals whose rights were violated, rather than on abstract ideas. According to them, "This led to strong identification between the victim and the public."[12] Its concentration on a small number of gross violations enabled it to utilize issues on which significant international consensus existed. By selecting its urgent action cases equally from First, Second, and Third Worlds, Amnesty established independence from Cold War politics. And, in its documentation, AI established and maintained a reputation for careful cross-checking. However, the organization has increasingly emphasized situations as contrasted with attention to individual victims of human rights abuses. Although Urgent Action appeals and the regular letter-writing campaigns for prisoners of conscience continue to provide the stuff for groups' meetings, the tasks of the central research office relate increasingly to systematic abuses.

Thakur[13] notes that Amnesty carries out the first four of five distinct NGO roles in international relations: (1) consciousness-raising or value promotion; (2) agenda setting; (3) lobbying to shape delegates' instructions at forums and to implement international commitment; (4) monitoring; and (5) direct action.[14] As a "sovereignty-free" actor, AI (like the vast majority of human rights NGOs) is primarily concerned with states' internal behavior, rather than with their international behavior. Amnesty can monitor states' performance better than the United Nations due not only to its independence from government pressures,[15] but also to "the more intensely personal com-

mitment of its members, its cost-effectiveness and flexibility of management and structure."[16] Thakur does not comment on AI's behind-the-scenes role in proposing treaty
language, which is in many respects the organization's area of most lasting impact.

Cook directs her attention to Amnesty International's impact on the United Nations, the most important political intergovernmental organization. AI's work within
IGOs "is a core element of its efforts to secure universal observance of the [Universal]
Declaration [of Human Rights] and the organisation devotes considerable time, expertise and resources to these activities."[17] Although AI *promotes* all human rights, it seeks
to *protect* specific areas, calling upon governments to free all prisoners of conscience; ensure fair and prompt trials for all political prisoners; abolish the death penalty, torture,
and other cruel treatment of prisoners; and end extrajudicial executions and disappearances. Combining national action and direct input to UN bodies, especially through
AI's professional staff, "has greatly enhanced Amnesty's impact."[18] Cook details specific contributions in (1) standard-setting, (2) strengthening UN mechanisms and procedures (including the establishment, following the 1993 Vienna World Conference,
of the High Commissioner for Human Rights) and (3) raising country situations at the
Commission on Human Rights (through the 1503 procedure,[19] thematic mechanisms,
and the treaty-monitoring bodies). She concludes, "The profile and recognition that
Amnesty has established at the UN have created tremendous scope for action and influence. At the same time this has a price; it leads to heavy demands on the organisation
and expectations that it can and will act on every issue, sometimes making it difficult
to focus Amnesty's own priorities."[20]

Clark[21] concentrates on Amnesty's role in the development of new norms of international practice. To her, such norms (1) impose international standards on internal
state matters, despite the long heritage of noninterference and domestic sovereignty,
(2) have proliferated in the past half century, (3) have been pressed by NGOs that make
bold attempts to influence states, (4) are codified and applied in intergovernmental
arenas, and (5) arise from insufficiently studied nonstate actors. Clark considers three
issue areas in which Amnesty has made significant contributions to these norms: torture, disappearances, and extrajudicial executions. In the case of torture, already pro-
hibited in international law when AI was founded, public awareness and information
about torture as a government practice were missing.[22] Amnesty's seminal Campaign
for the Abolition of Torture "was a new kind of endeavor for AI, and its success provided
a blueprint for the organization's further growth."[23] These lessons were applied well
in the "new phenomenon" of disappearance[24] that surfaced in Latin America in the
mid-1970s. Conceptualization was essential, for the traditional case-oriented approach
proved far better in dealing with "single cases of government ill-treatment of individuals."[25] Tracing governmental denial and accountability proved essential. A new organizational strategy had to be developed. AI's investigation of extrajudicial executions,
coupled with its extensive cooperation with the International Commission of Jurists
and the Minnesota Lawyers Human Rights Committee, led to new technical standards
for investigation. These case studies, Clark concludes, "show that AI was a leader rather

than a follower of states on the normative front. . . . In the choice to work in intergovernmental channels, AI takes on the conscious role of the third party."[26] Her chapter in this volume on Guatemala further illuminates how Amnesty has adapted its strategy.

Korey[27] devotes considerable attention to Amnesty International, stressing its promotional accomplishments. He deems the collection, organization, preparation, and presentation of information "critical to the organization," with credibility based on this information its "most important value."[28] AI gained its "influence and potency" through "the power of exposure of damaging information, or its threatened use."[29] Amnesty gradually expanded its mandate from prisoners of conscience to ending the death penalty in 1973; its Campaign for the Abolition of Torture became "one of the most successful initiatives ever undertaken by an NGO."[30] The organization received the 1977 Nobel Peace Prize as a result in part of its report on killings and disappearances in Argentina. This report was based on the visit of a three-member team, in Iain Guest's words, "one of the most significant human rights missions ever undertaken by a non-governmental organization."[31] AI continues to bombard UN special rapporteurs with information. Korey points out that 80–90 percent of the material received by them came from NGOs, with Amnesty "far and away the principal supplier of documentation."[32] Behind the scenes, it has lobbied extensively for UN peacekeeping operations to ensure human rights.[33] Amnesty maintains a large membership base, to which I shall return below and in the concluding chapter. With the growing prominence of Human Rights Watch, AI has expanded its campaign and advocacy efforts,[34] again an item that merits further discussion. Finally, AI Secretary-General Pierre Sané has advocated new priorities in women's rights and in the connection of poverty and powerlessness[35]—evidence of the gradual edging toward recognition of economic and social rights that, I believe, marks the major Western-based human rights NGOs.

Analysis of AI's Influence and Effectiveness

This sampling of the increasing professional literature on Amnesty International underscores the organization's importance in global and national efforts to enhance human rights. More than any other NGO, it has carried the torch to end specific abuses. Utilizing its superb research staff, AI has without question made a difference. But how can its influence be measured? Let us turn, in accordance with the earlier acronym, to Amnesty's ROLES.

Resources. As readers of this volume are well aware, Amnesty International and its national sections rely heavily on voluntary donations by members and their dues. The organization's policy manual sets forth the guiding principles in detail. Corporations, foundations, and especially governments are suspect sources of support and, quite simply, are not solicited save in special circumstances.[36] Fund-raising is decentralized. National sections do the work of finding the bulk of resources, paying assessments to the International Secretariat. As the former chair of AIUSA noted, the average gift it receives is forty-eight dollars.[37] Any gift amounting to more than 5 percent of a national

Table 1. Amnesty International USA budgets, 1995–98

	1998	1997	1996	1995
Support/revenue				
Contributions from individuals	$20,939,582	$19,942,772	$19,154,956	$18,982,345
Foundation grants	566,334	351,760	499,842	391,616
Bequests/planned giving	2,197,610	1,187,312	1,367,461	2,214,466
Donated services and assets	8,256,877	5,957,214	2,702,232	1,435,551
Literature/merchandise/rental	366,871	355,275	387,713	380,260
Investment gains	854,837	741,640	365,738	188,277
Other	675,333	660,569	99,870	75,575
Assets no longer restricted	655,058	1,134,873	863,665	
Total support	$32,942,040	30,331,415	24,519,147	23,731,226
Expenses				
International	5,761,395	5,590,810	5,123,412	5,321,738
Campaigns, actions	3,645,241	3,112,760	3,772,540	2,922,788
Membership programs	7,394,603	5,913,205	2,960,778	2,396,075
Communications/publications	9,481,233	9,096,514	7,258,955	5,881,301
Management/general	2,086,233	2,339,891	1,529,279	2,113,323
Fund-raising	4,306,675	3,751,360	3,316,984	4,007,303
Total expenses	$32,675,380	29,804,540	23,961,948	22,642,528

Source: Calculated from annual reports; fiscal years end September 30.

section's annual budget, or exceeding £2,500, requires higher approval for acceptance. The advantage of membership dues and voluntary donations is that there are few if any strings attached to such gifts. On the other hand, there are relatively high fund-raising costs associated with direct mail solicitations.

Greater budgets and increased scope have come hand in glove for both national sections and the International Secretariat. The London-based International Secretariat is the heart—and the brain—of AI. Critically important is its careful research. Only four full-time researchers were on the budget in 1968; a decade later, there were fourteen, in a department of fifty-six.[38] Similar increases can be noted in the national sections and the groups within them. The number of groups increased from 70 in 7 countries (1961–62) to 400 in 19 states (1965) to 850 in 27 countries (1970) to 2,283 in 39 states (1979).[39] By 1998, the organization claimed "more than 1,000,000 . . . members and supporters in over 140 countries and territories," in some 4,200 local AI groups and 3,200 youth and student and professional groups. Approximately 330 cases were launched during the year, some 200 cases of prisoners of conscience were closed, and 425 new Urgent Action appeals were initiated.[40]

The best-heeled of Amnesty's national sections is the American one. Remittances from AIUSA account for a quarter of the International Secretariat's budget. With a current annual budget hovering around $30 million, AIUSA disposes of double the funding for Human Rights Watch (although a significant portion is immediately remitted to London). Table 1 indicates the major sources of support and categories of expenditure for AIUSA, from which the London-based central organization draws substantial resources.

Organization. Amnesty International combines centralization (the International Secretariat) and decentralization (groups and national sections). Policy consistency is assured by the supervisory role of the International Executive Committee, by the lobbying of IGOs carried out largely from London, and by the all-important research effort. Membership involvement comes through the groups.

Amnesty International couples a patina of popular participation in establishing priorities with the reality of centralized authority. Its divided nature was well captured by former secretary-general Ennals, quoted extensively a few paragraphs back. On the one hand, he deemed AI "a movement so strictly controlled by its participating membership"—while on the facing page he stressed how the organization "applies to all its membership a very strict discipline in terms of its common actions, common voice and the independence of its finances."[41] Clark and McCann have discussed the high level of control applied to initiatives from members.[42] As the heated debate over whether persons imprisoned for homosexual practices should be considered prisoners of conscience illustrated, some degree of internal differentiation is permitted.[43] And, as Clark has noted, Amnesty's search for greater dynamism "may lead to greater diversity of creative member-initiated action."[44] The jury is thus still out on the impact of members in terms of establishing and revising goals—but my strong inclination is to view this as a prerogative of the International Secretariat and International Executive Committee.

The complex structure of Amnesty International allows for multiple types of leadership. National sections run periodic elections. Participation rates vary markedly among them. Every three years (originally annually), the International Council meets; among its crucial powers are setting assessments for funding the International Secretariat. The International Executive Committee stands at the pinnacle of elected AI leadership. Consisting of the treasurer, a representative of the secretariat, and seven elected individuals, the International Executive Committee appoints and receives reports from the secretary-general (now Pierre Sané of Senegal).

In this bureaucratic maze, what is the significance of individual members, or of particular leaders? Keeping in mind the dictum of Montesquieu that "First men make institutions, then institutions make men,"[45] I shall turn now to the key founders of Amnesty International.

Leadership. AI founder Peter Benenson cast a long shadow. A British advocate (in the lawyerly sense), Benenson had long been identified with liberal political causes. His article "The Forgotten Prisoner" appeared in the *Observer* in late May 1961. By alerting citizens around the world about unjust incarcerations (especially of advocates of peaceful political change), Benenson hoped to preclude abuses. As he argued, "The important thing is to mobilise public opinion quickly and widely before a government is caught up in the vicious spiral caused by its own repression. . . . The force of opinion, to be effective, should be broadly based, international, non-sectarian and all-party."[46] Such an identification with individual victims, based on careful research and political neutrality, became a hallmark of Amnesty's modus operandi.

The 1967 dispute between Benenson and Sean MacBride (chair of AI's International Executive Committee) became the low point in the organization's history.[47] As Tolley comments, members of Amnesty International were feuding over alleged British secret service penetration of the organization.[48] The startling revelation that the International Commission of Jurists (ICJ), which MacBride also headed, had received funding from the CIA early in its history threatened to torpedo both organizations. Amnesty International and the ICJ faced simultaneous crises of confidence, with their leaders in the crosshairs. Had they compromised with the Devil in their search for resources? Could they claim neutrality with such suspicions about support having arisen? Benenson became a casualty, resigning from AI, the organization he had founded and led with such distinction in its early years. MacBride retained his position with the ICJ—and went on to receive the Nobel Peace Prize and the Lenin Peace Prize, no mean feat. But for Amnesty members and leaders alike, the message was clear. The disinterested support of individual members was infinitely to be preferred to suspect government or foundation grants, despite the far higher costs of raising funds in a highly decentralized way. Leaders had to develop and implement policies in a transparent manner.

Execution of objectives. Despite these vicissitudes in leadership, AI has remained remarkably consistent in its goals, broadening them only rarely and on the basis of careful study. It has directed primary attention to those issues emphasized in its statute. The mandate calls for (1) promotion of, and adherence to, the Universal Declaration of Human Rights and other internationally recognized human rights instruments; (2) opposition to violations of everyone's rights to freedom of opinion, to expression of these opinions, and to freedom from discrimination; (3) release of prisoners of conscience;[49] (4) fair and speedy trials for political prisoners; and (5) an end to the death penalty, torture, and other cruel, inhuman, or degrading punishment for all prisoners. Expansion of the mandate requires years of patient, worldwide lobbying of national sections, a point stressed earlier by Winston.

The mandate, in short, provides Amnesty a clear set of issues to which it devotes considerable resources. While it theoretically promotes a full range of human rights within close to 200 countries or territories, its research and annual reports concentrate on the rights mentioned in the mandate. With limited resources and an understandable desire for results, the organization must choose among specific countries as targets. To maximize its effectiveness, what choices does it make? For example, would or should a country with particularly severe abuses but with a government resistant to external pressure attract greater attention than a country marked by less severe abuses but with a government more sensitive to such pressure?

Writing in the early 1980s, Ripp concluded that selections of AI targets were not determined solely by the level of human rights violations in that country, but by a combination of factors. Detailed, accurate information is a sine qua non for Amnesty International. Hence, closed societies present much greater difficulties for research and lesser likelihood of success in liberating POCs or changing government practices. Situations of internal war, where nonstate actors are prominent, pose exceptional challenges for successful influence—yet are highly likely to be marked by widespread abuses. According to Ripp, there is a higher potential for effectiveness within countries with extensive political, economic, and cultural relations with the West.[50] A major campaign by AI means that previous efforts were "ignored, rebuffed, or were met with a counteroffensive by the government." When a major campaign is started, AI expects that (1) the target government will perceive the campaign as having a detrimental effect on its prestige; (2) Western countries with strong AI national sections will actually be able to limit ties with the offending government, and (3) the campaign will generate discussion and concern within the target country.[51] Thus, choice of strategy is based to some extent on desires for success. Although Ripp completed his research nearly two decades ago, these conclusions remain tenable today.

Choice of strategies. With its highly effective Campaign for the Abolition of Torture, initiated in 1972, Amnesty International fundamentally broadened its strategy. What had started as an organization focused on release of prisoners of conscience—a casework type of approach—became an organization increasingly concerned with human rights situations, a broad-brush type of approach. As did Helsinki Watch a decade later with the establishment of other regional groups, AI expanded its outreach soon after its founding.

The statute was formally amended in 1968 to include the right not to be subjected to torture (UDHR, Article 5) and the right to be free from arbitrary arrest, detention, or exile (UDHR, Article 9).[52] A well-timed report on Greece, released January 27, 1968 (three days after the European Commission on Human Rights agreed that human rights complaints against the Greek government by four states were admissible), provided useful information. Nearly five years later, on December 10, 1972, Amnesty launched its landmark Campaign for the Abolition of Torture, initially a one-year campaign which, "by all accounts, changed the course of AI's destiny as an organization and the process of global standard setting by governments."[53] Its work in Guatemala late in the 1970s manifested shortcomings in the "normal" approach of adoption of prisoners of conscience following lengthy study.

No organization can stand still—and Amnesty International has made other adaptations, to which Winston and Clark have already alluded. Torture, the death penalty, extrajudicial executions, disappearances, and "deliberate and arbitrary" killings by governments were explicitly adopted.[54] It has turned increasingly to campaigns focused on single countries or issues. Compared with Human Rights Watch, however, AI appears to have been both less flexible and less focused in its advocacy, a point to which I shall return. It also paid little heed to post-Helsinki changes in eastern Europe, the arena in which Human Rights Watch initially took shape. On the other hand, AI worked far earlier and more effectively within the IGO context, particularly the United Nations, than did HRW. Later in this chapter, I shall suggest this may have been due to the different views of early leaders as well as the constituencies each organization sought to serve.

Human Rights Watch

Given the importance of this organization, especially in the United States, the lack of academic attention to it seems surprising. Amnesty International has attracted many times the comment given Human Rights Watch. The definitive analysis of HRW has yet to be written. It has received extensive, laudatory treatment from Korey, who charts its expansion from a small, U.S.-based public interest group concerned with freedom of publication and eastern Europe to a global organization with a far broader mandate, primarily in civil and political rights. More must be said, however.

Founded in 1978 in the wake of the Final Act of the Helsinki conference, Human Rights Watch initially had a limited geographic focus—especially in contrast to Amnesty International—as noted in Chapter 3. Founded by persons "uncomfortable with the slowness and conservatism of AI in responding to changing patterns of [human rights] violations,"[55] what was called "Helsinki Watch" took its title from one of this century's most unusual human rights documents. "Basket III" of the Final Act of the Conference on Security and Cooperation in Europe—the Helsinki Act—was entitled "Cooperation in Humanitarian and Other Fields." The seventh of the ten "guiding principles" of Basket III was entitled "Respect for Human Rights and Fundamental Freedoms, Including Freedom of Thought, Conscience, Religion or Belief." Little was new in the text of the document, but its political context was all-important. In the words of an internationally distinguished expert, "By linking human rights to peace and friendly relations, the participating states transformed human rights from a marginal item on the pan-European political agenda into a subject of central importance to it."[56]

What was conceived of as a process of *international* negotiation among governments based on a recognition of a territorial status quo became, instead, a far more complex series of *national* discussions between governments and their populations, in which NGOs played increasingly important roles. Citizen organizations were formed in numerous Central European states to support the full realization of the agreement, such as Charter 77 in Czechoslovakia and the Public Group to Assist the Implementation of the Helsinki Accords in the USSR.[57] These developments received international attention. Follow-up conferences to the initial gathering at Helsinki were scheduled at regular intervals to "review compliance by participating states." According to Buergenthal, this "unique negotiating process has permitted the instrument to be amplified, amended, reinterpreted and extensively revised over time while focusing public attention on the failure of certain states to live up to their human rights commitments."[58] As Donnelly has aptly noted, "In hindsight, the Helsinki process can be seen as a chronicle of the gradual demise of the cold war and Soviet-style communism in the face of increasing national and international demands to implement internationally recognized human rights."[59] Largely absent, however, was Amnesty International.[60]

Who or what focused public attention on the human rights implications of the Final Act and Basket III? A large part of the answer in the United States was Helsinki Watch. The founders—including wealthy Random House publisher Robert L. Bernstein and American Civil Liberties Union head Aryeh Neier—wanted to pressure the United States government into a more proactive human rights role. Their attention was thus concentrated in a dual sense on criticizing specific human rights infractions in Eastern and Central Europe and on pressuring Washington officials (through the media and by direct lobbying) for greater action on behalf of human rights. The major initial funder, the Ford Foundation, was the inaugurating its major human rights efforts, as delineated below in Chapter 13. At its start, Helsinki Watch had "limited horizons," in Korey's phrase.[61] While Amnesty International drew attention to prisoners of conscience,[62] Helsinki Watch emphasized restrictions on publication in the Soviet bloc, and would-be emigrants from communist rule who had been denied exit visas. Two texts proved particularly important for this emphasis: the Final Act, to which reference has already been made, and the Jackson-Vanik Amendment, which denied most favored nation status in trade to communist countries that denied the right of free emigration to their citizens.

The establishment of Helsinki Watch was affected by its historical context. With post-Watergate congressional initiatives that highlighted patterns of gross violations of human rights, with Jimmy Carter's voice on this subject, and (later) with the strident anti-Soviet rhetoric of Ronald Reagan, the United States was poised in the late 1970s and early 1980s for new foreign policy emphases. The Cold War remained a fact, despite détente. And, with patent abuses of human rights in Argentina, Chile, and several Central American states among other Western Hemisphere nations, plus the 1979 ouster of bloodthirsty dictators in Central African Empire, Equatorial Guinea, and Uganda, and continued abuses in several Asian countries, ample opportunity existed for NGO initiatives. And, as noted, the Ford Foundation was also ready to provide significant funding. Its initial support for Helsinki Watch was channeled through the Fund for Free Expression, which Bernstein had founded in 1964.[63]

Within a decade, Human Rights Watch had grown from its initial Helsinki focus to a global enterprise covering all regions; within two decades, it had cautiously broadened its civil and political rights agenda, established overseas offices, attained greater managerial efficiency, established new initiatives, and given greater emphasis to advocacy. All these developments arguably enhanced the organization's effectiveness; they certainly increased its claim to international coverage. None of this could have occurred, however, without steadily increasing financial support.

Analysis of HRW's Influence and Effectiveness

Resources. Comparison between tables 1 and 2 highlights the most significant contrast between AI and HRW. Amnesty International derives a substantial portion of its funding from individual members; Human Rights Watch is far more dependent on other

Table 2. Revenues and Expenses, Human Rights Watch

	1998–99	1997–98	1996–97	1995–96	1994–95
Operating Revenues					
Foundations/corporations	$4,432,803	$4,271,722	$3,893,607	$3,678,200	$3,994,572
Individuals	7,403,754	6,201,674	4,967,311	4,105,700	3,354,777
Special events	1,859,673	1,555,778	697,391	744,700	766,728
Direct mail			149,477	91,700	52,527
Investment income	121,709	185,377	197,006	18,000	375,595
Publications	263,972	324,717	336,011	305,400	246,425
Other		30,000	27,500	32,800	61,716
Total Revenues	14,081,911	12,569,268	10,268,303	9,376,500	8,852,340
Operating Expenses					
Human Rights Watch/Central	1,403,706	1,505,187	650,542	513,200	593,362
Africa	1,034,995	808,215	1,087,272	946,500	1,150,055
Americas	988,254	975,187	1,170,380	1,134,200	1,069,803
Asia	1,206,577	1,066,509	1,322,035	1,318,400	1,224,434
Europe and Central Asia	1,794,844	1,530,371	1,270,425	1,122,221	1,305,900
Middle East and North Africa	908,680	879,736	1,097,580	1,164,800	1,098,940
Arms[a]	861,993	853,624	689,099	639,100	300,252
Women's Rights[a]	621,023	932,917	410,925	345,200	290,239
Children's Rights[a]	863,864	427,158	203,857	185,400	92,380
Total regional and thematic	9,484,936	6,765,205	6,598,234	6,383,000	6,258,815
Prisons/Drugs	94,557	90,123	90,089	69,200	
International Criminal Court	179,537	31,507			
Rwanda	137,831	108,251	150,749		
Former Yugoslavia/Bosnia[b]	177,557	244,544	117,388		208,290
Commonwealth of Independent States projects[c]	329,968	160,215	70,006	70,800	177,310
Translations	157,491	90,432	57,378		
Brussels office			355,025	247,700	141,304
Ken Saro-Wiwa Fund	107,890	55,432	15,270		
Hellman/Hammett Grants	175,861	219,473	135,211	197,600	215,687
New Direction Projects	500,000	500,000	500,000		
Other projects	41,373	37,186	33,762	14,700	146,998
Grants to others	44,400	123,755			
Total special projects	1,981,090	1,732,483	2,832,679	2,044,500	1,572,460
Management and general	589,827	522,137	207,533	181,900	264,357
Fund-raising	1,784,922	1,342,950	629,857	766,300	755,738
Total Operating Expenses	14,080,775	12,576,474	10,268,303	9,375,700	8,851,370

Sources: Annual reports for years cited.

[a] Included prior to 1997–98 annual report under programs rather than projects; total expenditure that year for program services hence shows in annual report as $8,987,904.

[b] Retitled Bosnia in 1997–98, Kosovo in 1998–99.

[c] A combined category for expenses budgeted separately for Belarus, Caucasus, Kurdistan, Tajikistan, and Uzbekistan in various years.

sources. Let me illustrate by using AIUSA, with the assumption that it potentially appeals to a similar American audience as does HRW. Where individual donors are concerned, HRW will, for efficiency, draw from the well-heeled; it devotes limited resources to the costly direct solicitation methods AIUSA utilizes. On the other hand, there is some degree of convergence. For example, AIUSA has increasingly utilized the stratagem of mounting prestigious, large, and costly benefit dinners.[64]

As table 2 demonstrates, foundation grants and corporate sponsorships run a close second to private benefactions in the budget of Human Rights Watch—a sharp contrast with Amnesty International. There, as already noted, the International Secretariat does not seek such private funding, although national sections may be permitted to do so, under strict guidelines approved by the secretariat.[65]

As Osviovitch has documented, Human Rights Watch received over $8.5 million between 1990 and 1996 from the Ford, Carnegie, and MacArthur Foundations[66]—three entities that both dispose of enormous assets and give substantial amounts to support human rights NGOs. Of the three, Ford ranks first among donors to HRW, its grants averaging $513,286 per year.[67] This is not surprising, given the foundation's interest in this area.[68]

Organization. The explicit mandate of Human Rights Watch appears significantly broader than its actual scope of operations. Its aspiration for global coverage collides with the need to focus resources on a limited number of countries and key human rights issues. HRW's formal mandate starts with the ringing statement that the organization "is dedicated to protecting the human rights of peoples around the world" (although its activities essentially involve promotion rather than direct protection). Human Rights Watch "stand[s] with victims and activists to prevent discrimination, to uphold political freedom, to protect people from inhumane conduct in wartime, and to bring offenders to justice." It "investigate[s] and expose[s] human rights violations and hold[s] abusers accountable"; challenges governments and those who hold power "to end abusive practices and respect international human rights law"; and seeks to "enlist the public and the international community to support the cause of human rights for all."[69]

These are very broad objectives. Application is, necessarily, more selective. Carrying out the mission has evolved over time, through waves of successive expansion that have seen new divisions and special initiatives added to the original Helsinki Watch. Through its divisions[70] and special initiatives, HRW can give the impression of a hydra-headed organization, with numerous foci and offices vying for attention. In reality, Human Rights Watch is a centralized organization, though less so as its overseas personnel and its coalitions with other NGOs increase. Nearly two-thirds of the staff work on two floors in the Empire State Building, while most of the rest are housed in the District of Columbia office, near trendy Dupont Circle. Most notably, all but thirteen of the eighty members of departments are located in New York City. Of the five geographic divisions, the Americas is housed in Washington, D.C., Europe/Central Asia is in New York City, Middle East/North Africa is split evenly, and Africa and Asia are based mostly in New York City. The Arms project is on Connecticut Avenue in Washington, D.C., Children's Rights on Thirty-fourth Street in Manhattan, Women's Rights divided between the two. A variety of reasons accounts for such placements. For example, a Washington presence helps in lobbying Congress and the executive, and is advantageous for Latin American matters, given the location of the OAS (Organization of American States); a New York locus brings the division or project closer to the Human Rights Watch's center of decision making and power and to major U.S. media contacts. Preference of directors has affected placement (for example, the Africa division wended its way from London to Washington to New York, reflecting leaders' desires). Increasing cooperation with other human rights NGOs, greater funding, and conscious efforts to reduce the American dominance within Human Rights Watch have resulted in gradual but steady increases in HRW's visibility outside the United States. Overseas offices have taken on greater significance as Human Rights Watch has boosted its advocacy, NGO liaison, and research efforts.

As of September 1998, about 45 percent of the more than 180 staff members of Human Rights Watch (a figure including some volunteers) worked in departments such as communication, development, or finance/administration, 55 percent in the five geographic entities and the three thematic divisions (Table 3). Areas of special initiative include academic freedom, antinarcotics campaigns and human rights, business and human rights, free expression, prisons, and human rights in the United States. (The initiative on business strikes me as especially important; HRW's occasional reports on domestic abuses of rights help counter the criticism the organization's investigations start outside U.S. borders.) The dynamics of HRW cannot be obtained simply from an organizational chart. To assume that "departments" meant mainly administrative duties and that the geographic and thematic divisions meant mainly research would be wrong. The programmatic side of Human Rights Watch counts for the great majority of staff.[71] Communications and advocacy, for example, are essential to all NGOs. Only those sections of HRW devoted to development and to finance and administration should be construed as totally administrative—and clearly they provide the essential budget support of the organization.

HRW's focus on civil and political rights has been constant since its founding. The standards the organization employs are "universal civil and political rights as embodied in international laws and treaties." So-called second-generation rights do not fall within HRW's mandate save as they impact on the rights protected in the International Covenant on Civil and Political Rights (ICCPR)—although it is manifestly impossible to overlook economic and social conditions in its reports and press releases. In common with other classic INGOs, Human Rights Watch has been edging cautiously toward a broader mandate. An important 1992 report, "Indivisible Human Rights," discussed in Chapter 7 by Makau Mutua, started this gradual broadening of emphasis. Subtitled "The relationship of political and civil rights to survival, subsistence and poverty," this seventy-two-page study "demonstrated links between the enjoyment of certain human rights on the one hand [specifically, freedom of expression, association and assembly; free and competitive elections; and freedom of movement and residence], and freedom from

Table 3. Staffing of Human Rights Watch, September 1998

Departments	New York City	Wash-ington, D.C.	Los Angeles	London	Brussels	Rwanda	Hong Kong	Moscow	Total
Advocacy	3				2				5
Communication	7			1					8
Development	10		3						13
Executive	4								4
International film festival	4								4
Finance/ administration	11	3		1	1				16
General counsel	4								4
Program	17	1							18
United Nations	4								4
Divisions									
Africa	7	3		2		1			13
Americas		12[a]							12
Asia	7	4		2			1		14
Europe/Central Asia	22	1						4	27[b]
Middle East/North Africa	7	7							14
Arms division		9							9
Children's rights	6								6
Women's rights	4	5							9
Total	117	45	3	6	3	1	1	4	184

Source: Calculated from roster available on Web, *http://www.hrw.org/about/info/staff.htm*, accessed September 5, 1998.
[a]This figure includes three persons whose specific locale is not indicated.
[b]One person in Tblisi office, and two listed for both New York City and Sarajevo, included in New York total.

famine and socioeconomic well-being on the other."[72] Democratic accountability, free-dom of movement and residence, and freedom from arbitrary deprivation of livelihood would have mitigated the four issues studied, Human Rights Watch asserted.

Human Rights Watch thus stands in the mainstream of Western-based human rights NGOs. Few of them seek to protect or even promote second-generation eco-nomic, social, and cultural rights, as defined in and protected by the International Covenant on Economic, Social, and Cultural Rights (ICESCR). But to many critics, the distinction between "generations" of rights harks back to the Cold War era, and fails to reflect the 1993 endorsement of the indivisibility of rights by the Vienna World Confer-ence. The Vienna Declaration and Programme of Action stated—admittedly after much debate—that "all human rights are universal, indivisible and interdependent and inter-related. The international community must treat human rights globally in a fair and equal manner, on the same footing, and with the same emphasis."[73] A person who dies of starvation in a government-induced famine is every bit as much a victim of human rights abuses as an individual forcibly disappeared by political authorities.[74] Yet second-generation rights occupy only a small and recent place in the mantles of protection major human rights NGOs seek to wrap around individuals. (The exceptions in terms of humanitarian assistance and development NGOs were noted in the Introduction, and are also explored by T. Jeffrey Scott in Chapter 10.) I shall return to the issue of second-generation rights in the concluding chapter.

Leadership. The development of Human Rights Watch is inseparable from the crucial roles played by Aryeh Neier, long-term executive director, and Robert L. Bernstein, founding chair.[75] Neier, born in Berlin in 1937, immigrated to the United States in 1947, becoming naturalized in 1955. His human rights involvement started at a tender age; by twenty-one, he had become executive director of the League for Industrial Democracy (1958–60). As executive director of the New York Civil Liberties Union in 1965–70, and as executive director of the American Civil Liberties Union in 1970–78, Neier brought to these organizations both a keen sense of what deprivation of civil and political rights could entail, and indefatigable commitment to these rights. He also brought a strongly personal sense of leadership. As the "prime builder of HRW," [76] Neier was also marked by a "rather authoritarian manner" and a "tendency to inadequately consult," according to a 1993 management study.[77] Neier and Bernstein (who served as president, chair, and CEO of Random House in 1967–89) cooperated effectively in launching Helsinki Watch, then in carrying out its geographic expansion. In slightly over a decade, the four other regional divisions were established, with the three thematic divisions following from 1990 on. Bernstein was an activist chair, interacting regularly with staff as research projects advanced and the organization achieved greater recognition in the halls of Congress and in the American press. His contacts through the media helped in publicizing HRW's research and, perhaps no less important, assisted in obtaining gifts and grants for the organization.

HRW has not faced traumatic leadership succession, although strains were evident late in Neier's more than fifteen years of leadership. When Neier departed in order to head the Open Society Institute (funded by George Soros), he was succeeded by his extremely able deputy, Ken Roth, first on an acting basis, then permanently. The divisions (the geographic entities) have manifested greater turnover, with the exception of Asia Watch, headed since its inception by Sidney Jones. On the whole, HRW has never suffered a crisis of leadership comparable to the 1967 trauma of Amnesty International. Thus, not only has the basic philosophy of Human Rights Watch remained stable, but its top office has been held by only two people in twenty years, and its first board chair served for most of this period. Roth has presided over several successes, discussed below under choice of strategy.

Execution of objectives. Central to Human Rights Watch—and to Amnesty International—has been careful study, leading to publicity about human rights abuses. What occurred, as precisely as possible? Who was responsible? In particular, what government involvement can be found, whether in perpetration, failure to prevent occurrence, or unwillingness to assist the victims? What are the responsibilities of governments (for HRW can direct its censures far more readily at governments that have signed international human rights treaties than at international financial institutions [IFIs], hydra-headed corporations, or resistance movements)? What potential remedies exist? These questions can be answered only after detailed analysis has been carried out; hence, the centrality of accurate documentation.

Human Rights Watch has established a solid foundation of respect for its research. Its mandate, firmly in the traditional paradigm of major Western human rights NGOs, allows for detailed reports. Promotion of civil and political rights fits well with many American foreign policy objectives and with funding priorities of several major foundations. Lacking a substantial base of members and the equivalent of national sections, Human Rights Watch cannot claim the geographic breadth and citizen support of Amnesty International. HRW has nonetheless scored significant successes in its twenty-year history, the result in large part of its effective, focused research, its expansion into new areas, its media savvy, and its major roles in several NGO coalitions (discussed below). But has its emphasis on reports become a bankrupt strategy, as a widely circulated *New York Times* article alleged? [78]

Choice of strategy. The 1992 study of Human Rights Watch, "Indivisible Human Rights," opened the door (slightly) to economic, social, and cultural rights. It recognized that survival, subsistence, and poverty were human rights issues to which HRW might give attention, yet in a clearly subordinate fashion, as Mutua emphasizes in Chapter 7. After several years' further discussion, the organization established a one-year interim policy. Under this, attention would be given to protection of economic, social, and cultural rights violated as "the direct and immediate product of a substantial violation of an ICCPR right," in which the violation was a "direct product of state action, whether by commission or omission," in which the principle of applying an ICESCR right is "one of general applicability," and where there exists "a clear, reasonable and practical remedy . . ." [79] It was a modest start toward what are, to this point, modest changes. Clearer standards are evolving for economic and social rights. [80] This should, over time, ease the task of any classic NGO broadening from civil and political rights— assuming the will to do so is present.

During the 1990s, Human Rights Watch has taken important steps in the following areas:

- It has actively participated in several joint campaigns with other NGOs, with pressure on behalf of establishing international tribunals for the former Yugoslavia and Rwanda, creating an international criminal court, and banning land mines.
- It has helped create networks with NGOs of developing countries, with India as a leading example. [81] (I shall return to this initiative in the final section of this chapter.)
- It has combated what might be termed its "ugly American" image through increased joint research with NGOs in several states, rather than "parachuting in" researchers.
- It has creatively used procedures under NAFTA (the North American Free Trade Agreement) to force the Mexican and American governments to reexamine policies of some companies. [82]

- It has given increased attention to advocacy, through creation of a new position of advocacy director, and through new offices established for the United Nations and European Union. On the other hand, Amnesty International focused on pressuring the UN from early in its history, establishing a formidable reputation for behind-the-scenes effectiveness.
- And, last but certainly not least, Human Rights Watch has implemented recommendations of management consultants, resulting in clearer lines of authority and identification of the organization.

Before concluding this chapter, let us briefly draw together the organizational factors and see how AI and HRW compare in specific areas.

Comparisons: Amnesty International and Human Rights Watch

Although the two organizations share a fundamental commitment to improving human rights globally, and although both have developed formidable reputations for their thorough research, several contrasts remain. Amnesty International and Human Rights Watch typify somewhat different approaches to promotion and protection of human rights. Their mandates are restricted in distinctive ways. In this concluding section, I draw together the threads of comparison implicit above, to show how similar objectives and dissimilar bases of support and governance mark them.

Each, naturally, carries important traces of the founders' philosophies and respective modus operandi. In Table 4, I have summarized descriptive points, each of which merits at least a paragraph.

Initial focus. The description of Martin Ennals, writing in the early 1980s, can provide a starting point for comparison. "Since those early inventive days [of the early 1960s], Amnesty International has really changed very little in its main purposes and its methods. The central theses remain: prisoners of conscience, freedom of expression and beliefs, impartiality of research and concern, financial independence and independence from governmental influences."[83] Ennals's statement would now be modified in the following ways:

- AI now lays far greater emphasis on campaigns, particularly on countries in which patterns of gross violations of human rights can be observed, *and* for which there is reasonable likelihood of success. However, it retains its policy of carrying out these campaigns with limited direct involvement of the national section, a policy dating from its early days.
- Amnesty seeks greater involvement with IGOs and other NGOs in proposing and drafting standards for new international human rights instruments.
- Internally, there has been increasing pressure from national groups to explore means of gaining financial support other than reliance on members' dues and con-

Table 4. Comparison of Amnesty International and Human Rights Watch

Characteristic	Amnesty International	Human Rights Watch
Initial focus	Individual prisoners of conscience	Freedom of expression in Eastern Europe; Soviet Jews and others denied Helsinki Accords rights
Major funding	Membership dues	Personal gifts; foundations
Fund-raising strategy	Decentralized	Centralized
Center of operations	London	New York City
Mandate	Prisoners of conscience; torture; death penalty; disappearances, extra-judicial executions	Civil and political rights
Dominant paradigm	Liberal	Liberal
Links to members	National chapters Groups	(n.a.)
Major target audiences (in rough priority order)	Governments (esp. abusers) AI members IGOs Public opinion globally	U.S. Congress, executive Public opinion mostly in the U.S. Other governments Major global media Other human rights NGOs
Governance structure	council; executive committee secretary-general national sections	executive director board of directors advisory committees

tributions—although the concern about "strings" on foundation and government grants remains strong.

What about Human Rights Watch? Its transformations have been largely geographic (keeping within the framework of civil and political rights), and to a lesser extent thematic (through the projects and special initiatives). Additional attention has been given to major governments and, to a very limited extent, cooperation in field research with other NGOs has developed.

The following modifications seem to have resulted from the growth of Helsinki Watch into Human Rights Watch:

- HRW can rightfully claim to be concerned about human rights globally, although its near-total civil and political rights focus remains at odds with the Vienna Declaration and Programme of Action.

- There is greater willingness to cooperate with other human rights NGOs in research and publicity, manifested most strongly in analyses of India and Rwanda.[84]
- Thematic approaches, notably in the projects and special initiatives, offer some potential for broader approaches to human rights.

Funding and fund-raising strategies. While Human Rights Watch has successfully pursued a focused strategy that might be called "Fewer is More," Amnesty International has remained committed to a highly decentralized fund-raising strategy. The amounts raised will naturally never suffice in terms of the needs. Strategies, staffing, and success all depend on dollars (or pounds, ringgits, yuan, marks, etc.) raised.

Financial support from governments is unacceptable, for them and for many other human rights groups. Human Rights Watch, as noted earlier, shares AI's deep concern about potential compromise of its objectivity were government funding accepted. Their worry runs counter to some important trends—notable ones if we look globally at how human rights NGOs are funded:

- Several governments, such as the Dutch or Swedish and Norwegian, have proven willing to offer "no-strings" assistance to nongovernmental organizations, including several active in human rights. Interesting to note, Human Rights Watch in 1996 did accept a grant from NOVIB, the Dutch organization for international development linked to Oxfam, whose prime support comes from the Dutch government.[85]
- Where funds are offered through autonomous government-chartered and government-funded organizations, and when disbursement is based on peer review (as in, for example, National Science Foundation or National Institutes of Health research grants), opportunities for political influence are significantly reduced.
- Government grants for humanitarian assistance, obviously a matter of deep concern to human rights, are often channeled through NGOs.

Intriguing international contrasts exist. Western European human rights NGOs have appeared somewhat more willing to seek government and government-linked support than American NGOs. Why? More research clearly is required.

What about foundation support? Earlier in this section, I alluded to the Carnegie, Ford, and MacArthur foundations in relation to Human Rights Watch. It would appear that similar goals motivate these grants. HRW and the three foundations employ similar strategies and pursue related or identical objectives. Does this congruence mean there are alliances of interest, where there is little mutual shaping of goals and hence lack of direct influence? Would, say, Amnesty International-USA find it easier than the London-based secretariat of Amnesty International to solicit support from major U.S. foundations? For the moment, and pending further research, the answer seems to be yes. But the observations of William D. Carmichael, formerly a leading official of the Ford Foundation and for many years a central participant in the volunteer leadership of Human Rights Watch, must be kept in mind (see Chapter 3).

Center of operations. What lies at the centers of AI and HRW—and of almost all human rights NGOs[86]—is their documentation of abuses. Both utilize field missions, in which a researcher or small team spends a few weeks in intensive on-site investigation.[87] Both have long recognized that credibility is difficult to achieve and easy to forfeit if reports are hasty or inadequately checked. Hence, the research and editorial operations have been centralized for ease of quality control, access to a variety of media, and distance from the abuses themselves (AI in London, HRW primarily in New York). Within both organizations, draft reports are subject to extensive vetting for consistency and accuracy. The process can be ponderously slow, particularly for Amnesty International.[88] Yet both NGOs know that lives may be at stake, necessitating rapid intervention as well as the drafting and circulating of detailed reports. Amnesty International and Human Rights Watch can move with surprising agility and speed when necessary. And rapid action is often essential. Benenson's original concept for Amnesty International, quoted earlier in this paper, recognized the critical significance of the first few days of incarceration of prisoners of conscience. Amnesty International has developed its Urgent Action network on behalf of individuals at risk.[89] Human Rights Watch has issued increasing numbers of news releases calling attention to acute abuses.[90] The rise of electronic communications, which Laurie S. Wiseberg examines in Chapter 12, has had significant impact here. The tension that exists between rapid response based on partial information and reasoned response based on extended research must be addressed by all human rights NGOs. No satisfactory abstract answer can be given.

Cooperation in research with other NGOs is increasing, as standards of professionalism rise in the human rights community. Human Rights Watch and Amnesty International are aware of the resentment felt by some indigenous NGOs when they feel excluded from research and publicity. Why should they share their contacts and findings with staff members of well-heeled northern NGOs parachuted in for brief periods of study? Centralization of core research will continue to prevail, I believe, but field research will be increasingly carried out by decentralized teams of activists drawn primarily, but not exclusively, from AI and HRW.

Two valuable examples come from India. Recent Human Rights Watch reports on bonded child labor and caste violence have broken new ground for the organization. Research for these reports drew in numerous local NGOs; social and economic issues received detailed attention; and Indian NGOs have started to develop their own networks for advocacy and further cooperation. A few sentences on each change is appropriate.[91]

With 60–115 million working children, India "has the largest number of working children of the world . . . [most of whom] are working under compulsion, whether from their parents, from the expectations attached to their caste, or from simple economic necessity."[92] Far and away the most severely affected are the 15 million bonded child laborers, who face years of unrelenting toil to pay off debts usually incurred by their relatives or guardians. Dalits (as the 160 million people often called "untouchables" prefer to be called) face a staggering array of abuses in their daily lives, including exploitative forms of labor, rural violence by upper-caste militias, and attacks on women by landlords and police. India has specific constitutional provisions and numerous laws on the books that are supposed to provide social, economic, and political justice for all, and to preclude abuses of the sort so fully documented in the reports. These legal safeguards do not work. Hence, what might initially be viewed as essentially economic and social issues fit within the mandate of Human Rights Watch, as it is being more broadly interpreted. The researchers for HRW worked with Indian NGOs to develop the areas in which study could best be carried out. More important, they cooperated in developing follow-up steps. Two conferences of NGOs, in south and north India, went beyond suggesting strategies for implementation, but resulted in creation of a campaign. As Smita Narula of HRW commented, "it was the first time to get such NGO input face to face. . . . Implementation is as important as research itself."[93] The campaign for Dalit rights was launched on December 10, 1998, the fiftieth anniversary of the adoption of the Universal Declaration of Human Rights; the report on caste violence was released April 14, 1999, a day of special significance to Dalits.[94] Indian NGOs are writing "Black Papers" to document abuses further, the choice of term deliberate as a riposte to government "White Papers" and as a way to reinforce a type of "Black is Beautiful" message among the oppressed.

Mandate. In broadest terms, both Amnesty International and Human Rights Watch *promote* a broad range of human rights, and give particular emphasis on key rights that must be *protected.* Their inspiration comes from the international bill of rights (the Universal Declaration of Human Rights and the International Covenant on Civil and Political Rights in particular, far less the International Covenant on Economic, Social, and Cultural Rights) and from specific international treaties and declarations (for example, the Convention Against Torture and the Declaration on the Protection of All Persons from Enforced Disappearance[95] particularly for Amnesty International; the regional human rights agreements for Africa, the Americas, and Europe).

This surface similarity should not obscure the distinctive ways in which the two organizations have interpreted their mandates. Amnesty International has a significantly narrower focus than does Human Rights Watch when it comes to abuses of rights that are investigated in detail; HRW covers a smaller number of countries than does AI. Take their most recent reports (at time of writing) as examples. Human Rights Watch examines the full range of civil and political rights, albeit for approximately 65 states;[96] Amnesty International concentrates on prisoners of conscience, torture, the death penalty, disappearances, and other parts of its analyses of about 142 countries.[97] Such important issues as freedom of expression or the right to political participation are central to HRW, not to AI.

Both organizations utilize what Keck and Sikkink term "accountability politics," based on conventions states have accepted. The beauty of utilizing international or regional standards, as embodied in widely ratified treaties, should be obvious to the beholder. A human rights NGO can say to a ratifying government that has failed to counter abuses, "You are not meeting commitments you made in accepting these treaty obligations." Mobilization of shame is a strategy central to all organizations working to improve human rights.

This strategy has worked spectacularly well—up to the present, and in certain areas. According to a recent journalist's account, "human rights seems to have become the dominant moral narrative for thinking about world affairs."[98] This revolution, which occurred with "amazing swiftness," seemed to testify to the value of "releasing shocking reports detailing abuses, [and] exploiting the media to shame Western leaders into action . . ."[99] Outrage over the wrongs committed by governments has been made possible by careful research and excellent media contacts. But limits exist to accountability unless linked to popular mobilization. In the stinging words of Rieff, "Human rights is one of the major ideas to emerge from the 20th century. But it has yet to become an integral part of the fabric of American democracy. So far, what power the human rights movement has obtained [in the United States] derives not from an evolution in popular sentiment—as occurred, for example, with regard to civil rights or the environment—but from the press and the political elite."[100]

A need clearly exists for Human Rights Watch to build a solid, committed, and large constituency among citizens. For Amnesty International, the main issue seems to be protecting its own membership base, which has not grown in recent years. Additional details appear later in this chapter, and in the Conclusion.

Alas, accountability is a strategy that works best with governments willing to acknowledge their responsibility to protect human rights and able to take effective action when abuses occur. Countries torn by civil war, or headed by authoritarian rulers impervious to external pressure, are far less likely to respond. Hence, the acuteness of human rights abuses is *not* an accurate guide to the extent of NGO involvement or its effectiveness. Criticisms carefully orchestrated by human rights groups against determined giant states such as China, or even against small countries such as Myanmar (Burma), seem to have produced limited results.

Amnesty International and Human Rights Watch utilize networks extensively. HRW seems to be the more willing partner, it is my impression. The evidence cited above about India and the new campaign on abuses against untouchables are a case in point. Indigenous NGOs were catalyzed by the efforts of Human Rights Watch to obtain information and develop areas about strategies. The effort launched early in 1999 had a far stronger foundation within India than Amnesty International's own campaign on India, carried out a few years earlier. AI's restrictive mandate means that national sections cannot work directly on issues involving their own countries, for reasons pointed out by Winston (Chapter 1). Thus, while Amnesty participates in numerous networks of NGOs, it does so more for its international than its national campaigns, and cannot readily tap into the knowledge and interests of local members for the latter.

Dominant paradigm. As noted in Table 4, and as discussed at length by Mutua (Chapter 7), AI and HRW alike follow what Mutua,[101] Steiner,[102] Donnelly and Howard,[103] and several others have deemed a Western, liberal perspective on their actions. The philosophical roots of their human rights activism lie in documents such as the Declaration of the Rights of Man and Citizen.[104] Civil and political rights, it is argued, are first-generation rights that can be enforced at low cost, are essential for the accomplishment of other rights, and fit well with a rule-of-law philosophy. The point need not be belabored, as it is commonplace in the academic and popular literature alike. Far more important are the implications for what NGOs seek and achieve.

I have already commented upon the political contexts in which Amnesty International and Human Rights Watch developed. Benenson, MacBride, and their fellow founders of AI consciously sought to balance POCs from first, second, and third worlds in their appeals. Political balance was essential to establish Amnesty's reputation of impartiality. Members multiplied the efforts of the International Secretariat through their letter-writing efforts. Neier, Bernstein, and their colleagues in Helsinki Watch deliberately concentrated on human rights advocates in Eastern and Central Europe. Political focus and specific policy recommendations seemed important to create HRW's basis of credibility with potential donors, to gain attention from the American media and government officials, and to shepherd limited resources appropriately. AI began in Great Britain but campaigned globally, seeing in the growth of national sections the best avenue for public involvement. HRW started (and to a substantial extent remains) in the United States, but broadened its Helsinki focus geographically by adding new divisions and opening overseas offices. Amnesty International saw its membership base as the focus of funding (see next paragraph) and a major factor in successful pressure on governments. Human Rights Watch concentrated its fund-raising on large foundations and donors. Its growing influence brought both increased budgets and wider ambits of action, but was not accompanied by major efforts to build a large membership base, unlike AI. Substantial contrasts thus existed between Amnesty International and Human Rights Watch in their manner of growth, not readily explicable either by the contrasting perspectives of 1962 and 1978, or by the political cultures of England and the United States. The answer probably lies in the specific leadership of the two organizations in their early days and the successes they achieved, confirming their choices of strategy.

Links to members. Especially in contrast to Amnesty International, the concept of a "member" of Human Rights Watch has limited meaning. HRW was created as a public interest group, speaking on behalf of the cause of human rights. It did not seek mass support from its inception. This is not to say that the organization, whether in its initial Helsinki guise or in its subsequent formats, has neglected individuals. Attention has always been given to human rights defenders, concentrated first on Eastern European refuseniks and would-be emigrants, later broadened globally. AI and HRW have both sought to establish solidarity with advocates of human rights. Where the difference between the organization lies is in their conceptions of *dues-paying members*—important in theory for Amnesty, nonexistent for Human Rights Watch.

Financial information examined above partially illuminates the contrast. Amnesty International and its scores of national sections draw heavily on membership dues and contributions. Average gifts are small. Human Rights Watch receives greater support from individuals than from foundations and corporations. Yet in many cases those who give as individuals influence foundation grants; and average gifts are higher.[105] Human Rights Watch has tapped into Hollywood largesse from time to time.[106] Fund-raising costs differ markedly, and each organization had important historical and organizational reasons for its choices. Both have sedulously avoided becoming dependent on governments; both have tried to reduce the percentage of their budgets coming from a single donor, such as a major foundation.

Does the piper decide the tune? Do large foundations or individual donors dictate policy directions for AI and HRW? Probably not. We must look inside the organizations themselves. Contrary to announced intent, the policies of organizations deeply committed to member participation are determined essentially by staff, not by members—the noted "iron law of oligarchy." Although AI's International Council examines broad policy matters, including the mandate, and although the International Executive Committee supervises national sections, the overwhelming majority of operational decisions are made within the International Secretariat. Human Rights Watch likewise acts upon priorities and projects deemed important by its highly qualified researchers and administrators. Policies are shaped respectively in London and in New York, and, at headquarters, largely by the leaders. Amnesty International and Human Rights Watch have been strengthened by the visions of their heads.

Do the titles of the two organizations' chief executives reflect differences between them? A "secretary-general" such as Pierre Sané would appear to exercise more limited responsibilities than an "executive director" such as Kenneth Roth—far more limited than a "president" such as Aryeh Neier (Open Society Institute). But I believe the issue should be formulated differently. More significant is the degree of "institutionalization."[107] The longer an organization survives, the greater the likelihood that its permanent employees rather than its members determine the goals. Amnesty International puts a rhetorical premium on participation, but copes with the realities of relatively high fund-raising costs and of limited involvement by members apart from letter-writing. Human Rights Watch has utilized advisory committees for its divisions, combining academic specialists, interested (and often affluent) laypersons, and various notables.[108] Still a matter of concern is reaching to wider publics.

Major target audiences. Broadly speaking, Amnesty International and Human Rights Watch seek to influence public opinion and governmental actions. They wish to defend and protect victims and preclude others from suffering, through creation of a "human rights culture." Ideally, they hope to preclude human rights offenses from being committed. Prevention of abuses is obviously preferable to ex post facto analysis of them. Though they centralize their media and research efforts in the North—since both AI and HRW recognize the importance of what Keck and Sikkink term "leverage" politics—their ultimate targets lie in rights-abusing countries. Those responsible for the infractions, especially governments, constitute the primary focus. However, as already noted, many governments are reluctant to acknowledge pressure from NGOs.

Both organizations make specific recommendations to rights-abusing governments for corrective actions, HRW more forcefully in most cases. But there are other states to which reports are directed. Since its inception, Human Rights Watch has targeted the American government and major shapers of public opinion. Its news releases have been timely, focused, and policy specific. Once again, because of its size, mandate, and more ponderous means of action, Amnesty International has less impact on the American government than Human Rights Watch. However, due to its large membership base, AI wields considerable influence, significantly greater in Western Europe than in North America.

But how does one measure their impact, as organizations, on target states? Do AI and HRW have a discernible impact on government policies and private actions? It is easier to ask these questions than to give precise answers to them. One avenue is to determine the main foci of pressure, and assess how specific messages are directed toward them. Have the priorities of the NGOs been accepted as priorities of the targets? Adoption of new policies by rights-abusing governments along the lines favored by NGOs suggests success. Is there specific mention of the organization in the major media and centers of political power? Amnesty International and Human Rights Watch alike carefully compile press cuttings and parliamentary or congressional references citing their studies. But is a mention of HRW in a *New York Times* editorial as significant as a British MP's reference to AI in a House of Commons debate? In the absence of accurate polling data, how can changes in public opinion about human rights be charted—and if such data are available, can the impact of individual organizations be discerned? These questions cannot readily be answered, although Chapter 11 by David L. Cingranelli and David L. Richards suggests criteria of effectiveness. Suffice it to say that (despite their cooperation in several campaigns) there is a sense of competition between Amnesty International and Human Rights Watch—and it is my belief that this rivalry has been generally healthy, in terms of making each organization more effective within its chosen mandate.[109]

Attitudes of the two organizations to intergovernmental organizations (IGOs) provide a final contrast in terms of targets. From early in its history, Amnesty International leaders regularly lobbied United Nations bodies. AI representatives worked closely with the Commission on Human Rights, the Subcommission on the Prevention of Discrimination and Protection of Minorities, the myriad of working groups and special rapporteurs, and the treaty bodies established under the various conventions. Several scholars have documented these roles.[110] The diplomatic orientation of Sean MacBride, whose importance to Amnesty's growth was discussed earlier, may have accounted for this emphasis.[111] AI monitored, encouraged, pressured, and invested time and staff resources in regional human rights organizations as well. Human Rights Watch, by contrast, paid little heed to the United Nations until the mid-1990s. HRW's orientation toward pressing the United States government, its limited resources, and perhaps Aryeh Neier's personal conviction that the UN and its many subsidiary bodies were more talk than action, accounted for this relative lack of attention. Better to invest, the organization seemed to reason, where advocacy efforts could pay off in terms of concrete steps. However, this attitude shifted with the end of the Cold War, as the United Nations became a far more prominent actor in peacekeeping and other respects. Ken Roth's increasing emphasis on advocacy led to the appointments of well-qualified persons who lobbied directly at the UN, the European Union, and other IGOs. AI had paved the way, and HRW belatedly learned the lesson that intergovernmental organizations do count.

Conclusions

In the final analysis, leaders of Amnesty International and Human Rights Watch have taken numerous steps to change and expand their organizations, and thereby make them more effective in carrying out their objectives. Both have grown substantially by any criterion, expanded their geographic range and policy mandates, and engaged in policy influence. The early imprint of their founders remains. Strategies developed in the early days of the year-long "Campaign for Amnesty" and of Helsinki Watch have been refined, but not discarded. Expansion and development, not basic reformulation, have marked their histories. The resources Amnesty International and Human Rights Watch now deploy are exponentially larger than their initial budgets. Organizationally, both have efficient, highly skilled professional researchers, for documentation remains their underlying strategy. Transitions in leadership have occurred, but their fundamental approaches continue, with civil and political rights clearly dominant. Their importance in appealing to and shaping public opinion about human rights cannot be denied. The quality of their written output remains high, and their savvy in working with networks of NGOs on behalf of expanded human rights has increased. Although they continue to differ in terms of their commitment to working with and through the United Nations, some convergence in lobbying strategies and cooperation has emerged.

The bottom line, then, is this: The two organizations have proven themselves to be entities worthy of policy attention. Amnesty International and Human Rights Watch have become significant actors on the global political stage, which now gives NGOs far greater opportunity for influence. They play bit parts relative to major states, but their asides to the international audience make clear that the main actors do not always or fully determine what occurs. For the roles AI and HRW fulfill, we should all be thankful.

Notes

1. The fact that encouraging human rights figures among the four specific purposes of the United Nations, as stated in its charter, can be attributed largely to NGO pressure on the American government. Such diverse entities as the American Jewish Committee, the Federal Council of the Churches of Christ, the Carnegie Endowment, the National Association of Manufacturers, the Chamber of Commerce, the American Bar Association, the NAACP, and the League of Women Voters counted among the observers in the hectic opening days of the San Francisco conference that drafted the UN Charter. Their influence on Secretary of State Edward Stettinius was marked. See the summary in Felice D. Gaer, "Reality Check: Human Rights NGOs Confront Governments at the UN," in Thomas G. Weiss and Leon Gordenker, eds., *NGOs, the UN, and Global Governance* (Boulder, Colo.: Lynne Rienner, 1996), p. 52, and the details in William Korey, *NGOs*

and the Universal Declaration of Human Rights: "A Curious Grapevine" (New York: St. Martin's Press, 1998), pp. 31–41. Korey points to "the remarkable impact that the ideas and language of NGOs exerted on the genesis of human rights in the UN system" (p. 41).

2. Amnesty does not, of course, outweigh the International Committee of the Red Cross (ICRC) in terms of these criteria. As David Forsythe notes in his forthcoming book *Human Rights in International Relations: Liberalism in a Realist World* (Cambridge: Cambridge University Press, 2000), AI employs around 300 in London, the ICRC circa 450 in Geneva. The ICRC supervises the four Geneva Conventions and their optional protocols, the former being arguably the most widely ratified extant human rights treaties, while Amnesty is one of many NGOs providing input to UN treaty bodies, the Subcommission and Commission on Human Rights, and the General Assembly. But since the ICRC has traditionally operated in the area of humanitarian law rather than human rights, and has generally eschewed publicizing the abuses it is seeking to have corrected, it occupies a different, in fact unique, position among nongovernmental entities concerned with human rights.

3. Early works include Egon Larsen, *A Flame in Barbed Wire: The Story of Amnesty International* (New York: Norton, 1979); Jonathan Power, *Amnesty International: The Human Rights Story* (New York: McGraw-Hill, 1981); and Rudolph K. Ripp, "Transnationalism and Human Rights: The Case of Amnesty International" (Ph.D. diss., City University of New York, 1982). Also worthy of note is Ramesh Thakur, "Human Rights: Amnesty International and the United Nations," in Paul C. Diehl, ed., *The Politics of Global Governance: International Organizations in an Interdependent World* (Boulder, Colo.: Lynne Rienner, 1997), pp. 247–69.

4. Martin Ennals, "Amnesty International and Human Rights," in Peter Willetts, ed., *Pressure Groups in the Global System: The Transnational Relations of Issue-Oriented Non-Governmental Organisations* (London: Frances Pinter, 1982), pp. 63–83.

5. Ibid., p. 82.

6. Ibid., p. 79.

7. Ibid.

8. Ibid., p. 67.

9. Ibid., p. 73.

10. Morton Winston, letter to the author, August 26, 1997.

11. Margaret E. Keck and Kathryn Sikkink, *Activists Beyond Borders: Advocacy Networks in International Politics* (Ithaca, N.Y.: Cornell University Press, 1998).

12. Ibid., p. 88.

13. Ramesh Thakur, "Human Rights: Amnesty International and the United Nations," *Journal of Peace Research* 31, no. 2 (1994), 143–60.

14. Ibid., p. 153.

15. As a matter of policy, Amnesty International and its national branches do not accept government funding. Membership dues provide the great majority of the budgets of national sections in developed countries; subventions are given to sections in poorer developing countries. The central secretariat of AI does not accept foundation grants either, although individual national sections may do so, under conditions previously approved by the International Executive Committee. As former secretary-general Martin Ennals explained, "There has been a long and continuing argument as to whether AI should accept—at any level within the organization— funds from well-known public foundations such as Ford, Rockefeller, Volkswagen, etc. This is not because there is fear that such public foundations would seek to influence Amnesty, but because in other parts of the world their reputation as being government-linked would be prejudicial to the work of AI for prisoners of conscience and would influence the attitude of AI of either governments or their victims. There was some doubt as to whether AI should have accepted the Nobel Peace Prize in 1977 for this specific reason." Ennals, "Amnesty International and Human Rights," pp. 69–70.

Human Rights Watch, discussed below, also does not solicit or receive government grants; its limited membership base makes HRW heavily reliant on private foundations and donations from well-heeled individuals. However, some Western European states have established nonpartisan, government-supported foundations that have provided extensive support to human rights NGOs without interference in their internal operations. Are funds provided by smaller powers such as Denmark, the Netherlands, or Norway bound to be less "political" than any given by, say, a permanent member of the UN Security Council such as the United States or the United Kingdom?

16. Thakur, "Human Rights," p. 158.

17. Helena Cook, "Amnesty International at the United Nations," in Peter Willetts, ed., *"The Conscience of the World": The Influence of Non-Governmental Organisations in the UN System* (Washington, D.C.: Brookings Institution, 1996), p. 181.

18. Ibid., p. 186.

19. The 1503 procedure is the means by which the commission reviews, on confidential basis, communications that "appear to reveal a consistent pattern of gross and reliably attested violations of human rights."

20. Ibid., p. 208.

21. Ann Marie Clark, "Strong Principles, Strengthening Practices: Amnesty International and Three Cases of Change in International Human Rights Standards" (Ph.D. diss., University of Minnesota, 1995).

22. Ibid., pp. 89–90.

23. Ibid., p. 139.

24. Ibid., p. 143.

25. Ibid., p. 151.

26. Ibid., pp. 233–34.

27. Korey, *NGOs and the Universal Declaration of Human Rights.*

28. Ibid., p. 166.

29. Ibid., p. 167.

30. Ibid., p. 171.

31. Iain Guest, *Behind the Disappearances: Argentina's Dirty War Against Human Rights and the United Nations* (Philadelphia: University of Pennsylvania Press, 1990), p. 85; quoted in Korey, *NGOs and the Universal Declaration of Human Rights*, p. 179.

32. Korey, *NGOs and the Universal Declaration of Human Rights*, p. 260.

33. Ibid., p. 300.

34. Ibid., pp. 303, 305.

35. Ibid., p. 306.

36. There are, however, exceptions, including acceptance of funds from intergovernmental agencies designated for specific purposes (e.g., prison relief funds received from the European Community), if authorized by the International Executive Committee.

37. Winston, letter to author, August 26, 1997.

38. Ripp, *Transnationalism and Human Rights*, pp. 23–24.

39. Ibid., p. 37.

40. Amnesty International, *Report 1999* (London: Amnesty International, 1999), p. 404.

41. Ennals, "Amnesty International and Human Rights," pp. 66, 67.

42. Ann Marie Clark and James A. McCann, "Enforcing International Standards of Justice: Amnesty International's Constructive Conflict Expansion," *Peace and Change* 16 (1991), pp. 389–90.

43. Peter Baehr, "Amnesty International and its Self-Imposed Limited Mandate," *Netherlands Quarterly of Human Rights* 12 (1994), pp. 5–22.

44. Clark, *Strong Principles, Strengthening Practices*, p. 67.

45. Quoted in Samuel P. Huntington, "Political Development and Political Decay," *World Politics* 17 (1965), p. 421; author's translation.

46. Power, *Amnesty International*, p. 13.

47. Ripp, *Transnationalism and Human Rights*, p. 25. Also see Larsen, *A Flame in Barbed Wire*, pp. 31–35.

48. Howard B. Tolley, Jr., *The International Commission of Jurists: Global Advocates for Human Rights* (Philadelphia: University of Pennsylvania Press, 1994), pp. 125–26.

49. Persons detained "for their beliefs, colour, sex, ethnic origin, language or religion" who have not "used or advocated violence," in the words of Article One of the statute. For discussion of AI's decision not to adopt Nelson Mandela as a prisoner of conscience, see Edy Kaufman, "Prisoners of Conscience: The Shaping of a New Human Rights Concept," *Human Rights Quarterly* 13 (1991), pp. 339–67, esp. pp. 350–54.

50. Ripp, *Transnationalism and Human Rights*, p. 318.

51. Ibid., p. 319.

52. Clark aptly comments that the 1968 revision dropped references to the (European) Convention for the Protection of Human Rights and Fundamental Freedoms, citing instead the Universal Declaration of Human Rights, "in order to reflect AI's new, self-consciously global vision." Clark, *Strong Principles, Strengthening Practices*, p. 93, citing the 1968–69 annual AI report.

53. Clark, *Strong Principles, Strengthening Practices*, p. 105.

54. Korey, *NGOs and the Universal Declaration of Human Rights*, p. 302.

55. Winston, letter to author, August 26, 1997.

56. Thomas Buergenthal, "The Helsinki Process: Birth of a Human Rights System," in Richard Pierre Claude and Burns H. Weston, *Human Rights in the World Community: Issues and Action*, 2nd ed. (Philadelphia: University of Pennsylvania Press, 1992), p. 258.

57. Arie Bloed and Pieter Van Dijk, eds., *Essays on Human Rights in the Helsinki Process* (Dordrecht: Martinus Nijhoff, 1985).

58. Buergenthal, "The Helsinki Process," p. 259.

59. Jack Donnelly, *International Human Rights*, 2nd ed. (Boulder, Colo.: Westview Press, 1998), p. 79.

60. "Where Amnesty's neglect was especially pronounced was in relation to the crucial Helsinki process, which had contributed greatly to transforming Europe in 1989–90. Amnesty hardly was involved in that process and its representatives avoided showing up at its various and historic follow-up meetings and special conferences." Korey, *NGOs and the Universal Declaration of Human Rights*, p. 345.

61. Ibid., p. 341.

62. Korey also observes that not until 1975 did AI issue a long report on prisoners of conscience in the USSR. Ibid., p. 169.

63. Ibid., pp. 342, 341.

64. Let me cite two examples. At a Human Rights Watch dinner honoring Robert Bernstein in November 1998, tickets for individual patrons started at $500; a true "Friend of Bob" could purchase a table for ten at $25,000. At the Third Annual Media Spotlight Awards of AIUSA, to which I was invited in the final days of revising this chapter, a well-heeled individual or group could fork over $25,000 for a Human Rights Defender Table, which, in the words of the invitation, "Includes prime seating for 10 guests, listing as a Human Rights Advocate and Vice Chair in the evening's program, and a full-page ad in the evening's program." Those to be honored were Quincy Jones, Paul Fireman (Reebok), Susan Sarandon, Ed Bradley (*60 Minutes*), the *New Yorker*, and the *St. Louis Post Dispatch*. A "limited number of tickets" at $250 were available for the September 1999 dinner, for which "festive attire" was specified. The "Human Rights Defenders" included American Airlines; AT&T; Craven, Matthews, Smith and Co.; the Paul and Phyllis Fireman Charitable Foundation; the Mayflower Hotel; Joanne and Jim Moore; and Reebok International.

65. Strikingly, AIUSA received about fifty-five times as much money from individuals compared with foundations in a recent fiscal year, contrasted with HRW's far closer to even split.

66. Jay S. Osviovitch, "Feeding the Watchdogs: Philanthropic Support for Human Rights NGOs," *Buffalo Human Rights Law Review* 4 (1998), p. 356.

67. Ibid., p. 357.

68. Richard Magat, "Confronting Man's Inhumanity," *Foundation News* (December 1978), p. 9, cited in ibid., p. 342.

69. Text drawn from Web site *http://www.hrw.org/about/about.htm* August 20, 1999.

70. (Sub-Saharan) Africa (established 1988), the Americas (established 1981), Asia (established 1985), Europe/Central Asia (established as Helsinki Watch in 1978), and Middle East/North Africa (established 1989).

71. Kenneth Roth, HRW executive director, interview by author, New York City, December 14, 1998.

72. "Indivisible Human Rights: The Relationship of Political and Civil Rights to Survival, Subsistence and Poverty," New York: Human Rights Watch, 1992, p. 72.

73. "Vienna Declaration and Programme of Action," UN Document A/CONF.157/23 (July 12, 1993), para. 5. This ringing statement is, I must note, followed by a partial disclaimer: "While the significance of national and regional particularities and various historical, cultural and religious backgrounds must be borne in mind, it is the duty of States, regardless of their political, economic and cultural systems, to promote and protect all human rights and fundamental freedoms." The subordinate clause at the start of the quoted sentence was the object of heated, protracted wrangling at the Vienna World Conference.

74. Thanks to human rights advocates, especially Amnesty International, "disappear" has become a transitive verb in English.

75. Information in the following sentences is drawn from *Who's Who in America.*

76. Korey, *NGOs and the Universal Declaration of Human Rights*, p. 345.

77. Quoted in ibid., p. 347.

78. David Rieff, "The Precious Triumph of Human Rights," *New York Times Magazine*, August 8, 1999, pp. 36–41.

79. "Human Rights Watch's Proposed Interim Policy on Economic, Social, and Cultural Rights," September 30, 1996; quoted in Makau Mutua, "The Ideology of Human Rights," *Virginia Journal of International Law* 36 (1996), p. 619. As Mutua pungently comments, "this policy statement can be seen as a continuation of the history of skepticism toward economic and social rights HRW has long demonstrated. . . . The policy also continues HRW's stress on state-related violations, such as businesses and international corporations." Ibid., pp. 619–20.

80. Since the drafting of the 1986 Limburg Principles, the serious work undertaken by the committee established under the International Covenant on Economic, Social, and Cultural Rights, and the recent codification of specific guidelines, substantial progress has been made in clarifying measures of progress and areas of governmental responsibility. For details, see the Limburg Principles on the Implementation of the International Covenant on Economic, Social, and Cultural Rights, reprinted in *Human Rights Quarterly* 9 (1987), pp. 122–35, and the Maastricht Guidelines on Violations of Economic, Social, and Cultural Rights, *Human Rights Quarterly* 20 (1998), pp. 691–705.

81. These networks were central in the preparation of two major reports about India, on child labor and on caste violence. More details appear in the concluding section of this chapter.

82. Specifically, a Mexican firm with strong trade links to the United States had been giving pregnancy tests to job applicants, a discriminatory practice barred under the NAFTA treaty; HRW was a pioneer in use of this treaty for human rights objectives.

83. Ennals, "Amnesty International and Human Rights," p. 64.

84. For India, see the "The Small Hands of Slavery: Bonded Child Labor in India" (New York: Human Rights Watch, 1996) and "Broken People: Caste Violence Against India's 'Untouchables' " (New York: Human Rights Watch, 1999). The International Commission of Inquiry on Rwanda included not only HRW, but also FIDH (*Fédération internationale des droits de l'homme*, now becoming more commonly known by its English title, of International Federation of Human Rights). For details, see Alison Des Forges, *Leave None to Tell the Story: Genocide in Rwanda* (New York: Human Rights Watch and Paris: International Federation of Human Rights, 1999).

The failure of global human rights efforts in Rwanda has been sharply criticized by Alex de Waal, former HRW-Africa researcher associated with the NGO African Rights. In several stinging reports, he condemned the ways in which international humanitarian operations, reports by Human Rights Watch, and my own book on African human rights NGOs (*Protecting Human Rights in Africa*) supposedly failed to come to grips with the horrors of the Rwanda situation. See, among others, "Humanitarianism Unbound? Current Dilemmas Facing Multi-Mandate Relief Operations in Political Emergencies" (London: African Rights, Discussion Paper No. 5, 1994); "Witness to Genocide: Burying the Truth in the Name of 'Human Rights' " (London: African Rights, 1997); and his critical review of *Protecting Human Rights in Africa* (London: *Times Liter-*

ary Supplement, February 21, 1997). For responses to the latter review, see the letter from Ken Roth, "Human Rights Abuses in Rwanda" (*Times Literary Supplement,* March 14, 1997) and my own response (*Times Literary Supplement,* March 21, 1997).

85. HRW, *1996/97 Annual Report,* p. 20.

86. According to one of the world's best-known advocates and analysts of human rights, human rights NGOs perform "two absolutely indispensable functions": information gathering, evaluation, and dissemination; and keeping the political process open or creating political space for democratic forces. Laurie S. Wiseberg, "Defending Human Rights Defenders: The Importance of Freedom of Association for Human Rights NGOs" (Montreal: International Centre for Human Rights and Democratic Development, 1993), pp. 4–6.

87. At the risk of offending some hard-working special rapporteurs and others designated by the Subcommission and the Commission on Human Rights, the quality and depth of reports written by AI and HRW staff and observers seem superior, at least to me. For some dated insights into such reporting, see Hans Thoolen and Berth Verstappen, *Human Rights Missions: A Study of the Fact-Finding Practice of Non-Governmental Organizations* (Dordrecht: Martinus Nijhoff, 1986) and B. G. Ramcharan, ed., *International Law and Fact-Finding in the Field of Human Rights* (Dordrecht: Martinus Nijhoff, 1982).

88. For example, drafting and publishing the annual report for Amnesty International consumes as much as eighteen months, while that for Human Rights Watch takes closer to two months. Interview by the author with Mike McClintock (responsible for preparing the annual reports for both organizations at various points in his career), New York, December 14, 1998. Confirming evidence comes from Korey, *NGOs and the Universal Declaration of Human Rights,* pp. 365–66.

89. In 1997, 583 new urgent actions were issued, involving individuals from ninety-nine countries; in addition, further appeals on existing actions were requested 351 times. *http://www.web.amnesty/org/web/aboutai,* accessed August 5, 1999.

90. Korey quotes HRW's associate director as estimating that the organization "sends out ten releases per week, eight of which are responsive to specific events that are taking place or having just taken place." Korey, *NGOs and the Universal Declaration of Human Rights,* p. 366. Thus, while AI continues its stress on individuals, HRW maintains its focus on situations.

91. Information in the following paragraph comes from "The Small Hands of Slavery," "Broken People," and, most important, from telephone interviews by the author with two members of the HRW's Asia Division, Jeannine Guthrie (August 9, 1999), and Smita Narula (August 10, 1999).

92. "The Small Hands of Slavery," p. 1.

93. Narula, interview.

94. It is the birthday of Dr. B. R. Ambedkar, the most famous "untouchable" leader. Among his accomplishments were founding the Scheduled Caste Federation in 1942 and chairing the drafting committee for the 1950 Constitution of India, which includes numerous articles relevant to Dalit concerns (see "Broken People," pp. 208–17). Dr. Ambedkar died in 1956. According to Hardgrave, the word Dalit means "oppressed" in Marathi (Robert L. Hardgrave, Jr., and Stanley A. Kochanek, *India: Government and Politics in a Developing Nation,* 4th ed. [San Diego: Harcourt Brace Jovanovich, 1986], p. 171); Human Rights Watch and Indian NGOs translate the term as "broken." Releasing "Broken People" in London recognized the large, influential Indian community there—and furthered the identity Human Rights Watch is trying to develop as an international rather than American organization.

95. Adopted by the General Assembly, it is worth noting, without a vote—in Clark's words, "an indication that no government was willing to go on record opposing it." Clark, *Strong Principles, Strengthening Practices,* p. 185.

96. *Human Rights Watch World Report 1999* (New York: Human Rights Watch 1998), covering events from December 1997 to November 1998.

97. *Amnesty International Annual Report* (London: Amnesty International, 1999).

98. Rieff, "The Precarious Triumph," p. 37.

99. Ibid., pp. 37–38.

100. Ibid., p. 41.

101. Makau Mutua, "The Politics of Human Rights: Beyond the Abolitionist Paradigm in Africa," *Michigan Journal of International Law* 17 (1996), pp. 591–613 (an extended review of my own *Protecting Human Rights in Africa*); "The Ideology of Human Rights," pp. 607–26, focused on what Mutua calls "conventional doctrinalism"; and Mutua's Chapter 7 in this volume.

102. Henry J. Steiner, *Diverse Partners: Non-Governmental Organizations in the Human Rights Movement* (Cambridge, Mass.: Harvard Law School Human Rights Program and Human Rights Internet, 1991), p. 19.

103. Rhoda E. Howard and Jack Donnelly, "Introduction," in Donnelly and Howard, eds., *International Handbook of Human Rights* (New York: Greenwood Press, 1987), pp. 23–25.

104. Stephen P. Marks, "From the 'Single Confused Page' to the 'Decalogue for Six Billion Persons': The Roots of the Universal Declaration of Human Rights in the French Revolution," *Human Rights Quarterly* 20 (1998), pp. 459–514.

105. For example, while Susan and George Soros gave over $100,000 in 1996 to HRW, so did the Open Society Institute. Of the twenty-two donors at this level, seven were individuals or couples, the remaining fifteen foundations, funds, or trusts.

106. Again utilizing the 1996 annual report, donors between $5,000 and $10,000 included American Movie Classics, Castle Rock Entertainment, Phil Collins, Creative Artists Agency, FOX Filmed Entertainment, Home Box Office, Joanne Woodward and Paul Newman, Sony Pictures Classics, Jane Pauley and Garry Trudeau, and the Walt Disney Company. Danny Glover, NBC, Ted Turner and Jane Fonda, and Universal Studios gave between $10,000 and $25,000 each. Alas, according to the 1997 annual report, the only media figures who gave again were Danny Glover and Jane Pauley and Garry Trudeau, who contributed between $5,000 and $10,000.

107. Albeit focused on political institutionalization, Huntington's four criteria—adaptability-ridigity; complexity-simplicity; autonomy-subordination; and coherence-disunity—merit mention in this context. See Samuel P. Huntington, *Political Order in Changing Societies* (New Haven: Yale University Press, 1968), pp. 12–24.

108. I have been a member of the Advisory Committee for the Africa Division since its inception; meetings are irregular, rarely more than two per year, devoted largely to discussing plans of action prepared by the professional staff. The Advisory Committee has also urged greater emphasis on economic and social conditions, and on links with African NGOs—both of them areas of broader concern to Human Rights Watch as a whole.

109. Korey quotes Susan Osnos, HRW's associate director, as deeming Amnesty International to be less effective (*NGOs and the Universal Declaration of Human Rights*, p. 367); I concur. But this is a relative matter. AI enjoys enormous credibility, based on its reputation for careful research and its massive membership base (although the American, Dutch, and German sections together account for half of the frequently cited 1,000,000 figure). (The latter figure comes from ibid., p. 302.)

Korey is right on the mark in noting the "impressive competition" AI has faced from HRW, a competition recognized most readily by AIUSA. Since 1995, Amnesty has tried both to speed up and enliven its documents. It has changed its emphasis, according to a story published in the *New York Times*, from "get it right" to "get it out and fast." Raymond Bonner, "Defining and Proving Rights Abuses: Debate Splits Amnesty International," *New York Times*, July 26, 1995, quoted in ibid., p. 304.

110. Peter Baehr, "Human Rights Organizations and the United Nations: A Tale of Two Worlds," *Paradigms: The Kent Journal of International Relations* 8 (1994), pp. 92–110; Rachel Brett, "The Role and Limitations of Human Rights NGOs at the United Nations," *Political Studies* 43 (1995), pp. 96–110; Cook, "Amnesty International at the United Nations"; Diane Otto, "Nongovernmental Organizations in the United Nations System: The Emerging Role of International Civil Society," *Human Rights Quarterly* 18, no. 1 (1996), pp. 197–241; Nigel S. Rodley, "The Development of United Nations Activities in the Field of Human Rights and the Role of Non-Governmental Organizations," in Toby Trister Gati, ed., *The US, the UN, and the Management of Global Change* (New

York: New York University Press, 1983), pp. 263–82; and Ramesh Thakur, "Human Rights: Amnesty International and the United Nations," *Journal of Peace Research* 31, no. 2 (1994), pp. 143–60.
    111. I owe this observation to Ann Marie Clark.

Chapter 5
The Role of the International Commission of Jurists

Nathalie Prouvez and Nicolas M. L. Bovay

The International Commission of Jurists (ICJ)[1] was founded in 1952 with a broad mandate to promote the legal protection of human rights throughout the world under the rule of law. From the outset, the ICJ undertook the task of defining the requirements of the rule of law.[2] Law, as all other human institutions, is never static and the rule of law is a dynamic concept for the expansion and fulfillment of which jurists are primarily responsible.

The rule of law embraces a broader conception of justice than just the mere application of legal rules, whatever they might happen to be in any given state at any given time. The rule of law must be employed to safeguard and advance all human rights, which are universal, indivisible, interdependent, and interrelated. While recognizing the significance of national and regional particularities and various historical, cultural, and religious backgrounds,[3] the premise for the activities of the ICJ is the duty of states, regardless of their political, economic, and cultural systems,[4] to promote and protect all human rights and fundamental freedoms, whether civil and political or economic, social, and cultural in a democratic society.[5] The promotion and protection of economic, social, and cultural rights constitutes one of the objectives defined by the ICJ in its program of activities on the same level of priority as civil and political rights. The promotion and protection of an independent judiciary is also at the core of the organization's mandate. There can be no rule of law—and therefore no respect and protection of human rights—in a system where the judiciary is in any way subservient to executive authority or other organized interests.

In nearly half a century of existence, the ICJ has sought to link its activities at the international level with proactive work at the local level. This chapter highlights chief goals and the strategies utilized by the ICJ to achieve them over recent years[6] in several areas within its mandate: promoting and protecting economic, social, and cultural rights; combating impunity; promoting and protecting the independence of judges and lawyers; strengthening human rights through international and regional organizations;

and strengthening human rights through empowerment and education and ensuring legal protection of human rights at the national level.

Organizational Profile

The ICJ consists of up to forty-five jurists representative of the different legal traditions of the world.[7] New members are elected to the commission by existing members. Candidates are selected on the basis of their commitment to human rights. The commission is convened on a triennial basis and elects an Executive Committee of up to seven members which meets twice a year. The Executive Committee appoints the secretary-general.[8]

The Geneva-based international secretariat ensures the daily running of the organization and implements a broad program of activities defined on a two-year basis. The current secretary-general, Adama Dieng, is from Senegal. He was selected for the position in October 1990, having previously served nearly a decade with the ICJ as legal officer for Africa.

The secretariat is composed of a small team of fourteen full-time staff members—seven lawyers and seven administrative staff members—but also includes interns working either on a voluntary basis or for a stipend when special funding is obtained for the implementation of specific projects. Legal officers of the ICJ are recruited in the regions for which they are responsible in order to ensure thorough knowledge and experience of national and regional activities and human rights concerns. The Centre for the Independence of Judges and Lawyers (CIJL) was created by the ICJ in 1978.

The ICJ depends on foundations, selected governmental grants, and donations and contributions from some of its members and national sections and affiliates. The ICJ budget includes core funding as well as special project funds. Several foundations and governments provide the essential basic support for ICJ activities, while most funds are allocated to projects. The ICJ is conscious of the fact that diversification of financing is vital to its independence and preserves it from being a "donor driven" organization. The annual budget of the ICJ's international secretariat reaches approximately $3 million—$1.3 million for the core budget and $1.7 million for the program budget. Some of its major funders include the Swedish International Development Cooperation Agency (SIDA), the Ford Foundation, the Dutch Organization for International Development Cooperation (NOVIB) and the German Evangelical Church (EKD).

The ICJ maintains contact with the legal profession at the local level through a network of national sections and affiliated organizations. Most national sections and affiliates are countrywide in nature; some are regional groupings, such as the Andean Commission of Jurists. There are currently seventy-four national sections and affiliates of the ICJ—fifteen sections and affiliates on the American continent, twenty-three in Europe, ten in Africa, and twenty-six in Asia and Australia—plus nine affiliates of the CIJL in all continents. National sections are financially independent from the ICJ, and also devise their own programs.

The rate of activities of the sections and affiliates varies a great deal, depending on whether they operate exclusively on a purely voluntary basis, or whether they have full-time staff. National sections and affiliates implement their own projects in areas of domestic or regional concern such as cases of miscarriage of justice, asylum and refugees, criminal justice legislation, racial discrimination, gender issues, and issues related to economic and social rights. In many cases, human rights advocacy and training and lobbying state institutions are their prime methods of action.

The international secretariat cooperates with and enhances the activities of national sections and affiliates by taking up issues on their behalf at the international level and involving section members in the implementation of its own programs. Joint trial observation, needs assessment, and election monitoring missions are organized by the international secretariat with its national sections and affiliates. The latter also cooperate with one another in the implementation of programs and try and promote the creation of new sections in countries which have recently established democratic systems.[9]

Promoting Economic, Social, and Cultural Rights and Their Justiciability

The principle of indivisibility, interdependence, and interrelatedness of economic, social, cultural, civil, and political rights was restated in 1993 at the World Conference on Human Rights in Vienna. However, in spite of this, the implementation and monitoring of economic, social, and cultural rights are still lagging behind in comparison with the implementation and monitoring of civil and political rights.

The major concern of the ICJ for the promotion and the protection of economic, social, and cultural rights is far from recent. The conferences organized by the ICJ in New Delhi in 1959, Lagos in 1961, and Rio de Janeiro in 1962, which were instrumental in shaping and defining the rule of law, emphasized the use of law in the advancement of human rights and the establishment of economic, social, and cultural conditions under which individuals may achieve their dignity and realize their legitimate aspirations. The Congress of Rio adopted principles relating to the role of lawyers in a changing world. The Rio principles established that lawyers have "a social obligation to concern themselves with the prevalence of poverty, ignorance and inequality in the world and to play a leading role in the eradication of those evils, for while they exist, civil and political rights cannot of themselves ensure the full dignity of man. . . . The lawyer today . . . cannot remain a stranger to important developments in economic and social affairs if he is to fulfill his vocation as a lawyer: he should take an active part in the process of change."

Such a statement makes it imperative for lawyers to be involved in the global campaign for the protection of economic, social, and cultural rights, in full recognition of the promulgated tenet of the unity, indivisibility, and interdependence of all "equal and inalienable" human rights. The ICJ was also closely involved with the emergence of the right to development.[10] During the conference held in The Hague in 1981 on "development, human rights and the rule of law," the ICJ concluded that "human rights organizations have tended to concentrate mainly on violations of civil and political rights. In keeping with the growing demand for a fuller realisation of human freedoms in our times, they should now become involved in the more complex field of social, economic and cultural rights."

Action in the field of economic, social, and cultural rights has, accordingly, assumed priority ranking among the various projects undertaken by the ICJ over the past few years. This, as we shall see later in this chapter, has been intensified by the ongoing trend of globalization and the powerful emergence and influence of nonstate economic actors.

Bangalore Plan of Action

In October 1995, at the triennial meeting of the ICJ held in Bangalore, India, more than a hundred jurists from all continents debated the role of lawyers in the implementation of economic, social, and cultural rights and adopted the Bangalore Declaration and Plan of Action. This conference examined, discussed, and formulated recommendations on the justiciability of economic, social, and cultural rights and what should be done at the international and national levels to increase it and to enhance the use of the International Covenant on Economic, Social, and Cultural Rights (ICESCR) and elevate it from its tacit second-class status. It was stated that lawyers and judges should not concentrate on the familiar territory of civil and political rights and should ensure protection of economic, social, and cultural rights, using instruments such as the ICESCR. The Bangalore Plan of Action made proposals at three levels:

- At the international level, the ICJ called for universal ratification of the ICESCR. It was stressed that the justiciability and violations of economic, social, and cultural rights, which are increasingly acknowledged at the national level, also ought to be acknowledged at the international level through the adoption of an optional protocol providing for the examination of individual cases.
- At the national level, the ICJ highlighted the central role of an independent judiciary in the implementation of economic, social, and cultural rights. Also deemed necessary was to render judges, lawyers, civil servants, and legal institutions aware of their obligations in this field; to empower disadvantaged groups and provide educational programs; to help judges to apply international norms domestically; to incorporate economic, social and cultural rights into domestic law; and to ensure their justiciability.
- At the individual level, jurists were urged not to focus exclusively on civil and political rights and to promote the ICESCR and other treaties enshrining economic and social rights.

Action at the Universal Level on Economic, Social, and Cultural Rights

Over the years, in its interventions before the UN Committee on Economic, Social, and Cultural Rights, and the UN Commission on Human Rights and its subcommission, the ICJ has highlighted the necessity of developing a legal framework to implement economic, social, and cultural rights, and reemphasized the importance of a violations approach that would enhance their justiciability. Furthermore, it has endeavored to contribute directly to developing this legal framework through various initiatives.

The International Covenant on Economic, Social, and Cultural Rights, adopted by the UN General Assembly in 1966, has suffered from the assumption that it places no real and legal obligations on states and that the instrument is merely a statement of aspirations. In order to dispel this erroneous notion, the ICJ, in collaboration with the Urban Morgan Institute on Human Rights (Cincinnati) and the Centre for Human Rights of the Faculty of Law of the University of Limburg (Maastricht, the Netherlands), convened a meeting of experts in Maastricht in 1986. The Limburg Principles that emerged from this meeting identified the nature and scope of state obligations, the role of the implementing mechanism—the United Nations Committee on Economic, Social, and Cultural Rights—and set out possible guidelines for the consideration of state reports by the committee. The principles have become a point of reference, both for states and for the committee.

Since the adoption of the Limburg Principles in 1986, economic and social conditions have declined at alarming rates for over 1.6 billion people. The gap between the rich and the poor has doubled in the last three decades. Furthermore, since the end of the Cold War, there has been a trend in all regions of the world to reduce the role of the state and to rely on the market to resolve problems of human welfare, often in response to conditions generated by international and national financial markets and institutions and in an effort to attract investments from the transnational corporations whose wealth and power exceed that of many states. While the challenge of addressing violations of economic, social, and cultural rights is rendered more complicated by these trends, it is more urgent than ever to take these rights seriously and, therefore, to deal with the accountability of governments for failure to meet their obligations in this area.

On the occasion of the tenth anniversary of the Limburg Principles,[11] a group of more than thirty experts met in Maastricht in January 1997 at the invitation of the ICJ, the Urban Morgan Institute on Human Rights, and the Centre for Human Rights of the Faculty of Law of University of Maastricht. The objective of this meeting was to elaborate on the Limburg Principles as regards the nature and scope of violations of economic, social, and cultural rights and to identify appropriate responses and remedies. The Maastricht Guidelines on Violations of Economic, Social, and Cultural Rights drawn up at the meeting are designed to be of use to all concerned with understanding and determining violations of economic, social, and cultural rights and in providing remedies, in particular monitoring and adjudicating bodies at the national, regional, and international levels.

In the Bangalore Plan of Action, the ICJ emphasized that renewed efforts should be directed toward the adoption of an optional protocol to the ICESCR which would make it possible for individual and group complaints alleging violations of these rights to be submitted for examination by the UN Committee on Economic, Social, and Cultural Rights. The ICJ believes that a system for the examination of individual cases offers the only real hope to move towards the development of a significant body of jurisprudence; this is absolutely indispensable if economic, social, and cultural rights are ever to be taken seriously. An individual complaints procedure will be the best opportunity, by means of developing case law, to define the precise meaning and the limits of economic, social, and cultural rights. Unfortunately, the proposal for the adoption of an optional protocol to the ICESCR providing for a system of individual complaints has not, so far, received the support it deserves.

The ICJ launched a global campaign to promote the draft optional protocol in 1999, together with other international and national NGOs, including Habitat International Coalition, FoodFirst Information and Action Network (FIAN), and Terre des Hommes. Activities in the framework of this campaign include government lobbying and oral interventions during meetings of the UN Commission of Human Rights [12] and its subcommission, and the organization of workshops for NGOs and state representatives. [13]

Action at the Regional and National Levels

The ICJ has organized several meetings over the past few years at the regional and national levels in Latin America, [14] Africa, and Europe to implement the Bangalore Plan of Action and complement activities at the universal level.

In Africa, preliminary discussions on how to monitor economic, social, and cultural rights have taken place in various meetings, including some workshops organized by the ICJ prior to the ordinary sessions of the African Commission on Human and People's Rights. The workshops concluded that the right to development is almost meaningless if adequate attention is not given to the enjoyment of economic, social, and cultural rights. The Regional Seminar on Economic, Social and Cultural Rights, organized by the ICJ and the African Development Bank (ADB) in 1998 in Abidjan, gathered representatives from governments, financial institutions, IGOs, and NGOs. It identified more clearly the obstacles to the realization of economic, social, and cultural rights in Africa, strategies to overcome them, and determined the role of different actors, particularly jurists, in promoting these rights.

The Law of Abidjan adopted at the end of the meeting highlights the need to initiate a campaign against corruption and impunity of its perpetrators by developing normative strategies, and recommends the drafting of an African Convention Against

Corruption, together with the establishment of a monitoring system in the form of an "observatoire." This mechanism should have representation from the Organization of African Unity (OAU), governments, civil society, the legal profession, the African Commission on Human and Peoples' Rights (ACHPR), the ADB, and other subregional economic communities.[15] Long term follow-up action after the Abidjan seminar will include subregional meetings to be organized in collaboration with the regional economic communities and participants of the Abidjan seminar from their respective regions; these meetings are expected to assist in developing advocacy strategies and skills. The report of the Abidjan seminar was brought to the attention of the OAU and resulted in the OAU Summit of Heads of State and Government request to its secretary-general, in cooperation with the ACHPR, to convene a high level meeting of experts to "consider ways of removing obstacles to the enjoyment of economic, social and cultural rights, including fight against corruption and impunity and propose appropriate legislative and other measures."

In Europe, the ICJ is committed to playing a leading role in the promotion of economic and social rights as provided in the European Social Charter. Compared with the European Convention on Human Rights, the 1961 European Social Charter has, for many years, appeared as the poor relative. Over the last ten years, however, it has undergone a major revitalization process. The European Social Charter is very important for the consolidation of democracy, human rights, and the rule of law in Europe. Application of it has already prompted progress in the legislation and practice of several countries.[16]

The revised charter (adopted in 1996 and which entered into force on July 1, 1999) affirms thirty-one economic and social rights shared by European democracies, both old and new, and should become one of the major points of reference for social rights in the twenty-first century. The adoption in 1995 of an additional protocol providing for a system of collective complaints against states in violation of provisions of the charter is particularly important. It introduces a valuable extra dimension to the machinery for the international supervision of compliance with the European Social Charter. Unfortunately the number of states which have ratified the revised charter and the 1995 protocol is still very limited. Furthermore, additional steps should be taken in order to speed up the supervisory procedure, to strengthen its democratic nature, and to ensure that measures are taken if governments do not properly implement their commitments under the charter.

The ICJ was the first international NGO to use the collective complaint mechanism by lodging a complaint against Portugal only a few weeks after the 1995 additional protocol entered into force in July 1998. In its complaint, the ICJ stated that children are illegally employed in many sectors of the Portuguese economy despite legislative and other steps taken by that country to prohibit the employment of children under fifteen years of age as required by the charter. On March 10, 1999, the European Committee of Social Rights, a committee of independent experts constituted under Article 25 of the European Social Charter, declared admissible the complaint brought by the

ICJ against Portugal. The report containing the decision of the European Committee of Social Rights on the merits of the complaint was adopted on September 10, 1999.[17] The ICJ is currently preparing to submit complaints against other countries that violate the charter.

The ICJ has become the main partner of the Council of Europe for the promotion of the European Social Charter and the protocol providing for a system of collective complaints within civil society.[18] In 1998, the ICJ started a cooperation program with the Council of Europe to promote the European Social Charter in Eastern and Central Europe. In this part of Europe, the negative impact on economic and social rights of the transition to market economies over the past ten years has made it crucial and urgent to provide local human rights defenders with training and information on useful tools, such as the International Covenant on Economic, Social, and Cultural Rights and the European Social Charter.[19] The cooperation program between the Council of Europe and the ICJ has already led to the organization of several multilateral and national seminars gathering advocates and human rights defenders from Eastern and Central Europe.[20] The importance and totally innovative character of these seminars stems from the fact that both international and national NGOs working in this region have, over the past ten years, focused nearly exclusively on civil and political rights.

Combatting Impunity: The International Criminal Court, Reparation, and the African Court

Internal and international armed conflicts result in impunity for gross violators of human rights. In Bosnia, Rwanda, Chechnya, Sierra Leone, Kosovo, and East Timor, civilians and unarmed persons have been specifically targeted. Lack of accountability for human rights crimes is an immutable feature of countries which undergo internal conflict or high levels of latent violence.[21] Three decades ago, ICJ Secretary-General Sean MacBride observed: "In protecting human rights, it is not sufficient to enunciate the rights involved; it is essential to provide a judicial remedy accessible to those affected. In curbing cruelty and crimes against humanity it is not sufficient to deplore them; it is essential to pass judgement and if necessary outlaw the individuals responsible."[22]

One of the purposes of any penal system is to ensure that perpetrators are made responsible for the crimes they commit. The same is true under international law, as was recognized in Principle I of the Charter of the Nuremberg Tribunal: "[a]ny person who commits an act which constitutes a crime under international law is responsible therefor and liable to punishment."[23]

Impunity lessens and even eliminates the legal effect of the norms that define conduct as criminal. It also undermines the principle of equality before the law by absolving certain individuals from all responsibility. On the contrary, crime becomes less attractive to potential offenders when punishment results from their actions as a matter of course. It was based on this axiom that, in 1992, the ICJ held an international multidisciplinary meeting on impunity. The meeting strongly supported the idea that creating a permanent, independent, and effective International Criminal Court (ICC) would strengthen the fight against impunity.[24]

At the same time, the unravelling tragedy in the Balkans prompted political will, dormant since Nuremberg, into action. The ad hoc International Criminal Tribunal for the former Yugoslavia is the result.[25] By the early 1990s also, the political climate had changed and the notion of noninterference in another state's affairs was on the wane. However, transition from dictatorship to democracy in Latin America was, to a large extent, made at the expense of justice. Impunity for human rights violations became, tacitly or not, the general norm. It illustrated the failure of national courts to provide sanctions for the former oppressors and remedies for their victims. In Eastern Europe and the former USSR, transition to democracy was, in most cases, not even accompanied by any form of judicial call to account whatsoever.

In advocating the establishment of an international criminal court, the ICJ recalled that, under international law, it was well accepted that "individuals have international duties which transcend the national obligations of obedience imposed by the individual State."[26] Gross violations of human rights, such as genocide and torture, fall under international jurisdiction by their very nature.[27] Such crimes strike at the inner core of legality by negating the very conscience of humanity. They contradict the principles and objectives of the United Nations Charter and constitute, more often than not, threats to international peace and security. Such matters transcend the claim of national sovereignty and beg for international adjudication.

A statute for the International Criminal Court was finally adopted in Rome on July 17, 1998, by a Conference of Plenipotentiaries in which the ICJ fully expressed its views. At present, the ICJ is contributing to the work of the Preparatory Commission which is finalizing practical arrangements for the establishment of the court and preparing the court's rules of procedure and evidence, as well as the elements of crimes. In campaigning for the statute's ratification, the ICJ organizes and participates in seminars to explore and discuss the statute at the national level.[28]

Impunity should be eliminated not only so that the guilty be prosecuted, but, more importantly, so that the victims receive compensation, reparation, or restitution.

It is significant that in tackling gross violations of human rights in the international system, most attention used to be paid to violations as facts and practices, but that the persons behind the facts and practices, the perpetrators and the victims, remained largely outside the spectrum of national and international concern.

The establishment of ad hoc International Criminal Tribunals for the former Yugoslavia and for Rwanda and the current endeavor to set up a permanent International Criminal Court are indications of the determination of the international community to combat impunity, while insisting on the criminal responsibility of perpetrators.

In a parallel process, more consistent attention has been given to the rights of victims of gross violations of human rights, in particular to their rights to reparation. The United Nations Commission on Human Rights is considering a set of basic principles and guidelines on the right to reparation for victims of gross violations of human rights and international humanitarian law.[29] The ICJ is involved in the efforts to draw up a coherent normative framework on the right to reparation.[30] The principles and guidelines are intended, no more and no less, as an affirmation and an elaboration of principles which are already largely recognized. Finally, the decision of the Assembly of Heads of State and Government of the Organization of African Unity (OAU) on June 9, 1998, to establish an African Court on Human and Peoples' Rights, is the result of a process in which the ICJ played a central role.

Given the slow pace of change in international law, the speed with which the OAU moved toward a court is remarkable. In 1994, the Assembly of Heads of State and Government of the OAU requested the secretary-general of the OAU to convene a meeting of the organization's legal experts to look into means of strengthening the African human rights system, including the possibility of establishing a human rights court. The ICJ provided technical assistance to the three meetings of legal experts in which the draft protocol was prepared and finalized. The draft protocol was adopted in Addis Ababa in December 1997, at the third and last of the OAU meetings of legal experts. It was approved by the Conference of Ministers of Justice and Attorneys General which followed.

At the outset, thirty member states of the OAU signed the protocol to the African Charter on Human and Peoples' Rights establishing the new court. In December 1998, a meeting of experts was convened in Ouagadougou (Burkina Faso) by the ICJ in collaboration with the OAU in order to reflect on how to ensure early ratification of the protocol establishing the court. The protocol requires fifteen ratifications to enter into force and had been ratified by two countries in August 1999. It is widely expected that the African Court will give a practical meaning to the justiciability of human rights on the continent.

Promoting and Protecting the Independence of Judges and Lawyers

In response to the growing number of attacks on judges and lawyers, the ICJ created the Centre for the Independence of Judges and Lawyers (CIJL) in 1978 as a means to establish an international solidarity network among members of the legal professions. The mandate of the CIJL is to promote the independence of the judiciary and the legal profession and organize support for judges and lawyers who face harassment and persecution. The first part of the mandate involves the analysis of legal and constitutional structures with a view to encourage reform.

The establishment of practical mechanisms to promote and protect judicial and legal independence and normative development in the field of judicial independence are comparatively recent. In addition to being instrumental in the formulation and adoption of the 1985 UN Basic Principles on the Independence of Judiciary and the

1990 UN Basic Principles on the Role of Lawyers, the CIJL has, for years, intervened directly with governments in cases of persecution. Its lobbying efforts also led to the establishment by the UN Commission on Human Rights of the Special Rapporteur on the Independence of Judges and Lawyers in 1994.

Cases that are brought to the attention of the CIJL are subject to factual verification, and the legality of the measures taken by the state against any judge or lawyer is assessed on the basis of the two UN Basic Principles on the Independence of the Judiciary and the Role of Lawyers. If it is found that the measure in question violates these standards, the CIJL requests the government to remedy the violation. Public disclosure and condemnation are used as a last resort, only when it becomes obvious that a situation is serious enough to warrant open protest and manifest action from jurists internationally. Alerts are released to denounce a situation that affects the legal community as a whole.[31]

Traditionally, the CIJL has focused on the role of the state in promoting and protecting judicial independence. Yet, during the last few years, various international financial institutions, as well as development and funding agencies, have been involved in judicial reforms that directly related to the independence of judges and lawyers. Recognizing the growing significance of these activities, the CIJL has undertaken to explore the impact of the activities of these bodies on the independence of the judiciary and the legal profession, as part of its fact-finding efforts.

The CIJL is also considering the possibility of developing a method to monitor and report on judicial corruption. Experience reveals the complex dimensions of the phenomenon. On the one hand, while allegations of corrupt judicial practices are widespread in many counties, it is difficult to find concrete evidence of corruption. Corruption has many forms and stems from many situations, in particular the lack of adequate resources. On the other hand, some governments have used the existence of corrupt practices to take drastic measures against the judiciary as an institution as well as against individual judges.

Missions to investigate the status of the bar and the judiciary in countries where the situation gives rise to concern are regularly sent by the CIJL. Such missions make governments aware of the international vigilance over the principles of judicial and legal independence.[32] The CIJL also sends observers to the trials of jurists. This method exposes particular flaws in legal systems to international scrutiny. It is also an effective way of demonstrating solidarity between jurists—and, if need be, public disapproval of governmental interference in the course of justice.[33]

The CIJL regularly reports on all cases of the harassment and persecution of judges and lawyers that it is aware of. Findings are published in an annual report, *Attacks on Justice*. Although it focuses primarily on the independence of the judiciary, the report provides an overview of the state of the rule of law in each of the countries it covers.[34]

Meetings are organized on subjects that are deemed particularly relevant and timely. In 1999, for instance, the ICJ and CIJL held a workshop in Belfast reviewing the criminal justice system in Northern Ireland. The idea emerged when exploring practical ways to express support for the agreement reached in Belfast on Good Friday 1998, which provides for a "wide-ranging review of criminal justice."[35]

The CIJL publishes a *Yearbook*, which serves as a forum for discussion on the subject of independence of judiciary and the legal profession. Each *Yearbook* explores specific themes. To date, volumes have explored such critical subjects as the media and the judiciary, the judiciary in transition, Asian perspectives on judicial independence, and the judiciary in a globalized world.

Strengthening Human Rights Through International Organizations

Geneva is the center of United Nations human rights activities. As a Geneva-based organization, the ICJ considers one of its main objectives to be working with the United Nations to promote and protect human rights. The ICJ works closely with the United Nations Office of the High Commissioner for Human Rights (UNHCHR), providing it with information, and serving as a main source of reference concerning human rights law and policies. The ICJ participates in the work of the United Nations Commission on Human Rights and its Subcommission on the Promotion and Protection of Human Rights,[36] the Human Rights Committee, and the Committee on Economic, Social, and Cultural Rights, as well as the United Nations High Commissioner for Refugees (UNHCR), UNESCO, and the International Labor Organization (ILO).

The ICJ endeavors to enhance the effectiveness of these bodies. In addition to promoting action on situations in particular countries with a view to protecting the victims of human rights violations, the ICJ encourages the Commission on Human Rights and its subcommission to strengthen their work with regard to themes that fall within their own program objectives. These include impunity; economic, social, and cultural rights; the administration of justice; gender; racial discrimination; and globalization and human rights. The ICJ also organizes parallel activities to raise matters of concern and to advocate specific action on issues within its mandate.[37]

Standard setting. Elaborating norms and standards and creating mechanisms for the universal protection of human rights is a vital part of ICJ activities.[38] It contributed or is currently contributing to the drafting and promotion of several universal instruments recently adopted or still under discussion.[39]

One example of ICJ involvement in these standard-setting exercises is the role it played in the discussion and drafting of the Declaration on Human Rights Defenders, adopted by the United Nations General Assembly in December 1998.[40] This instrument aims to highlight and reinforce existing rights (e.g., freedom of association) essential for promoting and protecting human rights. Nonetheless, negotiations in the relevant UN working group lasted thirteen years, because a few states used the consensus procedure to seek new limitations on human rights defenders, especially NGOs.

The ICJ was one of four or five NGOs central to the initiation, drafting, safeguarding, and promotion of the declaration. In the early 1990s, only two NGOs participated strongly in the negotiations, Amnesty International and the ICJ;[41] other NGOs attended the working group as observers. With time, more NGOs became involved, in particular the International Service for Human Rights, which facilitated the attendance of national NGOs at the working group.

The ICJ delegation was active in all pivotal working group discussions throughout the 1990s, except in those limited to governments. To encourage broader NGO input, the ICJ increased awareness about the draft declaration through articles in human rights periodicals and other means. A resolution adopted by a plenary of 300 NGO delegates at the 1993 World Conference on Human Rights urged greater protection for defenders, including a UN special rapporteur.

As more NGOs became interested in the possible achievement of a Declaration on Human Rights Defenders in the mid-1990s, a cooperative pattern emerged. NGOs joined in convening strategy sessions in Geneva and other venues and in promoting public education about the declaration and the barriers it faced. The ICJ shared in these important endeavors, but its representatives concentrated on continuing the lawyers' role in negotiations, proposing tactics and drafting wording for the declaration and for joint NGO statements. The ICJ opposed any proposed "compromises" that would undermine defenders' freedoms. In the 1990s, the ICJ issued annual working group statements concerning progress recorded in the yearly reports of the chairman, so that future researchers could understand the background and meaning of agreed wording.

Inspired by the declaration, the UN Commission on Human Rights has added human rights defenders as an agenda item. In following this item and related tactical and educational activities, the ICJ continues to promote understanding and implementation of the declaration.[42] By monitoring its application into the twenty-first century, the ICJ will strive to ensure that the instrument becomes a source of real protection.

Collaboration with regional mechanisms in Africa and Europe.[43] In recognition of the ICJ's contribution and expertise in the development of human rights in Africa, a far-reaching cooperation agreement was signed between the ICJ and the OAU in autumn 1996. This agreement signaled a new era in an already long-lasting bilateral relationship which can be traced back to the early 1960s. The ICJ provides assistance to the OAU and its organs in strengthening human rights and the rule of law in Africa.

The first thirty years of ICJ activities tending to promote and protect human rights in Africa culminated with the adoption in 1981 of the Charter on Human and Peoples' Rights (which entered into force in 1986) by the Assembly of Heads of States and Government of the OAU and the establishment in 1987 of the African Commission on Human and People's Rights (ACHPR, or African Commission). The ICJ then adopted a plan of action aiming at strengthening and improving the work of the African Commission. It also developed a general objective of close and fruitful cooperation between the African Commission and NGOs, notably by means of consultation, submission of communications to the commission, and NGO participation in the commission's sessions.

Over the past decade, the ICJ has organized a workshop every six months, before the commission's ordinary sessions, to bring together members of the African Commission on Human and Peoples' Rights, representatives of the NGO community and, more recently, African ambassadors accredited to the OAU in their capacity as representatives of the policy organs of the OAU. The workshops tackled emerging and ongoing human rights concerns and strategies for improving human rights and supporting the work of the commission. A critical evaluation of these workshops was conducted in October 1996.[44] One of the main achievements of the workshops was their contribution to the capacity building and empowerment of NGOs. A far greater number of African NGOs can now use the regional system quite efficiently. They are also able to educate the human rights communities in their respective countries about it. The increasing use of the charter in national legal systems provides at least partial evidence for this conclusion. The workshops also contributed to strengthening the African Commission and highlighting major human and peoples' rights problems.

ICJ representatives participate in the major annual sessions of the policy-making organs of the OAU, to lobby and ensure that human rights issues are addressed at these levels. In addition, the ICJ works closely with the OAU secretariat and policy organs toward the development of legislative measures for dealing with obstacles to the enjoyment of economic, social, and cultural rights in Africa.

Seminars for African ambassadors on strengthening the African human rights system are held in Addis Ababa, Ethiopia, jointly with the OAU. The objectives are to initiate and follow up on discussions related to strengthening the protection and respect of human rights, taking into account their importance to peace, stability, and economic development in Africa.

Following a request by the African Commission for assistance in the preparation of a draft protocol to the African charter on the human rights of women, the ICJ organized a meeting of experts to prepare an initial draft in 1996. The draft was modified during 1997 and submitted to the African Commission, which appointed a working group to finalize the draft for presentation to the political organs of the OAU. The ICJ is now one of the two NGO members of the working group which has been set up to work on the draft.

In Europe, the ICJ has also cooperated with regional entities.

The Council of Europe strives to be a world leader in the field of human rights protection. Its importance stems from its broad membership (forty-one states), from human rights instruments such as the European Convention on Human Rights and the European Social Charter, and existence of the European Court of Human Rights and the European Committee of Social Rights.

The ICJ follows closely all developments related to human rights at the Council of Europe. It is one of only three NGOs that have observer status with the Steering Committee on Human Rights (CDDH).[45] The ICJ has gained access to the committees of experts and working groups of the CDDH in which preparatory drafting work and in-depth discussions are taking place. The ICJ is the only NGO to send a representative to the meetings of the Committee of Experts on Developments in Human Rights of the Council of Europe (DH-DEV). Participation in these meetings has, for instance, allowed the ICJ to play a crucial role for the past three years in lobbying for the adoption and contributing to drafting of an additional protocol to Article 14 of the European Convention on Human Rights on equality and the prohibition of discrimination on all grounds. The work related to the draft protocol is done in close cooperation between the international secretariat and the European sections of the ICJ, which lobby governments in their respective capitals.

The ICJ attaches great importance to the adoption of this protocol. A resurgence of nationalism, racism, and xenophobia is witnessed in many European countries. However, the European Convention on Human Rights lacks a provision equivalent to Article 26 of the International Covenant on Civil and Political Rights (ICCPR) providing comprehensive protection against discrimination in all those activities which the state chooses to regulate by law. The Council of Europe must reinforce the international protection of victims of discrimination on the European level rather than fall short of contemporary international standards, particularly in the light of the tragic events in Bosnia and Kosovo. Effective protection of human rights in Europe can only occur if nondiscrimination and de jure and de facto equality, which constitute fundamental principles in the protection of human rights, are secured through the adoption of a binding legal instrument and through a mechanism which will ensure full justiciability of these principles.

Over the last two years, the ICJ has played a key role as NGO representative in various colloquies organized by the Council of Europe, and the NGO forums that have preceded them. For instance, the ICJ is currently part of a group of seven NGOs preparing the NGO forum to precede the European Conference against Racism, and the NGO input to this governmental conference, which will take place in 2001.

Strengthening Human Rights Through Empowerment and Education: Ensuring Legal Protection of Human Rights at the National Level

Enhancing human rights groups and providing legal services for the disadvantaged. Capacity building of local NGOs is an important goal for the ICJ. The empowerment of national NGOs strengthens networks of local human rights groups by exchanging information for mutual benefit and developing cooperation.

Gender issues, poverty, the rights of the child, and the rights of indigenous peoples constitute fields of cooperation with local NGOs. Jointly organized meetings on these themes are designed to acquaint disadvantaged groups with their rights under international law. These meetings also help the ICJ maintain and expand its links with local human rights NGOs. They provide an opportunity for the ICJ to keep abreast of current concerns in these countries, and serve as forums for evaluating ICJ activities, setting its priorities, and defining follow-up programs.

Seminars on the rights of indigenous peoples in Latin America constitute a typical example of these activities. Bolivia and Guatemala, which have overwhelmingly indige-nous populations, have provided the scene for a number of seminars, organized by the ICJ within the context of the UN Decade of the Indigenous Peoples, on the human rights of indigenous peoples.

The ICJ provides support to local and national groups involved in the provision of legal services in rural areas. In 1996, the ICJ evaluated a decade of such activities in Africa,[46] which involved the organization of a series of workshops and seminars to en-courage the development of legal services in rural areas. A manual for paralegal trainers was published in 1994,[47] and support was also provided to local and national initiatives. The primary objective of these projects was training paralegals to act as a bridge be-tween lawyers and the urban and rural poor. The 1996 evaluation was inspired by the need to take stock of what had been accomplished so as to assist the ICJ in determining its future focus. The evaluation report recommended that seminars continue on areas of need. It highlighted the necessity to promote law as an instrument of development through multidisciplinary activities and to encourage networking among organizations providing legal services in rural areas in order to ensure the sustainability of their work.

Promoting the legal protection of human rights at the national level. Respect for the human rights enshrined in the Universal Declaration of Human Rights must be ensured pri-marily at the national level. Bringing national legislation and practice into conformity with universal and regional human rights standards and promoting these standards at the domestic level lies at the inner core of the ICJ mandate. This concern has led the ICJ to carry out projects on the domestic implementation of international human rights norms and to provide technical assistance to governments. The latter has involved assis-tance in constitutional reform, drafting legislation on the judiciary, mediation mecha-nisms, or other institutions for the promotion and protection of human rights.

Experience has shown that in all regions of the world, there is limited knowledge or application of international human rights norms. While implementation is primarily the responsibility of national governments, the ICJ endeavors to inform and train local judges, prosecutors, lawyers, and law enforcement agents on international and regional human rights norms and how to apply them.

An evocative example of the blending of the two activities—the organization of domestic implementation meetings on the one hand and the provision of technical as-sistance on the other—is the project carried out in Kyrgyzstan. This country hosted two separate workshops following a needs assessment mission conducted by the ICJ in 1995. The first one was a seminar on the domestic application of international human rights standards held in Bishkek in 1996. It was organized in cooperation with the Kyrgyz Constitutional Court and attended by judges of the constitutional and supreme courts, government officials, law academics, and representatives of local NGOs. During the seminar, a recommendation was made to provide technical assistance to the state au-thorities in charge of drafting reports to the UN human rights treaty bodies and to NGOs on drafting alternative reports. A second workshop devoted to these issues was organized in cooperation with the ministry of foreign affairs in 1997.

The ICJ in a Changing World: Meeting New Challenges

The ICJ has elaborated a dynamic concept of the rule of law and endeavored to extend and diversify its activities in order to meet the emergence of new challenges and opportunities.

Very early on, specific attention was given to social, economic, and cultural rights and the rule of law as a determinant for development. The fundamental principles of interdependence, indivisibility, and interrelatedness of all human rights molded the organization's own program of activities. In 1995, a conference held in conjunction with the organization's triennial meeting in Bangalore (India), on the role of lawyers and economic, social, and cultural rights, laid an emphasis on those rights in the program of activities at the dawn of the new millennium.

Globalization has prompted the ICJ to reconsider the role of the rule of law, and its own role, in the context of the new "global village" marked by the decline of the state and the concomitant emergence and rise of powerful global economic nonstate actors. The rapid trend toward a globalized economy affects economic, social, and cultural rights and has implications for many other aspects of the rule of law. There is a growing interdependence of peoples and national economies. Unbridled economic liberalism and privatization, the weakening regulatory capacity of states—notably in the domain of human rights—and the growing impact of global economic actors on the enjoyment of human rights, have created new challenges for human rights organizations.

The ICJ decided to assess these challenges and the impact of globalization on the rule of law and human rights at its triennial conference in Cape Town in July 1998. The resulting Cape Town Commitment stresses the need to develop strategies for monitoring the activities of global actors, in particular, international financial institutions and trade and investment organizations. The ICJ intends to lobby in order to ensure that international trade and investment agreements conform with international human rights standards. The ICJ plans to contribute to strengthening existing international human rights mechanisms and instruments to ensure accountability of corporations for human rights violations resulting from their activities. The ICJ is also linking up with other organizations to begin a campaign against corruption and the impunity of its perpetrators by developing normative strategies at the national, regional, and universal levels. Corruption in the judiciary is a primary concern for the ICJ; it is a serious impediment to the success of any anticorruption strategy. Both at the international and at the national levels, it is necessary to ensure the accountability of judges and to clean up corrupt judicial services within the framework of the constitutional guarantees of judicial independence.

The contribution of the ICJ to upholding human rights under the rule of law in a globalized context must be made not only through specific programs on the impact of globalization, but also and mainly by following up on what has already been implemented, bearing in mind the spirit of the work of the ICJ over the past five decades.

The lawyer has not merely a professional responsibility, but owes a definite social and ethical duty to society and the individual. Just as a doctor has a duty to preserve and prolong life, so has the lawyer a duty to protect the physical, moral, and intellectual integrity of the human being. The ICJ aspires to be the organized expression of this idealism and of the social responsibility of jurists throughout the world.

Notes

1. The ICJ is a Geneva-based international nongovernmental organization in consultative status with the United Nations Economic and Social Council (ECOSOC), the United Nations Educational, Scientific, and Cultural Organization (UNESCO), the Council of Europe, and the Organization of African Unity (OAU).

2. See International Commission of Jurists, *The Rule of Law and Human Rights—Principles and Definitions as Elaborated at the Congresses and Conferences Held under the Auspices of the ICJ, 1955–1966* (Geneva: International Commission of Jurists, 1966).

3. See the report of the seminar held in Kuwait in December 1980 in which the ICJ set out to investigate Islam's stance on a number of vital issues concerning human rights. International Commission of Jurists, *Human Rights in Islam* (Geneva: International Commission of Jurists, 1982).

4. See, on the issue of universality of rights and the concept of cultural relativism, the following observation made by Higgins: "It is sometimes suggested that there can be no fully universal concept of human rights, for it is necessary to take into account the diverse cultures and political systems of the world. In my view, this is a point advanced mostly by States, and by 'liberal' scholars anxious not to impose the Western view of things on others. It is rarely advanced by the oppressed, who are only too anxious to benefit from perceived universal standards." Rosalyn Higgins, *Problems and Process: International Law and How We Use It* (Oxford: Clarendon Press, 1994), p. 96: See also B. G. Ramcharan, "The Universality of Human Rights," *ICJ Review* 58–59 (1997), p. 105; and Dato' Param Cumaraswamy, "The Universal Declaration of Human Rights—Is It Universal?" *ICJ Review* 58–59 (1997), p. 118.

5. While the earlier congresses and conferences of the ICJ focused their attention on the political, administrative, and legal aspects of the rule of law, the Conference of Bangkok, held in February 1965, stressed social and economic problems. One year before the adoption of the International Covenant on Economic, Social, and Cultural Rights, the Conference of Bangkok called upon the United Nations to safeguard economic, social, and cultural rights by relevant conventions.

6. For a historical perspective, see Howard B. Tolley, Jr., *The International Commission of Jurists: Global Advocates for Human Rights* (Philadelphia: University of Pennsylvania Press, 1994).

7. The commission currently has thirty-nine members with the following geographical distribution: two North Americans, eight South Americans; eleven Australasians; eight Africans; ten Europeans. The current president is Mrs. Justice Claire l'Heureux Dubé, judge of the Supreme Court of Canada. Vice presidents are: Dr. Dalmo de Abreu Dallari, professor of law at the University of Sao Paulo, Brazil; Mr. Justice Enoch Dumbutshena, former chief justice of Zimbabwe; Mr. Desmond Fernando, barrister and former president of the International Bar Association, Sri Lanka; Mr. Justice Lennart Groll, former judge of the Stockholm Court of Appeal, Sweden; and Professor Theo van Boven, professor of law at Maastricht University, the Netherlands.

8. The current executive committee was elected in July 1998 and its mandate will end with the convening of the next triennial meeting in 2001. The chairperson is Professor Kofi Kumado, professor of law at the University of Ghana. The executive committee also includes Dato' Param Cumaraswamy, UN special rapporteur on the independence of judges and lawyers, Malaysia; Dr. Jerome Shestack, president of the American Bar Association, United States; Mrs. Justice Vera V. de Melo Duarte, a judge of the Supreme Court of Cape-Verde; Dr. Diego Garcia Sayan, executive director of the Andean Commission of Jurists: Peru; Lord Goodhart, Q.C., member of the House of Lords, United Kingdom; and Asma Khader, a leading human rights advocate from Jordan.

9. The European sections have established a standing committee which organizes biannual conferences of the European sections during which issues of common interest and joint projects are discussed and which provide an opportunity to introduce the ICJ to the members of potential new sections and affiliates, in particular in Eastern and Central Europe.

10. In 1978, the ICJ held a conference in Dakar (Senegal), on "Development and Human Rights" in which the then ICJ president, Keba Mbaye, spoke on the place and role of human rights in development and on the right to development, a concept authored by him and which was subsequently adopted by the UN in the 1986 Declaration on the Right to Development.

11. See International Commission of Jurists, *Economic, Social and Cultural Rights—A Compilation of Essential Documents* (Geneva: International Commission of Jurists, November 1997).

12. The ICJ is lobbying for further consideration of the draft optional protocol to take place in a working group of the UN Commission on Human Rights.

13. In February 1999, a workshop on the draft optional protocol to the International Covenant on Economic, Social, and Cultural Rights (ICESCR) was organized by the ICJ under the auspices of the UN High Commissioner for Human Rights. Some fifty-five states sent representatives, and eleven international NGOs also attended. It was the first meeting ever organized on the promotion of the draft optional protocol. A seminar was held in August 1999 at the Palais des Nations in Geneva for NGOs attending the Subcommission on the Promotion and Protection of Human Rights, during which a discussion was held on devising strategies toward strengthening the protection of economic, social, and cultural rights through the adoption of the optional protocol.

14. In Latin America, from May 14 to 17, 1996, the ICJ and the Colombian Commission of Jurists held a joint Seminar on Economic, Social, and Cultural Rights in Bogotá, Colombia, in which various indigenous peoples' organizations, NGO representatives and trade unionists participated. One of the areas covered during the meeting was how to approach and utilize the opportunities offered by the Inter-American institutions to redress human rights violations. See International Commission of Jurists, *Seminario sobre derechos económicos, sociales y culturales* (Bogotá: International Commission of Jurists, May 1996).

15. See International Commission of Jurists, *Report of a Regional Seminar on Economic, Social and Cultural Rights* (Geneva: International Commission of Jurists, May 1999).

16. The European Social Charter has prompted, inter alia, Cyprus to introduce a proper social security system, France to raise the age limit for family reunion to twenty-one, Ireland and the United Kingdom to adopt legislation on equal rights for children born in and out of wedlock, and the Netherlands to have a law securing at least twelve weeks' maternity leave.

17. The content of the report was still confidential when this chapter was completed. According to Article 8, para. 2 of the 1995 protocol to the European Social Charter, the report is made public when the Committee of Ministers adopts a resolution or recommendation on the basis of the report of the European Committee of Social Rights, or at the latest four months after the transmission of the report to the committee.

18. The ICJ legal officer for Europe presented the NGO viewpoint on the collective complaint mechanism during the intergovernmental colloquy on the European Social Charter held at the Council of Europe in May 1997 as part of the relaunch of the charter. See Natalie Prouvez, "The Implementation of the Collective Complaints Procedure: Opinion of the Non-Governmental Organizations," in *The Social Charter of the Twenty-First Century* (Strasbourg: Council of Europe Publishing, 1997), p. 140.

19. See the report by the United Nations Development Program entitled "Transition 99," in which it is stressed that one quarter of the 410 million people living in the former eastern bloc live in extreme poverty.

20. A first seminar was held in August 1998 in Kyiv, Ukraine, with the Ukrainian-American Bureau for the Protection of Human Rights and the Human Rights Directorate of the Council of Europe, and gathered jurists and human rights defenders from six Eastern and Central European states. A second seminar was held in December 1998 in Slovenia in cooperation with the Slovenian Legal and Information Center for NGOs. This seminar was attended by advocates and human rights defenders from thirteen countries of Eastern and Central Europe. A national

seminar organized by the ICJ with the Council of Europe and the Inter-regional Association of Women Lawyers took place in July 1999 in Saratov, Russia, gathering jurists and NGOs from ten regions of the Russian Federation.

21. In Colombia, for instance, impunity in human rights-related cases reaches 100 percent, according to ICJ affiliate, the Colombian Commission of Jurists.

22. Sean MacBride, "Introduction," *Journal of the ICJ* 8 (1968), pp. iii, iv–vi.

23. *Principles of International Law Recognized in the Charter of the Nuremberg Tribunal and in the Judgment of the Tribunal.*

24. In 1993, the ICJ published a study in which it advocated the establishment of such a court. International Commission of Jurists, *Towards Universal Justice* (Geneva: International Commission of Jurists, 1993). It also placed the ICC on the agenda of the World Conference on Human Rights which took place in Vienna in 1993. The quasi-consensus that emerged in Vienna on the issue was reflected in the final Declaration and Programme of Action. It paved the way for the draft statute of the International Criminal Court elaborated by the International Law Commission to be considered by the ad hoc preparatory committee meetings in New York, where the ICJ position on the draft statute was voiced. At the same time the ICJ lobbied governments to support the ICC in the UN Commission on Human Rights and its Subcommission.

25. In the past, punishment of human rights abuses has not been a priority in postconflict peace building. A notable exception is the establishment of the International Criminal Tribunal for the former Yugoslavia. From 1994 to 1997, the ICJ provided twenty-two legal assistants to the tribunal in order to assist it in its operation through a project funded by the European Commission.

26. International Commission of Jurists, *Trial of the Major War Criminals Before the International Military Tribunal—Nuremberg: 14 November 1945–1 October 1946* (Geneva: International Commission of Jurists, 1947), pp. 168–69; see also Nanette Dumas, Note, "Enforcement of Human Rights Standards: An International Human Rights Courts and Other Proposals," *Hastings International and Comparative Law Review* 13 (1990), pp. 585, 593.

27. The arrest and detention in London in October 1998 of former Chilean dictator Augusto Pinochet constitutes more than a symbolic blow to the solid edifice of impunity. The ICJ issued statements recalling that the United Kingdom had the right and obligation to prosecute suspects such as Pinochet when they were within its jurisdiction. The ICJ recalled that treaties and customary international law on human rights obligated states to do so in cases of crimes against humanity and genocide. It asserted that no domestically entrenched immunity could protect Pinochet against detention and prosecution in England, or against his extradition to Spain or another state. International Commission of Jurists, *Crimes Against Humanity: Pinochet Faces Justice* (Geneva: International Commission of Jurists, July 1999).

28. The ICC Statute requires sixty instruments of ratification, acceptance, approval, or accession to enter into force. By the end of August 1999, eighty-five states had signed the statute and four had ratified. A major effort is now underway to encourage ratification and the ICJ is at the center of this collective endeavor.

29. These basic principles and guidelines were initially prepared by the Subcommission on Prevention of Discrimination and Protection of Minorities on the basis of a study carried out by the Subcommission's former special rapporteur, Professor Theo van Boven (UN document E/CN.4/Sub.2/1993/8).

30. The ICJ and the Maastricht Centre for Human Rights organized a workshop in 1996 for experts from all regions of the world to discuss and review the basic principles and guidelines that had been drafted by the then special rapporteur of the subcommission on the subject, Professor Theo van Boven. The suggestions made by the workshop were taken into consideration by the special rapporteur in a revised draft. The ICJ continues to work closely on this subject with the commission's independent expert on the subject, Professor Cherif Bassiouni. The fifty-fifth session of the UN Commission on Human Rights, held in 1999, requested a final draft be made available at the fifty-sixth session in 2000. The ICJ campaign for reparation included the publication of a compilation of relevant materials. International Commission of Jurists, *The Right*

to Reparation for Victims of Human Rights Violations (Geneva: International Commission of Jurists, January 1998).

31. This was the case in Sudan in 1988, where elections to the national bar association were tampered with in clear pursuit of a political agenda which had little to do with the freedom of association of the country's lawyers.

32. Missions were sent to Sri Lanka in 1997, Egypt in 1998, and Malaysia in 1999, to report on the situation of the judiciary and the legal profession in the three countries. In the two first cases reports have already been published with a view to publicize recommendations on how to improve the situation. Sir William Goodhart, *Judicial Independence in Sri Lanka, Report of a Mission, 14–23 September 1997* (Geneva: Centre for the Independence of Judges and Lawyers, 1998); Neil Q. C. Davidson, *Egypt: The Sequestration of the Bar, Report of a Mission, 10–16 March 1998* (Geneva: Centre for the Independence of Judges and Lawyers, 1998).

33. The case of Advocate Radia Nasraoui, a highly respected Tunisian human rights lawyer, is an illustrative one. Ms. Nasraoui was charged and sentenced to a six months suspended sentence by the first instance court in Tunis. The CIJL sent an observer to attend two hearings that took place in this case in 1999. The observer concluded that allegations of torture on some of Ms. Nasraoui's codefenders and the inadequate manner in which all the judicial authorities examined the case had marred the proceedings. Based on the reports, the CIJL concluded that the trial was unfair. The CIJL brought the case before the UN Subcommission on Human Rights, which specifically named Ms. Nasraoui in its resolution on human rights defenders.

34. The ninth and latest edition documents and analyzes the situation of judges and lawyers in forty-eight countries from March 1997 to February 1999. During this period, the CIJL found that 876 judges and lawyers had been harassed or persecuted for carrying out professional functions. The CIJL also received reports of an additional 508 jurists who suffered reprisals in 1997 and 1998 but was unable to conclusively confirm them.

35. The workshop was attended by members of the Criminal Justice Review Group, foreign and local experts, and representatives of the organizers.

36. Formerly the Subcommission on Prevention of Discrimination and Protection of Minorities.

37. For instance, during the 1999 session of the Commission on Human Rights, the ICJ organized, with the sponsorship of the Council of Europe and the European Union, a seminar on the death penalty in order to support and promote discussion on the resolution against the death penalty that was adopted by the Commission on Human Rights. It also organized a roundtable on the International Criminal Court during the same session, together with Human Rights Watch.

38. The ICJ monitors the review process of the UN human rights mechanisms—which are the cornerstone in the universal protection and promotion of human rights—that was established by the 1998 session of the UN Commission on Human Rights. While advocating the strengthening of UN human rights mechanisms during the 1999 session of the commission, the ICJ denounced those states which continued to relentlessly advocate measures designed to reduce the effectiveness of the commission.

39. (1) *The Draft Convention on the Protection of All Persons from Enforced Disappearances*: The ICJ was instrumental in setting up the UN Working Group on Enforced Disappearances in 1980. In December 1992, after years of lobbying and involvement of the ICJ in the drafting process, a Declaration on the Protection of All Persons from Enforced Disappearance was adopted by the UN General Assembly. Since then, the ICJ has been lobbying to promote the drafting and final adoption of a Convention on the Protection of All Persons from Enforced Disappearance. The ICJ assumed a vital coordinating role in the drafting process leading to a new convention. In June 1996, together with Amnesty International and the International Service for Human Rights, the ICJ organized a international meeting of experts at the ILO headquarters in Geneva to prepare the draft of the convention. The debate's main focus was on defining "disappearance," as well as discussing disappearance as a crime against humanity, the universal jurisdiction concerning the crime of forced disappearance, and the most effective system to supervise the application of the provisions of the convention. The draft convention was submitted in August 1996, for the first

time, to the UN Subcommission. The draft has now been referred to the Commission on Human Rights for action. In parallel, the ICJ been a driving force behind the elaboration of the Inter-American Convention on the Forced Disappearance of Persons approved by the OAS General Assembly in 1994. (2) *The Optional Protocol to the Convention Against Torture:* This new instrument is designed to provide on-site visiting missions to various countries by members of a UN expert committee. The ICJ is systematically represented in the meetings of the working group of the UN Commission on Human Rights, which is currently working on the text. (3) *The Draft Optional Protocol to the International Covenant on Economic, Social, and Cultural Rights Providing for a System of Individual Complaints* (see text above). (4) *The Basic Principles and Guidelines on the Right to Restitution, Compensation, and Rehabilitation for Victims of Violations of Human Rights* (see text above).

40. Declaration on the Right and Responsibility of Individuals, Groups, and Organs of Society to Promote and Protect Universally Recognized Human Rights and Fundamental Freedoms, adopted December 9, 1998 by the UN General Assembly, without a vote.

41. During the 1990s, the official representative of the ICJ in UN negotiations on the declaration was Allan McChesney, member of the Canadian section of the ICJ.

42. At The Hague Appeal for Peace in May 1999, the ICJ representative participated in a session discussing the declaration and its implications.

43. In the Americas, the ICJ attends meetings of the Inter-American human rights system, including the General Assembly of the Organization of American States, the Inter-American Commission on Human Rights and the Inter-American Court on Human Rights. Although the Inter-American system does not provide formal accreditation for NGOs, ICJ presence is felt through lobbying activities, participation in the setting of human rights standards, the promotion of human rights, and the domestic application of international norms. ICJ representatives—usually members of an affiliate organization of the ICJ in an American country—attend these meetings. This allows the Secretariat in Geneva to monitor and participate in the consideration of matters relevant to its work; for instance, in drafting human rights instruments such as the Inter-American Convention against Forced Disappearances, the draft American Declaration on Indigenous People, and the draft American Convention on Human Rights Defenders. It also allows the ICJ to submit petitions and communications to the Inter-American Commission on Human Rights and amicus curiae briefs before the Inter-American Court of Human Rights.

44. Shadrack Gutto, *ICJ workshops on NGO Participation in the African Commission on Human and People's Rights 1991 to 1996: A Critical Evaluation* (Geneva: International Commission of Jurists, 1996).

45. The other two NGOs are Amnesty International and the International Federation for Human Rights.

46. In January 1997 this resulted in the publication of *Legal Services in Rural Areas in Africa,* which provides a comprehensive review and evaluation of a series of ICJ enlightenment workshops and seminars held over the past ten years in Africa. International Commission of Jurists, *Legal Services in Rural Areas in Africa* (Geneva: International Commission of Jurists, 1997).

47. Amy S. Tsanga and Olatokumbo Ige, *A Paralegal Trainer's Manual for Africa* (Geneva: International Commission of Jurists, 1994).

Chapter 6
The International Human Rights Law Group
Human Rights and Access to Justice in Postconflict Environments

Mark K. Bromley

As a nonprofit human rights organization that has sought to link international human rights programming with a development-oriented approach to human rights, the International Human Rights Law Group (the Law Group) has initiated a slate of field programs in a variety of postconflict and transitional societies. While other human rights NGOs have proven effective in reporting abuses, garnering media attention for reports, and flooding international bodies with complaints, the Law Group operates on the assumption that over the long term, local NGOs, progressive lawyers, and other dynamic local professionals must decisively challenge their own government's human rights policies. The Law Group's projects are designed accordingly, with its programs emphasizing the importance of mobilizing technical capacities and resources worldwide to strengthen local NGOs.

The Law Group employs approximately one hundred staff, representing eighteen nationalities, in offices in Bosnia and Herzegovina, Cambodia, the Democratic Republic of the Congo, Morocco, Nicaragua, Nigeria, and Washington, D.C. In addition, new Law Group field programs are scheduled to begin in Burundi and Yemen in 2000. The Law Group's professional staffing component is also augmented by a pro bono advocacy network that links human rights advocates, lawyers, law firms, and other professionals to its worldwide program activities. Its anticipated budget for fiscal year 2000 surpasses $5 million.

The Law Group's overall size and budget have both grown substantially since it was founded as a small legal research and advocacy institution in 1978. The Law Group is now solidly classified as a medium-sized NGO by U.S. standards. Since in-country field programs tend to be more expensive than traditional human rights documentation and advocacy initiatives, the Law Group's budget reflects the fact that it receives broad-based support from both private foundations and a number of different governments. This public-private mix of funding has been indispensable to the Law Group's development-oriented approach, and without this healthy mixture of government and private foundation support, it seems unlikely that the Law Group could otherwise have established a long-term presence in a number of the countries where it has now developed in-country programs.

This chapter focuses on the Law Group's model for access-to-justice programs, highlighting programs in postconflict legal environments. It should be noted, however, that the Law Group defines its access-to-justice programs in broad terms. Its current access-to-justice programs include a Defenders Project in Cambodia that provides comprehensive legal representation in Cambodian courts for the indigent and for victims of human rights abuses; capacity-building programs working with human rights and legal service providers in the Democratic Republic of the Congo and Nicaragua; international litigation support for NGOs bringing cases within the Inter-American human rights system; support for legal reform initiatives that address gender discrimination in inheritance laws in Africa and potentially abusive trafficking or forced-prostitution laws world-wide; and an expansive training and mentoring program that supports the human rights litigation efforts of legal advocates in Bosnia and Herzegovina. The Law Group has also initiated a program addressing the application of international human rights treaty obligations in the United States.

In addition to these legally focused programs, the Law Group maintains related programs and activities that are not generally characterized, even by nontraditional standards, as access-to-justice programs, including more traditional human rights documentation, training, and advocacy programs around the world. Owing to the synergies that often emerge when these various programming components intersect, this broad range of programs may actually account, in some respects, for the Law Group's particular successes in its access-to-justice programs. Nonetheless, this chapter concentrates on access-to-justice activities as a case study exploring the Law Group's overall approach to human rights work.

The Law Group Model of Advocacy

The Law Group has concluded, based on its experiences in several contexts, that access-to-justice programs are most successful when they are linked to complementary advocacy programs that seek to build the talents and resources of local actors, thereby animating civil society and testing the capacity of local institutions, including legal institutions, to implement basic human rights protections and legal guarantees. Indeed, the ultimate challenge of any access-to-justice program is to identify activist lawyers and other human rights professionals who will support social change through their own professional networks. As a result, while the Law Group may temporarily import outside experts, and such experts often have an important role to play, all Law Group initiatives ultimately seek to identify and support local change agents who will fight for change on the ground within the context of their own societies.

In supporting such local activists in postconflict environments, the Law Group recognizes that paralysis is an all-too-common reaction to the often daunting array of social, political, and infrastructure-related obstacles that must be overcome in the aftermath of conflict. Working with activists to confront this paralysis, the Law Group's programs emphasize that little steps and small victories can have an enormous impact, producing exponential and often unpredicted effects. Small NGOs, for example, may initiate effective judicial sector interventions through carefully chosen, impact-oriented human rights cases. More important, small successes at the local level may build momentum and self-confidence around local victories, thereby developing a level of engagement where such a response may not have been expected.

An example of just such an unexpected success was evident in the Law Group's education initiative in Bosnia and Herzegovina in 1997. Working with Bosnian activists, the Law Group identified pernicious forms of de jure and de facto ethnic segregation in Bosnian schools as an important issue in the context of the peace and reconstruction process in Bosnia and Herzegovina. Once the Law Group began to raise the issue within the legal community in Bosnia and Herzegovina, local Bosnian support for an antisegregation advocacy campaign grew rapidly, leading eventually to one of the first street petition drives in Sarajevo in the postwar period. In November 1997, in the face of significant local and international protest, officials in the Federation of Bosnia and Herzegovina[1] withdrew official orders that had permitted and in fact furthered ethnic segregation in the Federation's schools. Given the acute ethnic identifications that were reinforced, and in some cases created, by the years of ethnic conflict in the former Yugoslavia, the Law Group did not anticipate such broad public support within the legal and nonlegal communities for a unified education system. The education issue has since become a leading policy issue in Bosnia, and the Council of Europe has indicated that the country's education policies will be viewed as an important indicator of Bosnia's capacity to accede to it as a full member state.

At the same time, despite such unexpected advocacy successes, it is also important to recognize that in some respects most NGO interventions will initially appear modest. This is true of both the Law Group's comparatively large legal assistance and advocacy programs in Cambodia and its more contained advocacy and access-to-justice programs on the Atlantic coast of Nicaragua. No matter how large the program or how many successes may be recorded, any national NGO initiative, particularly when viewed in isolation, will appear limited in comparison to the magnitude of the problem and the overwhelming influence of government policies or attitudes on the pace of both judicial and civil society development. Nonetheless, considering the daunting and even seemingly insurmountable limitations that must necessarily be overcome in any post-conflict environment, such progress *must* often emerge from the margins. The role of the Law Group, then, has been to support activities and activists working at the margins of official policies and programs.

In philosophical terms the Law Group's access-to-justice programs in countries as diverse as Bosnia and Herzegovina, Cambodia, the Democratic Republic of the Congo, and Nicaragua recognize that laws and legal institutions, as abstract ends in themselves, are almost always insufficient as a base for building a human rights culture. Nazi Germany harbored a peculiarly odd and almost sentimental attachment to the rule of law, and the Soviet bureaucracy could be remarkably efficient, when measured by at least some legal barometers. Yet both of these systems established the legal and bureaucratic environments within which unimaginable abuses were committed, often with shocking efficiency, under the color of law. Indeed, the human rights movement in the post–World War II era evolved as a response to human rights abuses committed *within* such a legal framework.[2] Assuming therefore that the mere emergence of functioning legal mechanisms within a postconflict reconstruction program should not be characterized as a sufficiently worthy end in itself, the Law Group's model seeks, instead, to address access-to-justice issues from a human rights framework. This means, in more concrete terms, that the legal system in any society, but most essentially in a postconflict environment, must be seen as addressing basic inequalities in that society, as unaddressed inequities are potential sparks of future conflicts.

As the 1993 UN World Conference on Human Rights emphasized, human rights norms are "universal, indivisible and interdependent and interrelated." A human rights approach to the rule of law demands basic recognition and respect for economic, social, and cultural rights, as well as for the often more familiar civil and political rights. The Law Group model also emphasizes, accordingly, that ultimately judicial reform and access to justice may only be expected to lead to a stabilizing environment in which peace and development are possible if such legal initiatives begin to address the full spectrum of economic, social, and cultural rights within any society, as well as the underlying civil and political inequities. For example, through a thematic program in West Africa, the Law Group has supported NGO advocacy initiatives around women's inheritance rights, as gender-biased inheritance laws and practices have consistently undermined the economic rights of millions of women across Africa. Moreover, by impacting women's access to property ownership and, as a result, to many forms of economic credit, these laws and practices have had a significant negative effect on the global struggle to eradicate poverty.

Operational Elements of the Law Group Model

In addition to emphasizing the conceptual link between human rights advocacy and access to justice, other elements have emerged as hallmarks of the Law Group's access-to-justice model: a focus on supporting local NGOs and local advocates in the legal sector; recognition of the key roles that dynamic local professionals must play in all access-to-justice programs; careful consideration and identification of essential external benefits; and an emphasis on enforcing judgments and building the credibility of a judicial system in the eyes of its users. These elements are described here in brief detail to provide a more comprehensive overview of the Law Group's approach to access-to-justice programs.

Supporting Local NGOs

As already noted, the Law Group's approach to all human rights activities, including all access-to-justice programs, stresses the importance of in-country projects that seek to strengthen the capacity of local groups to transform their own societies. In particular, the Law Group recognizes that NGOs have advanced some of the most successful human rights campaigns over the past ten years, and that NGOs have also won important social and legal victories both in their own countries and on the international stage.[3] Many of these victories are discussed in this book.

To be effective, local NGOs must have access both to technical and to financial support. Such access may be frustrated, however, by domestic governmental efforts to restrict the work of NGOs in many postconflict societies. For example, limitations on the freedom to organize or on freedom of expression may severely impact the effectiveness or even the existence of NGOs in many regions. Tax policies and limits on international or local charitable giving may similarly impact the activities of national and international NGOs. Law Group programs in many countries have sought to challenge such restrictive NGO laws, often as a component of a larger access-to-justice program, since these laws or regulations may have a vastly destabilizing effect both on NGO development and, by extension, on long-term judicial reform.

International support for local NGOs from organizations such as the Law Group may also lend important protection to these NGOs, allowing them to function more effectively and without undue political interference or harassment from their own governments. In some situations, however, the reverse may also be true. During Franjo Tudjman's presidency in Croatia, for example, NGOs affiliated with international organizations were often specifically targeted for particular harassment by local authorities.

Supporting Dynamic Local Leaders

As a corollary to support for local NGOs, the Law Group's in-country access-to-justice programs also emphasize that, when compared to international technical advisors, local and regional experts clearly have a more personal, longer-term commitment to the rule of law and to the creation of a human rights culture within their own society. Although it may be difficult in many postconflict situations to identify local leaders with the necessary skills and talents to lead an access-to-justice initiative, there is simply no long-term substitute for dynamic local leadership.

The relative scarcity of legal experts in many postconflict environments often relates to the facts that educated professionals generally enjoy greater opportunities to leave their homes or countries during periods of escalating conflict and that educational opportunities and training for future legal professionals often remain inaccessible during such periods. It is important to recognize, however, that the international community often overlooks the local expertise that may exist, including leading talents within a local NGO community. The efficient local translator who makes a project run may also be able to assume a more significant project leadership role with proper training or encouragement. Quite simply, without the input of local actors, Law Group programs could never develop an adequately refined understanding of the social, political, and human rights landscape in a country, a factor that would significantly reduce the effectiveness of any in-country program.

An example of this local approach is evident in two Law Group pilot programs in Morocco and Yemen, where the Law Group is currently attempting to establish an informal network of legal advisors who will, in turn, facilitate women's access to basic legal advice in nonurban or para-urban communities. In each country, this network will be augmented by community liaisons drawn from the small but important cadre of women who already enjoy some level of professional respect in these communities, including school teachers, medical professionals, and others. To a large extent, therefore, the program seeks to build the skills and legal literacy of a network of professional women who are already accepted and trusted within their communities, and are ideally placed to provide basic legal advice and to refer legal issues to urban-based legal professionals.

At the same time, one consideration in all Law Group programs is the difficult issue of whether international organizations drain talent from local NGO communities by offering competing employment offers or higher salaries to major NGO activists. In the final analysis, the Law Group model postulates that local experts must play a leading role in all in-country programs and that, to the extent that local NGOs are already assuming leadership roles in access-to-justice or civil society sectors, these local institutions should be supported as a matter of priority. In such cases, the Law Group seeks to work directly with local experts, rather than diverting resources to competing or parallel programs. In most cases, however, where the Law Group is clearly responding to needs that are not being addressed by local institutional actors, the Law Group still aims gradually to transform its in-country programs into locally driven initiatives at an appropriate point. As an example, after five years of operations, the Law Group's Cambodia Defenders Project is slated to become an independent Cambodian-run NGO in 2000.

Building Inclusive Demand for Access-to-Justice Programs

Law Group programs also emphasize that all access-to-justice initiatives should seek, at their most basic level, to challenge the attitudes and the relationships of ordinary citizens to a nation's judicial structures. Such a demand-side approach, which seeks to build trust in legal institutions at the grassroots level, ultimately struggles to build a citizen and NGO constituency for judicial reform. This is particularly important in societies where, historically, legal institutions have served as a primary obstacle to protection of human rights, rather than as a champion of fundamental rights.

Efforts aimed at building demand for access to justice must also recognize that the constituency for the rule of law must be as diverse as the society itself. Capacity-building programs should recognize, for example, that women and men often have vastly different experiences in bringing human rights abuses to the attention of judicial institutions, and similarly different experiences in interacting with the judicial system. As a result, access-to-justice programs must specifically address both de jure and de facto impediments that women may face in accessing justice. In Cambodia, the Law Group has established a Women's Resource Centre to offer legal services tailored to meet the needs of victims of domestic violence and to provide legal education and outreach around domestic violence, family law, and other women's rights issues. The Women's Resource Centre was formed out of the experiences of a women's litigation unit that was originally established within the Law Group's Cambodian Defenders Project and which was successful in advancing important domestic violence trial practices. For example, the unit succeeded in obtaining the first-ever interim order issued by a Cambodian court to prevent property dispersal by an abusive husband. The Law Group's legal advocates in Cambodia have also fought vigorously to persuade courts to issue restraining orders and other provisional measures in domestic violence cases. More recently, building on this model, the Law Group has organized a unit within the Defenders Project to address cases relating to trafficking in persons.

Similarly, access-to-justice initiatives must also reach out to minority communities, as minorities are often underrepresented within the legal system and restricted in their access to judicial mechanisms. Indeed, to build confidence in legal institutions and greater demand for legal reform at the grassroots level, the judiciary must not be identified as the protector of specific business interests or of a dominant social or ethnic group. Rather, access-to-justice programs emphasize that the judiciary, acting through all of its many branches and agents, must truly hold itself out as an impartial arbiter of nondiscriminatory laws and policies. Unless justice programs address those social inequities that are so often starkly apparent in moribund judicial systems, human rights will not be protected—particularly the right to equality and dignity on a nondiscriminatory basis—and the judiciary will enjoy little, if any, grassroots support.

Based on this model, in Nicaragua the Law Group has supported access-to-justice initiatives that have sought to strengthen both civil society and judicial mechanisms within the marginalized indigenous and Afro-Caribbean communities on Nicaragua's Atlantic Coast. Through two offices in Nicaragua—in Bluefields in the Southern Autonomous Area (RAAS) and Puerto Cabezas in the Northern Region (RAAN)—the Law Group supports the work of Afro-Caribbean, indigenous, and women's groups to access the institutional structures established by the government of Nicaragua that provide for limited regional autonomy and protection of indigenous and Afro-Caribbean rights.

External Benefits

Access-to-justice programs may also be designed to accomplish a number of related or subsidiary goals, including important efforts at reconciliation in postconflict environments. For example, in the context of legal training in Bosnia and Herzegovina, the

Law Group's legal director in Bosnia often raised questions concerning the use of the three "national languages" in the legal system. Article 6 of the European Convention on Human Rights states that everyone charged with a criminal offense has the right "to have the free assistance of an interpreter if he cannot understand or speak the language used in court." Thus, the Law Group's legal director has asked participants in legal training programs whether this provision should be interpreted as affording minority defendants in criminal proceedings the opportunity to request translations into one of the languages of Bosnia's three "constituent peoples," as specifically enumerated in the Dayton Agreement's Constitution. Surprisingly, after some rather predictable nationalistic responses, a consensus always developed to support the view that, with the exception of certain documents that may be produced in Cyrillic, "everyone understands each other," as one participant noted, and that in most cases, therefore, a request for an interpreter would in fact be an abuse of the rights enshrined in the European Convention on Human Rights.

Discussions such as these, especially when they involve professionals and raise legal or technical points, have often engendered remarkably tolerant dialogues among seeming adversaries. In short, such discussions in Bosnia at least have produced encouragingly moderate responses. As such, these legal exchanges represent an important vehicle for encouraging a broader national dialogue around the need for cooperation and reconciliation. The importance and the value of building such goals into all in-country programs should not be underestimated.

Enforcing Rights-Protective Decisions

Attention must also be devoted to the actual enforcement of rights-protective decisions. Simply winning a human rights case can be an important but meaningless and in some cases even a harmful step, if that victory is not given legal effect and merely adds to a backlog of unimplemented cases at the local or national level. A large backlog of such rights-protective decisions will ultimately undermine the credibility of the judiciary as a whole, particularly in the eyes of those who must vest their trust in the legal system to protect their basic human rights. In many instances, therefore, access-to-justice programs, particularly demand-side or legal aid programs, must also focus on activities aimed at improving the enforcement of judicial decisions. This may include developing or adapting litigation strategies that are useful in seeking the enforcement of rights-protective legal judgments at the local or national levels, including comprehensive litigation strategies focusing on the accumulation of unenforced judgments.

Measuring Results

In measuring results, the Law Group has sought to develop longer-term indicators of success that emphasize the domestic impact of the activities of the Law Group's partners. The most useful of these indicators of accomplishment generally relate to evolving attitudes to the judicial sector within minority or historically disadvantaged communities, and the willingness of all segments of society to rely on the formal legal sector to address social inequities through legal mechanisms. Benchmarks reflecting such social change are not easily quantified, however, particularly where the ultimate aim of a program is to build respect for basic human rights standards and a rule-of-law culture within a community. Nonetheless it remains important to measure success in this broad context. For example, in many environments specific legal victories should only be viewed as successes to the extent that they are actually implemented and begin to effect social change at the grassroots level. In the aggregate, therefore, rights-protective legal victories may represent a significant step in a longer-term process of building a human rights culture, but specific judicial decisions themselves are often merely half successes, at least to the extent that they remain unimplemented and ineffective.

Conclusion

The Universal Declaration of Human Rights challenges us to recognize the "inherent dignity" and the "equal and inalienable rights of all members of the human family." In achieving these lofty goals, the UDHR has much to say about the central importance of access to justice in building a human rights culture. The UDHR recognizes, for example, that "it is essential, if man is not to be compelled to have recourse, as a last resort, to rebellion against tyranny and oppression, that human rights should be protected by the rule of law." Today, unfortunately, we find that in many societies, where the rule of law has been neglected or has otherwise broken down, rebellion has indeed taken hold. Even more disturbingly, today, more than fifty years after the Universal Declaration of Human Rights was adopted in the wake of the Holocaust, we must still bear witness to the possibility of resurgent genocide in many corners of the world. From the Balkans in Europe, to the Great Lakes region of Central Africa to ethnic conflicts in Asia, the horrors of the first half of the century *are* being repeated.

If we are to make greater strides in achieving the promise of the UDHR over the course of the next fifty years, we must redouble our efforts to support the rule of law within a human rights context. To achieve this, the Law Group is devoting significant attention to a broad range of in-country access-to-justice programs, but much more work remains to be accomplished in implementing such programs over the long term.

Notes

These reflections are based on the author's personal observations in working with the International Human Rights Law Group for nearly four years. At the same time, the author wishes to recognize the visionary role that Gay McDougall has played, as Executive Director of the International Human Rights Law Group, in identifying and developing the human rights model described in this chapter, and to thank her for her comments on earlier drafts of the chapter. The author similarly wishes to thank Stephen Bowen, former Program Director of the Law Group, for his reflections on this chapter. Despite the comments and contributions of these and other Law Group staff members, any errors in fact or judgment are solely the responsibility of the author.

1. As established under the Framework Agreement for Peace in Bosnia and Herzegovina (the Dayton Agreement), the unified State of Bosnia and Herzegovina is divided into two entities: the Federation of Bosnia and Herzegovina, where Bosnian Muslims (or Bosniaks) and ethnic Croats constitute a majority of the population; and the Republika Srpska, where Bosnian Serbs constitute a significant majority population.

2. In fact, human rights lawyers have struggled for many years to describe a human rights framework in which nonstate actors committing grave abuses could be held accountable for their actions under traditional human rights and humanitarian law norms. In some respects it has only been through the work of the ad hoc International Criminal Tribunals for the former Yugoslavia and Rwanda, and as a result of the negotiations leading up to the adoption of a statute for an International Criminal Court, that many of the issues surrounding individual liability for these abuses and corresponding state responsibility for preventing and redressing such abuses have been settled.

3. Some remarkable NGO victories have included the campaign to establish an International Criminal Court; campaigns to support and advance gender-specific prosecutions within the UN International Criminal Tribunal for the former Yugoslavia and the International Criminal Tribunal for Rwanda, the campaign to ban landmines, and ongoing campaigns to recognize the human rights implications of female genital mutilation. NGOs have also brought life, momentum, and new ideas to important international human rights discussions, including the 1993 World Conference on Human Rights in Vienna and the 1995 Fourth World Conference on Women in Beijing. In particular, Southern NGOs lent credibility and an important perspective to these significant international forums.

Chapter 7
Human Rights International NGOs
A Critical Evaluation

Makau Mutua

The human rights movement can be seen in variety of guises. It can be seen as a movement for international justice or as a cultural project for "civilizing savage" cultures. In this chapter, I discuss a part of that movement as a crusade for a political project. International nongovernmental human rights organizations (INGOs), the small and elite collection of human rights groups based in the most powerful cultural and political capitals of the West, have arguably been the most influential component of the human rights movement. They have led the promotion and "universalization" of human rights norms, even though the formal creation and promotion of human rights law is carried out by collections of states—the so-called international community—acting in concert and separately within and outside the ambit of the United Nations. Indeed, INGOs have been the human rights movement's prime engine of growth. INGOs seek to enforce the application of human rights norms internationally, particularly toward repressive states in the South, in areas formerly colonized by the West. In this chapter, I call INGOs conventional doctrinalists because they are marked by a heavy and almost exclusive reliance on positive law in treaties and other sources of international law.

INGOs are ideological analogues, both in theory and in method, of the traditional civil rights organizations that preceded them in the West. The American Civil Liberties Union (ACLU), one of the most influential civil rights organizations in the United States, is a classic example of a Western civil rights organization.[1] Two other equally important domestic civil rights organizations in the United States are the National Association for the Advancement of Colored People (NAACP)[2] and the NAACP Legal Defense and Educational Fund (LDF).[3] Although these organizations are called civil rights groups by Americans, they are in reality human rights organizations. The historical origin of the distinction between a "civil rights" group and a "human rights" group in the United States remains unclear. The primary difference is that Western human rights groups focus on abusive practices and traditions in what they see as relatively repressive, "backward" foreign countries and cultures, while the agenda of civil rights groups concentrates on domestic issues. Thus, although groups such as Human Rights

Watch publish reports on human rights abuses in the United States, the focus of their activity is the human rights problems or abuses of other countries.

The half-dozen leading human rights organizations, the prototypical conventional doctrinalists, have arisen in the West over the last half century with the express intent of promoting certain basic Western liberal values—now dubbed human rights—throughout the world, especially the non-Western world. These INGOs were the brainchildren of prominent Western civil rights advocates, lawyers, and private citizens.

The International League for the Rights of Man, now the International League for Human Rights (ILHR), is the oldest such organization, founded in New York in 1942.[4] At various times it has focused on victims of torture, religious intolerance, the rights of human rights monitors at its affiliates abroad, the reunification of Eastern Europeans with relatives in the West during the Cold War, and the human rights treaty state reporting system within the United Nations, and it even got interested in anticolonial struggles in Africa and Asia.[5] Roger Baldwin, the founder of the ACLU, also founded the ILHR.[6] The ILHR itself was responsible for establishing in New York the Lawyers Committee for International Human Rights, now known as the Lawyers Committee for Human Rights (LCHR), another of the more important Western INGOs, in 1975. The LCHR claims to promote the human rights standards contained in the International Bill of Rights.[7] The New York–based Human Rights Watch, discussed in earlier chapters, has developed into the most dominant American INGO working to expose violations of basic liberal freedoms. The last major American INGO is the Washington D.C.–based International Human Rights Law Group, which was established by the Procedural Aspects of International Law Institute, a private American organization that explores issues in international law.[8] Some American domestic civil rights NGOs are acutely aware of their pioneering role in the creation of similar organizations abroad.[9] Until recently, and to a large extent even today, none of these American INGOs focused on human rights issues in the United States, except to seek the reform of U.S. foreign policy and American compliance with aspects of refugee law.[10]

The two other leading INGOs are located in Europe, in the United Kingdom and Switzerland. The Geneva-based International Commission of Jurists (ICJ) was "founded in 1952 to promote the 'rule of law'[11] throughout the world."[12] The ICJ has been accused of being a tool of the West in the Cold War, spending considerable resources exposing the failures of Soviet bloc and one-party states.[13] Today, however, it is regarded as a bona fide INGO, concerned with rule of law questions in the South and other issues, as discussed in Chapter 5.

Lastly, the London-based Amnesty International (AI), the most powerful human rights INGO, is today synonymous with the human rights movement and has inspired the creation of many similar human rights groups around the world. It was launched by Peter Benenson, a British lawyer, writing in the May 28, 1961, issues of the *Observer* and *Le Monde*. Benenson's article, "Forgotten Prisoners," urged moral outrage and appeals for amnesty for individuals who were imprisoned, tortured, or executed because of their political opinions or religion.[14] The recipient of the 1977 Nobel Peace Prize,

AI claims that its object is "to contribute to the observance throughout the world of human rights as set out in the Universal Declaration of Human Rights" through campaigns to free prisoners of conscience; to ensure fair trials within a reasonable time for political prisoners; to abolish the death penalty, torture, and other cruel treatment of prisoners; and to end extrajudicial executions and disappearances. In the last few years, AI has done substantial work in the West, including exposés of police brutality and the application of the death penalty in the United States.

Social Support and Political Bias

Some structural factors provide evidence of the ideological orientation of INGOs. They concern the sources of their moral, financial, and social support. The founding fathers of major INGOs—they have all been white males—were Westerners who either worked on or had an interest in domestic civil and political rights issues; they sought the reform of governmental laws, policies, and processes to bring about compliance with American and European conceptions of liberal democracy and equal protection. Although the founders of the INGOs did not explicitly state their "mission" as a crusade for the globalization of these values, they nevertheless crafted organizational mandates that promoted liberal ideals and norms. In any case, the key international human rights instruments such as the Universal Declaration of Human Rights (UDHR) and the International Covenant on Civil and Political Rights (ICCPR) pierced the sovereign veil for the purposes of protecting and promoting human rights. The mandates of INGOs are lifted, almost verbatim, from such instruments. AI also deploys jurisprudential arguments developed in the context of Western liberal democracy to cast the death penalty as the "ultimate form of cruel, inhuman and degrading punishment."[15]

The pool for the social support of INGOs has therefore come from the private, nongovernmental, and civil society segments of the industrial democracies: prominent lawyers, academics at leading universities, the business and entertainment elite, and other professionals. In the United States, these circles are drawn from the liberal establishment; the overwhelming majority vote for and support the Democratic Party and its politics and are opposed to the Republican Party. The board of directors of Human Rights Watch, for example, counts among its members such luminaries as Robert Bernstein, formerly the top executive at Random House; Robert Joffe, the managing partner at Cravath, Swaine and Moore; Jack Greenberg, the former director-counsel at LDF and professor of law at Columbia University; and Alice Henkin, an important human rights advocate and spouse of the acclaimed professor of international law Louis Henkin. The board of directors of the Lawyers Committee for Human Rights includes its chair, Norman Dorsen, the prominent New York University law professor, former ACLU president, and First Amendment expert; Louis Henkin; Sigourney Weaver, the actress; Kerry Kennedy Cuomo, the founder of the Robert F. Kennedy Memorial Center for Human Rights, named for her father; Marvin Frankel, formerly the chairman of the board and a named partner in a major New York City law firm; and Tom Bernstein, the committee's president, a senior business executive, and son of Robert Bernstein. The board of directors of the International Human Rights Law Group is composed of similar personalities. These boards are predominantly white and male and almost completely American; some, such as those of the Lawyers Committee or HRW, typically have one or several African Americans or a member of another nonwhite minority.

The boards of the European-based INGOs, the ICJ and AI, tend to differ, somewhat, from American INGOs, although they too are dominated by Westerners, Western-trained academics, professionals, and policy makers, or non-Westerners whose worldview is predominantly Western. Thus, even these Asians and Africans—who, though nonwhite, nevertheless "think white" or "European"—champion, usually uncritically, the universalization of the human rights corpus and liberal democracy. In 1997, for example, the seven members of the executive committee of the ICJ included a British lawyer, a Dutch law professor, a Peruvian (a Westerner), and four establishment figures from India, Ghana, Cape Verde, and Jordan. The non-Westerners in the group were prominent legal professionals steeped in either the common law or the civil law traditions. AI's International Executive Committee, its principal policy-making organ, is arguably more global looking—it includes a number of members from the South—although it too has historically been dominated by Westerners.[16] The staffs of all the major INGOs, including AI's headquarters in London, are similarly dominated by Westerners, although both AI and the ICJ now have African heads.[17] The selection of the boards and staffs of INGOs seems designed to guard against individuals, even if they are Westerners, who may question the utility or appropriateness of the conventional doctrinalist approach. This vetting perpetuates their narrow mandates and contradicts the implied and stated norms of diversity and equality, the raison d'être for the existence of these organizations.[18]

The relationship between social, financial, and other material support provides further evidence of the political character of INGOs. Except for AI, which relies heavily on membership dues, most INGOs are funded by a combination of foundation grants, private donations, corporations, businesses, and governments. While most do not accept government funds, some, among them the ICJ and the International Human Rights Law Group, have accepted financial support from governmental sources such as the United States Agency for International Development (USAID) and its Canadian and Nordic counterparts.[19] Those who reject government funds cite concerns for their independence of action and thought. It seems fair to conclude that to be considered for acceptance financial support must come from an industrial democracy with a commitment to promoting human rights abroad; presumably, support from Saudi Arabia or the Democratic Republic of the Congo, clearly authoritarian states, would be unacceptable.

The value of the board of directors is critical for groups that rely on private funding. Those networks and associations signify an INGOs's reputation and acceptability by political and business elites. In the past decade, some INGOs, especially those based in the United States, have devised a fund-raising gimmick. At an annual dinner they present an award to a noted activist from a repressive country in the South or to a Westerner with superstar quality, such as Senator Edward Kennedy or George Soros, the philanthropist, and invite well-to-do, if not wealthy, citizens, corporations, law firms, and foundations to "buy a table," a euphemism by which it is meant an invitee purchases the right to the dinner by reserving a table for a certain number of guests for a substantial donation. This tapestry of social and business ties, drawn from leading Americans who believe in liberal values and their internationalization through the human rights regime, underlines the agenda of INGOs.[20]

Mandates of INGOs

Substantively, conventional doctrinalists stress a narrow range of civil and political rights, as is reflected by the mandates of leading INGOs like Amnesty International and Human Rights Watch. Throughout the Cold War period, INGOs concentrated their attention on the exposure of violations of what they deemed "core" rights in Soviet bloc countries, Africa, Asia, and Latin America. In a reflection of this ideological bias, INGOs mirrored the position of the industrial democracies and generally assumed an unsympathetic and, at times, hostile posture towards calls for the expansion of their mandates to include economic and social rights.[21]

In the last few years since the collapse of the Soviet bloc, however, several INGOs have started to talk about the "indivisibility" of rights; a few now talk about their belief in the equality of the International Covenant on Economic, Social, and Cultural Rights (ICESCR) and the International Covenant on Civil and Political Rights (ICCPR), although their rhetoric has not been matched by action and practice. Many, in particular Human Rights Watch, for a long time remained hostile, however, to the recognition of economic and social rights as rights. HRW, which considered such rights violations "misfortunes," instead advanced its own nebulous interpretation of "indivisible human rights," which related civil and political rights to survival, subsistence, and poverty, "assertions" of good that it did not explicitly call rights.[22] It argued that subsistence and survival are dependent on civil and political rights, especially those related to democratic accountability.[23] According to this view, civil and political rights belong to the first rank because the realization of other sets of concerns or rights, however they are termed, depend on them.[24]

In September 1996, however, Human Rights Watch abandoned its long-standing opposition to the advocacy of economic and social rights.[25] It passed a highly restrictive and qualified policy—effective January 1997—to investigate, document, and promote compliance with the ICESCR. Under the terms of the new policy, HRW's work on the ICESCR will be limited to two situations: where protection of the ICESCR right is "necessary to remedy a substantial violation of an ICCPR right," and where "the violation of an ICESCR right is the direct and immediate product of a substantial violation of an ICCPR right." Furthermore, HRW will intervene to protect ICESCR rights only where the violation is a "direct product of state action, whether by commission or omission";

where the "principle applied in articulating an ICESCR right is one of general applicability"; and where "there is a clear, reasonable and practical remedy that HRW can advocate to address the ICESCR violation."

While an important step by HRW, this policy statement can be seen as a continuation of the history of skepticism toward economic and social rights HRW has long demonstrated; it sees economic and social rights only as an appendage of civil and political rights. Its construction seems to condition ICESCR rights on ICCPR rights—in other words, economic and social rights do not exist outside the realm of civil and political rights. Thus, one interpretation of the HRW policy could be that civil and political rights are the fundamental, primary rights without which other rights are less meaningful and unattainable. The policy also continues HRW's stress on state-related violations, an orientation that does not place emphasis on important violators, such as businesses and international corporations. What is important about the policy, however, is the commitment by the largest and most influential American INGO to begin advocacy of economic and social rights. No other major INGO has gone that far in its practical work. Experimental for the first year, the policy now appears to be part of HRW's mandate, although it remains marginal to its work.[26]

Steiner has described the character of INGOs succinctly:

The term "First World" NGOs both signifies an organization's geographical base and typifies certain kinds of mandates, functions, and ideological orientations. It describes such related characteristics as a concentration on civil and political rights, a commitment to fair (due) process, an individualistic rather than group or community orientation in rights advocacy, and a belief in a pluralist society functioning within a framework of rules impartially applied to protect individuals against state interference. *In a nutshell, "First World" NGOs means those committed to traditional Western liberal values associated with the origins of the human rights movement.* Many of these NGOs work exclusively within their home countries, but the "First World" category also includes most of the powerful international NGOs that investigate events primarily in the Third World.[27]

Traditionally, the work of INGOs has typically involved investigation,[28] reporting,[29] and advocacy.[30] Investigation usually takes place in a Third World country, while reporting and advocacy aim at reforming policies of industrial democracies and intergovernmental agencies to trigger bilateral and multilateral action against the repressive state. Some INGOs now go beyond this denunciatory framework and work to foster and strengthen processes and institutions—rule of law, laws and constitutions, judiciaries, legislatures, and electoral machineries—that ensure the protection of civil and political rights.[31] Although the ideological commitment of these INGOs seems clear through their mandates and work, they nevertheless cast themselves as nonideological. For example, Amnesty International refused to condemn apartheid as a political system or to adopt Nelson Mandela, the century's most prominent prisoner, as a prisoner of conscience. They perceive themselves as politically neutral modern-day abolitionists whose only purpose is to identify "evil" and root it out. Steiner again notes that "although committed to civil-political rights and in this sense taking clear moral and political positions, First World NGOs prefer to characterize themselves as above the play of partisan politics and political parties, and in this sense as apolitical. . . . Their primary self-image is that of monitors, objective investigators applying the consensual norms of the human rights movement to the facts found. They are defenders of legality."[32]

Thus, although INGOs are "political" organizations that work to vindicate political and moral principles that shape the basic characteristics of a state, they consciously present themselves as disinterested in the political character of a state. When HRW asserts that it "addresses the human rights practices of governments of all political stripes, of all geopolitical alignments, and of all ethnic and religious persuasions," it is anticipating charges that it is pro-Western, procapitalist, and unsympathetic to Islamic and other non-Western religious and political traditions. The first two charges could have been fatal to a group's credibility at the height of the Cold War. In reality, however, INGOs have been highly partial: their work has historically concentrated on those countries that have not attained the stable and functioning democracies of the West, the standard for liberal democracy. Target states have included the Soviet bloc and virtually the entire South, where undemocratic or repressive one-party states and military dictatorships have thrived.

The content of the work of INGOs reveals their partiality as well. The typical INGO report is a catalogue of abuses committed by a government against liberal values. As Steiner notes, "given the ideological commitments of these NGOs, their investigative work naturally concentrates on matters such as governmental abuses of rights to personal security, discrimination, and basic political rights. By habit or established practice, NGOs' reports stress the nature and number of violations, rather than explore the socioeconomic and other factors that underlie them."[33]

Reports further document the abridgement of the freedoms of speech and association, violations of due process, and various forms of discrimination. Many INGOs fear that explaining why abuses occur may justify them or give credence to the claims of some governments that civil and political rights violations take place because of underdevelopment. Such an argument, if accepted, would destroy the abolitionists' mission by delaying, perhaps indefinitely, the urgency of complying with human rights standards. Abolitionists fear that this argument would allow governments to continue repressive policies while escaping their obligations under human rights law. INGOs thus demand the immediate protection and respect of civil and political rights regardless of the level of development of the offending state. By taking cover behind the international human rights instruments, INGOs are able to fight for liberal values without appearing partisan, biased, or ideological.

Law Versus Politics

Conventional doctrinalists also perpetuate the appearance of objectivity by explicitly distinguishing themselves from agencies, communities, and government programs that promote democracy and democratization. The democracy and human rights communities see themselves in different lights.[34] The first is made up of individuals and institutions devoted to "democracy assistance programs" abroad, while the second is primarily composed of INGOs. The human rights community has created a law-versus-politics dichotomy through which it presents itself as the guardian of international law, in this case human rights law, as opposed to the promoter of the more elusive concept of democracy, which it sees as a political ideology.[35] A complex web of reasons, motivations, and contradictions permeates this distinction.

The seeds of the dichotomy are related to the attempt by the human rights community not to side with the two protagonists of the Cold War, and in particular Ronald Reagan's crusade against communism and his efforts to pave the way for democracy and free markets across the globe. The human rights community, whose activists and leaders are mostly Democrats or sympathetic to the Democratic Party, in the case of the United States, or Social Democrats and Labor Party sympathizers in Europe—liberals or those to the left of center in Western political jargon—viewed with alarm Reagan's and Margaret Thatcher's push for free markets and support for any pro-Western government, notwithstanding its human rights record. This hostility was exacerbated by the Reagan administration's attempts to reverse the rhetorical prominence that the Carter administration had given to human rights in American foreign policy. Although INGOs delighted in Reagan's opposition to communist rule within the Soviet bloc— their own human rights reports on Soviet bloc countries were scathing—they sought "impartiality" and a "principled" use by the administration of human rights as a tool of foreign policy. INGOs also feared that "democracy programs" would focus only on elections without entrenching basic civil and political rights.[36] In addition, INGOs believed that the focus on democracy blurred the focus on violators and dulled the clarity of physical violations of rights.

The differentiation between democratic and free-market crusades and human rights had another advantage: Western governments and human rights groups could play "good cop, bad cop" roles in the spread of Western liberal values. While the West in bilateral agreements and projects opened up previously closed or repressive one-party societies to markets and "encouraged" democratization, human rights groups would be unrelenting in their assault on the same government for violating civil and political rights. Ordinarily, staffs of INGOs consulted extensively with the State Department or relevant foreign ministry, Western diplomats[37] in the "repressive" state, and elements of the United Nations charged with human rights oversight, such as the Commission on Human Rights, the Committee Against Torture, and the Human Rights Committee.

Other factors indicate the commitment of INGOs to liberal democracy as a political project. At least one American NGO, the Lawyers Committee for Civil Rights Under Law, a domestic NGO with an INGO dimension, expressly linked the survival of its international operations to the "attainment" of democracy by, for example, shutting down its Southern Africa Project after the 1994 South African elections. Some INGO reports explicitly lament the failure of democratic reform.[38] They defend and seek to immortalize prodemocracy activists in repressive states.[39] At least one former leader of an INGO recognizes that the distinction made between democracy and human rights is a facade:

This determination to establish impartiality in the face of human rights violations under different political systems led Amnesty International to shun the rhetorical identification of human rights with democracy. But in fact the struggle against violations, committed mostly by undemocratic authoritarian governments, was closely bound up with the struggle for democracy. Thousands of prisoners of conscience for whom Amnesty International worked in its first three decades were political activists challenging the denial of their rights to freedom of expression and association.[40]

Conclusion

In the past decade, some INGOs have started seeking the deployment of the resources of other institutions, in addition to those of the United Nations, in their advocacy for liberal values. The Lawyers Committee for Human Rights, for example, has instituted a project that explores ways of encouraging international financial institutions such as the World Bank to build human rights concerns into their policies.[41] Perhaps INGOs should openly acknowledge the inescapable and intrinsic linkage between human rights and democracy, a fact consciously recognized by quasi-governmental agencies in the North.[42]

The facade of neutrality, the fiction that INGOs do not seek the establishment of a particular political system, in this case, a liberal democracy, must be abandoned immediately. No one should be expected to believe that the scheme of rights promoted by INGOs does not seek to replicate a vision of society based on the industrial democracies of the North. Only after openly conceding that INGOs indeed have a specific political agenda can discussions be had about the wisdom, problems, and implications for the advocacy of such values. And only then can conversations about the postliberal society start in earnest.

Notes

1. Initially founded in 1920 to advocate the rights of conscientious objectors, the ACLU sees itself as the "guardian of the Bill of Rights which guarantees fundamental civil liberties to all of us." These rights include the freedoms of speech, press, and religion (First Amendment); freedom from abuses by the police, domestic spying, and other illegal intelligence activities (Fourth Amendment); equal treatment and fair play (Fifth Amendment); fair trial (Sixth Amendment); prohibition against cruel and unusual punishment (Eighth Amendment); and privacy and personal autonomy (Fourth, Fifth, and Ninth Amendments). See Laurie S. Wiseberg and Hazel Sirett, eds., *North American Human Rights Directory* (Garrett Park, Md.: Garrett Park Press, 1984), p. 19.
2. The NAACP, the oldest U.S. civil rights organization, was founded in 1909 to seek equal treatment—the removal of racial discrimination in areas such as voting, employment, housing, business, courts, and transportation—for African Americans through peaceful reform. See ibid., p. 161.
3. Although today the LDF and the NAACP are separate legal entities, the LDF was founded in 1939 as the legal arm of the NAACP. It has initiated legal action in courts to challenge discrimi-

nation and promote equality in schools, jobs, the electoral system, land use, and other services and areas. Ibid., p. 159.

4. See Wiseberg and Sirett, eds., *North American Human Rights Directory*, p. 135.

5. Ibid. The ILHR was also involved, albeit paternalistically, in anticolonial struggles in Africa and Asia, particularly in South-West Africa, now Namibia. See William Korey, *NGOs and the Universal Declaration of Human Rights: "A Curious Grapevine"* (New York: St. Martin's Press, 1998), p. 101.

6. See Rita McWilliams, "Who Watched Americas Watch?" *National Interest* 19 (1990), pp. 45, 53. Jerome Shestack, a prominent American lawyer who long served as the president of the ILHR and is the organization's current honorary chair, was replaced in May 1996 by Scott Horton, a partner in a New York law firm. Telephone interview with the ILHR, September 13, 1996.

7. On the mandate of the LCHR, see Lawyers Committee for Human Rights, *Critique: Review of the Department of State Country Reports on Human Rights Practices for 1990* (New York: Lawyers Committee for Human Rights, 1991), back leaf.

8. See Wiseberg and Sirett, eds., *North American Human Rights Directory*, p. 133. The institute itself was established in 1965 and has devoted considerable resources to the promotion of the idea of human rights. Richard Lillich, its former president, is a professor of law at the University of Virginia School of Law and one of the leading writers on human rights.

9. At a 1992 LDF symposium of public interest law NGOs from around the world, Julius Chambers, then director-counsel of the LDF, recalled how Thurgood Marshall, his most celebrated predecessor, had in 1959 helped write the Kenya Constitution, and had helped to endow it with doctrines of due process, equality, and justice. Chambers also remembered how Jack Greenberg, another predecessor, had laid the groundwork for the Legal Resource Centre of South Africa, one of that country's leading public interest law firms under apartheid. Instructively, he noted that he did not view the symposium "primarily as an occasion for the LDF to *teach* others." See National Association for the Advancement of Colored People Legal Defense and Educational Fund, *Public Interest Law around the World: Report of a Symposium held at Columbia University in May 1991 with Descriptions of Participating Legal Organizations from Twenty Countries* (New York: Columbia Human Rights Law Review, 1992), p. 1; emphasis added. Noting the progress made in establishing human rights NGOs around the world and arguing for the removal of restrictions on NGOs to allow them to operate more freely, see also Lawyers Committee for Human Rights, *The Establishment of the Right of Non-Governmental Groups to Operate* (New York: Lawyers Committee for Human Rights, 1993).

10. American INGOs argue, with some justification, that there is a glut of civil rights organizations addressing civil (human) rights problems in the United States. They therefore see little purpose in duplicating the excellent work of local NGOs. This posture is self-defeating in several respects. First, charges of "imperialism" undercut the effectiveness of American INGOs, even with some of their kindred spirits in the South and the former Soviet bloc. Secondly, domestic American NGOs remain unaware of the uses of the international rights regime and the solidarity of advocates elsewhere, facts which conspired to delay the ratification by the United States of major international human rights treaties. The absence of domestic U.S. NGOs from the international human rights movement served, among other things, to delegitimize the movement in the eyes of other cultures. Nevertheless, in a rare effort, Human Rights Watch and the ACLU in 1993 produced a report on human rights abuses in the United States. See Human Rights Watch and American Civil Liberties Union, *Human Rights Violations in the United States* (New York: Human Rights Watch and American Civil Liberties Union, 1993). Two things were unusual about the effort: first, that an American INGO produced a human rights report on the United States, and second, that it did so in collaboration with a domestic American NGO. In a rare call, Dorothy Thomas, formerly the director of the Human Rights Watch Women's Project, urged the use of international human rights norms in protecting human rights in the United States. Dorothy Q. Thomas, "Advancing Rights Protection in the United States: An Internationalized Advocacy Strategy," *Harvard Human Rights Journal* 9 (1996), pp. 15–26. Amnesty International also launched an extensive campaign on human rights in the United States in 1998.

11. This term is commonly understood to describe a state that is accountable to the governed through the application of fair and just laws enforced by an independent and impartial judiciary.

See Andrea J. Hanneman, "Independence and Group Rights in the Baltics: A Double Minority Problem," *Virginia Journal of International Law* 35 (1995), pp. 485, 523: "The extent to which a society protects human rights in general and minority rights in particular has been called the 'litmus test of liberty and the rule of law' "; citing Ralf Dahrendorf, "Minority Rights and Minority Rule," in Ben Whitaker, ed., *Minorities: A Question of Human Rights?* (New York: Pergamon Press, 1984), p. 79. For a history of the ICJ, see Howard B. Tolley, Jr., *Global Advocates for Human Rights: The International Commission of Jurists* (Philadelphia: University of Pennsylvania Press, 1994).

12. Laurie S. Wiseberg and Hazel Sirett, eds., *Human Rights Directory: Western Europe* (Washington, D.C.: Human Rights Internet, 1982), p. 216.

13. See Issa G. Shivji, *The Concept of Human Rights in Africa* (London: Codesria, 1989), p. 34. At its inception, the ICJ was funded in part by covert CIA funds. "It followed an essentially American set of priorities in its early years, then expanded and became less politically partial." Claude E. Welch, Jr., *Protecting Human Rights in Africa: Roles and Strategies of Non-Governmental Organizations* (Philadelphia: University of Pennsylvania Press, 1995), p. 163.

14. See Ian Martin, *The New World Order: Opportunity or Threat for Human Rights?* (Cambridge, Mass.: Harvard Law School Human Rights Program, 1993), pp. 4–5. From 1986 to 1992, Martin was the secretary-general of Amnesty International. Benenson's article accompanied photos of six political prisoners: three were imprisoned in Romania, Hungary, and Czechoslovakia; the other three were a Greek communist and unionist imprisoned in Greece, an Angolan doctor and poet incarcerated by the Portuguese colonial rulers in Angola, and the Rev. Ashton Jones, an American who had repeatedly been beaten and jailed in Louisiana and Texas for advocating the civil rights of black Americans. Ibid. Although AI now focuses most of its attention on Africa, Central America, and South America, the trigger for its creation was, ironically, the official conduct of Soviet bloc and Western governments, including the United States.

15. Ibid., p. 21. In addition, AI attacks the "arbitrary and irrevocable nature of the death penalty," its use as a "tool of political repression," and its disproportionate imposition on "the poor and the powerless." It disagrees with the argument that the death penalty has a deterrent effect on crime. Ibid.

16. See Henry J. Steiner, *Diverse Partners: Non-Governmental Organizations in the Human Rights Movement: The Report of a Retreat of Human Rights Activists* (Cambridge, Mass.: Harvard Law School Human Rights Program and Human Rights Internet, 1991), pp. 61–64.

17. Ibid. Pierre Sané, a Senegalese, became AI's first non-European secretary-general in October 1992. Adama Dieng, also a Senegalese, became the secretary-general of the ICJ in 1991. Although both AI and the ICJ accepted non-Western heads, the choices were more "safe" and less radical than they initially appeared. Sané came from the International Development Research Centre, a Canadian development aid organization, for which he had worked since 1978. Dieng was working for the ICJ before his appointment. Both were nationals of Senegal, with a reputation in the West as a stable formal democracy, and one of the most Francophilic countries in Africa.

18. When INGOs engage Southerners, it is ordinarily for area-specific responsibilities, usually their native region. For example, Africa Watch, the division of Human Rights Watch that addresses sub-Saharan African human rights problems, has been headed by Africans since its founding in 1988. Similarly, Americas Watch has been headed by Latin Americans virtually since its inception in 1981. This author, an African, was in 1989–91 the director of the Africa Project at the Lawyers Committee for Human Rights, having succeeded Rakiya Omaar, another African. This ghettoization—conscious or not—seeks to legitimize the organization in the particular region while retaining its commitment to Western liberal values. It also pigeonholes non-Westerners as capable of addressing issues in only their native region and incapable of dealing with questions from other regions. In effect, these hiring patterns leave the impression that only Westerners have the ability to develop a universal outlook.

19. In 1993 this author led a USAID-funded "rule of law" study mission to Ethiopia for the International Human Rights Law Group and wrote a report on the mission's findings. International Human Rights Law Group, *Ethiopia in Transition*.

20. In 1986, for example, the Lawyers Committee for Human Rights honored President Cora-

zon Aquino of the Philippines for "her achievement in leading the people of her nation to peacefully reclaim democracy." See Lawyers Committee for Human Rights, *Tenth Anniversary Annual Report* (New York: Lawyers Committee for Human Rights, 1988). In 1987, it honored Robert Bernstein, senior executive at Random House and the founder of Human Rights Watch. NBC news anchor Tom Brokaw was the master of ceremonies at the 600-guest event which attracted prominent businessmen and lawyers. Ibid.

21. See Aryeh Neier, "Human Rights," in Joel Krieger, William A. Joseph, James A. Paul, et al., eds., *The Oxford Companion to Politics of the World* (New York: Oxford University Press, 1993), pp. 401, 403.

22. See Human Rights Watch, *Indivisible Rights: The Relationship of Political and Civil Rights to Survival, Subsistence and Poverty* (New York: Human Rights Watch, 1992). In 1993, Neier, the former executive director of HRW, expressed his opposition to the deployment of rights rhetoric to economic and social concerns: "When it comes to the question of what are called economic rights, I'm on the side of the spectrum which feels that the attempt to describe economic concerns as rights is misguided. I think that when one expresses this opinion, it is often thought that one is denigrating the significance of economic misery and inequities. I would like not to be accused of that. I regard economic equity and economic misery as matters of enormous significance. I just don't think that it's useful to define them in terms of rights." Aryeh Neier, "Remarks to East Asian Legal Studies & Human Rights Program Symposium, Harvard Law School, May 8, 1993," in *Human Rights and Foreign Policy: A Symposium* (Cambridge, Mass.: Harvard Law School Human Rights Program, 1994), p. 16. For a critique of NGOs and their restrictive mandates, see James Gathii and Celestine Nyamu, "Note, Reflections on United States-based Human Rights NGOs' Work on Africa," *Harvard Human Rights Journal* 9 (1996), p. 291.

23. See Human Rights Watch, *Indivisible Rights*, pp. vi–vii. One of the most coherent rationalizations of the opposition to economic and social rights was expressed in a meeting of American INGOs: "One participant felt strongly that it would be detrimental for U.S. human rights NGOs to espouse the idea of economic, social and cultural rights. Although they refer to important issues, they concern distributive justice rather than corrective justice, like civil and political rights. But distributive justice is a matter of policy, rather than principles; and human rights NGOs must deal with principles, not policies. Otherwise, their credibility will be damaged. Supporting economic demands will only undermine the ability of NGOs to promote civil and political rights, which are indispensable." M. Rodriguez Bustelo and Philip Alston, unpublished report of a conference held at Arden House, 1986, p. 26; quoted in Philip Alston, "U.S. Ratification of the Covenant on Economic, Social and Cultural Rights: The Need for an Entirely New Strategy," *American Journal of International Law* 84 (1990), p. 390, n. 107. The credibility of American INGOs to which the speaker referred was unlikely to be credibility among those whose economic and social rights are denied. It seems fair to suppose that the concern here was the reputation of NGOs with the governments of industrial democracies and the elites who support the INGO community.

24. Human Rights Watch, *Indivisible Rights*, pp. vi–vii.

25. Human Rights Watch, "Human Rights Watch's Proposed Interim Policy on Economic, Social, and Cultural Rights," internal document, September 30, 1996. All quotations in this paragraph are from this document.

26. Ibid. HRW has been reluctant to expand this mandate to cover more ICESCR rights for a number of reasons, including the lack of adequate human resources. Kenneth Roth, executive director, Human Rights Watch, telephone interview with author October 8, 1996. See generally, Human Rights Watch, *Human Rights Watch World Report 1999* (New York: Human Rights Watch, 1999).

27. Steiner, *Diverse Partners*, p. 19; emphasis added.

28. An investigation, known as human rights fact-finding mission, is conducted by the staffs of INGOs who typically spend anywhere from several days to a number of weeks in a Third World country interviewing victims of repression, government officials, local activists, local media, and academics. See, generally, Diane F. Orentlicher, "Bearing Witness: The Art and Science of Human Rights Fact-Finding," *Harvard Human Rights Journal* 3 (1990), p. 83.

29. Reporting involves compiling data and information from the fact-finding mission and cor-

relating them to human rights standards to bring out discrepancies and disseminating the results through reports or other media. This method is also called "shaming" because it spotlights the offending state to the international community. See, e.g., Lawyers Committee for Human Rights, *Zimbabwe: Wages of War: A Report on Human Rights* (New York: Lawyers Committee for Human Rights, 1986); Human Rights Watch, *World Report 1995.*

30. This includes lobbying governments and international institutions to use their leverage to alleviate violations.

31. For example, according to its statute, Amnesty International works to "promote as appears appropriate the adoption of constitutions, conventions, treaties and other measures which guarantee the rights contained in the provisions referred to in Article 1 hereof." Amnesty International, *Report*, appendix 2, p. 333. The International Human Rights Law Group undertakes rule of law assessments which aim at identifying institutional weaknesses and proposing structural reforms. See, generally, International Human Rights Law Group, *Ethiopia in Transition.*

32. Steiner, *Diverse Partners*, p. 19.

33. Ibid.

34. For a comprehensive journalistic account of the differences between the two communities, see Thomas Carothers, "Democracy and Human Rights: Policy Allies or Rivals?" *Washington Quarterly* 17 (1994), p. 109.

35. Ibid., p. 111.

36. See Lawyers Committee for Human Rights, *United States Draft Human Rights Action Plan*, p. 4.

37. Meetings at the request of INGOs with State Department officials responsible for policies in particular countries are indispensable to INGOs, whose clout often comes from their association with rich and powerful Western states. Ordinarily, INGO fact-finding missions also meet with Western diplomats to raise concerns and seek inside information about political issues in the country.

38. See, e.g., Amnesty International USA, *Zaire: Violence Against Democracy* (New York: Amnesty International USA, 1993), p. 23; Africa Watch, *Zaire: Two Years Without a Transition* (Washington, D.C.: Africa Watch, 1992), pp. 45–46.

39. The Robert F. Kennedy Memorial Center for Human Rights, for example, has often given its annual award to prodemocracy activists, including Gibson Kamau Kuria of Kenya, a leading figure in the struggle to end repressive one-party rule by introducing multiparty democracy in his country. See Robert F. Kennedy Memorial Center for Human Rights, *Justice Enjoined: The State of the Judiciary in Kenya* (Washington, D.C.: Robert F. Kennedy Memorial Center for Human Rights, 1992); Makau Mutua, *Confronting the Past: Accountability for Human Rights Violations in Malawi* (Washington, D.C.: Robert F. Kennedy Memorial Center for Human Rights, 1994).

40. Martin, *The New World Order*, p. 6.

41. See Lawyers Committee for Human Rights, *The World Bank: Governance and Human Rights* (New York: Lawyers Committee for Human Rights, 1993), pp. 2–3.

42. David Gillies, *Human Rights, Democracy and "Good Governance": Stretching the World Bank's Policy Frontiers* (Montreal: International Centre for Human Rights and Democratic Development, 1993).

Part II
Economic, Social, and Cultural Rights
An Increasingly Significant Emphasis

Chapter 8
FoodFirst Information and Action Network

Brigitte Hamm

FoodFirst Information and Action Network (FIAN) is an international NGO (INGO) committed to strengthening economic, social, and cultural rights.[1] Traditionally, states and international organizations as well as NGOs perceive human rights as civil liberties and political rights. Together with other domestic and international NGOs active in the field of economic, social, and cultural rights, FIAN is working to reframe this traditional understanding. In their book *Activists Beyond Borders*, Margaret Keck and Kathryn Sikkink describe the effort of reconstructing frames of meaning as one of the main endeavors of principled NGOs such as FIAN.[2] Increasingly, human rights is being rethought to include economic, social, and cultural rights, an indication of the "frame resonance" of these efforts.[3]

Definition of Human Rights

The Universal Declaration of Human Rights links human rights and human dignity. A life in dignity requires participatory rights known as civil liberties, the protection from state interference in the private sphere, as well as protection from arbitrary acts such as torture and other illegal measures by state actors. However, not only are adequate political conditions considered necessary to lead a life in dignity, but the economic, social, and cultural environment is seen as a precondition as well. FIAN expresses this view in the sentence: "Hunger kills like a bullet, only more slowly."[4] Thus in the language of human rights, states have the responsibility and the duty to respect and provide political, economic, social, and cultural rights for a life in dignity.

By including these different dimensions, the Universal Declaration of Human Rights expresses the indivisibility, interrelation, and interdependence of human rights. Among the economic, social, and cultural rights mentioned in the declaration are the rights to social security; work; just and favorable remuneration; a decent standard of living including food, clothing, housing, and medical care; education; and the right to participate freely in the cultural life of the society. However, only six articles of the declaration concern economic, social, and cultural rights, while nineteen articles are dedicated to political rights and civil liberties.

The Development of Human Rights Since 1948

According to Renteln, the consideration of economic, social, and cultural rights in the Universal Declaration of Human Rights was possible because consent to this document implies only a moral commitment without the binding duty of an international treaty.[5] The United States was notable among countries which declared opposition to the inclusion of economic, social, and cultural rights in the declaration.[6] In contrast to the U.S. position, socialist states criticized the emphasis on civil liberties and political rights as a Western bias.

While the Universal Declaration of Human Rights is—at least in principle—based on a holistic view of human rights, two international treaties, namely the International Covenant on Civil and Political Rights (ICCPR) and the International Covenant on Economic, Social, and Cultural Rights (ICESCR) divided these rights in international law. Both treaties went into force in 1976. Many authors contend that this separation was caused by the intensification of the Cold War.[7]

In contrast to political rights, the institutionalization of economic, social, and cultural rights is much weaker. Originally, the International Covenant on Economic, Social, and Cultural Rights did not provide for a committee to monitor the compliance of the treaty by its member states, while such committees had been installed for other human rights treaties. The Committee on Economic, Social, and Cultural Rights (CESCR) was established only in 1987 to survey the covenant. Political rights are further strengthened by an optional protocol allowing for individual communications to the Human Rights Committee when member states of the International Covenant on Civil and Political Rights violate political rights. Such an optional protocol is still lacking for the International Covenant on Economic, Social, and Cultural Rights (but the draft is pending before the Commission on Human Rights).

One often mentioned rationale for the weaker institutionalization of economic, social, and cultural rights is that they are not really rights but are of programmatic character, as mentioned in the Introduction to this book. In this sense, these rights are understood as aspirational goals that governments should pursue for the welfare of their people. In contrast to this view, NGOs such as FIAN emphasize the rights character of economic, social, and cultural rights, and understand them as immediately applicable and as policy guidelines that require governments to create the conditions for their realization. There are three obligations that governments have for all human rights, namely to *respect* these rights, to *protect* them against third parties such as multinational companies, and to *fulfill* them.

FoodFirst Information and Action Network (FIAN)

It was exactly the separation of human rights into political and economic, social and cultural rights that members of a number of national sections of Amnesty International (AI) (in particular Austria, Belgium, and Germany) criticized when discussing the relationship between hunger and repression in the course of a debate on Amnesty's mandate in the early 1980s.[8] In Heidelberg, Germany, a working group on the right to food was started on the district level of AI in 1982. This initiative was strengthened by the outcome of an internal study commissioned by AI to investigate links between land rights and the work of Amnesty. However, AI denied the consideration of economic, social, and cultural rights because of the organization's mandate and because of scarce resources.[9] By March 1983 the Heidelberg working group had given up hope that the right to food could become a major matter of concern of AI, and accordingly founded an urgent action network in Geneva jointly with representatives of NGOs from Austria, France, Germany, and Switzerland. This network explored human rights work centered on the right to food. It steadily increased its membership from different parts of the world and developed its mandate in two international conferences in France and Sweden. In Heidelberg, on June 6, 1986, this urgent action network founded a new human rights organization—FoodFirst Information and Action Network, known as FIAN—the first international human rights organization in the field of economic and social human rights.[10] Most of the founding members of FIAN International remained as members of AI as well.

Similar to Amnesty, FIAN International is independent of governments, political parties, and religions.[11] FIAN International is based on worldwide voluntary membership. Above all, the organization is financed by contributions of the country sections to the head branch. Depending on their size and financial situation they deliver 20–40 percent of their resources, which are mainly membership fees and individual donations, to the International Secretariat (IS). About half of the money at the central level is spent for personnel. The budget in 1998 was 530,000 DM (about $285,000), and for 1999 740,000 DM (about $400,000), an increase mainly due to money coming from outside sources to finance major projects.[12] Among these is a project on the code of conduct (duration of two years) and one on agrarian reform (duration of three years). Outside money for projects comes from various sources, such as church-based NGOs active in the development field, and foundations. In 1999, the European Commission gave 100,000 Euro to the European sections of FIAN International for human rights education in the member states of the European Union.[13]

The authority for the conduct of the affairs of FIAN such as a change in mandate lies with the International Council (IC), which meets every two years. The IC is composed of delegates of all sections and elects the International Executive Committee (IEC). Since 1998 no person can be reelected to the IEC more than twice in a row.[14] This new rule led to a generational change with implications for the geographical composition of the IEC; for the first time in the short history of FIAN a majority of the nine members of the IEC now come from the South. The IEC is responsible for implementing the decisions of the IC and conducting the affairs of FIAN. It meets twice a year to deal with finances and planning as well as programmatic issues. It also nominates and controls the IS, seated in Heidelberg, Germany. At present, the IS consists of seven persons. Three work on a full-time and four on a half-time basis. The IS heavily relies on volunteers and interns. About 60 percent of the activities of the IS can be described as work to increase FIAN's capability for urgent actions and interventions. The rest of the work is divided evenly into education and seminars and work at the UN.

In its thirteen years of work, FIAN has grown steadily in membership, resources, and activities. Today, the organization counts roughly 6000 members. Of these about 80 percent belong to sections in the North and 20 percent in the South. Country sections work in ten states of the Americas, Asia, and Europe, but no section exists in Africa yet. Windfuhr gives two reasons for this.[15] First, hunger in Africa often is caused by armed conflicts and civil wars and is less rooted in ownership rights to land. Armed conflicts and civil wars generally necessitate humanitarian help rather than support in organizing demands. In contrast to humanitarian aid, the relationship between hunger and land rights may be described as the main issue of FIAN's work. Second, few domestic peasant and women's organizations in Africa work as yet on the right to food. This implies that the domestic structure for networking in respect to the right to food is quite weak in Africa. However, African organizations concerned with economic, social, and cultural rights are growing, as is networking on a regional basis. Especially, the World Food Summit that took place 1996 in Rome offered chances for intensified networking among African organizations and with INGOs. FIAN was invited to participate in the founding conference for the Coalition on Sustainable Food Security that took place in Dar es Salaam in 1998. At present, FIAN International has contacts with African organizations in South Africa, Tanzania, Zimbabwe, Cameroon, and Ghana. Most of these contacts involve the support of domestic organizations in concrete casework.

The largest sections of FIAN are those in Austria, Belgium, and Germany. Based on the demand of domestic members and considering its size and the different languages, India has two sections; a third one is on the way. New sections under formation are called coordinations. The United States has a coordination, which is supported by the Institute for Food and Development Policy, known as FoodFirst Institute, in California. However, FIAN and this institute are independent from each other.[16]

FIAN's mandate focuses on the right to (adequate) food, which is considered as the fundamental element of all social rights. For FIAN the right to adequate food is not a matter of charity that depends on others for support, but it means access to productive resources as a precondition to feed oneself and to lead a life in dignity.

FIAN's mandate can only be changed by the International Council (IC). In addition to the biannual meetings of the IC, the IEC organizes an international conference to discuss the mandate and other FIAN International issues in the years without an IC. As within AI, FIAN's mandate is almost always under debate, implying continuous reflection over meaning and norms. One main demand is to extend the mandate to

Table 1. Regional Distribution of FIAN International in 1998

Sections	Coordinations
Austria	Italy/South Tyrol
Belgium	Brazil
Germany	Honduras
France	United States
Norway	Sri Lanka
Sweden	Delhi (North India)
Switzerland	Philippines
United Kingdom	
India (Tamil Nadu)	
India (West Bengal)	
Mexico	

Source: FIAN International Secretariat, *Annual Report 1998*.

workers' rights. Another call comes from sections of the South, asking that FIAN work on the violation of the right to food in countries of the North. A further discussion revolves around the question of what sections should be allowed to do in their own countries. The present agreed-upon program says that they may do research and lobbying, but—as with AI—they cannot organize concrete actions in their countries.

FIAN's Activities: Research and Intervention, Campaigns and Lobbying

The multiple tasks of international human rights NGOs, noted earlier in the Introduction, include human rights education, agenda and standard setting, monitoring compliance with international standards, lobbying governments and international organizations to enforce international human rights standards, and creating and strengthening public opinion against human rights violations. These different fields are separated for analytical purposes, but in reality they overlap, as the activities of FIAN demonstrate.[17]

FIAN's work can be described as the "classic" human rights work of an INGO. FIAN organizes national and international campaigns including urgent actions, letters of protest, lobbying, and advocacy. The aim is to put pressure on governments and other actors to take measures against concrete violations of social human rights. The tactics involved can be described as the following:

1. *information politics,* or the ability to quickly and credibly generate politically usable information and move it to where it will have the most impact;
2. *symbolic politics,* or the ability to call upon symbols, actions, or stories that make sense of a situation for an audience that is frequently far away;
3. *leverage politics,* or the ability to call upon powerful actors to affect a situation where weaker members of a network are unlikely to have influence; and

4. *accountability politics*, or the effort to hold powerful actors to their previously stated policies or principles.[18]

The activities of FIAN International are structured within two main work areas, namely research/intervention and campaigns/lobbying.[19] The organization of these activities is in the responsibility of the IS. Research and intervention are closely related because FIAN carries out its own investigations before taking action. Research and intervention are divided into the following three levels.[20]

1. Urgent actions—mainly carried out as letter actions (by region in 1998)
- Forced expulsions for construction of a dam in Mokhada, Maharashtra, *India*
- Land evictions for industrial estate in Tamil Nadu, *India*
- Legal land claim by the Mapalad farmers cooperative denied by Supreme Court, *Philippines*
- Violent oppression of landless peasants, Paraná, *Brazil*
- Evasion of enforcing a decree of regularization of forest reserve, Ciríaco, *Brazil*
- Failed implementation of agrarian reform, *El Salvador*

2. Hot lines—fast letters (by region in 1998)
- Eviction of villagers for construction of a dam, Maheshwar, *India*
- Evasion of agrarian reform, Char Lota, *Bangladesh*
- Nonimplementation of agrarian reform in Toledo, Cebu, *Philippines*
- Forced eviction of small-scale miners from ancestral land, Mindanao, *Philippines*
- Reservation for the Tagaeri to secure their livelihood, *Ecuador*
- Destruction of forest reserve threatens the right to food, Imataca, *Venezuela*
- Right to food threatened for indigenous people by oil exploitation, Tabasco, *Mexico*
- Destruction of indigenous land by hydroelectric power plant, Sinú River, *Colombia*
- Evasion of agrarian reform, Pariaba, *Brazil*
- For a reconstruction oriented toward economic and social human rights, *Central America*
- Draft amendment of refugee law violates right to food, *Germany*

3. Special interventions—direct, small, and short-term interventions (by region in 1998)
- Violations of the right to food, Irian Jaya, Puncak Jaya, and East Timor, *Indonesia*
- Forced evictions of tribal, peoples North Mindanao, *Philippines*
- Evasion of agrarian reform, Bondoc, *Philippines*
- Violations of human rights, Chiapas, *Mexico*
- Implementation of agrarian reform, *Bolivia*
- Insufficient compensation in favor of mining, Cajamarca, *Peru*
- Failed recognition of indigenous land, Salta, *Argentina*
- Evasion of agrarian reforms, Pariaba, *Brazil*
- Destruction of forest reserve threatens the right to food, Imataca, *Venezuela*

- Land-grabbing of indigenous land, Jalisco, *Mexico*
- Land rights threatened by oil exploitation, Khanty-Mansi, *Russia*

FIAN International organizes about fifty to sixty such actions per year, in contrast to about 500 new actions taken by Amnesty International every year. In 1998, the number of actions decreased slightly due to a reduction in available staff time in the IS.

FIAN International regularly evaluates its activities in a qualitative manner. The criteria are changes or improvements that have taken place upon the conclusion of these activities. According to FIAN, in 30 to 40 percent of these actions substantial next steps were taken, such as the solution of a problem or important steps in this direction. In 20 to 30 percent of the actions steps were taken, such as the reopening of legal proceedings.[21] In 1998, the IS started to publish FIAN Action Updates to provide follow-up information on previous interventions in the Philippines, Costa Rica, Mexico, Colombia, Venezuela, and Egypt.

While hunger is predominantly a problem of the South, it increasingly occurs in industrial countries as well. Therefore, to fight hunger, FIAN monitors the right to food all over the world. The organization is mainly engaged in campaigns on long-term issues such as land rights and for the further elaboration of specific economic, social, and cultural rights and their implementation. It has organized campaigns against the violation of the right to food in the United States and campaigns to protect social rights that relate to the right to food. One example is the campaign against the planned cutback of basic social services for asylum seekers in Germany. Some country sections engage in their own campaigns, as will be described below.

To support its campaigns and to inform the public and FIAN's members about the organization's work, FIAN International regularly publishes the magazine *HUNGRY for what is right*. Country sections may have their own magazines. The goal of articles by FIAN members and books on the right to food is to strengthen economic, social, and cultural rights. The organization also prepares expert papers relating to social rights on the request of institutions. Among these are foundations and organizations related to churches and UN panels.[22] Furthermore, the organization participates in conferences concerning development and human rights issues.

Keck and Sikkink consider that "networks operate best when they are dense, with many actors, strong connections among groups in the network, and reliable information flows. . . . Effective networks must involve reciprocal information exchanges, and include activists from target countries as well as those able to get institutional leverage."[23] The network for the strengthening of economic, social, and cultural rights has been developed by manifold efforts on the local, national, regional, and international levels.

FIAN International is strongly engaged in networking with domestic organizations such as unions and NGOs, and with other INGOs. Domestic groups (e.g., peasants, women, and indigenous peoples) often ask for help to organize international solidarity in concrete cases. For example, after checking a request for support from a human rights group in Cairo, FIAN started an international letter campaign in four languages to help Egyptian peasants in their struggle against a law that was supposed to lift limitations on the lease of land.[24] The case demonstrates the so-called boomerang pattern of influence, where channels from the outside are used by domestic groups to put pressure on their own government.[25] In a long-term campaign for land rights, FIAN International is cooperating with the international small peasants' organization, La Via Campesina, to organize a Global Campaign on Agrarian Reform. In 1998, both organizations cooperated to demand an agrarian reform in marches and demonstrations before Brazilian embassies in countries from Mexico to the Philippines. Peasant organizations from the South participated in this Global Action Day.

In addition to such cooperation, FIAN tries to strengthen and contribute to the development of networks through education. In 1999, for example, FIAN organized five regional seminars in Brazil on human rights and lobbying at the UN, where thirty to fifty domestic organizations participated.

Networking with other INGOs is important to strengthen leverage potential and to organize the international division of work in lobbying national governments and the UN. An example of such networking is the International NGO Network for Human Rights in Trade and Investment that was founded in 1998 by Habitat International Coalition, Peoples' Decade for Human Rights Education, the Lutheran World Federation, and FIAN International. The network delivered a submission on the possible impact of the Multilateral Agreement on Investment (MAI) to the UN Subcommission on Prevention of Discrimination and Protection of Minorities. This was followed by a very influential resolution of the subcommission which contributed to stopping the MAI negotiations within the Organization for Economic Cooperation and Development (OECD).

The Right to Food and Land Rights

Violations of the right to food often coincide with the threatened expulsion of peasants and other groups in the interests of landed proprietors and multinational companies, and for big, often multilateral projects such as dams. Indigenous peoples are especially threatened by eviction from their land. Therefore, in the context of food, one major concern is land rights for small and landless peasants in Third World countries, where land and access to clean water are indispensable. In the view of FIAN, states parties to the International Covenant on Economic, Social, and Cultural Rights (ICESCR) will be obliged to execute agrarian reform to secure land rights for poor peasants, if this is necessary to implement the right to food.

The closeness of the right to food to land rights also relates to group rights, because indigenous peoples are being evicted from their land worldwide for various reasons. An example is the solidarity campaign to support the indigenous Suminao of the Philippines in their effort to gain the right to live on their traditional land. Suminao families were threatened and massacred by a landed proprietor family while the government failed to provide help. Amnesty International and FIAN International informed the public about the threat to the Suminao in 1998.

Demands for land rights for indigenous peoples include adjusting the prevailing human rights concept and considering group rights as human rights. Group rights are highly questioned in the human rights debate, as they contradict the traditional view of human rights as individual rights. Furthermore, the concept of group rights leaves open questions such as who represents the group and how to shape the relationship between leaders and the group in order to be in accordance with human rights standards. Therefore, the rights of minorities are not perceived of as collective group rights, but as the rights of the individual members of minorities to practice their group customs. In a similar way land rights of indigenous peoples are understood as the individual rights of the members of these traditional communities. This view of the CESCR is also supported by NGOs and INGOs active in the field of economic, social, and cultural rights. More and more this view has been established in constitutions of Latin American states.

The Right to Food and Globalization

The impact of globalization on human rights is a main issue in discussions among human rights NGOs and INGOs, as was shown at the Vienna Plus Five International NGO Forum in 1998 in Ottawa. Economic, social, and cultural rights are especially threatened by the effects of economic globalization. Above all, this concerns people living in the eighty-two low-income food-deficit countries in Sub Saharan Africa, Asia/Pacific, Latin America, and the Near East.[26] In many campaigns on the right to food, FIAN fights negative outcomes of economic globalization.

Because of multilateral agreements such as GATT and the WTO, countries of the South cannot protect themselves by tariffs against cheap agricultural imports. Such imports from the European Union (E.U.) and the United States to countries of the South often destroy local food production. One example is the importation of cheap (because subsidized) E.U. beef to West African coastal states such as Côte d'Ivoire and Ghana. European meat has pushed aside the more expensive meat of the cattle-breeding nomads from Burkina Faso, Mali, and Niger, who traditionally had supplied the local markets of this region, and thus has destroyed the nomads' existence. Another example is cheap wheat exported to developing countries, especially in sub-Saharan Africa. Here, both the United States and the European Union compete against each other by dumping prices, which has negative results for the industries and agricultures of the importing countries. Such information is made available to a broader public in industrial countries by FIAN International and by country sections in order to create public opinion against such policies.

Structural adjustment programs imposed by the International Monetary Fund

(IMF) and the World Bank weaken national and local production for self-supply in favor of an export orientation. FIAN coordinates an international lobby campaign against a law imposed by the World Bank for modernizing the agricultural sector of Honduras which would be implemented at the cost of local peasants.[27] The organization—as well as other NGOs and INGOs—strives for the IMF and World Bank to base their policies on human rights standards.

Adjustment policies also mean that traditional agricultural land is more and more often turned into land for the production of export goods. For example, the shrimp industry in India has boomed at the cost of local rice production since the early 1990s. In Irian Jaya (Indonesia), several indigenous peoples are threatened by expulsion from their land because of the gold mining of a U.S. company. FIAN Germany has organized campaigns to support these local peasants and indigenous peoples in their struggle for land and resources. In 1994 it started a successful campaign with letters of indignation in support of a village in Turkey. There, the traditional olive tree plantations were threatened by a gold-mining project. One consequence of this campaign was that the European Parliament passed a resolution against the plans of the Turkish government and its financing by the Dresdner Bank, Germany. The efforts of the European Parliament ended the project.

In the 1990s, FIAN Germany extended its support of the rural population in their claim for the right to food and land to workers in rural industries. This enlargement of FIAN's approach to economic, social, and cultural rights also relates to the fast changes that disintegrate traditional agrarian structures in Third World countries because of economic globalization. FIAN links the demand for the right to food to traditional workers' rights to organize in unions and to just wages. This extension is considered to be within the mandate of FIAN because workers' rights are included in the International Covenant on Economic, Social, and Cultural Rights. However, according to Jecht, FIAN Germany's first campaign to support women in the flower industry of Colombia and to demand the protection of their workers' rights and higher wages was debated within the organization as it referred only indirectly to the right to food.[28] Today, FIAN's flower campaigns are carried out in cooperation with other NGOs and INGOs, religious groups such as Christian Aid in England, and international and local union organizations. FIAN monitors the production of flowers in countries such as Colombia, Ecuador, and Kenya.

In addition to workers' rights, one important aim of these campaigns is to increase international pressure to reduce social and ecological damage by clean flower production. Moreover, these campaigns are designed to raise the awareness of consumers and to induce ethical consumer attitudes that will affect multinational companies in their worldwide ways of production. According to FIAN, product-related campaigns such as the flower campaign are efficient, because companies and entrepreneur associations can be influenced to agree to social and ecological standards.[29] However, FIAN also sees a danger that the protection of social human rights might be privatized if UN and ILO instruments are not strengthened at the same time.[30]

FIAN's Lobbying for Economic, Social, and Cultural Rights at the UN

FIAN International has consultative status on the Roster of the UN Economic and Social Council (ECOSOC). This lowest of three categories of consultative status of INGOs (and since 1996 also NGOs) equals the status of a passive observer, but how this status is used is largely up to the organization itself. "NGOs on the Roster are not excluded from being read or heard, but they must receive a Council invitation for each debate."[31]

Together with other INGOs and NGOs mainly from the South, FIAN has contributed in putting economic, social, and cultural rights on the human rights agenda of the UN. Although there has been some progress in this respect, within the UN the understanding of human rights as political rights still prevails. In its lobby and support work at the UN, FIAN focuses on food-specialized agencies, especially the Food and Agriculture Organization (FAO), the World Food Programme (WFP), and the International Fund for Agricultural Development (IFAD), and to some extent also the United Nations Development Program (UNDP). For example, as a follow-up to the World Summit on Food in 1996, FIAN was invited by FAO and the UN High Commissioner for Human Rights to participate in expert seminars to develop a clear definition of the right to adequate food and the respective state obligations. The results of these seminars influenced substantially the drafting of General Comment 12 presented by the CESCR in May 1999.

Support of the Committee on Economic, Social, and Cultural Rights

The CESCR, which is responsible for surveying the International Covenant on Economic, Social, and Cultural Rights, is the most important board for these rights within the UN. It consists of eighteen independent experts and meets twice a year in Geneva. Its chairperson for most of its history has been Philip Alston, an Australian professor of international law who also has contributed to strengthening economic, social, and cultural rights with his many publications. He was succeeded in 1999 by Virginia Bonan-Dandan from the Philippines. From the beginning of its work, the committee has had to rely on the knowledge and expertise of NGOs to execute its multiple tasks because of a lack of resources. It "considers the participation of NGOs such as FIAN, Oxfam, or Habitat International Coalition as indispensable for the committee's work."[32] FIAN International cooperates with other INGOs such as the humanitarian organizations Oxfam and CARE to present concrete cases to the committee (see Chapter 10).

Every five years member states of the covenant report on the implementation of economic, social, and cultural rights in their countries. The committee regularly analyzes and discusses concrete human rights situations on the basis of these reports. A special focus is on disadvantaged regions and on vulnerable groups. Parallel reports of NGOs supplement the reports of governments. In cooperation with national peasant and human rights organizations, FIAN has handed in reports on many countries, including Kenya, the Philippines, Paraguay, Guatemala, Colombia, El Salvador, Peru, Nigeria, Sri Lanka, Mexico, Israel, and Germany, and on the food situation of indigenous peoples in Siberia.[33] Often governments neglect their duties to deliver these reports. In such cases, and also if no government representative is sent to the meeting, the committee discusses compliance with the treaty on the basis of UN information and of contributions of NGOs. From the year 2000 onwards, FIAN International will deliver parallel reports to the Committee for the Convention on the Rights of the Child as well.[34]

In addition to the discussion of state reports and to concrete cases that INGOs such as FIAN International bring forward to the committee, one regular topic of the agenda of the committee's meeting is the further operationalization and definition of economic, social, and cultural rights.[35] This is especially important because even treaty member states still consider these rights as political goals and not as judiciable rights. Among the topics considered have been the right to food and to housing, as well as indicators for the realization of economic, social, and cultural rights. NGOs such as FIAN have participated in these discussions, which resulted in several general comments of the CESCR (e.g., adequate housing, forced evictions, adequate food).[36]

The 1993 World Conference on Human Rights

The 1993 World Conference on Human Rights in Vienna may be considered a turning point not only for emphasizing the indivisibility and interdependence of human rights, but also for putting economic, social, and cultural rights on the agenda. This was only possible because of the intensive lobbying before the conference and in Vienna by NGOs from the South and INGOs such as FIAN.

One important topic in Vienna was strengthening the International Covenant on Economic, Social, and Cultural Rights by the establishment of an optional protocol. Years before the world conference, FIAN International, together with other INGOs (e.g., International Commission of Jurists [ICJ], and Terre des Hommes, France), had started lobbying to bring the demand for an optional protocol onto the agenda of the conference. This protocol would allow for individual communications against the violations of those human rights covered by the treaty. The optional protocol was not included as a concrete demand in the Final Declaration and Programme of Action of the Vienna conference, but was only recommended for further consideration. Since Vienna, the optional protocol has increasingly become part of the agenda of the UN. In 1997 the CESCR presented its draft of such a protocol modeled after the optional protocol for the International Covenant on Civil and Political Rights. In 1998, the Commission on Human Rights passed a resolution asking the member states to express their views on this draft. Only a few governments did so. Among them were Germany and Canada, which first rejected an optional protocol for economic, social, and cultural rights, arguing that these rights cannot be sued for. However, the new German government, convinced by the arguments of NGOs, now supports the establishment of such a protocol. Lobbying of FIAN International continues for the optional protocol. Leaflets are distributed in several languages and sections are asked to lobby their governments to support further study of the issue when it comes up in the Commission on Human Rights in 2000.[37] In August 1999, INGOs such as FIAN, Habitat International Coalition, the ICJ, and Terre des Hommes have intensified their lobby work by starting an international campaign. Consent to the optional protocol is slowly increasing.

After Vienna, the Office of the High Commissioner for Human Rights was established. Mary Robinson, the second high commissioner, has emphasized the importance of economic, social, and cultural rights. Measures to strengthen these rights were taken by the Commission on Human Rights in 1998. The commission decided to establish a Special Rapporteur on the Right to Education. An independent expert will analyze the relationship between human rights and extreme poverty.

In spite of these positive signs, pressure on the part of NGOs and INGOs is necessary to keep economic, social, and cultural rights on the agenda. While there was no follow-up conference on the state level, NGOs and INGOs came together at the Vienna Plus Five International NGO Forum that took place in 1998 in Ottawa.[38] The NGO forum critically reviewed the human rights work of the UN since Vienna and formulated demands for the future. Economic, social, and cultural rights were at the center of the conference.

Code of Conduct for the Right to Food

A code of conduct was one major demand of NGOs and INGOs at the World Food Summit that took place in 1996 in Rome. FIAN drafted a code of conduct on the request of a preparatory seminar for the conference consisting of several Latin American states, FAO members, and NGOs/INGOs. Included in the draft is the demand for better instruments to control the implementation of the right to food.[39] FAO published a booklet, "The Right to Food in Theory and Practice," to commemorate the fiftieth anniversary of the Universal Declaration of Human Rights. It carried an article by FIAN with excerpts from the code of conduct.[40] The NGO forum in Rome decided that such a code should become the central issue of the follow-up process of this world summit. Its main aim is to establish the duties of governments to implement the right to food. The document also demanded that nonstate actors such as multinational and transnational companies and multilateral organizations be made accountable to this code of conduct.

Conclusion

By its work on various levels, FIAN has contributed to reframing the understanding of human rights, and has helped to strengthen the indivisibility, interrelation, and interdependence of human rights. Networking is a main strategy in this endeavor. It is indispensable for concrete casework but it is also used to influence UN agencies. FIAN itself considers concrete casework, such as urgent actions, the dominant and most important part of its work and puts most of its time into these activities. The work at the UN is considered to be relevant to influence understanding of human rights and to give leverage to their legal development. This involves a long-term perspective, as the actions for the optional protocol demonstrate.

Using the strengthening of economic, social, and cultural rights as criteria, FIAN's effectiveness is reflected in its differing activities:

- FIAN supports the claim for the right to food and for economic, social, and cultural rights more generally through domestic and international NGOs. These campaigns have influenced decision makers; specific projects were cancelled. These activities have also been helpful in raising the consciousness of main causes of the violations of the right to food.
- The expertise of FIAN is sought to strengthen human rights, especially economic, social, and cultural rights. This includes the drafting of a code of conduct for governments, international organizations, and nonstate actors in response to negative outcomes of globalization.
- Through information FIAN works for ethical consumer attitudes to effectively implement protection of the right to food.

Economic, social, and cultural rights are still in the phase of agenda and standard setting within the human rights system of the UN. NGOs and INGOs such as FIAN have contributed to this process in the following ways:

In cooperation with local NGOs and other organizations FIAN delivers highly respected reports and information to the CESCR.

Its expertise is helpful for operationalizing economic, social, and cultural rights.

FIAN is active in the further institutionalization of these human rights, such as the establishment of an optional protocol to complement the International Covenant on Economic, Social, and Cultural Rights.

Notes

1. Contact information: e-mail: *fian@fian.org*; Web site: *http://www.fian.org*.

2. Margaret Keck and Kathryn Sikkink, *Activists Beyond Borders: Advocacy Networks in International Politics* (Ithaca, N.Y.: Cornell University Press, 1998).

3. Ibid., p. 17.

4. FIAN, ed., *Food First: Mit Menschenrechten gegen den Hunger* (Bonn: Dietz Verlag, 1998), p. 18.

5. Alison Dundes Renteln, *International Human Rights: Universalism Versus Relativism* (Newbury Park, Calif.: Sage Publications, 1990), p. 30.

6. Tony Evans, *U.S. Hegemony and the Project of Universal Human Rights* (New York: St. Martin's Press, 1996).

7. For example, Paul Sieghart, *Die geltenden Menschenrechte* (Kehl am Rhein: Engel, 1988).

8. Sabine Jecht, "Respect, Protect, Provide: Zur Entwicklung der Menschenrechtorganisation FIAN," *iz3w* (blätter informationszentrum 3. welt) 232 (1998), p. 30; Michael Windfuhr, executive director of FIAN International, interview with the author, Duisburg, Germany, May 6, 1999.

9. At the meeting of the International Council in South Africa in 1997, AI decided to differentiate the organization's mandate as one of opposition and promotion. The mandate of opposition is the well-known mandate that guides the actions of AI. The mandate of promotion refers to all human rights. For example, it allows AI to support the demand for an optional protocol to complement the International Covenant on Economic, Social, and Cultural Rights. For further details, see the chapters above by Winston and Welch.

10. Today, both organizations cooperate in concrete campaigns. E-mail messages from Rolf Kuennemann, cofounder and secretary-general of FIAN International, August 17 and 19, 1999.

11. FIAN, ed., *Food First*, p. 17.

12. According to the statute of FIAN, only clearly defined projects, seminars, travel, and campaigns may be financed by outside grants. Michael Windfuhr, interview, Duisburg, May 6, 1999.

13. Ibid.

14. FIAN International Secretariat, *Annual Report 1998*, internal document.

15. Michael Windfuhr, interview, Duisburg, May 6, 1999.

16. Ibid.

17. See, for example, Franz Nuscheler in cooperation with Brigitte Hamm, *Die Rolle von NGOs in der internationalen Menschenrechtspolitik: Gutachten für die Friedrich-Ebert-Stiftung* (Bonn: Friedrich-Ebert-Stiftung, 1998); Jackie Smith, Ron Pagnucco, and George A. Lopez, "Globalizing Human Rights: The Work of Transnational Human Rights NGOs in the 1990s," *Human Rights Quarterly* 20 (1998), p. 387.

18. Keck and Sikkink, *Activists Beyond Borders*, p. 16.

19. Michael Windfuhr, interview, Duisburg, May 6, 1999.

20. FIAN International Secretariat, *Annual Report 1998*.

21. Michael Windfuhr, interview, Duisburg, May 6, 1999.

22. FIAN, ed., *Food First*, p. 182.

23. Keck and Sikkink, *Activists Beyond Borders*, pp. 28–29.

24. FIAN, ed., *Food First*, p. 185.

25. Keck and Sikkink, *Activists Beyond Borders*, pp. 12ff.

26. FIAN, cd., *Food First*, p. 23.

27. FIAN, ed., *Food First*, p. 127.

28. Jecht, "Respect, Protect, Provide," p. 32.

29. FIAN, ed., *Food First*, p. 91.

30. Michael Windfuhr, "Social Standards in World Trade Law: A Situation Report on Controversial Debate," *Economics* 55/56 (1997), pp. 113–31.

31. Declan O'Donovan, "The Economic and Social Council," in Philip Alston, ed., *The United Nations and Human Rights: A Critical Appraisal* (Oxford: Clarendon Press, 1992), p. 110.

32. Cited in FIAN, ed., *Food First*, p. 165.

33. FIAN, ed., *Food First*, p. 165; Michael Windfuhr, interview, Duisburg, May 6, 1999.

34. Michael Windfuhr, interview, Duisburg, May 6, 1999.

35. FIAN, ed., *Food First*, p. 164.

36. The operationalization of economic, social, and cultural rights has also been discussed by expert conferences in cooperation with NGOs and INGOs. Their results are set forth in the Limburg Principles of 1986 and the Maastricht Guidelines of 1997. See, respectively, "The Limburg Principles on the Implementation of the Covenant on Economic, Social and Cultural Rights," *Human Rights Quarterly* 9, no. 9 (1987), pp. 122–35; "The Maastricht Guidelines on Violations of Economic, Social and Cultural Rights," *Human Rights Quarterly* 20, no. 3 (1998), pp. 691–705.

37. FIAN International Secretariat, *Annual Report 1998*.

38. See *Human Rights Tribune* 5, no. 3 (1998).

39. Windfuhr, "Social Standards in World Trade Law."

40. FIAN International Secretariat, *Annual Report 1998*.

Chapter 9
Action for Development in Uganda

Susan Dicklitch

Nongovernmental organizations (NGOs) have a certain mystical, venerable quality to them. They are often portrayed as fighting for the poor and helpless, especially in developing countries. After all, they are usually the main actors helping out in refugee camps, genocidal conditions, or war zones.[1] It is thus sometimes difficult to develop a clear, unbiased, and realistic understanding of what role NGOs really do play in the context of democratic transition and human rights protection. It is, in fact, sometimes difficult to distinguish their promise from their performance.

National and international NGOs have operated in the developing world for a long time. But the number of NGOs that have evolved in the last decade is astounding. There are an estimated 4,000–5,000 indigenous human rights NGOs alone in the Third World.[2] This development can be attributed to several global trends including the so-called third wave of democratization,[3] the end of the Cold War, and the globalizing trend of economic liberalization calling for state withdrawal from social service provision. NGOs are the new actors—the new favored partners of governments unwilling to channel funds through bilateral (government-to-government) ties. Increasingly, donors and international NGOs have targeted indigenous NGOs for poverty alleviation as well as democratization and human rights programs. But how effective have NGOs been in achieving their stated objectives as well as contributing to more rights-protective societies?

In the civil society and democratization literature, NGOs have four key normative roles to fulfill: empowerment,[4] educative,[5] political,[6] and watchdog[7] roles.[8] More and more case study evidence has determined that NGOs experience considerable bottlenecks in achieving these idealistic roles.[9] This chapter attempts to measure the effectiveness of one indigenous NGO, Action for Development (ACFODE), in promoting a rights-protective society in Uganda. A rights-protective society strives to ensure basic rights for all, including the right to physical security, the right to minimal economic security, and the right to political participation. The creation of a rights-protective society does not depend exclusively on the state and the reduction of state abuse of human rights. A rights-protective society depends on the development of a rights-protective culture, similar to the development of a democratic society or culture. This cannot simply be imposed from above or from outside, but must be cultivated from below as well. NGOs can help to secure a more rights-protective society and state through education, local empowerment, and lobbying, focusing on building trust, compromise, and cooperation.

ACFODE is one of the more successful indigenous NGOs operating in Uganda. It has been one of the most active NGOs in engaging the rural population and government. It is concerned primarily with women's advocacy and women's rights and economic empowerment, but it functions for both its members and the wider community. ACFODE is an unusual African NGO. It is not a human rights organization in the orthodox sense, nor is it a grassroots self-help organization. ACFODE most closely resembles an intermediate-level "people's organization."[10] Ironically, ACFODE emphatically claims that it is apolitical; however, its actions have been far from apolitical.[11]

ACFODE is a particularly interesting case study because it does have a significant impact on the development of a rights-protective society in Uganda, yet it does not focus exclusively on civil and political rights. ACFODE, of course, is not the only indigenous NGO operating in Uganda that has an impact on the development of a rights-protective society.[12] ACFODE's focus is on empowerment—empowering women within Ugandan society economically, culturally, socially, and even politically. But an NGO's effectiveness cannot be gauged without also recognizing the contextual constraints imposed by the social, political, and economic milieu in which it operates. I argue that the effectiveness of ACFODE and other indigenous NGOs in Uganda is limited by three major factors: structural bottlenecks, regime impediments, and internal shortcomings. I will examine the first two impediments briefly, but focus more intensively on the internal bottlenecks.

The Social, Political, and Economic Milieu

From the basket case of Africa in the 1970s to the success story of the 1990s, Uganda defies classification. It is neither strictly authoritarian, nor completely democratic; perhaps it is best described as a "guided democracy."[13] The National Resistance Movement (NRM, renamed "The Movement" in 1995) stormed into power in 1986 after a protracted bush war (1980–86), ushering in a new era for Ugandan politics. The first priority of the new regime was to implement its Ten-Point program, which summarized the basic ideology of the Movement.[14] Citing politicized ethnicity as one of the major hurdles to stabilization, the Movement identified political parties as the culprits. Subsequently, President Yoweri Museveni and the Movement temporarily banned political party activity. Instead, the Movement installed what it called a "no-party system" (which increasingly looks like a one-party regime) which co-opted leaders from other opposition parties as well as important national leaders, giving it the semblance of a broad-based movement. Political parties are severely restricted within the Movement's no-party system. They are allowed to exist, but are not allowed to hold national conventions, issue platforms, endorse candidates, or open branch offices outside of the capital until after the Year 2000 Referendum on multiparty politics.[15]

The fear of sectarianism is not unfounded. Uganda's postcolonial history is rife with examples of the politicization of ethnicity. During the two regimes of Milton Obote (1962–70 and 1980–85), as well as the regime of Idi Amin Dada (1971–79), ethnicity, religion, and regionalism were the mobilizing forces in politics. Coups d'état, counter-coups, and civil war became the instruments by which an ethnic group and political party would attempt to secure its dominance of the political system. This is illustrated by the fact that since 1962 alone, Uganda has suffered from five violent overturns of power.[16]

This political decay had significant economic and social repercussions. For example, Amin's 1972 expulsion of Asians—over 49,000 Indo-Pakistani merchants, manufacturers, and civil servants[17]—virtually eliminated the entire middle class. These Asians (along with the foreign multinational subsidiaries which were also nationalized by Amin in 1972) had provided the foundation for industrial capital in Uganda. In their place, Amin promoted his kinsmen and military men, called the *mafuta mingi*, a Swahili term literally meaning "dripping with oil," or "get rich quick." They squandered their new-found wealth and helped to destroy the once productive Ugandan manufacturing and commercial base. The mold was cast: once in power, promote yourself, your kinsmen, and your ethnic group, often to the detriment of the rest of the country. No sense of civic nationalism or duty developed in Uganda during the pre-NRM period; instead, ethnic nationalism, regionalism, and religious animosity were promoted—hardly a breeding ground for trust, cooperation and compromise.

Given the chaotic and extremely divisive nature of the past, the Movement regime has focused on stabilizing the political and economic arena, claiming that it is an African alternative to multiparty democracy. It allows for political participation, but that participation is filtered through its hierarchical Local Council (LC) system.[18] Individuals run for office on the basis of personal merit, not political party affiliation. Autonomous associations like NGOs are allowed to operate in Uganda, but the regime frowns upon overtly political NGOs.[19] The Movement regime has permitted the proliferation of NGOs, but has attempted to regulate and monitor their activities by establishing the 1989 NGO Registration Board[20] and to control more vocal and critical NGOs through the use of varying degrees of coercion.[21] It has also integrated many NGOs into its local development plans at LC3 (county level). Many NGOs in Movement-ruled Uganda prefer to remain apolitical and presumably on good terms with the Movement regime. Ultimately, NGOs cannot function effectively (or at all) without at least the acquiescence of the regime. Because NGOs often exist only at the whim of the regime in power (particularly if they are engaged in political advocacy), they are often subjected to co-optation or at least conformity with rudimentary regime policy. Because of their relative dependence and weakness, NGOs cannot hope to be very effective if the regime feels threatened by their activities and growth.

One of the more positive aspects of Movement rule has been the promotion of women to national and local politics. The Movement has instituted guarantees for women's participation in the Local Councils as well as at the parliamentary level.[22] For example, Uganda boasts the first female vice president in Africa, Dr. Specioza W. Kazibwe (1994).[23] There have been mixed reactions to this Movement initiative. Some simply perceive this as a Movement attempt to co-opt the women's vote in Uganda and achieve political maneuvering, since women make up more than 50 percent of the population in Uganda.[24] Whatever the case, the Movement's affirmative action strategy has heightened women's role in Ugandan politics. The Movement's strategy also complements ACFODE's mandate, thereby undermining any potential tension between the regime and ACFODE.

The Context of NGO Operations in Uganda

Decades of brutal rule and civil war have helped to precipitate societal disengagement from politics and the formal economy. Even though the political climate in Uganda has considerably warmed since the dark days of Idi Amin and Milton Obote, Ugandans are still hesitant to become too political, or to be perceived by the regime as too political. This hesitancy further reinforces the unwillingness of people in NGOs to engage the regime, directly or indirectly, on a plethora of issues. Linked to these years of repression and civil war, suspicion and lack of trust still permeate the Ugandan polity and society. This does not provide fertile ground for the development of democratic values, trust, or compromise, or a rights-protective society. ACFODE has been significantly affected by the context of its operations.

Furthermore, the existence of a society, economy, and polity driven by survival has helped to undermine voluntarism and the development of a democratic political culture and rights-protective society. The psychological impact of years of civil war and terror have weakened the basis for mutual trust, understanding, and compromise: all fundamental components of a democratic civil society and rights-protective society. NGOs can be important actors in the process of slowly rebuilding trust, understanding, and compromise. However, an economy of survival that necessitates, for example, that individuals have more than one job, significantly undermines the development of a spirit of voluntarism often necessary to sustain a strong voluntary sector. A growing number of individuals are drawn to the NGO sector in pursuit of profit, often generating both public and regime suspicion of NGO motives.

Uganda has experienced a flood of both foreign international and national NGOs since 1986 when the Movement regime came to power. In fact, some suggest that foreign and indigenous NGOs have invaded Uganda.[25] This invasion of NGOs has affected almost every sector of Ugandan life and every region of Uganda, although some districts, such as Luwero and Kampala, have higher concentrations of NGOs.[26] No complete record of NGOs is available, but it is estimated that there are more than one thousand registered NGOs (foreign and indigenous) operating in Uganda.[27]

Indigenous NGOs face several common bottlenecks to effectiveness in Uganda.

These bottlenecks can be divided into three mutually reinforcing categories: structural/historical, regime impediments, and internal constraints. Structural constraints include unstable financial bases, mutual suspicion and societal suspicion, relative youth, and state and donor pressure to focus on service provision or gap filling rather than advocacy and empowerment issues.[28] The structural constraints are reinforced by state impediments, particularly fear of regime co-optation or repression. And finally, NGOs have their own internal limitations which also stem from the context in which they operate. For example, indigenous NGOs in Uganda face accountability and legitimacy issues. They are primarily accountable to their donors (whose funds often keep them running). NGOs often lack a stable, regular, or independent source of funding, which makes their programs very irregular and dependent on external funding; and there is cutthroat competition for funding which impacts on their willingness to coordinate with other NGOs.[29] But NGOs in Uganda have still played an important role in rebuilding civil society, particularly in the context of post–civil war Uganda.

The Human Rights Context

Although far from perfect, the Movement's record on human rights abuses has been a vast improvement from the past. During the regimes of Idi Amin Dada and Milton Obote, human rights abuses committed by the state abounded. Most of the Movement-related human rights abuses are linked to Uganda People's Defence Force (UPDF, formerly called the National Resistance Army) campaigns against renewed insurgencies in the North ("operational sweeps") and West (Allied Democratic Forces, ADF). Human rights violations, including deaths, torture, and scorched-earth tactics have characterized these sweeps.[30] New armed rebel attacks in the West, spilling over from the conflict in the Democratic Republic of Congo and Rwanda, have frustrated government attempts at creating political stability and human security in the region.[31] Security forces are accused of using excessive force throughout the country.[32] However, the regime has cooperated with NGOs on legal and prison reforms.[33]

In addition to these obvious abuses, there are some troubling, more subtle abuses, such as the use of the charge of treason to silence opposition,[34] as well as use of the outdated law of sedition to silence overly critical journalists.[35] But state abuse of human rights is not the only problem in Uganda. Societal abuse of fundamental human rights also occurs. For example, there has been a disturbing rise of vigilante justice throughout Uganda.[36] Violence against women is also a significant problem in Uganda, with women often viewed as chattels, or mere possessions of husbands and fathers. The prevalence of bride price and widow inheritance serve to reinforce this widely held perception. There still exists widespread traditional and societal discrimination against women, especially in the rural areas. Customary laws tend to discriminate against women, especially in the areas of "adoption, marriage, divorce, and devolution of property on death. In most areas, women may not own or inherit property, nor retain custody of their children under local customary law."[37] The abuse of women's rights is much more complicated since it is usually not the state doing the abusing, but customary laws and society overall. In fact, the 1995 Ugandan Constitution guarantees equality in citizenship, fundamental human rights and freedoms, and in structures of representation. It not only prohibits gender discrimination, but also allows for affirmative action for marginalized groups, especially women. Thus, organizations like ACFODE have been working with the Movement government to promote the status of women in Uganda. ACFODE has made significant strides in empowering women and bringing women's issues to the forefront of Ugandan politics and society.

Action for Development (ACFODE)

The concept of Action for Development (ACFODE)[38] originated during the 1985 United Nations Decade for Women's Conference in Nairobi.[39] It was officially founded on November 19, 1985.[40] Although the initial composition of ACFODE reflected a focus on the Makerere University community, over time its membership broadened to represent a wider cross section of Ugandan women. There still remains, to some extent, a perception (shared by many male and female Ugandans) that ACFODE is an elite women's organization rather than a broad-based, nonsectarian, women's NGO. ACFODE has fought hard to try to erase this negative perception and to some extent it has been successful in discrediting those accusations.

Major Goals

ACFODE was formed to address a gap that existed in Ugandan society. There was "no forum uniting all categories of women in Uganda where women could meet and discuss matters concerning themselves."[41] Although there were many other women's organizations, such as the Mother's Union, Muslim Women's Association, FIDA (Uganda Association of Women Lawyers), and the former National Council of Women (now NAWOU, National Association of Women's Organizations of Uganda), these organizations tended to *exclude* other women on the basis of marital status, religion, politics, or profession. This is not to say that these organizations were not effective, but rather to suggest that they did not address the broader societal needs and concerns of women as ACFODE aspired to do. As Miria Matembe, a former chairperson of ACFODE stated, ACFODE seeks to "bridge the gap between rural and urban women, rich and poor, elite and illiterate."[42] This statement is reflective of the broad objective of ACFODE: "To uplift the status of women in all spheres of public life; politically, socially, economically and spiritually and to integrate them into National Development."[43] These objectives are achieved through ACFODE's programs and activities, which are directed by three central decision-making and implementing bodies: the standing committees, the secretariat and the general membership. The general membership is the "policy and decision-making body" of ACFODE. The ACFODE secretariat is composed of a full-time staff that is paid by ACFODE to essentially run the organization.[44]

Governance

In order to achieve its broader objective as outlined above, ACFODE devised nine specific objectives, which were divided into two groups: advocacy and education. ACFODE advocates women's representation and participation at all levels of decision making; it advocates law reform and improvement of and enforcement of women's rights; and it campaigns for a positive portrayal of women in all areas of life. ACFODE also tries to educate the wider population through research and dissemination of that research to relevant sectors, policy makers and policy implementers. It attempts to conscientize Ugandan society about women's needs, potential, and problems. From a coordination perspective, ACFODE arranges workshops and seminars on women's issues and activities and cooperates and interacts with other national and international women's organizations and other relevant bodies to offer assistance to women's organizations.[45]

The general membership of ACFODE is composed of voluntary (almost exclusively female) members.[46] There are over three hundred members but only one hundred active members as of 1998.[47] The members constitute the general meeting which is the "policy and decision-making organ of ACFODE." General meetings occur monthly at the ACFODE headquarters in Bukoto, Kampala, with retreats annually and elections biannually. Although membership is open to all categories of women, the majority of members tend to be professional, middle-class, urban women, coming from Makerere University, private enterprise, the public service, and government. The rural counterparts, especially the "contact women" (who mobilize and help organize ACFODE's networking trips to their county) tend to occupy leadership roles within their area, and are usually involved in the Local Council system.

Restructuring

ACFODE totally restructured its operations and governance structures in 1993 and more recently in 1998. Before 1993, there were eight standing committees: legal, research, projects, education, finance, publicity, health, and executive. These standing committees were devised in order to deliberate on policy making and implementation of programs. The executive committee was the most powerful committee in ACFODE.[48] This was the policy-making body of the organization as well as the partial implementer of policies.

The 1993 restructuring evolved from recommendations suggested by an ACFODE ad hoc restructuring committee (composed mainly of the executive members of ACFODE) set up to reevaluate its approach and structure. The committee was reacting to a self-evaluation effort that attempted to address concerns about the smooth functioning of the organization. More specifically, the committee wanted to examine the waning nature of voluntarism and participation within the organization, the structure of decision making and implementation, bottlenecks in the channels of communication, and the overall "lack of action in Action for Development."

Over the years, there has been a distinct drop in voluntarism and participation within the general membership and on particular standing committees.[49] To combat this tendency, the ad hoc committee recommended that new members attend half day seminars to initiate them into the organization. To combat decreasing participation, it was suggested that a new approach be taken during general meetings, whereby discussion about issues would be conducted in small groups and members would be encouraged to get to know one another better through informal meetings. Because this waning participation and voluntarism impacted on decision making and implementation of policies, ACFODE also needed to reexamine the role of its standing committees. In the past, the standing committees made decisions not only about program activities but were also involved in program implementation. Because of waning voluntarism and participation, there were concomitant problems associated with decreases in committee attendance and consequent delays in decisions about program implementation. Consequently, the ad hoc committee recommended strengthening the secretariat so that it would undertake program implementation. The research, legal, education, projects, publicity, and health standing committees were reduced to one committee: the program committee. The program committee would discuss all the programs while implementation would be executed by the secretariat. Networking would be conducted by the secretariat only, although the members would "from time to time" take part in such activities. The ad hoc committee argued that these changes would cut down on bureaucracy, ensure the quick implementation of decisions, and would also ensure proper program coordination.[50]

The 1993 restructured ACFODE had four standing committees—an executive committee, a finance committee, a program committee, and an advisory committee. In addition, there were four subcommittees—a staff committee, a welfare committee, a selection committee, and an editorial board in charge of publications. The new executive committee had a chairperson, vice-chairperson, legal advisor, finance chairperson, chairperson of the program committee, and four committee members. A completely new committee called the advisory committee was set up to "promote, ensure, cultivate and maintain the mission, ideology, principles and philosophy with which the organization was founded." It would also "give advice and guidance to the executive committee on matters of philosophy or ideology whenever called upon to do so," and if necessary arbitrate between conflicting parties. The program focus of ACFODE would also be narrowed to cover only five areas—information and documentation, research, legal education, education and training, and health. This program restructuring was recommended to avoid duplication and increase clarity of purpose.

To address bottlenecks in the channels of communication, the ad hoc committee recommended that all communication from the executive committee go through the executive secretary (representing the secretariat) or program coordinator. Any communication from the staff would go through the executive secretary to the executive committee. Similarly, any communication from the membership would go through the executive secretary and vice versa. Team leaders for networking trips would be decided by the program coordinator and program officer responsible. This formulation would make the channels of communication much more transparent, structured, and effective.

In the past, the executive committee was responsible for the execution of all programs, including finances. With restructuring, this responsibility shifted to the secretariat, although the general membership still generates the ideas that are developed through the different committees and formulated into policies. Before the policies were carried out, they would have to be considered and approved by the executive committee, which was responsible to the general membership. With the proposed restructuring of standing committees and the increased involvement of the secretariat in the implementation of ACFODE programs, the general membership became further removed from the actual functioning of the organization.

Although this restructuring arose from a need to address waning voluntarism and participation on behalf of the general membership, the restructuring created a more bureaucratic and rigid structure at the expense of voluntarism. Unfortunately, this left ACFODE in a catch-22 situation: it could no longer rely so heavily on voluntarism because it was dwindling, but then by restructuring to this degree, a bureaucratic structure was created that tended to further alienate the general membership.

The latest restructuring in 1998 reflected a perceived turning point for ACFODE members. The restructuring process involved self-assessment as well as external facilitation through an Organizational Development intervention.[51] Three painful interventions of self-diagnosis and prognosis occurred in September 1997 and January and March 1998. Overall, several important changes were implemented. There was a greater centralization and decentralization of ACFODE activities at the same time. On the one hand, the ACFODE secretariat was given even more authority, especially in the administrative decision-making process, but a decentralization of the ACFODE structure was implemented so that ACFODE would have a permanent presence in various parts of the country. This was a fundamental change in ACFODE's philosophy vis-à-vis networking versus branches up-country. By decentralizing ACFODE in this way, there was a hoped-for attempt to implement different unit activities in different districts at the same time. Most important, the new transformation of ACFODE reflected the "perceived benefits of being more beneficiary focused."[52]

How Are ACFODE's Goals Assessed?

Whether decision making is implemented by the secretariat, the general membership, or the various committees, one thing remains clear: decisions are made from ACFODE headquarters, based in Kampala, even though a large number of ACFODE's endeavors are rural oriented. Although ACFODE engages in self-evaluation sessions (retreats) and has even started to include participatory workshops between their contact people and head office (participatory evaluation of rural area programs), most if not all of the decisions about programs and approach are made without the participation of target

Table 1. Restructuring of ACFODE Programs and Committees

Before 1993	*1993–98*	*1998–Present*
Legal Committee	Program Committee: Health Education and Training Information and Documentation Research Legal Education	Legal and Human Education and Training Program[a]
Research Committee	Finance Committee	Research Program
Projects Committee	Executive Committee	Training Program
Education Committee		Economic Empowerment Program[b]
Finance Committee		Information and Publications
Publicity Committee		Awareness Program
Health Committee		Three Departments: Advocacy Capacity Building Administration
Executive Committee		

Sources: ACFODE, *Action for Development*; ACFODE, "A Profile"; ACFODE, "Women Breaking Through: Proceedings of the Seminar on the Follow-up of the UN Decade for Women's Conference 1985 and Uganda's International Women's Week," Bishop Tucker Theological College, Mukono, March 1–8, 1986 (Kampala: ACFODE, 1988); AFCODE, "A Report of the Restructuring Committee (ADHOC)," internal document, 1993.

[a]This is one of the newest ACFODE programs. It includes a legal education program, workshops for law enforcement officers, civic education (particularly geared to promoting women's participation in the LC elections (1996–97), capacity-building seminars for elected women councilors, a domestic violence project, an in-house legal publication, information and advocacy against rape and defilement, involvement in the development of the Domestic Relations bill and the Land Act. ACFODE, *Action for Development*. This program is mainly funded by Oxfam and the Ford Foundation.

[b]This program focuses on training and capacity building for micro-finance programs, particularly in the Kiboga and Pallisa Districts. Ibid.

groups. This is a problem that is characteristic not only of ACFODE's approach but of most urban-based NGOs.

ACFODE does engage in what they term "needs assessments," where its representatives go into different rural areas, invited by women leaders in the area, and ask their target groups what they feel are the most pressing issues facing women.[53] But ACFODE determines who their "target group" is, as well as where they will operate and for how long. Similarly, often the targeted groups simply tell ACFODE what they think it wants to hear and not actually what the rural women need. Although ACFODE does evaluate programs after completion to determine what impact they had on the target group, there tends to be a long gap in time between the actual work in the area and the assessment afterward. The input that the targeted groups actually have is therefore rather limited. To a certain degree, there is a "big sister" approach to dealing with the less advantaged rural women. To be fair to ACFODE officers, however, they have adopted a wide range of activities and programs and cannot have input from every sector and every group in decision making.[54]

Part of the problem arises from ACFODE's method of implementing its programs. ACFODE does not establish branch offices in the different districts that it operates in. Instead, it engages in what is termed "networking." ACFODE's philosophy has been that "women groups have their own agendas and should be directly assisted in what they are doing rather than segregate them by forming branches."[55] Buttressing this philosophy is the practical limitation of funds which inhibits ACFODE from establishing branches. It remains to be seen how the 1998 restructuring of ACFODE will change this.

Although ACFODE has made an almost indelible mark wherever it has gone, its long-term impact in terms of empowering rural women is uncertain. ACFODE is aware of the limitations of its networking approach, including its heavy reliance on contact people, and the insufficient amount of time spent networking. Empowerment of course can occur on many different levels, but the question remains whether ACFODE has helped to change women's position in society generally, and specifically in the targeted areas, and whether it has helped to promote the development of a rights-protective society. In order to determine this, ACFODE's approach and programs must be examined.

Output and Outreach

For ACFODE, education is one of the key means of uplifting women. This entails educating them about virtually "everything; the laws and rights of women, the potential of women in the development process; the indispensability of women's contribution in nation-building; the plight of women and other issues."[56] Its programs have focused on both rural and urban women, elder and adolescent, educated and uneducated. ACFODE adopts a two-pronged strategy for empowering women: a broad-based approach and a more specific projects-based approach.

In terms of the broad-based approach, ACFODE focuses on lobbying the power brokers, building awareness of women's position in society, and cooperating with other organizations in the pursuit of empowering women on a collective level by attempting to change perceptions, culture, and discriminatory political structures affecting the actual and potential role of women in Ugandan society.[57] ACFODE has been involved in various national campaigns to sensitize the Ugandan population to these issues. For example, it instituted the first candlelight vigil to commemorate World Human Rights Day and women's rights (especially violence against women) in December 1992. ACFODE has held regional and national workshops on legal awareness and women's legal rights, and has been instrumental in lobbying the government for the successful creation of a Ministry of Women In Development (now the Ministry of Gender, Labour, and Social Development), a Department of Women's Studies and Gender at Makerere University, and the establishment of a women's desk (now termed gender desk) in all ministries. ACFODE also successfully lobbied for the reconstitution of the National Council of Women (which was previously government controlled) into an independent body called the National Association of Women's Organizations in Uganda (NAWOU). In addition, ACFODE was instrumental in instituting the 1.5 point admission criterion for women students entering Makerere University,[58] and in lobbying for gender equity in universal primary education, which started in 1997. ACFODE also successfully lobbied for the deletion of a clause in the Local Government Bill (1996) which would have disempowered women on the basis of their education status to contest for decision-making positions, as provided for in the Constitution.[59]

ACFODE has been quite involved in civic education as well. For example, ACFODE spearheaded the "Link" program during the Constitution-making process, which generated dialogue between civil society and the Constituent Assembly (the body established to debate the Draft Constitution). ACFODE also conducted sensitization and awareness-raising seminars in several districts[60] to encourage women to contest the one-third decision-making positions on all Local Councils during the 1998 Local Council elections.[61] In its legal and human rights education and training program, ACFODE aims to increase women's awareness of their human, legal, and civil rights as well as their civic responsibilities.[62]

ACFODE attempts to sensitize Ugandan society to the issues and concerns facing Ugandan women. It works from the realization that in order to have real and sustained change, cultural biases and injustices towards women have to be addressed, in addition to lobbying for legislative change that is more favorable to women's rights. Even if the laws that exist are changed to become more progressive and gender sensitive, unless the culture is subsequently gender-sensitized as well, those institutional and legislative changes will not affect the lives of the rural women, who are often unaware of their rights. ACFODE is quite aware of this, which is evident in its motto: "Break Through, Build Up and Bind." ACFODE has to "break through" the cultural barriers that inhibit Ugandan women's progress; "build up" or empower the members by building courage, self-confidence, and dispersing information and knowledge; and "bind," or bring women together in "love and solidarity."[63] Hence, ACFODE has also become involved in working on several projects which affect women's social rights. For example, ACFODE worked with the Law Reform Commission on issues such as rape and defilement, where ACFODE lobbied against the proposal to reduce the age of defilement to sixteen years; and ACFODE collaborated with the Association of Women Lawyers and Uganda Women's Network in advocacy initiatives surrounding the Domestic Relations Bill, which focused on such issues as bride price, polygamy, and the distribution of property in intestate succession. ACFODE also advocated a more gender-sensitive law on the Land Act (1998), and worked on the Domestic Violence Project (funded by the Canadian International Center for Human Rights and Democratic Development) in training female participants in basic counseling skills.

ACFODE has not only focused on lobbying to effect change, but also on a broader level to make sure that the change it has helped effect will actually benefit the women that it is working on behalf of. ACFODE has thus also attempted to help women generally and specific groups of women through income-generating activities, education seminars in schools and remote areas, fund-raising for such needs as maternity wards,[64] and workshops on writing skills and leadership skills for women. It has sought to educate women on various health, legal education, and projects networking trips in several different districts of Uganda. A key component of this approach focuses on ACFODE's microfinancing program, which aims to empower rural women economically (initially in Kiboga, Pallisa, Lira, and Rukungiri districts). Women's groups are trained in business management skills, constitution drafting, record keeping, and loan tracking. In addition to training and education, ACFODE provides a credit loan of approximately $900.[65]

In general, ACFODE has tried to educate women to become aware of their rights and subsequently empower them with knowledge. The achievements of ACFODE on the broad and specific projects levels, and on the local and national levels, are far too many to outline in depth here. Nonetheless, ACFODE's programs have been ambitious, realistic, and far-reaching in impact. Effectiveness cannot be quantified, nor can impact be scientifically measured, because the creation of a rights-protective society takes years, if not decades. However, the impact of lobbying lawmakers as well as targeting local-level groups bodes well for the creation of a more gender-sensitive and rights-protective society in Uganda.

ACFODE's Relationship with the Regime and Other NGOs

Inevitably there is only so much that one organization can achieve. Consequently, ACFODE has attempted to cooperate with other NGOs and organizations in fulfilling its goals and objectives. It is affiliated with the former National Council of Women, now called the National Association of Women's Organizations of Uganda (NAWOU), it is involved in a management-training enterprise with the Uganda Rural Development and Training Program (URDT) and the Development Network of Indigenous Voluntary Associations (DENIVA),[66] and it has connections with the International Labor Organization and UNICEF. During its preparations for the Sixteen Days of Activism Against Violence, it coordinated with several human rights NGOs as well.[67] However, the degree of coordination and cooperation with other NGOs tends to be limited. This is a phenomenon that is not specific to ACFODE, but characterizes many indigenous NGOs in Uganda. Because of scarcity of funds and competition between the different NGOs for them, many NGOs chose to work independently of other organizations. As a result, many programs are duplicated and uncoordinated, somewhat diminishing the overall benefits to the target groups.

On the other hand, ACFODE frequently utilizes the Local Council (LC) system in order to mobilize women for networking meetings, recruit contact women in the field, and target women for future leadership roles. This helps maintain a close link between the organization and the government, allowing for greater input in decision making at the various LC levels. More specifically, the fact that several members of

ACFODE are National Resistance Council (NRC) members and LC officials at lower levels gives ACFODE an "inside" for pressuring and lobbying for change to benefit women. The former chairperson, Honorable Miria Matembe, NRC Women's Representative for Mbarara District and also a member of the Uganda Constitutional Commission, has been particularly active in promoting the name of ACFODE and pressuring for change.

ACFODE, however, relies heavily on foreign NGO and government funding. Its main funding sources have included the Konrad Adenauer Foundation (KAF), Swedish International Development Agency (SIDA), Danish International Development Agency (DANIDA), the United Nations Development Program (UNDP), UNICEF, Oxfam, the Ford Foundation, World Vision, the Uganda Development Bank, the Mennonite Central Committee, German Development Service (DED), Pathfinder, Humanist Institute for Cooperation with Development (HIVOS), Network of Ugandan Researchers and Research Users (NURRU), the Forum for Women Educationalists (FAWE), Population Concern, the National Executive Unit, British Council, the Department for International Development (Great Britain) Micro Credit, Royal Netherlands Embassy, and Ms. Uganda. In 1998, foreign donors accounted for approximately US $462,000 of ACFODE's budget. In addition to foreign donors, ACFODE was able to raise approximately 15,967,877 Ugandan shillings (approximately $16,000) independently.[68] Most of the donor money was project specific, with the Konrad Adenauer Foundation the largest single donor (approximately U.S. $100,000).[69] Funders not only keep ACFODE accountable for money spent, but also steer the NGO into programs that often reflect the interests of Western donors more so than indigenous concerns.[70] For example, ACFODE now produces an impressive annual report that in essence accounts for all of its spending and programs to foreign donors. It seems increasingly that ACFODE spends more time and effort on writing proposals for additional funds and paperwork overall than on critically assessing the needs of its constituents.

Degree of Effectiveness?

ACFODE is at a pivotal stage in its development. It has been a vocal women's organization for many years, targeting national and local levels, urban, semiurban and rural women alike. It has grown substantially in size, function, and focus. Consequently, ACFODE is now at the stage where it is reevaluating its purpose, approach, and future. There is a danger, however, that ACFODE may be overextending itself, or in other words, trying to do everything but not excelling at anything.

One of the greatest impediments to ACFODE's development and programs is the scarcity of funds. This is evident in ACFODE's programs. For example, because of high transportation costs and a reliance on volunteers, ACFODE is limited in what it can achieve during its networking trips. In addition, there is heavy reliance on contact women who are not paid for their help. Similarly, low salaries or wages for employees who are exceptionally qualified creates a situation where they may seek other employment because ACFODE's salaries are not comparable to those that other NGOs offer. The worst-case scenario actually occurred in 1998 when several key members of the ACFODE secretariat were fired because of misuse of funds.

The dependence on donor funding, and the competition between women's NGOs and other indigenous NGOs for this funding, establish an uncertain environment that engenders competition rather than cooperation between NGOs. More NGOs are thus inclined to work independently rather than together for the betterment of women's position in Uganda. ACFODE is now at a stage where it can reevaluate its dependence on donor funding and begin to seek alternative, domestic sources of income that may be more secure and long term than that offered by donors. ACFODE has already begun this process by building the ACFODE complex in Bukoto (a Kampala suburb). The complex can bring in income from renting out the conference hall for conferences and workshops.

ACFODE may ultimately have to decide whether it focuses on a few districts only (satisfying the need for a rural focus and addressing the concerns of its wider constituency, albeit to a more limited extent), or concentrates on a much broader national level while not focusing specifically on the needs of rural women. The dilemma is whether ACFODE should concentrate on making a greater impact on one area, or a lesser impact in many. A society cannot be gender sensitized overnight, or even in a year or two. If ACFODE is committed to making an impact in the rural areas and actually effecting change, it has to spend more time in the rural areas. Making women aware of their rights and of their subordinate status in Uganda but not giving them the tools to alter it only creates frustration for the women and elicits suspicion from the men. ACFODE needs to keep a close check on the impact of its networking trips on the local population.

One way to address this concern is for ACFODE to switch its orientation by working with other indigenous women's NGOs that are concerned with the same issues as ACFODE and which can offer services that ACFODE could utilize in its networking activities. Many organizations exist to provide such services, such as FIDA, NAWOU (National Association of Women's Organizations in Uganda), Uganda Women's Finance and Credit Trust (UWFCT), the AIDS Service Organization (TASO), Safe Motherhood, Uganda Human Rights Activists (UHRA), and the Foundation for Human Rights Initiative (FHRI). In addition, ACFODE could try to increase its work and contact with women trained by the Ministry of Gender, Labour, and Social Development in conjunction with their contact people in the various districts in which they operate. Unfortunately, donors are at fault here as well. They are more interested in funding individual NGOs and demonstrating concrete results than funding cooperation between NGOs and the more difficult to measure results of empowerment, for example.[71]

In addition to clarifying who its primary constituency is, ACFODE needs to determine how it will target them. For example, does it focus on mass rallies, as has been the case in the past, or does it focus on only a few women in rural areas and concentrate on training them? If ACFODE engages in more cooperative work with other indigenous NGOs, it may be able to do both, that is, continue with mass rallies and "preach the gospel of ACFODE" to as many women as possible, as well as train women so that they can continue to preach the gospel of ACFODE even when ACFODE is not there.[72] In this particular case, utilizing the services of the women trained by the Ministry of Gender, Labour, and Social Development may be helpful.[73]

The overall achievements of ACFODE far outweigh most of its limitations. ACFODE has helped the women and men of Uganda by educating, empowering, and sensitizing Uganan women and men to the pressing need for cooperation and change in Ugandan society. It is very difficult, however, to gauge the effectiveness of sensitization or awareness of ACFODE's programs quantitatively.[74] ACFODE is an important force in the development of a democratic society and polity as well as a rights-protective society in Uganda. Ultimately, a rights-protective society is not possible unless the female population is brought into the political process, is economically and politically empowered, and is given real (not just formal) access to land ownership. ACFODE has been instrumental in promoting women into positions of power in Uganda. Although ACFODE cannot solve all the country's human rights problems, it has come a long way in educating women and men on the status of women and women's rights in Uganda. The creation of a lasting rights-protective society takes time—a lot of time—especially in an environment that has not traditionally fostered respect for human rights.

Notes

1. Tvedt, in a critical assessment of NGO activities, examines the myths associated with NGO effectiveness in comparison to private business and the state, and the "articles of faith" that accompany many NGOs. Terje Tvedt, *Angels of Mercy or Development Diplomats? NGOs and Foreign Aid* (Trenton, N.J.: Africa World Press, 1998), p. 128.

2. Julie Fisher, *NonGovernments: NGOs and the Political Development of the Third World* (West Hartford, Conn.: Kumarian Press, 1998), p. 13.

3. See Samuel P. Huntington, *The Third Wave: Democratization in the Late Twentieth Century* (London: University of Oklahoma Press, 1991).

4. Empowerment is a "multifaceted process [which] involves transforming the economic, social, psychological, political and legal circumstances of the currently powerless." Richard Sandbrook, *The Politics of Africa's Economic Recovery* (New York: Cambridge University Press, 1993), p. 2. Empowerment can be measured by such indicators are the amount of "political clout" that the organization has acquired, by the ability of the collective to alter conditions (social, economic, political, or cultural) that it finds intolerable, by its success in an educative role (if applicable), and its ability to voice or address popular concerns or interests. Michael Bratton, "Non-Governmental Organizations in Africa: Can They Influence Public Policy?" *Development and Change* 21 (1990), p. 93. Whether there is a general feeling of constructive change among the members can also be used as a measure (albeit an imprecise one) of whether the NGO has been able to empower its constituents. Certain indicators can be used to measure the degree to which individuals or communities are politically or economically empowered. Economic empowerment can be partially gauged by visible improvements in the standard of living directly related to the activities of the NGO, as well as by attempts to educate and therefore empower individuals to help themselves economically and politically to achieve greater self-sufficiency. On the political level, whether an NGO or association has helped to empower an individual or community can be gauged by determining whether the constituency has more political voice in affecting its destiny through actions (direct or indirect) of the NGO, and whether people have greater access to policy makers and policy formulation and decision making because of NGO activities.

5. NGOs are particularly useful in educating individuals and groups about their rights. In addition, NGOs serve an important role as "schools of democracy" where leaders within the organization learn how to organize and motivate people, debate issues, and become accountable to their membership, while the membership in turn learns how to keep its leadership accountable and how, therefore, eventually to pressure the state for accountability and responsiveness. See Larry Diamond, "Rethinking Civil Society: Toward Democratic Consolidation," *Journal of Democracy* 5, no. 3 (1994), p. 9.

6. For example, NGOs can play an extremely important role of bringing together individuals of a similar ethnic group or community or different ethnicities together under the banner of common issues or concerns. Ideally, NGOs could pressure policy makers on behalf of these groups to effect change.

7. NGOs can serve as "gadflies" to the regime by ensuring that it is accountable to the wider population. Working with other nonstate actors like the media, political parties, legal associations, and the like, NGOs, for example, can threaten to expose corruption, human rights abuses, or general incompetence.

8. See Susan Dicklitch, *The Elusive Promise of NGOs in Africa: Lessons from Uganda* (New York and London: St. Martin's Press and Macmillan Press, 1998).

9. See Alison Van Rooy, ed. *Civil Society and the Aid Industry* (London: Earthscan Publications, 1998); Dicklitch, *The Elusive Promise of NGOs in Africa.*

10. People's organizations are usually more narrowly focused on a particular constituency, for example women, but aim to empower not only their membership but also the wider community. They are often driven by strong values and member interests, and are usually geared, among other things, toward empowering communities that have been traditionally disempowered (see Dicklitch, *The Elusive Promise of NGOs in Africa,* pp. 6–8).

11. Even though ACFODE considers itself an apolitical organization, it has been instrumental in lobbying the government successfully for the establishment of a Ministry of Women in Development, a Department of Women's Studies in Makerere University, and the establishment of a women's desk in every ministry. It has also been integral in empowering women at the grassroots level, for example, by educating them about their rights in relation to customary law, in organizing them into self-help groups, and in sensitizing the Ugandan government to the needs of Ugandan women.

12. There are several NGOs in Uganda that focus more directly on civil and political rights. For example, the more traditional human rights organizations include Uganda Human Rights Activists (UHRA); Foundation for Human Rights Initiative (FHRI); FIDA (Association of Women Lawyers, Uganda branch); Human Rights Focus (a Gulu-based human rights group); the African Center for Rehabilitation and Treatment of Torture Victims (ACTV); the Uganda Law Reform Commission; the Uganda Law Society; the Uganda Prisoners' Aid Foundation (UPAF); the National Organization for Civic Education and Election Monitoring (NOCEM); the National Association of Women's Organizations of Uganda (NAWOU); the Human Rights and Peace Center at Makerere University; HURINET, a human rights network and umbrella organization for nine human rights organizations; and Amnesty International (branch office). The government has also established the Uganda Human Rights Commission (UHRC), a permanent independent body that has quasi-judicial powers. U.S. Department of State, *Country Reports on Human Rights Practices for 1997* (Washington, D.C.: U.S. Department of State, 1998), p. 372.

13. A key component in guided democracy is the institutionalization of "democratization from above" usually by an "extremely powerful military leader." Peter J. Schraeder, "Elites as Facilitators or Impediments to Political Development? Some Lessons from the 'Third Wave' of Democratization in Africa," *The Journal of Developing Areas* 29 (1994), p. 80. Thus military leaders with other military elites set the timetable and agenda for democratic transition, "maintain[ing] tight control over the transition process" (ibid). This type of democracy borders on authoritarianism with society viewed as an "organic whole with common interests," led by leaders who claim to know what these interests are, with the state existing to "execute the general will without being inhibited by constitutional checks to protect minorities or even . . . by majorities who have a false perception of their real interests." Robert Pinkney, *Democracy in the Third World* (Boulder, Colo.:

Lynne Rienner, 1994), p. 9. Guided democracies even allow for contested elections, as long as they do not threaten the power of the executive (ibid). These limitations are often justified as necessary for the avoidance of political instability in ethnically politicized and divided states. True to form for a guided democracy, the National Resistance Movement (NRM) regime has effectively moved Uganda from chaos to a controlled consensus. This is evident when one examines the nature of the NRM consolidation of rule, the NRM's attempt to democratize from above, and the nature of economic liberalization.

14. The Ten-Point program included popular democracy, restoration of security, consolidation of national unity, defending national independence, building a national economy, restoration and rehabilitation of social services, elimination of corruption and misuse of power, resettlement of displaced people, regional cooperation and human rights, and a mixed economy. National Resistance Movement Secretariat, *NRM Achievements: 1986–1990* (Kampala: NRM Publications, 1990).

15. Ironically, a new pressure group has developed, calling itself the "Forum for Promotion of Movement Politics in Uganda" (FOPROMU). This pressure group is supposed to function separately from the government, but work towards promoting the continuation of Movement politics after the referendum. The *Monitor*, "The Monitor View: Way to go for NRM," March 9, 1999, p. 6. This recent development serves to increase the fears of some in Uganda that the Movement regime is becoming less tolerant of criticism and is attempting to use the Year 2000 Referendum as a tool of making the Movement regime a legitimate dictatorship. The *Monitor*, "Movement is Greedy—Abu Mayanja," March 10, 1999, p. 3.

16. Obote's 1966 "civil constitutional coup" that effectively removed power from the Baganda Kabaka (king); Amin's takeover of power from Milton Obote in 1971; the overthrow of Amin by the United National Liberation Army (UNLA) and Tanzanian forces and the imposition of Lule in 1979; the reign of the Okellos in 1985 which overthrew Milton Obote; and Museveni's guerilla bush war that overthrew the Okellos in 1986. See Phares Mutibwa, *Uganda Since Independence: A Story of Unfulfilled Hopes* (London and Kampala: Fountain Publishers and C. Hurst, 1992); Jan J. Jorgensen, *Uganda: A Modern History* (London: Croom Helm, 1981).

17. Jorgensen, *Uganda*, p. 247.

18. The Movement system is a five-level Local Council/Committee (LC) system, LC1–LC5 consisting of LC1 (village level), LC2 (parish level), LC3 (subcounty level), LC4 (county level) and LC5 (district level). Parliament (the National Resistance Council) with the National Executive Committee (cabinet) are at the apex of the system. See Dicklitch, *The Elusive Promise of NGOs in Africa*, pp. 76–78. The Movement system consists of a combination of direct participatory democracy (at LC1) and electoral colleges (LC2–LC5).

19. For example, security services dispersed three seminars on "Human Rights and Democracy" held by the Foundation for African Development (FAD), an indigenous NGO closely associated with the Democratic Party, claiming that the seminars had a "political content." *New Vision*, "Police Stop NGO Assembly," May 28, 1999, p. 2.

20. See Dicklitch, *The Elusive Promise of NGOs in Africa*, pp. 100–101.

21. Ibid., pp. 103–106.

22. For example, at every district level, there is a position reserved for Woman Representative to be filled by a woman. From 1989–96 the National Resistance Council included fifty women, and when it was renamed the National Assembly in 1996, it included fifty-one women parliamentarians. For an excellent overview of women's roles in Ugandan politics and society, see Sylvia Tamale, *When Hens Begin to Crow: Gender and Parliamentary Politics in Uganda* (Boulder, Colo.: Westview Press, 1999).

23. Museveni's appointment of Kazibwe as vice president also satisfied other political concerns, because she is a female Catholic from eastern Uganda, and a former Democratic Party member. See ibid., p. 111, n. 7.

24. See ibid., p. 91.

25. For example, one newspaper article claimed that NGOs have invaded Kumi district. *Weekly Topic*, "NGOs invade Kumi," March 5, 1993, p. 18.

26. See Dicklitch, *The Elusive Promise of NGOs in Africa*, p. 125.

27. J. B. Kwesiga and A. J. Ratter, "Realizing the Development Potential of NGOs and Community Groups in Uganda," report of a study commissioned by the Government of Uganda: Ministry of Finance and Economic Planning, 1993, p. 10; Z. Gariyo, "NGOs and Development in East Africa: A View from Below," in Michael Edwards and David Hulme, eds., *Beyond the Magic Bullet: NGO Performance and Accountability in the Post–Cold War World* (West Hartford, Conn.: Kumarian Press, 1996), p. 156.

28. See, for example, Dicklitch, *The Elusive Promise of NGOs in Africa*, chapter 5; Van Rooy, *Civil Society and the Aid Industry*.

29. See Dicklitch, *The Elusive Promise of NGOs in Africa*, chapter 5.

30. Amnesty International, *Uganda: The Failure to Safeguard Human Rights* (London: Amnesty International Publications, 1992); J. Oloka-Onyango, "Armed Conflict, Political Violence and the Human Rights Monitoring of Uganda: 1971–1990," *Working Paper No. 12* (Kampala: Kampala Center for Basic Research, 1990); U.S. Department of State, *Country Reports on Human Rights Practices for 1998* (Washington, D.C.: U.S. Department of State, 1999).

31. The Allied Democratic Forces (ADF) rebels have killed an estimated 400 people, while the Lord's Resistance Army, led by eccentric Joseph Kony, was responsible for approximately 200 murders. *New Vision*, "ADF Victims toll 400, says U.S. Human Rights Report," March 10, 1999, p. 1.

32. U.S. Department of State, *Country Reports on Human Rights Practices for 1998*, p. 363.

33. Ibid.

34. For example, Professor Isaac Newton Ojok was remanded in Luzira prison since 1987 on charges of treason. The Uganda High Court acquitted him on charges of treason only in January 1994. See *New Vision*, January 3, 1995, p. 10. The NRM also arrested eighteen government officials from the North in May 1991 on treason charges. These included the former minister of state for foreign affairs Daniel Atubo as well as several members of Parliament including Zachary Olum and Irene Julu. The government released fourteen of the eighteen in January 1992, but did not release the other four (including Olum and Julu) until August 1992. See the *Monitor*, August 17–20, 1993. In addition to these trumped-up charges of treason, a number of the detainees showed visible signs of torture. See *Weekly Topic*, May 17, 1991. In other cases, the Democratic Party secretary-general, Robert Kitariko, was charged with treason on January 13, 1993, but later released. Cecilia Ogwal, the secretary-general of the Uganda People's Congress, was also detained but not charged on January 21, 1993 along with fourteen other UPC party officials. *The Monitor*, August 17–20, 1993.

35. Perhaps one of the most infamous cases is that of Teddy Seezi Cheeye, outspoken editor of the biweekly *Uganda Confidential*. In an attempt to discredit Cheeye and his stories about government corruption, the government has charged him with sedition on several occasions as well as unsuccessfully tried him on the charges of having kidnapped a woman for sexual purposes. See U.S. Department of State, *Country Reports on Human Rights Practices for 1998*, p. 369.

36. One particularly disturbing encounter with vigilante justice in 1992 occurred in Kampala when a man was accused of stealing a woman's purse on a busy downtown Kampala street. An angry mob of people circled the man and kicked and punched him while a policeman looked the other way.

37. U.S. State Department, *Country Reports on Human Rights Practices for 1998*, p. 373.

38. The following sections draw heavily from Dicklitch, *The Elusive Promise of NGOs in Africa*, chapter 5.

39. ACFODE was registered as an NGO (certificate #50) under the NGO registration statue in 1989.

40. There were three main founding members: Dr. Maxine Ankrah, Dr. Hilda Tadria and Dr. Ruth Mukama.

41. ACFODE, "A Profile," internal document, 1992.

42. Miria Matembe, "ACFODE: Women Binding and Building," internal document, 1990, p. 6. ACFODE has been able to avoid some of the leadership transition issues that other NGOs have faced. The ACFODE constitution stipulates that a chairperson can only hold two consecutive

terms. Leadership transitions have been generally quite peaceful and amicable. During the 1993 chairperson elections marking the transition of leadership from Honorable Miria M. K. Matembe to Dr. Joy Kwesiga, there was a substantial amount of politicking and coalition forming before the elections. However, the transition was generally amicable. Matembe was a charismatic, vocal, and well-known chairperson because of her positions as National Resistance Council Women's Representative for Mbarara District and member of the Uganda Constitution Commission. There was some concern that ACFODE would lose some of its public spotlight with Matembe's retirement as chairperson, but there was also the fear that ACFODE was being overwhelmed by her persona. In other words, the public was not making the clear distinction between Matembe's sometimes extreme comments and opinions and ACFODE's policies. Fortunately, the separation of chairperson and executive director in ACFODE allows for a certain degree of continuity and smooth operations even with leadership transitions.

43. ACFODE's updated mission statement as of 1998 is that "ACFODE is a women's organization striving for gender equality and equity in Uganda. As a development organisation, ACFODE works through a strong sense of voluntarism and participative engagement within its ranks in spearheading efforts towards women's empowerment. ACFODE does this through advocacy and networking to create an enabling environment and at another level by increasing the capacities of women in local communities to manage their own activities and stand for their rights." ACFODE, *Action for Development: Annual Report 1998* (Kampala: ACFODE, 1998).

44. This staff is composed of an executive director (head of staff), a economic empowerment officer, training and awareness officer, research officer, legal officer, information and publications officer, administrative assistant, finance and administration officer, accounts assistant, two drivers and an office assistant/messenger. ACFODE, *Action for Development.*

45. ACFODE, "A Profile."

46. There were nineteen associate members (men) in 1998, and eight in 1997. ACFODE, *Action for Development.*

47. Ibid. All members are required to join at least one committee, or they are considered dormant members.

48. Within this committee there was the chairperson, vice-chairperson, secretary, assistant secretary, treasurer, assistant treasurer, legal advisor, chairpersons of the standing committees, and four other executive committee members.

49. For example, it was often difficult to recruit general members to participate in networking trips up-country. Many women could not leave their jobs or families to travel up-country for three to four days to engage in networking activities.

50. This concern was well justified. I attended many ACFODE committee and general meetings which were plagued by lack of voluntarism, time management, organization, and direction.

51. ACFODE, *Action for Development.*

52. Ibid.

53. For example, an ACFODE needs assessment trip to Mbarara and Kasese Districts from December 6 to 10, 1992, attended by the author, was characterized by lack of organization, minimal input from the intended beneficiaries, and a very rushed atmosphere. Three different counties were targeted for a Woman and Health Needs Assessment. In Kazo county, a large assembly of women and men awaited the ACFODE team, but the parallel desire to include men in the discussions backfired somewhat in that many women were hesitant to talk in front of their husbands or relatives. Much time was spent on political speeches made by members of the various LCs, and not enough on consulting the women on their problems. Because the political speeches lasted longer than scheduled, the needs assessment based on a general questionnaire was virtually rushed through. More time could have been spent encouraging the women to speak out about their problems rather than having ACFODE talking to the women. In Kabatunda-Busongora county, the last ACFODE destination, the meeting took place in a very small LC1 office (because of the rain) and included ten men and only two women. The questionnaire was rushed through, with the women in particular not really consulted, only the leaders (LCs). The majority of people stood outside in the rain, peering into the office. The follow-up on program success

also tends to be weak, although the secretariat recognizes these shortcomings, and is attempting to deal with the problem. There is, however, a substantial amount of participation within the organization itself, evident in the monthly general membership meetings.

54. For example, ACFODE created a 1991 self-evaluation report that was compiled from reports from twenty-three district representatives. Similarly, in April 1993 ACFODE conducted their first "participatory evaluation" involving ACFODE contact people from the various districts that they operated in during 1992–93.

55. Matembe, "Women Binding and Building," p. 14.

56. Miria Matembe, "Involvement of Grassroots Women and Women's Organizations in the Constitutional Reform Process in Uganda," unpublished paper, p. 11.

57. Luckily, the regime's policies toward women complement rather than compete with ACFODE's program. For example, many ACFODE programs focus on sensitizing women (and men) to the injustices suffered by women due to culture, economics, and politics. ACFODE attempts to empower more women to become involved in changing their political, economic, and social situation. The National Resistance Movement (NRM) launched a program in 1986 to make women more aware of their rights and increase their political power. It attempted to make them politically conscious, enabling women to be part of the policymaking in the country and contribute to the country's development. Betty Baliwa, "NRM to Launch Women Politicisation," *New Vision*, October 9, 1986, pp. 5–6. The pursuits of ACFODE and the NRM regime are therefore complementary rather than competing. This can partially explain why ACFODE has been so successful in lobbying the government on women's issues.

58. This admission criterion of positive discrimination in favor of women was deemed necessary in order to increase the chances of women in entering university. Studies showed that the dropout rate was very high among schoolgirls, leading to low female entry into university (only 25 percent of admissions). In order to encourage and enable more female students to apply to university, it was argued that women applicants be given a 1.5 percent increase in their grades to bring them up to the level of competing male students. This helped raise female students to 39 percent of the total applicants.

59. ACFODE, *Action for Development*.

60. These districts included Hoima, Kumi, Mbarara, Lira, Soroti, Pallisa, Kiboga, and Rukungiri.

61. ACFODE, *Action for Development*. ACFODE had to postpone its legal and human rights education training program in the districts of Soroti and Kisoro on the advice of local authorities to avoid ACFODE being accused of campaigning for candidates (the existing law in Uganda forbids election campaigning by party candidates).

62. Ibid.

63. Matembe, "Women Binding and Building."

64. In Lira District, a maternity ward was paid for by the money collected from a charity walk. ACFODE raised 2,500,000 shillings in funds and another 1,500,000 shillings in kind, the equivalent of almost $4,000.

65. ACFODE, *Action for Development*.

66. The URDT (Uganda Rural Development and Training Program) is an indigenous NGO engaged in training, input distribution, organization development for grassroots associations, and the development of technologies for creating awareness workshops. DENIVA (the Development Network of Indigenous Voluntary Associations) is an indigenous umbrella NGO, a consortium of local nongovernmental organizations and grassroots community groups actively engaged in development oriented programs in Uganda.

67. These NGOs included UHRA (Uganda Human Rights Activists); Legal-Aid Project; FIDA (Uganda Association of Women Lawyers); FHRI (Foundation for Human Rights Initiative); Ministry of Women in Development, Culture, and Youth; and the Makerere Law Society. The Sixteen Days of Activism Against Violence was in general an information and education campaign to sensitize Ugandans to the level of violence experienced in Uganda.

68. ACFODE, *Action for Development*.

69. One of my visits to ACFODE headquarters in 1993 involved a ceremony commemorating

the donation of a Toyota Landcruiser by the Konrad Adenauer Foundation. There was a lot of pomp and circumstance involved, with the Foundation obviously interested in ensuring that all realized that it had donated the money specifically to purchase the vehicle.

70. This donor preoccupation with displaying how their money was spent (often an important way of accounting to northern constituents for money dispersed to indigenous NGOs) often leads to a donor lack of support for indigenous NGO coordination of activities and programs, since it would be much harder to show the concrete results of such collaboration, especially if it focused on advocacy or empowerment concerns which are quantitatively more difficult to measure.

71. For other case study examples, see Van Rooy, *Civil Society and the Aid Industry.*

72. ACFODE's mass rallies in the rural areas were spectacular. Women would come by foot from miles away. There would always be food (at least for the visiting ACFODE guests), dance, song, and speeches involved, along with a lecture on the problems, for example, of bride price and widow inheritance. As a collective, we would all leave extremely happy and satisfied, but I always had the sinking feeling that we had sensitized women to their plight, but we had not given them any real tools to rectify the situation.

73. There is always the danger that other indigenous NGOs may not agree with the ACFODE "gospel" and refuse to promote it, or alter it.

74. For example, how does one gauge the impact of a Muganda woman from Kampala going to Lira to educate an Acholi woman about her rights vis-à-vis widow inheritance or the right not to be abused by her husband? How does one gauge the degree of compromise, trust, and cooperation that has developed from a networking trip up-country? These are long-term impacts, especially in a country that has had such a ghastly history of politicized ethnicity, civil war, and conflict.

Chapter 10
Evaluating Development-Oriented NGOs

T. Jeffrey Scott

Nongovernmental organizations (NGOs) that specialize in development and humanitarian assistance are commonly thought of distinctly and separately from human rights NGOs such as Amnesty International and Human Rights Watch.[1] This may be due in part to the fact that the right to development has not been established in international human rights law and practice in the way that civil and political rights, and even humanitarian assistance, have been. However, development-oriented NGOs address some of the most egregious human rights violations: failures of domestic and foreign governments to protect economic and social rights, to provide assistance, and to refrain from depriving the millions of people who struggle without the most fundamental means of subsistence. As Julius Nyerere's socialist conception of rights implies, "There can be no freedom without development, but without freedom there can be no development."[2]

Although there have been, and currently are, many national, regional, and international efforts directed toward development and humanitarian relief, these efforts are clearly insufficient. As a working hypothesis, I take it that this failure is due to both the nature of the efforts undertaken and their magnitude. Part of this problem thus relates to theoretical approaches, and part to the international community's reluctance to recognize that omissions concerning distributive justice result in human rights violations which are (at least) as equally detestable as widely (and properly) recognized commissions such as extrajudicial executions and arbitrary detentions.

The purpose of this chapter is to evaluate the effectiveness of human rights NGOs in their efforts to alleviate and eradicate poverty, and to assist people in meeting their basic needs of food, health, education, and housing.[3] In the first section of this chapter, sketches of two of the most prominent development-oriented human rights NGOs (Oxfam and CARE) are presented in order to convey the significance of their work, and to compare and contrast them with each other as well as with more politically oriented human rights NGOs. This examination is continued on a more general level with an analysis of the status and functions of development-oriented NGOs before discussing some of the problems with, and prospects for, evaluating the human rights impact of these NGOs.

A Look at Oxfam and CARE

The involvement of NGOs in relief and development work began at the end of the nineteenth century but is essentially a post–World War II phenomenon. After the reconstruction of Europe, some of these NGOs shifted their attention to the newly independent states of Africa and Asia, but remained peripheral actors until the early 1980s as most development aid was bilateral. They initially took on humanitarian assistance pertaining to drought, famines, and civil strife in these areas, and then remained to pursue development work with the goals of reconstituting the economic, social, and (eventually, in some cases) political structures. Let us now examine two of the largest and most distinguished of these NGOs, Oxfam and CARE.

Oxfam

Oxfam International was founded in 1995 to consolidate eleven autonomous Oxfam organizations, the first of which was founded in the United Kingdom as the Oxford Committee for Famine Relief in 1942.[4] Its aims are to unite Oxfam organizations in a partnership working to achieve the common vision of an end to the waste and pain of poverty; provide a common analysis of poverty based on experience; spearhead international campaigns and advocacy work; address global causes of poverty by working together; and support poor communities in response to humanitarian need in their struggle against hunger, disease, poverty, and exploitation. Individual Oxfams are independent organizations based in their own countries, but there is an international secretariat in Oxford and an advocacy office in Washington, D.C., to coordinate lobbying the International Bank for Reconstruction and Development (World Bank), the International Monetary Fund (IMF) and the United Nations on issues of common concern. Individual Oxfams fundraise, lobby, and campaign in more than 120 countries and together raised more than $335 million in fiscal year 1997.

Oxfam International's program expenditure by continental grouping for fiscal year 1997 was as follows: 46 percent in Africa, 24.34 percent in South America, 20.08 percent in Asia, 6.77 percent in Europe, 2.37 percent in the Middle East, 0.23 percent in North America, and 0.22 percent in the Pacific. In fiscal year 1998, individuals provided 70 percent of Oxfam America's funds (including 3 percent from bequests and legacies); foundations and corporations donated 18 percent; rent, interest, and dividends supplied 8 percent; and groups and events contributed 4 percent. Seventy-five percent of its revenue supported program work, 18 percent was spent on fund-raising, and 7 percent was invested in administrative functions such as bookkeeping and accounting. Among its expenditures for services, 84 percent was devoted to the global program, 9 percent to education, and 7 percent to policy.[5]

As early as 1960 Oxfam took a lead role in setting up the Freedom from Hunger Campaign/Action for Development, a specialized Food and Agriculture Organization (FAO) campaign. From 1966, starting with the Bihar (India) famine, it became directly involved in long-term emergencies by sending teams of young volunteers to help run major feeding programs and by supporting self-help schemes whereby communities improve water supplies, farming practices, and health care provision. Oxfam continues to provide financial, technical, and networking assistance to grassroots groups in support of self-help community development initiatives. It employs local people or refugees themselves rather than outsiders wherever possible, and ensures that people keep control of the schemes they are involved in. Realizing that many of the problems associated with poverty require government and international action, Oxfam campaigns on behalf of the people it works with and talks to decision makers who shape policy on relevant issues. The Public Affairs Unit, set up in the 1980s, provides research and analysis and lobbies on such issues as essential drugs, pesticides, food aid, and debt. The effective advocacy role of Oxfam has been pointed out by World Bank official Michael Cernea: "International NGOs—like Oxfam . . .—have repeatedly signaled to the Bank cases when resettlement under Bank-financed projects does not proceed satisfactorily . . . ; such signals have at many times triggered additional Bank efforts and have led to improvements in the standards and conditions of resettlement."[6]

Volunteer groups in several countries run a network of shops selling donated items and handicrafts from overseas, the latter derived through Oxfam Trading which gives small producers of handicrafts fair prices and support through training, advice, funding, and sanitation in emergencies. In parallel with support for development projects worldwide, increased resources are dedicated to policy, research, and campaigning work to address the structural causes of poverty in the South, such as crippling debt burdens, unfair terms of trade, and inappropriate agricultural policies. Recent major campaigns include "Debt Reduction," for which it has played a significant role in sustained lobbying resulting in a new framework for the debt reduction of the poorest countries (October 1996), and "Crisis in the Great Lakes Region of Africa." On March 22, 1999, Oxfam International launched its first ever international campaign, "Education Now! Break the Cycle of Poverty," which focuses on realizing the target of universal primary education by the year 2015.

In its mission statement Oxfam stresses that peace and substantial arms reduction are essential conditions for development, that poverty is a state of powerlessness in which people are unable to exercise their basic human rights, and that its ultimate goal is to enable people to exercise their rights. It has proven to be a very successful organization for developing new ideas, demonstrating their efficacy, publicizing them, and encouraging their widespread adoption. For example, Oxfam's water-harvesting experimentation in the Yatenga District of Burkina Faso "is now being adapted and applied by many agencies, including the World Bank, in arid regions throughout Africa."[7]

As discussed below, NGO research dissemination is almost as rare as self-evaluation; two functions which NGOs should increasingly be evaluated in terms of. *The Oxfam Field Director's Handbook* has proven to be an excellent means of research compilation, dissemination, and evaluation of initiatives it has undertaken.

CARE

Founded in 1945 as Cooperative for American Remittances to Europe and later renamed Cooperative for American Relief Everywhere, the current confederation Cooperative for Assistance and Relief Everywhere (CARE International) has headquarters in ten countries with country offices, individual public members, and civic, fraternal, philanthropic, denominational, and labor organizations in eighty countries.[8] CARE currently reaches 35 million people in sixty-four developing and emerging nations in Africa, Asia, Latin America, and Europe. It has a staff of over ten thousand people, most of whom are citizens of the countries in which they work.

CARE's revenue is generated by donations from the private sector, contributions in-kind, agricultural commodities donated by governments (e.g., through U.S. Public Law 480/Food for Peace provisions) and international organizations (such as the UN), ocean freight reimbursement, corporate and private donations, government grants, and multilateral contracts. Host governments share internal operating costs and may contribute material support and personnel. With total revenue and support of nearly $380 million in fiscal year 1998,[9] 91 percent of CARE USA's expenses went towards program activities; 9 percent was devoted to support services and fund-raising. Support from more than 400,000 American individuals and some three hundred U.S. corporations and foundations, along with supporters in Canada, Japan, Australia, and Europe, and funding and food commodities from governments and intergovernmental organizations (IGOs), made it possible for CARE USA to deliver $339 million in aid (81 percent of which went towards development assistance, the remaining 19 percent to emergency relief). The largest amount of CARE USA's resources is devoted to Asia and the Pacific (46 percent), followed by Latin America and the Caribbean (26 percent), Africa (24 percent), multiregional (3 percent), and Europe (1 percent).

CARE's aims are to assist people in less developed countries achieve long-term positive changes in their social and economic conditions through a process that promotes the development and use of indigenous resources, and to provide relief and rehabilitation support in times of emergency and disasters. CARE USA's accomplishments in 1998 can be summarized according to the main program areas:

Health: Thirty-four children's health projects in fourteen countries reached more than 5.4 million women and children. Forty-seven reproductive health projects in twenty-two countries reached 84.9 million men and women with family planning, maternal health, and STD/HIV interventions.

Water, Sanitation, and Environmental Health: Fifty-nine projects in thirty countries helped

1.4 million people gain access to clean water and sanitation services through the construction of wells, latrines, and sewers, and through the protection of watersheds.

Education: Thirty-one basic education projects in eighteen countries provided nonformal, literacy, primary, and other basic education to more than 250,000 participants, 39 percent of them girls and women.

Food: Twenty-two projects in nineteen countries provided food to 15.6 million people through programs in school feeding, food for work, and community kitchens.

Agriculture and Natural Resources: Ninety-three projects in thirty-one countries helped more than 667,000 farmers increase their livestock and crop yields to ensure food security and increase income. More than 520,000 people also benefited from natural resource conservation programs including agroforestry, integrated pest management, and soil conservation. Over 9.3 million trees were planted on both community and private lands.

Infrastructure: More than 85,000 kilometers of roads were repaired through food- or cash-for-work programs.

Small Economic Activity Development: Fifty-eight projects in twenty-five countries helped nearly 270,000 people through projects in credit, savings, and income-generating activities. Over $25 million in loans were disbursed with a repayment rate greater than 90 percent.

In addition, CARE has made progress in reaching the American people through public service announcements (PSAs), its Web site, and in national and international television and newspaper coverage. In fiscal year 1998, PSAs reached nearly 36,000 airings on national and local television stations for an estimated $9 million in station-donated time, and Web site hits increased more than 400 percent (roughly 5 million hits).[10] The mainstream media's coverage of CARE's work reached more than 170 million people worldwide, and CARE was often relied on for commentary on development and relief issues (thus generating international attention for humanitarian concerns).

Comparisons and Findings

NGOs that focus on economic and social rights tend to be more involved with the *fulfillment* of rights, while NGOs that focus on civil and political rights tend to be more involved with the *promotion* of rights. This may help to explain some of the differences between these two types of NGOs, such as the fact that a majority of the former type commonly rely more on funds from governments and IGOs.

Relative to other NGOs examined in this book, Oxfam and CARE are extraordinary in terms of budget, reach, and direct impact. For example, Oxfam International and CARE USA each generate about ten times as much revenue as Amnesty International USA, and more than twenty times as much as Human Rights Watch. In further contrast to Amnesty International, which focuses on individual prisoners of conscience, Oxfam and CARE concentrate their efforts solely on larger groups, issues, and situations. Unlike other development-oriented NGOs (such as ActionAid and Save the Children), neither Oxfam nor CARE employs misleading sponsorship programs in their fund-raising campaigns.[11]

Compared to one another, both Oxfam and CARE are at the forefront of NGO self-evaluation, and are to be commended for utilizing participatory approaches and employing large numbers of local workers. Both are international in character as the bulk of activity is conducted by national member organizations, such as fund-raising from which the international secretariats are maintained.[12] Consequently, opportunities for political influence by and on governments vary as well.

But the two are quite different in many ways. First, Oxfam's explicit emphasis on human rights provides a clear mandate and basis in international law. Second, with a smaller budget and a similar organizational structure, Oxfam has a broader support base than CARE, works in about twice as many countries, and is stronger in the areas of research innovation and dissemination. Whereas CARE devotes just under a quarter of its resources to Africa, almost half of Oxfam's program expenditure is alloted to this continent whose people are the poorest of the poor.[13] Third, while Oxfam has found it increasingly more difficult to devote at least 80 percent of its income to its overall program, CARE manages to spend over 90 percent of its resources on program activities and as of 1988 was able to turn every dollar contributed by a donor into $10.76 worth of overseas aid.[14] Fourth, Oxfam tends to favor providing funding and technical support for local initiatives over sending relief supplies such as CARE Packages. Last, while CARE relies heavily on government funding and has a long tradition of cooperation with the American government, Oxfam places a ceiling on governmental contributions of ten percent of the regular overseas program.[15] In order to maintain independence in its advocacy work before governments and multilateral bodies and bring a humanitarian perspective to policy debates, Oxfam America neither solicits nor accepts any funding from governments. Recognizing that it takes more than just seeds and tools to fight poverty, this policy allows Oxfam America to act with conviction and integrity when encouraging governments, IGOs, and international financial institutions (IFIs) to adopt policies that support long-term development (and criticizing them if they do not).

Development-Oriented Human Rights NGOs: Their Status and Functions

Before determining how human rights NGOs might best be assessed, it will be useful to determine how they should be categorized and to take account of their various roles and functions.

Status

NGOs frequently emphasize human rights as a means of development which is considered to be "the achievement of human rights through a process which respects human rights."[16] Thus while development and human rights may have presented competing goals in the past, the currently prevailing theory of sustainable development treats them as complementary. As Ian Smillie maintains, "the distinction between organizations working primarily as service providers and those whose role is primarily in advocacy does not work very well. Oxfam, for example, works in development and in emergencies, and has been a fierce advocate over the years for specific political action in such places as South Africa, Cambodia, and Rwanda."[17]

Take an example of an argument that is commonly considered to demonstrate a distinction between development NGOs and other human rights NGOs. The Ethiopian famines of the early 1970s resulted from government policies of the Derg under Mengistu, which employed starvation as a means of control.[18] Most of the NGOs working to alleviate this humanitarian crisis refrained from publicly challenging the government's human rights record, policies, cover-up of the cholera epidemic, and conduct of civil war in the northern part of the country based on the precept that they should avoid politics.[19] *Médecins sans frontières* (Doctors Without Borders) expressed opposition to the government in this case, and was expelled. Hence, it seems safe to assume that silence in the face of abuses was necessary if the starving were to be fed.

So one question is, should human rights NGOs remain silent about government oppression in order to achieve the "greater good" of assisting the people under the rule of that government? But this question is misdirected. A more relevant question is, given that publicizing abuses is a major weapon of human rights NGOs, should each and every human rights NGO use this strategy to combat injustice in every given situation? Framed in this light, a negative response to this question is easily understood. Different NGOs have different goals, different strategies as means of achieving those goals, and different geographical foci. No single human rights NGO can do all of the work that needs to be done. Where people are starving due to government oppression, some human rights organizations need to protect the rights of those affected by working directly with them, others by addressing the underlying causes of systematic deprivation. So even if some NGOs intentionally refrain from politics because it is outside the scope of their work, this does not mean that they are not human rights NGOs. The validity of this position is perhaps most apparent when one considers that much more egregious violations of human rights would have been left unchecked if only the publicizing strategy of "accepted" human rights NGOs was undertaken and not vice versa.

Functions

Since the advent of development-oriented NGOs, there has been an expansion of their role from implementation only to all stages of the development process—identification, design, appraisal and financing, implementation, and evaluation. This may be partially due to the fact that human rights NGOs that work in the field of development avoid the politics and ideological biases often associated with political rights. Therefore, their work is perceived as more neutral, and thus more desirable, by both major aid givers and states which govern the intended beneficiaries.[20]

The potential for human rights NGOs is significant in the field of development. While identification of development projects for specific populations requires the involvement of governments and aid donors, both of these entities face limitations and present obstacles when it comes to project identification—the crucial first step of any successful and sustainable development project. NGOs do not face the diplomatic restraints of governments when it comes to conducting needs assessments or publicizing problems; their projects generally involve participation from the intended beneficiaries; and they are much more efficient (partially due to their dedication and partially to their light administrative structures).[21] Governments obviously operate according to politics, and while this poses enough problems in transparent democratic societies, it can spell disaster in authoritarian ones. As Celia Taylor holds, governments (which in many cases are aid donors as well) may omit groups from consideration that they do not feel are worthy of recognition or that they fear may become popular (and more powerful) if given a voice (e.g., women, specific ethnic groups, or voluntary associations).[22] Both aid donors and governments may be too socially, economically, culturally, and geographically removed from the people who are being considered for development. When it comes to rural populations and even small cities that are distant from the capital, groups that consider themselves to be very distinct may be categorized together, resulting in counterproductive tensions and, most likely, a conflation of interests. It is in this representational capacity that NGOs can play a valuable role. Perhaps most importantly, they can serve as a means of communication and technology exchange between targeted populations and governments, or even between governments and aid donors, promoting accountability from both sides.

Many of the functions that NGOs can perform for the realization of the right to development are similar to those of advocacy of rights generally. NGOs can *encourage the recognition* of the right to development by familiarizing people with their rights, persuading states to ratify relevant international instruments and to include the right to development domestically as a constitutionally guaranteed right, and fostering the drafting of a Convention on the Right to Development by influencing relevant UN bodies. NGOs can *promote* the right to development by encouraging states, IGOs, and IFIs to incorporate specific goals leading towards progressive realization of this right based on resource availability. NGOs can *protect* the right to development by convincing states, IGOs, and IFIs to refrain from policies that result in maldevelopment; encouraging aid agencies and government ministries to adopt successful approaches developed within the voluntary sector; monitoring the progress of states, IGOs, and IFIs in implementing the right to development and in adopting recommendations made by the Working Group on the Right to Development; and identifying victims and violators and making their situations known to international organizations, the media, and the courts. NGOs can work to *fulfill* the right to development by promoting the reform of national and international institutions in order to influence local development policies, identifying remedial measures, acting as a conduit for public opinion and local experience in order to customize official programs to public needs, identifying groups which could form a network for activism relating to this right, and undertaking development projects on their own or in conjunction with states, IGOs, and international development agencies (IDAs).

The practice by IGOs and IDAs of contracting work out to NGOs is also a useful phenomenon by which to assess NGO functions. However, the autonomy of NGOs in contract arrangements may contribute to mixed results based on inconsistent priorities. One upshot of this is that where trade-offs are made in strategy from project to project, even within the same NGO, evaluation of performance will prove more difficult. Take two World Bank–contracted CARE projects in West Africa for example. A CARE road construction project in the Sierra Leone Eastern Integrated Agricultural Project was comparatively expensive due to adherence to high quality standards, whereas the construction of one hundred schools in the Liberia Second Education Project was estimated to be 30 percent less than the amount charged by private firms.[23] But in the Liberian case school use and maintenance were subsequently low because CARE did not adequately incorporate community participation.[24] Factors of cost, quality, and sustainability thus need to be prioritized or balanced for considerations of NGO evaluation. In addition, the impact of NGOs towards diverting employment opportunities away from local contractors may provide an additional relevant measure of impact assessment.

Evaluating the Work of Development-Oriented NGOs

As Smillie has remarked, it has become commonplace in discussions of NGOs to dismiss their positive attributes as unproven and focus on their obvious limitations. The 1993 UN Development Programme *Human Development Report*, for example, devotes six pages to "debunking—with faint praise and outright condemnation—the effectiveness of NGOs in tackling poverty, providing credit to the poor, reaching the poorest, empowering marginal groups, challenging gender discrimination; even in delivering emergency relief."[25] But as Smillie argues, "Failure should be regarded as a bad thing only if the same mistake is made over and over."[26] Unfortunately, repeated failure is common in the world of development, and one of the biggest causes is lack of evaluation and knowledge exchange. Few NGOs undertake self-evaluation, and while NGO evaluation is gaining increasing importance on the agendas of some donor governments, it is used more for reassurance and control purposes (i.e., evaluation qua audit) than to disseminate findings and advance development ideas.

Terje Tvedt argues that "development NGOs must be analyzed . . . as an outcome of complicated processes where factors like international ideological trends, donor policies and NGO agendas interact with national historical and cultural conditions in complex ways."[27] It is also important to recognize differences in NGO self-evaluations and donor-commissioned studies. Sten-Erik Kruse et al. remark that NGO self-evaluations tend to be colored by a participatory approach, an emphasis on evaluation as a learning tool, and a recognition of evaluation as a part of overall strategic planning.[28] While donor purposes of undertaking assessments as means for determining future funding are necessary and legitimate, evaluations may force NGOs to be less innovative and work only where projects are less costly and more guaranteed to be sustainable (i.e., not with those most in need).

Unfortunately, many NGOs do not examine the impact of their projects, or if they do, such reports only verify whether the project's outputs have been delivered or not, and any lessons learned are not shared with other NGOs. According to Smillie, NGOs avoid self-evaluation due to (1) complexity (intangibles such as empowerment and capacity building do not lend themselves to measurement), (2) inappropriateness (attempts to evaluate could demoralize workers), (3) time, and (4) cost. Off-the-record discussions among NGO workers reveal further explanations such as (1) actual overhead costs would have to be revealed to funders, (2) activities which are part of a larger program cannot be disaggregated for purposes of evaluation, (3) more is often promised than can be delivered, and (4) hints of failure and underachievement could result in major cuts.[29] Without evaluation, however, it is not possible to measure progress, identify strengths and weaknesses, share results, or improve effectiveness. As allocations to NGOs increase and they are placed under greater scrutiny, it is becoming increasingly more important to be able to discern their impact. As such, evaluations of development-oriented NGOs by donors have recently become much more common, but self-evaluation remains sparse.

On a more practical level, the private donor base for NGOs may have reached its limit. As NGOs must compete among themselves for funding, opportunities for coordination and cooperation may be threatened. They may inadvertently undermine public support of development assistance, public comprehension of development projects which do not relate to emergencies, and public trust of NGO fund-raising approaches (the overly dramatic tactics which Smillie has referred to as "the pornography of poverty"). As northern NGOs move closer to donors with regard to funding and policy analysis, "They have singularly failed . . . to persuade their supporters to become active citizens prepared to demand that their governments spend more on aid and spend it more effectively. [Northern] NGO lobbying and advocacy may even have backfired, fueling the right-wing agenda of reducing aid flows."[30]

NGO evaluation can be expected to vary with their goals and with the measures chosen by researchers in conducting assessments. Development NGOs usually have a plethora of interconnected aims, so when we talk about evaluation it is necessary to specify whether it is being considered at the project, institutional, national, regional, or even global level. Many appraisals focus on the percentage of an NGO's projects that have achieved their immediate objectives, but in a broader sense we are also interested in evaluating their objectives. Some general conclusions can be arrived at with regard to the approaches of different NGOs. For example, "NGOs are more successful when implementing social projects and delivering services, and considerably less successful when moving into the economic sphere. Relatedly, generalist NGOs often tend to be less effective at implementing more technical interventions than specialist ones." [31] Similarly, a European Union study in Ethiopia found that water and agricultural projects are more likely to be sustainable than health and education projects.[32] Are responsible NGOs to take their cue from such findings? Some forms of development activity are also more appropriate candidates for impact assessment than others. Kruse et al. note that "development interventions which focus on activities which aim to enhance livelihoods both over the longer term and less directly than discrete, concrete and more tangible projects are unlikely to be able to produce data and conclusions." [33]

Should NGOs be assessed on a comparative basis? If so, should it only be in relation to other NGOs or could it include states and IGOs as well? [34] Some factors of evaluation may pose chicken/egg type questions. For example, should access to decision-making bodies and resources be a measure of assessment or only taken into relative consideration when assessing other factors? For we would expect those NGOs with greater resources and political access to have more influence, but not all NGOs employ these strategies to achieve development goals and it thus may be inappropriate to evaluate them on these bases.

Some Factors that Affect Performance

Attention to cultural attitudes and customs is often essential to the successful implementation of rural community projects.[35] Ronald Cohen has documented and analyzed an example of this phenomenon in which an agricultural innovation succeeded technically, yet failed because the human components of the innovation experience were not taken into account.[36] As part of a 1956–57 general program of economic development in northern Nigeria, a foreign-trained Nigerian agricultural officer was interested in introducing superphosphate fertilizer into the agricultural practices of Kanuri cultivators to increase millet and groundnuts yields. Careful records of the trials were kept and there was a mean increase in the millet harvest from the fertilized test plot of 30.3 percent, and a mean increase of 35.1 percent for groundnuts (almost everyone obtained at least a ten percent increase while some received gains of up to 300 percent). But when the harvest season had ended there was a village-wide meeting with the district head at which the farmers unanimously rejected the innovation. Cohen offers five explanations from which we can gain valuable lessons for development projects more generally: (1) the farmers never expressed any dissatisfaction with the quantity of their crop yields using customary techniques; (2) superficially imposed colonial democratic procedures at the final meeting led the people to believe that fertilizer use was trivial and unimportant because it was not dictated in the traditional autocratic fashion; (3) in conjunction with (2), the Kanuri believe that advancement is made through profitable social relations and only secondarily through technology; (4) the insistence on using an acre for the test plot left portions of farms out of the experiment arbitrarily and emphasized the foreign character of the innovation; and (5) there was no follow-up of the successful demonstrations and little attempt to assess whether or not farmers were convinced of the utility of the fertilizer.[37]

The utilization of effective, established channels of authority such as voluntary associations and legitimate government structures are often necessary for initial implementation and continued sustainability. But it is also important to recognize that development efforts also face a dilemma here. Directing projects through established channels can also result in profiteering by officials and elites to the exclusion of the intended beneficiaries, resulting in the maintenance and strengthening of power imbalances rather than reform.[38] On a similar note, one basis of international NGO evaluation may be the extent to which they cooperate with, and act through, local structures, including domestic NGOs.

As no development can be sustainable and equitable without the participation of the people whom the project is intended to assist, one means of assessing the effectiveness of development NGOs is thus to determine the percentage of the "target population" that is actively involved in a specified project (or in all projects taken together). As stated in the 1990 Global Consultation on the Right to Development, popular participation is necessary for the exercise of human rights as "the principal means by which individuals and peoples collectively determine their needs and priorities, and ensure the protection and advancement of their rights and interests."[39] Without broad popular participation, development projects may be improperly conceived and designed, the targeted populations' sense of stakeholding in the project may be demoted (thus discouraging their long-term involvement and commitment), and the project may fall subject to co-optation by local elites and prohibit an equitable distribution of benefits among the intended beneficiaries.[40] Only with popular participation can true development, which results in distributive justice, increased autonomy, and even self-sufficiency in applicable areas as well as economic growth, be achieved.

The move from a "supply-side" to a "demand-side" approach is a recent change that emphasizes and encourages community participation in development projects. One means of evaluation which could therefore be very appropriate is surveying the people with whom the development NGO is working. An independent NGO review board might serve as an effective body for the distribution, collection, compilation, and presentation of surveys and corresponding responses for the various projects of the multitude of development NGOs. Further possibilities include NGO evaluation by other NGOs, for example, evaluation of international NGOs by domestic NGOs and vice versa, or evaluation of northern NGOs by southern ones and vice versa.

Internal or External Criteria?

Considering the extremely broad range of tasks, projects, and missions undertaken by human rights NGOs, it would hardly make sense to assess their effectiveness or impact according to a uniform set of standards. To some extent then, it seems that human rights NGOs must be evaluated on the basis of their own purposes and goals. However, there are problems of ambiguity with the assessment of project performance against internally defined objectives, which are generally inexplicit, varied, and vague. Roger Riddell et al. argue that a focus on the achievement of objectives tells us very little about development impact anyway. Anthony Bebbington and Adalberto Kopp concur that this provides "more of a description of what they have done than an analysis of the developmental relevance of what they have done." [41]

While assessments of human rights NGOs according to internal standards are important in that they should reflect the diversity of their work, the goal of all human rights action is ultimately that the people with whom and for whom an NGO is working be able to enjoy rights that currently are unprotected or unfulfilled. All human rights workers, and especially those whose task is development oriented, must remember that their ultimate job is to eliminate their job. Meaningful evaluations that convey the clearest possible pictures of the impact of human rights work need then to be based on objective standards of measurement and evaluation. Thus in addition to (or perhaps to the neglect of) subjective criteria, external indicators of performance are necessary.

One concern that can only be addressed by external assessment criteria is the selection of projects. Is it the case that, for the sake of their reputation and thus funding, some NGOs only undertake projects that they are certain to be successful with? Many NGO projects, and even their broader strategies, can be criticized on the basis that they do not reach the poor, or the poorest of the poor. Before we are too critical on this ground, however, it is important to recognize another dilemma facing development efforts—the apparent trade-off between achieving financial sustainability and reaching those most in need. For there is a fine line between continually providing the substantial amount of inputs necessary to make some projects sustainable with the extremely impoverished, and creating a counterproductive climate of dependency. Resolution of this dilemma may be aided by analyzing the similarly fine line between assisting the extremely impoverished with development projects, and providing emergency humanitarian relief. It should also be remembered that even the smallest gains for the poorest could have a relatively significant impact, perhaps as an initial catalyst, even though the absolute gains are minimal.

But while external criteria may provide us with necessary means of assessment, there are many problems associated with compiling, classifying, and interpreting data for human rights (and more specifically, development) indicators. Russel Lawrence Barsh has expressed the futility of such undertakings:

It would appear then, after all, that "there is extant today no single social accounting scheme that is adequate" for the measurement of human rights, and, as a consequence, no empirical basis for understanding the interrelationship between the development process and enjoyment of human rights. . . . More appropriate measures could be devised for testing a model of inter-action among "rights" and resources in development, but the model must precede the design of the measures. Specifying a new generation of arbitrary measures of "rights" will add nothing to our knowledge of development.[42]

Existing measures should thus be considered with an eye to their common unreliability, invalidity, and nonequivalence for purposes of understanding development because they do not assess the relationship between rights and resources in economic and social change.

Due to the complexity of etiological analysis in the development arena involving intricate interactions between various agents and external factors that are difficult to isolate, attempts to quantify the impact of NGOs do not seem promising. Subjective criteria are appropriate because they evaluate NGOs on the basis of the type of work that they actually pursue, but they are utterly useless for comparative purposes. On the other hand, objective criteria allow us to assess NGO strategies for work they do as well as to undertake metaevaluations of their missions, but they generally provide only a superficial, context-unrelated, and perhaps even biased assessment of an NGO, or can be applied only to a multiplicity of factors.

Conclusion

While advocating increased internal and external evaluation of NGOs, it is important to keep in mind that these evaluations require funds. Thus whether donors or NGOs conduct their evaluations, it could mean less money devoted to actual development projects. But the grounds for skepticism here are weak if, as hoped and expected, increased evaluation will mean better programs and improved human rights conditions for more people despite a 4 to 5 percent drop in project expenditure.[43] It is also important to recognize NGO limitations in the face of a multiplicity of external factors when considering their effectiveness. Many humanitarian crises and violations of economic and social rights are beyond the control and influence of NGOs, and because of the network context within which NGOs often operate, failure to act effectively may be due more to lack of coordination than to the approach of any given NGO.

While the moral imperative of the right to development is clear, steps toward a legally sanctioned global redistribution of wealth and other resources are necessary if it is to be fully realized.[44] The main point here is that voluntary charity (via states, IGOs, and NGOs) is insufficient to remedy problems of meeting people's basic needs on a global scale. Unfortunately, despite nine United Nations Conferences on Trade and Development and the work of intergovernmental organizations such as the Group of 77, the prospects for a just global redistribution of wealth appear worse now than they were in the mid-1970s when the UN General Assembly asserted that "the realization of the new international economic order is an essential element for the effective promotion of human rights and fundamental freedoms and should be accorded priority."[45] An unfortunate impediment to this process is the unwillingness of the United States to reaffirm the right to development (along with abstentions on this matter from nine other major Western states) as expressed in the final days of December 1998.[46] We can only hope that, as with so many other issues of human rights, the concerns of others (in this case, the 146 countries which originally voted in favor of the Declaration on the Right to Development) and the value of cross-cultural respect and consensus in a shrinking world will eventually be realized as legitimate national interests. The status of the right to development may adversely affect its promotion and protection by human rights NGOs. But at least from the literature I was able to locate and peruse, it seems that the work to promote internationally binding legislation pertaining to the right to development on the part of human rights NGOs has been inadequate.

Notes

I would like to thank Dr. Claude E. Welch, Jr., for the opportunity to be a part of this important book, and for his valuable comments on various drafts of this chapter.

1. For example, in Korey's book on the significance of NGOs in transforming human rights into an important international issue, neither Oxfam nor CARE is mentioned. While these NGOs may not seek to impact government policy in the way that, say, Amnesty International or Human Rights Watch does, their work toward information-gathering and publicizing of human rights abuses has certainly made human rights a "vital component of international concern and discourse." In fact, not only should development-oriented NGOs be acknowledged as part of the "curious grapevine" which has assumed the "function of implementing the demands of international morality," but they should also be recognized for establishing the basis for activism out of which the later human rights movement grew. William Korey, *NGOs and the Universal Declaration of Human Rights: "A Curious Grapevine"* (New York: St. Martin's, 1998), pp. x, 2.

2. Louis Henkin, "Rights Here and There," *Columbia Law Review* 81 (1981), p. 1608.

3. "Evaluate" is used synonymously with "assess" and "appraise"; the general idea is to determine and judge the rationale, relevance, impact, effectiveness, sustainability, equity, and efficiency of development-oriented NGOs.

4. Information for Oxfam is taken from Union of International Associations, ed., *Yearbook of International Organizations*, 35th ed. (Munich: K. G. Saur Verlag, 1998); *http://www.oxfam.org*. The eleven members consist of Oxfam America, Oxfam-in-Belgium, Oxfam Canada, Community Aid Abroad (Australia), Oxfam GB, Oxfam Hong Kong, Intermon (Spain), Oxfam Ireland, Oxfam New Zealand, Novib (The Netherlands), and Oxfam Quebec.

5. In comparison, Oxfam GB received 43 percent of its revenue from donations, 24.6 percent from the U.K. government, EU and UN, 16.5 percent from shops and trading, 9.5 percent from gifts-in-kind, 3 percent from other Oxfams, 1.7 percent from other organizations, and another 1.7 percent from miscellaneous. It spent 27.6 percent of its income on emergency relief, 25.1 percent on development, 18.8 percent on program development and support, 10.1 percent on fund-raising, 9.3 percent on transfer to reserves, 6.2 percent on education and campaigning, and 3 percent on administration and irrecoverable value-added tax.

6. Quoted in John Clark, *Democratizing Development* (London: Earthscan, 1991), p. 88.

7. Ibid., p. 59.

8. Except where noted, information on CARE comes from Union of International Associations, ed., *Yearbook of International Organizations*; Christine Maurer and Tara E. Sheets, eds., *Encyclopedia*

of Associations, 34th ed. (Detroit: Gale Research Co., 1999); *http://www.care.org* (primarily from the *1998 Annual Report*). As of 1990, CARE, as a cooperative, was owned by twenty-one other U.S. nonprofit organizations (since its inception, a total of forty-eight organizations have at one time or another been member-owners), and the work of the board and staff was supplemented by a corporate council of fifty-five corporations. The ten individual agencies that comprise CARE International are located in Australia, Austria, Canada, Denmark, France, Germany, Japan, Norway, the United Kingdom, and the United States.

9. Direct public support provided $52.3 million (360,000 individual donors made 700,000 gifts totaling $36.5 million; private foundations granted more than $8.1 million; contributions from cooperatives, civic associations, social clubs, religious bodies, and other groups totaled $4.8 million; and corporations gave $2.9 million). Other CARE International members provided $47 million. Government and other sources provided $273.5 million in support, including $156.0 million in cash grants and contracts, and $115.7 million in agricultural commodities ($224.4 million came from the U.S. government, $23.2 million from host governments, $10.3 from the Dutch government, $9.4 million from grants and contracts, and $6.2 million from the United Nations). The remaining $6.9 million came from interest, dividends, rents, etc. Fiscal year 1998 is from July 1, 1997, to June 30, 1998.

10. Darin Hyer, e-mail message to author, August 24, 1999.

11. It has been pointed out that both donors and recipients are exploited in sponsorship programs because while the funds from such programs are usually used in the community of the adopted person, they are often not used to benefit that person solely and directly. For a detailed account of problems with sponsorship programs (including cases in which sponsors unknowingly continued to support deceased children through Save the Children) see the series of articles by Lisa Anderson and Hugh Dellios in the March 15, 1998, *Chicago Tribune.*

12. In this respect, Oxfam and CARE are much like Amnesty International. See Chapter 1.

13. According to the human development index (HDI), the 22 lowest ranking countries (out of 174) are all African. Of the next 50 lowest (rankings 102–152), half are African. United Nations Development Programme, *Human Development Report 1999* (New York: Oxford University Press, 1999).

14. For example, CARE takes a $100 donation to pay for transportation and distribution costs of over $1,000 worth of commodities donated by the U.S. government under the Food for Peace program. See Wallace J. Campbell, *The History of CARE: A Personal Account* (New York: Praeger, 1990), pp. 4, 119.

15. CARE's association with the U.S. government includes relationships with many former presidents and first ladies, the Agency for International Development (USAID) and the Peace Corps. See Campbell, *The History of CARE.* Oxfam does accept additional funds in times of emergency and official aid sources such as Britain's Overseas Development Administration and the European Community have increasingly become a more important source of funds in recent years. See Maggie Black, *A Cause for Our Times: Oxfam: The First 50 Years* (Oxford: Oxfam and Oxford University Press, 1992), esp. pp. 293–96.

16. Quoted in Katarina Tomaševski, *Development Aid and Human Rights Revisited* (London: Pinter, 1993), p. 179. See UN document E/CN.4/1987/NGO/47, p. 2.

17. Ian Smillie, "NGOs and Development Assistance: A Change in Mind-set?" in Thomas G. Weiss, ed., *Beyond UN Subcontracting: Task-Sharing with Regional Security Arrangements and Service-Providing NGOs* (New York: St. Martin's, 1998), p. 184.

18. See Alex de Waal, *Evil Days: 30 Years of War and Famine in Ethiopia* (New York: Human Rights Watch, 1991).

19. Much of my discussion here is based on Welch's account which focuses on the Christian Relief and Development Association. Claude E. Welch, Jr., *Protecting Human Rights in Africa: Strategies and Roles of Non-Governmental Organizations* (Philadelphia: University of Pennsylvania Press, 1995), pp. 279–80.

20. Many NGOs, including Oxfam and CARE, are involved with both humanitarian assistance and development work. In many cases, such as in war-torn areas, any distinction between the two types of projects is very blurred, as relief and aid are essential as initial steps to any long-term

development. And because aid is often derived from major international powers, NGOs linked to such projects may often be perceived as more "political" in this aspect.

21. See Yves Beigbeder, *The Role and Status of International Humanitarian Volunteers and Organizations: The Right and Duty to Humanitarian Assistance* (Dordrecht: Martinus Nijhoff, 1990), pp. 92–93; cited in Welch, *Protecting Human Rights in Africa*, p. 46. However, Tvedt argues that NGO "articles of faith" (e.g., proximity to the poor, participatory nature, flexibility, and efficiency) "are untenable, firstly because of the heterogeneity of the organizations involved. . . . Secondly it is impossible to measure such advantages, partly because of methodological problems and partly because such a characterization presupposes that states, markets and NGOs have more or less identical objectives." Terje Tvedt, *Angels of Mercy or Development Diplomats? NGOs and Foreign Aid* (Trenton, N.J.: Africa World Press, 1998), pp. 5–6, 129. He concedes that under certain conditions NGOs may be flexible, cost-efficient and grassroots oriented, but in others less efficient and flexible because they do not have sanctions available to governments and they are founded on restricting values.

22. See Celia R. Taylor, "The Right of Participation in Development Projects," in Konrad Ginther, Erik Denters, and Paul J. I. M. de Waart, eds., *Sustainable Development and Good Governance* (Dordrecht: Martinus Nijhoff, 1995), esp. pp. 215–22.

23. Mark Robinson, "Privatising the Voluntary Sector: NGOs as Public Service Contractors," in David Hulme and Michael Edwards, eds., *NGOs, States and Donors: Too Close for Comfort?* (New York: St. Martin's in association with Save the Children, 1997), pp. 66–67.

24. See Lawrence F. Salmen and A. P. Eaves, "Interactions between Nongovernmental Organizations and the World Bank: Evidence from Bank Projects," in Samuel Paul and Arturo Israel, eds., *Nongovernmental Organizations and the World Bank: Cooperation for Development* (Washington, D.C.: World Bank, 1991), p. 121.

25. Ian Smillie, "Changing Partners: Northern NGOs, Northern Governments," in Ian Smillie and Henny Helmich, eds., *Non-governmental Organizations and Governments: Stakeholders for Development* (Paris: OECD, 1993), p. 15.

26. Ibid., p. 20.

27. Tvedt, *Angels of Mercy or Development Diplomats?* p. 4.

28. Sten-Erik Kruse, Timo Kyllönen, Satu Ojanperä, Roger C. Riddell, and Jean Vielajus with assistance from Anthony Bebbington, Denise Humphreys, and David Mansfield, "Searching for Impact and Methods: NGO Evaluation Synthesis Study," A Report prepared for the OECD/DAC Expert Group on Evaluation (*http://www.valt.helsinki.fi/ids/ngo*, 1997), § 8.1, 8.3.1. Examples of NGO initiatives in linking evaluation to experimentation and research include a 1995 joint Oxfam UK/I and Novib study to increase understanding of methods, and a Kenyan study which cites seven NGOs (including Oxfam and CARE) experimenting with new ways of evaluating projects.

29. Smillie, "NGOs and Development Assistance," p. 196.

30. David Hulme and Michael Edwards, "NGOs, States and Donors: An Overview," in Hulme and Edwards, eds., *NGOs, States and Donors*, p. 279.

31. Kruse et al., "Searching for Impact and Methods," Executive Summary.

32. Ibid., § 3.4. In § 8.2 they also note that "the failure of evaluations to provide reliable information on impact is rooted in the absence of baseline data and regular monitoring."

33. Ibid., § 8.1.

34. See, for example, Hans Thoolen and Berth Verstappen, *Human Rights Missions: A Study of the Fact-Finding Practice of Non-governmental Organizations* (Dordrecht: Martinus Nijhoff, 1986) and Farouk Mawlawi, "New Conflicts, New Challenges: The Evolving Role of Non-Governmental Actors," *Journal of International Affairs* 46 (1993), 391–413. As an aside, a 1996 British Overseas Development Administration study reported that NGO development projects have performed as well as, if not better than, official aid projects. See Kruse et al., "Searching for Impact and Methods," § 3.2.

35. In addition to their functions, an understanding of the factors that contribute to an NGO's success or failure is also necessary before evaluation methods can be analyzed. Kruse et al. list several in their Executive Summary which seem to offer a comprehensive account.

36. See Ronald Cohen, "The Success that Failed: An Experiment in Culture Change in Africa," *Anthropologica* 3 (1961), pp. 21–36.

37. Ibid., 30–35.

38. For examples of case studies attesting to this phenomenon, see Kruse et al., "Searching for Impact and Methods," § 3.3.1.

39. E/CN.4/1990/9 Rev. 1 of 9/26/90, pp. 65–66.

40. See Taylor, "The Right of Participation in Development Projects," pp. 206–07. Lappé et al. make a similar point about unintended effects of development projects due to disproportionate power structures within targeted areas. Frances Moore Lappé, Rachel Schurman, and Kevin Danaher, *Betraying the National Interest* (New York: Grove Press, 1987).

41. See, respectively, Roger C. Riddell, Anthony Bebbington, and Lennart Peck, *Promoting Development by Proxy: The Development Impact of the Swedish Government's Support to NGOs* (Stockholm: SIDA, 1995), p. 12; Anthony Bebbington and Adalberto Kopp, *Evaluation of the Swedish NGO Support Programme: Bolivia Country Case Study* (Stockholm: SIDA, 1995), p. 40.

42. Russel Lawrence Barsh, "Measuring Human Rights: Problems of Methodology and Purpose," *Human Rights Quarterly* 15 (1993), p. 121; quoting in part Michael Stohl et al., "State Violation of Human Rights: Issues and Problems of Measurement," *Human Rights Quarterly* 8 (1986), p. 593.

43. Based on the Norwegian and Netherlands studies from Kruse et al., "Searching for Impact and Methods," § 9.6.

44. In addition to ratification of a convention on the right to development, further progress would include the strengthening of regional governments and, eventually, a cosmopolitan democratic government (including, perhaps, an Economic Security Council).

45. General Assembly Resolution 32/130.

46. The United Kingdom, Germany, France, Italy, Canada, Australia, Denmark, Norway, and Sweden abstained from voting.

Part III
Analyzing and
Enhancing Effectiveness

Chapter 11
Measuring the Impact
of Human Rights Organizations

David L. Cingranelli and David L. Richards

No comparative, systematic, quantitative research has been conducted linking the activities of national or international nongovernmental human rights organizations (NGOs and INGOs) to improvements in the human rights practices of governments.[1] There is a substantial and convincing body of qualitative research demonstrating that international NGOs have been effective in putting new issues on the international human rights agenda, have affected the content of important human rights documents, have helped to monitor the human rights practices of national governments, and have assisted in the implementation of the provisions of human rights agreements.[2] Much of the existing research on human rights NGOs and INGOs consists of any of four types: case studies of individual organizations working for human rights;[3] comparative studies of a select number of organizations;[4] studies of the work of human rights organizations and institutions in specific countries or regions;[5] and studies of the political processes surrounding human rights standard setting and enforcement.[6]

Qualitative case studies of the effects of NGOs and INGOs on the human rights practices of specific governments are useful for answering questions about agenda setting and standard setting, and for developing and refining hypotheses about the effectiveness of NGOs in improving the human rights practices of governments. However, they cannot be used to provide scientific evidence of effectiveness of human rights organizations in improving the human rights practices of target governments.[7] We assume that the main question about the impact of human rights organizations on the practices of target governments may be stated as follows: Do the activities of NGOs and INGOs in a particular target country cause an improvement in the human rights practices of the government of the target country? If the answer to this first question is "yes," then we might also ask: What strategies, tactics, and organizational attributes of NGOs and INGOs are associated with the greatest improvement in the human rights practices of target governments?

To answer these questions about the effects of NGOs and INGOs on the human rights practices of target governments, one's research design would need to incorporate four elements. First, it must isolate the effects of NGOs and INGOs from the effects of other types of human rights organizations working toward similar goals in a given target state. Second, it must use relatively objective information about the human rights practices of target governments that is relevant to the mandate of the type of human rights organization of interest over an extended period of time. Third, it must possess information about human rights organizations from which measures of their efforts in different mandate areas could be constructed, also for an extended period of time. Finally, it must control for competing alternative explanations of the human rights practices of governments.

Separating Influences

Except in the improbable case that all human rights organizations attempting to affect the human rights practices of a given target government are concerned with mutually exclusive issues, it would be impossible to accurately assess the effectiveness of one NGO or INGO from another in changing the human rights practices of that government.[8] However, NGOs and INGOs are not the only types of human rights organizations, and it may be possible to assess the effectiveness of different types of human rights organizations. That is, on a general level it may be impossible to assess the effects of only, say, Amnesty International on a target government, but it may be possible to assess the effects of INGOs in general, as opposed to other kinds of human rights organizations, on a target government. Ball, Girouard, and Chapman distinguish among the following six kinds of human rights organizations: (1) governmental human rights bodies (e.g., the Honduran Human Rights Commissioner); (2) intergovernmental and regional organizations (e.g., UN human rights missions, the Inter-American Commission on Human Rights); (3) INGOs (e.g., Amnesty International); (4) regional, national, or local NGOs (e.g., Human Rights Foundation of Turkey, the Society for Community Organization in Hong Kong, the International Center for Human Rights Research-Guatemala); (5) quasi-governmental truth commissions (Haitian National Commission of Truth and Justice, Truth and Reconciliation Commission of South Africa), and (6) national or international criminal tribunals.[9]

To separate the effects of one type of human rights organization from the effects of another, one would need to collect information about the mandate (the types of government human rights practices they seek to change), strategies, and other organizational attributes of each type of human rights organization operating in a country. The caveat is that if there is overlap in the mandates of different types of human rights organizations, separating their effects becomes impossible. However, we expect more variation in the mandates among different types of human rights organizations than among separate organizations of a similar type. For example, we would expect more difference between the mandates of an INGO and a quasi-governmental truth commission than would exist between the mandates of Human Rights Watch and Amnesty International.

Collecting appropriate information about the all human rights organizations operating in a country or, even better, in several countries would be a major task. Recently, Smith, Pagnucco, and Lopez reported the results of a systematic survey of the leaders of human rights INGOs.[10] The survey asked questions about the organizational attributes of each INGO (e.g., its membership size), the scope of its human rights mandate, the amount of resources it had available, and the strategies it used. The Smith, Pagnucco, and Lopez study is ambitious, impressive, and valuable, but it only describes the organization and goals of one type of human rights organization—INGOs. In addition, some categories of organizations do not operate in some countries, and similar *types* of human rights organizations typically differ greatly in terms of their size, mandates, methodology, political leanings, and resources.

Information About the Human Rights Practices of Governments

Evaluating the human rights impact of human rights organizations on target governments requires that one have relatively objective information about the human rights practices of governments around the world over an extended period of time. A long time is needed because one would expect a time lag between NGO and INGO efforts and consequences. Thus, we should be most interested in those measures of human rights practices that already have been constructed and are available over a long period. Several have been available annually since the early or mid 1970s.

Over the last twenty-five years or so, a body of scientific research has developed focusing on the human rights practices of governments. To test hypotheses about those practices, various scholars have produced their own measures of human rights practices. The earliest research attempted to discover whether less developed countries with better human rights records received relatively more foreign aid from the United States. Later studies asked whether cutting off or drastically reducing aid for human rights reasons led to subsequent improvements in human rights practices by recipient governments. Most systematic research in the past few years has attempted to develop theories explaining variations in human rights practices among governments of the world.[11]

In each of the research projects noted above, scholars have attempted to develop relatively objective measures of the human rights practices of governments. One could ask the leaders of NGOs whether they think they have been effective in improving the human rights practices of different governments around the world. One could also ask government leaders the same question. The answers would provide us with interesting information, but would not provide the basis for a convincing objective test of the effectiveness of NGO activities, because the evaluations of effectiveness by both types of respondents would be too subjective. Moreover, to gather information about effectiveness over time, the survey would have to be repeated frequently.

Thus, the effort to develop objective measures of government respect for human rights relies on centralized, frequently updated sources of information about the human rights practices of a large number of countries. The most commonly used primary sources that contain fairly consistent information about the human rights practices of most countries of the world are the Amnesty International annual reports and the annually produced U.S. Department of State Country Reports on Human Rights Practices. Only the U.S. State Department reports systematically contain information about government respect for a wide variety of human rights over a long period of time. Though there were problems in the quality of the early State Department reports, the bias toward U.S. allies is generally regarded as having sharply declined since 1981.[12]

Even more important than the temporal aspect, however, is the imperative that we have measures of government respect for human rights that match the mandates of the human rights organizations that we would like to assess. One problem with the objective measures developed so far is that, to this point, empirical research has focused almost exclusively on the measurement of government respect for a category of human rights known as physical integrity rights. These are the rights human beings have not to be subjected to torture, political imprisonment, extrajudicial killing, and disappearance. Torture refers to the purposeful inflicting of extreme pain, whether mental or physical, by government officials or by private individuals at the instigation of government officials. Torture includes the use of physical and other force by police and prison guards that is cruel, inhuman, or degrading. Political imprisonment refers to the incarceration of people by government officials because of their ideas including religious beliefs, their nonviolent religious practices including proselytizing, their speech, their nonviolent opposition to government policies or leaders, or their membership in a group including an ethnic or racial group.[13] Extrajudicial killings are killings by government officials without due process of law. They include murders by private groups if instigated by government.[14] Disappearances refer to unresolved cases in which political motivation appears likely and in which the victims have not been found. Disappearances and killings are closely related practices. Many victims of human rights abuse who initially are categorized as having been disappeared are later found to have been killed.

The most frequently used measure of government respect for physical integrity rights is the Political Terror Scale (PTS), a five-category ordinal scale developed by Gastil and popularized by Carleton and Stohl.[15] The PTS measures the level of "terror," or physical integrity abuse, in a given country. The scale ranges from level one—meaning no terror, to level five—meaning widespread terror throughout the entire population. The PTS includes the rights against torture, extrajudicial killing, political imprisonment, and disappearance, and as a scale is assumed to be unidimensional, although this assumption has never been tested. The sources of data for the creation of the PTS are the yearly U.S. State Department Country Reports on Human Rights Practices and Amnesty International annual reports. Separate scales are created by coding the contents of each report for each country for each year. PTS data is now available for most countries of the world on an annual basis for the years 1976 through 1996.[16]

The other scale of government respect for physical integrity rights worth mentioning is a relatively new nine-category scale created by the authors using a probabilistic cumulative scaling technique known as Mokken scale analysis (MSA).[17] This measure is available for seventy-nine countries of the world for the years 1981–96, in three-year intervals. The scale runs from zero (no respect for any of the four physical integrity rights included) to eight (full respect for all four rights). Like the PTS, the sources of data for the creation of this measure are the annual U.S. State Department Country Reports on Human Rights Practices and Amnesty International annual reports. The scoring categories for the four physical integrity variables used to create this scale— extrajudicial killings, disappearances, political imprisonment, and torture—are as follows: (0) frequent violations; (1) some violations; and (2) no violations. Unlike the PTS, this measure is the only scale that has been empirically demonstrated to be unidimensional.

Both the PTS and the authors' scale are aggregated measures of government respect for physical integrity rights. That is, these measures provide one ordinal measure for each government's level of respect for all rights contained in these measures (combined) for each year on an ordinal scale. The problem is that unless these measures can be disaggregated by the user, one cannot be sure what the level of government respect is for any of the individual rights composing the scale. For example, if a human rights organization made a special effort to stop the use of torture by a government, one would not be able to assess the effectiveness of that particular effort by using the PTS. The authors' scale, however, provides information about the level of government respect for each of the individual rights used to create the aggregate scale, and thus circumvents this problem. Thus, each scale has its advantages. The PTS is available for more time points and countries, while the authors' scale can be disaggregated to study individual human rights abuses separately, and has been empirically demonstrated to be unidimensional.

This focus by previous scientific research on physical integrity rights, however, creates a problem for those who seek to evaluate the human rights impact of human rights organizations because most human rights organizations focus on other types of human rights as well as physical integrity rights—such as the rights of women or the rights of indigenous peoples. For those human rights organizations whose mandate finds them actively promoting rights such as the rights to freedom of opinion, expression, or thought, or the right to vote and to be elected in genuine periodic elections, the Freedom House annual survey of freedom around the world would be helpful.

Since the early 1970s, Freedom House has produced two seven-category scales, for political rights and civil liberties, indicating the level of government respect for these rights for every country in the world. It also produces a combined three-category "Status of Freedom" scale that rates countries as "free," "partly free," or "not free." One of the problems of the Freedom House measure in the context of measuring the effect of human rights organizations is that while the many items in both the political rights and civil liberties checklists used to provide the two scale scores are known, the individual scale scores are not. That is, we may know that a country scores a "5" on political rights, but we do not know how a country fares on the particular right to freedom of peaceful assembly and association.

In the realm of measuring women's rights, two measures have been recently produced that show great promise for assessing government respect for these particular rights. Poe, Wendel-Blunt, and Ho provide two five-category ordinal measures of women's political and economic rights based on information found in the 1994 U.S. State Department's Country Reports on Human Rights Practices.[18] Apodaca introduces what she calls the "Women's Economic and Social Human Rights Index" (WESHR).[19] The WESHR measures disparities between males and females as regards four rights: the right to work, the right to an adequate standard of living, the right to health and well-being, and the right to an education. WESHR is based on information found in both the U.S. State Department Country Reports and the United Nations' Human Development Report. It is available for 114 countries from 1975 to 1990 in five-year intervals.

It is important that efforts are being made to objectively measure the level of government respect for human rights other than physical integrity rights. Such efforts will help future efforts to assess the impacts of human rights organizations on the practices of target governments.

Whatever measure is being used, there are several potential problems that researchers must be aware of when assessing the influence of human rights organizations on governments, lest their inferences be tainted. We now discuss two of these problems, biased sources and human rights practices versus human rights conditions.

Biased Sources

As Bollen and Spirer have pointed out, human rights data are problematic by their very nature.[20] Out of the entire universe of human rights violations, few of these violations are reported to those who code, collect, or archive such information. Diplomatic relations, ideology, internal and/or external government regulations, geography, technology, media appeal, differences in the judgment of human observers, and fear all affect what information about human rights violations is available. Since we most often work with samples rather than with populations, we expect our sample data to be an unbiased indicator of the larger population from which it was culled. We wish to make unbiased inferences from our data. That means that on average, our inferences are correct, or to say it another way, not systematically incorrect. To do this, we must start with unbiased data. Data collection relying on information sources strongly affected by any one or more of the above factors may be biased in one manner or another; and it is reasonable to be skeptical of inferences garnered from questionable data.

Early empirical human rights research was often criticized as having used biased sources. One widely used source of data for these early studies was Taylor and Jodice's *World Handbook of Political and Social Indicators*.[21] Barsh points out that the *World Handbook*'s indicator of repression was a count of the "number of repressive 'events' reported in the *New York Times*."[22] Obviously, drawing inferences from a data source reliant on one U.S. newspaper, albeit a major paper, is a questionable practice. Davenport and

Galaich point out that all news coverage of human rights violations carries a heavy bias toward some regions and away from others.[23] For example, coverage is poor for China and even poorer for North Korea. News coverage of human rights violations also varies for a single country over time. An example would be the temporarily extensive coverage of Southeast Asian human rights violations during the 1960s.

Cingranelli and Pasquerello were criticized for using the annual U.S. State Department Country Reports on Human Rights Practices as their sole data source because of the alleged ideological bias of the U.S. government.[24] Critics of the State Department reports have alleged that they are biased toward putting a soft spin on human rights abuses in countries that are friendly to U.S. interests,a nd villainizing those countries hostile to U.S. interests. Thus, it is alleged, inferences drawn from this biased information are tainted. A recent empirical investigation shows that the State Department's reports "have, at times, favored friends and trading partners of the US, while discriminating against its leftist foes. The results [of the empirical analysis] strongly support many of the arguments of critics who, based on their examinations of the reports, have concluded that such biases exist. . . . However, consistent with other observations by these critics, our findings also appear to indicate that the well-chronicled biases of the *Country Reports* have faded with time; most likely the U.S. State Department has instituted improvements in response to its critics."[25]

While director of the *Comparative Survey of Freedom*, published by Freedom House, Raymond D. Gastil cited his information sources as being mainly those things that happened to be contained in the "more or less continuous flow of publications across the author's desk."[26] The fact that Gastil did not explicitly reveal his sources left him open to criticism that the *Survey* was influenced by the conservative ideology of its sponsor, Freedom House.[27] Gastil responds, "generally such criticism is based on opinions about Freedom House rather than detailed examination of survey ratings."[28] Were Gastil more explicit about his data sources, however, it would be easier to determine if this is true. As Bollen points out, "the political orientation of judges could lead them to give more credence to sources that are consistent with their predispositions."[29]

Practices Versus Conditions

One concern about the Freedom House scores and the Physical Terror Scale (PTS) is whether these scores measure human rights practices or human rights conditions. "Human rights practices" refers to the actions of government officials directly affecting the degree to which citizens can actually exercise various types of human rights. In other words, practices are what governments actually do, not what they claim to do or what consequences flow from what they do. Almost all of the scientific research in political science focusing on human rights as a concept is concerned about the causes or consequences of variations in the human rights practices of governments. "Human rights conditions" refers to the degree to which citizens can actually exercise various types of human rights. Human rights conditions are affected by phenomena other than government practices. For use in the research program looking at determinants of *government* respect for human rights, measures of government respect for physical integrity rights should focus exclusively on human rights practices. However, some do not.

For example, coders who collect information used to construct the PTS are told to "Try to measure government terror, but ultimately be sensitive to all forms of terror."[30] They are explicitly instructed not to ignore terror from nongovernmental actors. The aim of the Political Terror Scale is to reflect the human rights violations that exist in a country more generally.[31] Thus, PTS scores reflect some mixture of human rights practices and conditions. The authors' physical integrity rights scale, on the other hand, focuses exclusively on practices, not human rights conditions. It is not clear whether Freedom House scores reflect practices only, or both practices and conditions.

Many things will affect human rights conditions besides what governments intend and what they do. Nongovernmental groups such as revolutionaries, gangsters, or terrorists also may violate human rights. Independent from government practices, they may worsen the human rights conditions in a country. For example, in their 1992 reports, both Amnesty International and the U.S. State Department estimated that more than half the civilian deaths in Peru were caused by the Shining Path revolutionar group, not the government. Thus, theories constructed to explain the causes of variations in government human rights practices would be different from theories constructed to explain the causes of variations in human rights conditions. Moreover, for at least some countries, human rights conditions would be worse than government human rights practices.

Assessing the Effort of Human Rights Organizations

We are unaware of any attempt to objectively measure the effort expended by human rights organizations in trying to change the human rights practices of a target government. Thus, anyone attempting to do so would have to collect such information. We must ask ourselves, then, what characteristics these organizations might manifest that may be helpful in such a measurement effort. Here, we discuss three possible indicators that either alone, or in some combination, may be fruitful in examining the influence of human rights organizations on target governments.

Our first possibility is perhaps the most simple and intuitive: what level of resources has been spent trying to change the human rights practices of a target government? We might expect that human rights organizations would have the most influence in those places where they have committed the most resources. By resources, we mean money and personnel. By examining the financial records of human rights organizations, we may be able to tell how much money has been earmarked for or directed toward affecting a particular target government. In addition, the number of constant personnel in a particular country and the number of specific missions to a particular country might prove useful. The key to all of these possibilities lies with the cooperation of human rights organizations in making such information accessible.

The next two possibilities are based on the publications that human rights organizations regularly produce. One kind of publication regularly produced by these organizations is what we call the country-specific or situation-specific report. These reports detail either general human rights conditions within a particular country, or detail the specific plights of certain groups, individuals, or situations in a particular country. We would assume that human rights organizations would publish the most reports about countries where they have concentrated the most effort. An indicator might represent this either by the number of individual reports published about a country, or by the total number of pages published about a country among all the specific reports.

Some human rights organizations publish annual reports describing human rights conditions in many countries around the world. The most notable of these are Amnesty International and Human Rights Watch. Although these reports are annual they do not systematically include every country in the world. The copyright page of the 1998 Amnesty International Annual Report contains the statement: "This report documents Amnesty International's work and its concerns throughout the world during 1997. The absence of an entry in this report on a particular country or territory does not imply that no human rights violations of concern to Amnesty International have taken place there during the year. Nor is the length of a country entry any basis for a comparison of the extent and depth of Amnesty International's concerns in a country." In its introduction to its 1998 annual World Report, Human Rights Watch states that:

This volume . . . does not include a chapter on every country where we work, nor does it discuss every issue of importance. The failure to include a country or issue often reflects no more than staffing and funding limitations, and should not be taken as commentary on the significance of the related human rights concerns. Other factors affecting the focus of our work in 1997 and hence the content of this volume include the severity of abuses, our access to information about them, our ability to influence abusive practices, and our desire to balance our work across various political and regional divides and to address certain thematic concerns.[32]

These statements serve as disclaimers of compassion, serving notice to those not included that they are not forgotten. However, they also tell us much more. Amnesty notes that the report represents its "work and its concerns throughout the world during 1997," and Human Rights Watch notes that a country's absence or presence may be due to resource limitations, "the severity of abuses . . . access to information about them [or] ability to influence abusive practices." It is entirely reasonable to believe that the countries included in these reports are those that, for whatever reason, received the most attention from these organizations throughout a given year. Thus, over time, a dichotomous variable indicating a country's presence or absence in these reports may be useful in determining the effect of these organizations on the human rights practices of a target government.

Controlling for Alternative Explanations

Finally, to isolate the impacts of NGOs, one would want to control for competing alternative explanations of the human rights practices of governments, as there are many factors other than elections that might be associated with government respect for human rights. Bivariate models sometimes obfuscate the true picture of what is going on within a statistical relationship. One classic example of the need to employ control variables is Mitchell and McCormick.[33] In testing their hypothesis that there will be more human rights violations in those countries that are more involved with foreign capitalist interests, they found a significant relationship between foreign investment and the taking of political prisoners. Further tests, however, demonstrated that when a country's population size is controlled for, this statistically significant relationship disappears. Had they not taken the extra step of controlling for alternate explanations of variance in government respect for human rights, any inferences drawn from this part of their study would be incorrect.

Four studies are primarily responsible for a set of control variables that are now in common use in quantitative studies of government respect for human rights. This list includes level of economic development (Mitchell and McCormick);[34] presence of civil war, presence of international war, and level of past repression (Poe and Tate 1994);[35] population size (Henderson);[36] and level of democracy (Henderson).[37] Poe and Tate's work is the most well known piece that ties together all of these. Thus, to properly estimate the effects of human rights NGOs and INGOs, our research design must hold the effects of these competing explanations of government respect for human rights "constant."

Summary

There is a need for systematic, quantitative research linking the activities of national or international nongovernment human rights organizations (NGOs and INGOs) to improvements in the human rights practices of governments. Research of this type must satisfy four criteria. First, it must isolate the effects of NGOs and INGOs from the effects of other types of human rights organizations working towards similar goals in a given target state. Second, any study of impact must use relatively objective information about the human rights practices of target governments that is relevant to the mandate of the human rights organization of interest. Third, such a study must measure the degree of effort different human rights organizations devote to achieving different human rights goals. Fourth, it must control for competing alternative explanations of the human rights practices of governments.

Ideally, studies would be comparative across many countries and across an extended time. However, the availability of the above four types of information, particularly information about the efforts of human rights organizations, will dictate both the temporal and spatial scope of future empirical studies. In order to control statistically for alternative explanations of human rights practices of target governments, one would need the four types of information described above for each country under analysis over an extended time. Reliable information about the human rights practices of governments is readily available for almost all countries of the world for the last twenty-five years or so. Measures of other control variables needed for a systematic study of the effects of NGOs and INGOs such as national population and wealth are available for an even longer period of time and for more countries. However, a cross-national, cross-time study of the effects of human rights organizations on the actions of target governments would be very difficult at this time because there is currently no centralized source of information about the resources expended and goals of all human rights organizations in different countries over time. Because of this, conducting a rigorously scientific study of the human rights impacts of human rights organizations in even a single country or a few countries would be an ambitious task.

Notes

1. Though there are several types of NGOs and INGOs, we use those acronyms in this chapter to refer to human rights organizations only.

2. See, for example, Paul Wapner, *Environmental Activism and World Civic Politics* (Albany: State University of New York Press, 1996); Thomas G. Weiss and Leon Gordenker, eds., *NGOs, the UN and Global Governance* (Boulder, Colo.: Lynne Rienner, 1996); Margaret E. Keck and Kathryn Sikkink, *Activists Beyond Borders: Advocacy Networks in International Politics* (Ithaca, N.Y.: Cornell University Press, 1998).

3. See David Forsythe, "The Red Cross as a Transnational Movement: Conserving and Changing the Nation-State System," *International Organization* 30 (1976), pp. 607–30; Howard Tolley, "Popular Sovereignty and International Law: ICJ Strategies for Human Rights Standard-Setting," *Human Rights Quarterly* 11 (1989), pp. 561–85.

4. Harry Scoble and Laurie Wiseberg, "Human Rights NGOs: Notes Towards Comparative Analysis," *Revue des Droits de L'Homme* 9 (1976), pp. 611–44.

5. See Iain Guest, *Behind the Disappearances: Argentina's Dirty War Against Human Rights and the United Nations* (Philadelphia: University of Pennsylvania Press, 1990); Ron Pagnucco and John D. McCarthy, "Advocating Nonviolent Direct Action in Latin America: The Antecedents and Emergence of SERPAJ," in Bronislaw Misztal and Anson Shupe, eds., *Religion and Politics in Comparative Perspective: Revival of Religious Fundamentalism in East and West* (Westport, Conn.: Praeger, 1992), pp. 125–47; Kathryn Sikkink, "Human Rights, Principled Issue-Networks, and Sovereignty in Latin America," *International Organization* 47 (1993), pp. 411–41.

6. Jack Donnelly, "International Human Rights: A Regime Analysis," *International Organization* 40 (1986), pp. 599–642; David Forsythe, *The Internationalization of Human Rights* (Lexington, Mass.: Lexington Books, 1991); Jackie Smith, "Transnational Political Processes and the Human Rights Movement," *Research in Social Movements, Conflicts and Change* 18 (1995), pp. 185–219.

7. By "target government" we mean the national government of a country that is the focus of influence attempts by human rights organizations aimed at improving that government's human rights practices.

8. Based on individual casework, it may be able to assess the individual effectiveness of similar but separate human rights organizations. An example of this would be Human Rights Watch and Amnesty International both trying to free political prisoners, but concentrating on the cases of different prisoners. Success in individual cases is not indicative of success in changing policy, however.

9. Patrick Ball, Mark Girouard, and Audrey Chapman, "Information Technology, Information

Management, and Human Rights: A Response to Metzl," *Human Rights Quarterly* 19 (1997), pp. 836–59.

10. Jackie Smith, Ron Pagnucco, and George A. Lopez, "Globalizing Human Rights: The Work of Transnational Human Rights NGOs in the 1990s," *Human Rights Quarterly* 20 (1998), pp. 379–412.

11. See Steven C. Poe and C. Neal Tate, "Repression of Human Rights to Personal Integrity in the 1980s: A Global Analysis," *American Political Science Review* 88, (1994), pp. 853–72; Steven C. Poe, C. Neal Tate, and Linda Camp-Keith, "Repression of the Human Right to Personal Integrity Revisited: A Global Cross-National Study Covering the Years 1976–1993," *International Studies Quarterly* 43 (1999), pp. 291–313; William H. Meyer, "Human Rights and MNCs: Theory versus Quantitative Analysis," *Human Rights Quarterly* 18 (1996), pp. 368–97.

12. Steven C. Poe, Tonya Vasquez, and Sabine Zanger, "How Are These Pictures Different? An Empirical Comparison of the US State Department and Amnesty International Human Rights Reports, 1976–1995," unpublished paper presented at the Annual Meeting of the International Studies Association, March 17–20, 1998, Minneapolis, Minn.

13. Individuals who are imprisoned because they have committed violent acts, regardless of the reasons why they committed those acts, are not political prisoners.

14. Extrajudicial killings may result from the deliberate, illegal, and excessive use of lethal force by the police, security forces, or other agents of the state whether against criminal suspects, detainees, prisoners, or others. Extrajudicial killing excludes combat deaths.

15. Raymond D. Gastil, *Freedom in the World: Political Rights and Civil Liberties, 1980* (New Brunswick, N.J.: Transaction Books, 1980); David Carleton and Michael Stohl, "The Foreign Policy of Human Rights: Rhetoric and Reality from Jimmy Carter to Ronald Reagan," *Human Rights Quarterly* 7 (1985), pp. 205–29.

16. *www.ippu.purdue.edu/info/gsp/govern.htm.*

17. David L. Cingranelli and David L. Richards, "Measuring the Level, Pattern, and Sequence of Government Respect for Physical Integrity Rights," *International Studies Quarterly* 43 (1999), pp. 407–17. These data can be obtained at *www.polsci.binghamton.edu/hr.htm.*

18. Steven C. Poe, Dierdre Wendel-Blunt, and Karl Ho, "Global Patterns in the Achievement of Women's Human Rights to Equality," *Human Rights Quarterly* 19 (1997), pp. 813–35.

19. Clair Apodaca, "Measuring Women's Economic and Social Rights Achievement," *Human Rights Quarterly* 20 (1998), pp. 139–72.

20. Kenneth Bollen, "Political Rights and Political Liberties in Nations: An Evaluation of Human Rights Measures, 1950–1984," in Richard Pierre Claude and Thomas B. Jabine, eds., *Human Rights and Statistics: Getting the Record Straight* (Philadelphia: University of Pennsylvania Press, 1992), pp. 188–215; Herbert F. Spirer, "Violations of Human Rights—How Many?" *American Journal of Economics and Sociology* 49, no. 2 (1990), pp. 199–210.

21. Charles Taylor and David Jodice, *The World Handbook of Political and Social Indicators* (New Haven, Conn.: Yale University Press, 1983).

22. Russel L. Barsh, "Measuring Human Rights: Problems of Methodology and Purpose," *Human Rights Quarterly* 15 (1993), p. 101.

23. Christian Davenport and Glen Galaich, "What You See Might Be What You Get, But What You Get Ain't All There Is: Exploring News Coverage and the 'Observation' of Human Rights Violations," unpublished paper presented at the Annual Meeting of the American Political Science Association, September 3–6, 1998, Boston.

24. David L. Cingranelli and Thomas Pasquerello, "Human Rights Practices and the US Distribution of Foreign Aid to Latin American Countries," *American Journal of Political Science* 29 (1985), pp. 539–63; David Carleton and Michael Stohl, "The Role of Human Rights in US Foreign Assistance Policy," *American Journal of Political Science* 31 (1987), pp. 1002–19; Neil J. Mitchell and James M. McCormick, "Is US Aid Really Linked to Human Rights in Latin America?" *American Journal of Political Science* 32 (1988), pp. 231–39.

25. Poe et al., "How are These Pictures Different?" p. 11.

26. Raymond D. Gastil, *Freedom in the World: Political Rights and Civil Liberties 1987–1988* (New York: Freedom House, 1988), p. 25.

27. Harry M. Scoble and Laurie S. Wiseberg, "Problems of Comparative Research on Human Rights," in James R. Scarritt, Ved P. Nanda, and George W. Shepherd, Jr., eds., *Global Human Rights: Public Policies, Comparative Measures, and NGO Strategies* (Boulder, Colo.: Westview Press, 1981), pp. 147–71.

28. Raymond D. Gastil, "The Comparative Survey of Freedom: Experiences and Suggestions," *Studies in Comparative International Development* 25, no. 1 (1990), p. 26.

29. Kenneth Bollen, "Liberal Democracy: Validity and Method Factors in Cross-National Measures," *American Journal of Political Science* 37 (1993), p. 1224.

30. Mark Gibney and Matthew Dalton, "The Political Terror Scale," in David L. Cingranelli, ed., *Human Rights and Developing Countries* (Greenwich, Conn.: JAI Press, 1996), p. 79.

31. Ibid.

32. Human Rights Watch, *Human Rights Watch World Report 1998* (New York: Human Rights Watch, 1997), pp. xiii–xiv.

33. Mitchell and McCormick, "Is U.S. Aid Really Linked?"

34. Ibid.

35. Poe and Tate, "Repression of Human Rights."

36. Conway Henderson, "Population Pressures and Political Repression," *Social Science Quarterly* 74 (1993), pp. 322–33.

37. Conway Henderson, "Conditions Affecting the Use of Political Repression," *Journal of Conflict Resolution* 35 (1991), pp. 120–42.

Chapter 12
The Internet
One More Tool in the Struggle for Human Rights

Laurie S. Wiseberg

The Emergence of the Internet as a Channel of Communications

In the past five years, we have seen enormous advances in access to information as the Internet has become publicly accessible to more and more people in almost all areas of the globe. Millions of people "log on" regularly, whether to search for information or to post it. According to Professor Suman Naresh, about 120 million people throughout the world are using the Internet, and experts estimate that five million more come on-line every month.[1] While there are still some areas of the globe without access to this new channel of communication, this is rapidly becoming an anomaly. Today, the main barriers to access are illiteracy and poverty, not geographic location.

The Internet came into existence in the late 1970s as an outgrowth of a project of the U.S. Defense Department. Today, it is a global system of networked computers which allows communication and the transfer of data files from one machine to any other on the network.[2] Few dispute the fact that the speed with which the Internet has transformed both patterns of communications and the technology of communications is nothing short of revolutionary. By January 1999, it was estimated that there were more than 43 million hosts (i.e., computers or servers) on the Internet.[3] One scholar has compared the emergence of the Internet to Johannes Gutenberg's invention of the printing press, which "gave the world a device that expanded the mind without the need for travel."[4] Most notably, use of the Internet has fundamentally altered both the speed and the cost of communications. Others suggest that it is also helping to democratize access to information, an issue to which we will return.

With respect to the human rights movement, it is clear that the Internet has radically changed (1) the way in which human rights activists and organizations communicate with each other; (2) how they disseminate and/or "publish" their information (which is an aspect of their advocacy and campaigning work); and (3) how they do their research. Each of these three areas will be examined below.

First, however, it is necessary to briefly review the factors that have contributed to the exponential growth in the use of the Internet and its spread to all corners of the globe. Several factors have contributed to this dynamic.

The first is the development of the World Wide Web (the Web), a communications language (or protocol) of the Internet. Unlike other protocols such as Gopher and FTP (File Transfer Protocol), the Web is capable of displaying graphics in full detail and color and with multimedia features, including audio and moving images. Even more important, the Web is capable of presenting hypertext, or hyperlinked information. To the user, hypertext documents provide an endless web of linked information that can be followed in countless directions. In fact hyperlink capacity means that you can readily move between documents regardless of where they are located—whether that is a computer in a nearby city or a computer on the other side of the world.

The second factor contributing to the usability and usefulness of the Internet (directly related to the first) is the development of HyperText Markup Language (HTML). HTML is a simple coding language used both to prepare documentation for Web presentation, and to create the hypertext which links information together. Thus, the Web in general and a Web site in particular are actually a collection of HTML documents. Evidence that HTML is relatively easy to learn and being embraced by millions of individuals is given by Matthew Gray of the Massachusetts Institute of Technology, who notes that the number of Web sites increased from 130 in June 1993 to over 230,000 in June 1996 to over 650,000 in 1997.[5] In effect, HTML has made it possible for individuals, organizations, government bodies, commercial entities, and all persons to self-publish their information and documentation.

A third factor has enhanced the usability and effectiveness of the Web's massive body of information—the development of Web browsers. Browsers, or programs which display the contents of a Web page, are either graphical or text based. Graphical browsers, such as Netscape, Mosaic, and Internet Explorer, are capable of displaying both text and images, and many now play sound and video. Older text-based browsers displayed only text and ignored the graphical content of a Web page. Be it graphical or text based, a browser is the gateway to the World Wide Web, and it is also the means by which the user can obtain a printed version of a page viewed on-line. Overall, since their first limited network use in March 1991 and their commercial licensing in 1994, Web browsers increasingly simplify the task of "surfing" or "browsing" the World Wide Web. When an individual is supported by a good Web browser, minimal computer literacy is required to access information on-line.

Finally, in terms of making the Web's massive information collections more manageable, a fourth factor has enhanced the usability and usefulness of the Internet. The development of "search engines"—programs which routinely index a collection of Web pages—has provided Web users with the ability to tailor their search for information. Search engines on the Web are used as Web-wide indexes (or catalogues) of thousands of existing Web sites, and they are also used as limited, local indexing of any particular site or collection of Web pages. Examples of the former include Alta Vista (*http://www.altavista.com*), Yahoo! (*http://www.yahoo.com*), and Infoseek (*http://www.*

infoseek.com), to name a very few. An example of the latter is the search engine organizations use to render their site searchable by keywords.

The Human Rights Movement and the Internet

The legitimacy and effectiveness of the nongovernmental human rights movement have always rested squarely on the reliability, credibility, comprehensiveness, and timeliness of its information. It is, therefore, not surprising that the Internet, and especially the World Wide Web, have become tools that human rights activists and organizations have taken up to advance the cause of human rights. Initially, at least until late 1996, human rights NGOs regarded the new technology with some skepticism—after all, how helpful is e-mail if those you want or need to contact do not have e-mail addresses?

The Association of Progressive Communicators (APC), a consortium of not-for-profit information providers which began setting up low-cost networks in all regions of the world—for example, International Global Communications (IGC) in the United States, Web networks in Canada, Greenet in the U.K., GlasNet in Russia)[6]—was largely responsible for cajoling progressive movements and organizations into taking the first step in this direction. For example, during the World Conference on Human Rights in Vienna in June 1993, APC ran a training program to expose human rights activists to e-mail.[7] At the Fourth World Conference on Women in Beijing in August–September 1995, it was possible to register for an e-mail account and send and receive messages electronically. By 1996, a snowball effect had begun and, in the two-year period from mid-1997 to mid-1999, almost all major international, regional, and national human rights NGOs, and thousands of others, went on-line. At a minimum, they opened e-mail accounts, and many now have highly developed Web sites.

One landmark development in this process was the launching of a Web site, on December 10, 1996, by the UN Office of the High Commissioner on Human Rights. What was critical here was that, for the first time, NGOs could easily have access to UN human rights documents (e.g., the reports of the special rapporteurs of the Commission on Human Rights, or government reports to the treaty bodies) without having to visit UN headquarters in New York or in Geneva. Another landmark development took place in 1998 when the UN library in the Palais des Nations in Geneva established two large banks of computers with Internet access that could be used by NGOs accredited to the UN.

Impact on Communications

The advent of electronic mail had two immediately obvious effects: it vastly sped up the time it took to communicate with others, especially those at a considerable distance; and it dramatically reduced the cost of such communications. Prior to e-mail, one had to rely on telephone or fax (costly, and often difficult to connect to, because of both line problems and time differences), courier (very expensive) or snail mail (very slow and not always dependable). As the cost of computers fell dramatically, and the cost of line charges dropped significantly, one could be in almost instantaneous contact with colleagues practically anywhere in the world, for a modest price. Furthermore, once organizations mastered the skill of sending and opening attachments from different word-processing programs, very large amounts of data could be rapidly transmitted across the Internet, without any loss of formatting.

As well, with e-mail, and especially the advent of the "listserv"—a mass-mailing technique—information can be communicated to a very large number of people, and at little additional cost, by simply sending one message. It was with the help of e-mail and listservs that Amnesty International (together with the Dalai Lama and the Body Shop) was able to get over 12 million signatures from individuals in all corners of the globe, pledging a commitment to the Universal Declaration of Human Rights (UDHR). This petition was given to UN Secretary-General Kofi Annan during the Defenders Summit in Paris, to commemorate the fiftieth anniversary of the UDHR. Currently, there are hundreds of human rights listservs that one can subscribe to (generally at no cost), some private (which one can join only by invitation), and some public (that anyone can sign onto). Some of these listservs are general in nature (e.g., Huridocs-Gen-I or Derechos-I) but many are specialized, focusing on such subjects as violence against women in war, children's rights, or ethnic cleansing in Kosovo.

E-mail has also, of course, had very significant implications for campaigning and other advocacy work. For example, urgent action networks—of Amnesty International, Casa Alianza, Organisation Mondiale Contre la Torture, the Lawyers Committee for Human Rights, and others—used to rely on mobilizing individuals (often through telephone trees) to send letters, faxes, or telegrams when an individual was at risk of torture, death, or other serious harm. Now, far larger numbers of individuals can be mobilized much more rapidly, and with greater geographic spread, by use of e-mail. On a daily basis, Amnesty International sends Urgent Action cases to all of its national sections, generally by e-mail.[8] Casa Alianza, an organization working with street children in Central America, notes that its Rapid Response e-mail network of over 2,500 people from around the world "DOES WORK! Time and time again we have seen a cause and effect relationship between Rapid Response network letters and an immediate investigation of otherwise dormant cases of violence against street children. In such an integrated and shrinking world, no government—no matter how repressive they may be—can shy away from international pressure."[9]

To take another aspect of campaign work, organizations in different cities, countries, even continents, can now readily collaborate by working together on joint documents or statements, developing common strategies, and launching simultaneous events using electronic communications. While talking via e-mail will never fully replace the need for face-to-face contact—often necessary to build trust between individuals and organizations—once human contacts are established, the Internet has enormously facilitated our ability to stay in touch. This also means that groups or individuals that were largely isolated and cut off from frequent contact with, and information provided by, others can now more easily be brought into a network or relationship in a more systematic way. They can also now regularly send out information about their situation. For example, during the entire period that NATO was bombing Yugoslavia, we received daily e-mail reports from women's organizations in both Belgrade and Priština of the impact of the campaign on women's rights activists.

To some extent, e-mail communications also has an impact on the imperative to travel in order to network or share information. In a brief article on how NGOs can benefit from the Internet, Arun Mehta writes as follows:

Electronic mail cannot entirely replace travel, however, it can make it less frequently necessary and more productive. In decision making relating to policy matters, for instance, the positions of the different sides on an issue can be circulated to all the decision makers (perhaps even the entire membership), who can then discuss it via a mailing list. If consensus can be reached, a meeting becomes unnecessary. If not, a meeting is not avoided, but those who travel are much better informed: they will have all the relevant papers and the benefit of an active discussion and consensus-building process before they even leave home.[10]

One might also note that some human rights organizations have also begun to use tele-conferencing,[11] as a more cost-effective means of sharing information than travelling.

In this regard, we should note that, while in many parts of the world, e-mail communication is still dependent upon telephone lines—which can break down or be interrupted—e-mail can also now be sent via satellite transmission. Given the speed with which cell phones have spread into all corners of the globe, this technology will undoubtedly become cheaper and more accessible in the coming years.

The Internet does have at least one severe disadvantage for human rights organizations? In certain respects, it is easier for governmental authorities to monitor e-mail than it was for them to tap into, and disrupt, telephone or fax communications. However, while governments have become sophisticated enough to intercept—and even alter—e-mail transmissions, encryption technology has in some ways countered and provided some protection against this intrusiveness. Thus, with proper precautions, sensitive information can be transmitted relatively safely.[12]

The Internet as a Publishing Tool

The advent of the World Wide Web clearly had a revolutionary impact on communications and on our ability to disseminate information. Most significant in this respect was the Web's potential to democratize publishing and, therefore, access to information. Harry Cleaver describes, in vivid detail, what is now considered a classic case in this regard—use by the Zapatistas in Chiapas, Mexico, to get their message out to the world.

When the Zapatistas suddenly appeared in San Cristobal de las Casas . . . in the early hours of 1 January 1994, they brought with them a printed declaration of war against the Mexican state and for the liberation of the people of Chiapas and Mexico. News of that declaration went out through a student's telephone call to the Cable News Network; and then as journalists arrived to investigate, stories went out via the wire services, newspaper reports, and radio and television broadcasts all over the world. For the most part, however, readers and viewers of that reporting saw and heard only excerpts from the Zapatista declaration of war. They never saw the whole declaration, with all of its arguments and explanations for what were obviously dramatically surprising and audacious actions. Except for the rare exception, such as the Mexico City daily newspaper *La Jornada*, readers and viewers got only what the editors wanted them to get, according to their own biases.

As the Mexican state poured 15,000 troops into Chiapas and the fighting escalated, this kind of reporting continued. Even after the cease-fire, when the emphasis of the Zapatista offensive shifted from arms to words, the commercial media overwhelmingly refused to reproduce the striking and often eloquent communiqués and letters sent out by the EZLN. . . .

For those in Mexico who read those messages and found them accurate and inspiring, this blockage was an intolerable situation that had to be overcome in order to build support for the Zapatistas and to stop the government's repression. What the supporters did was simple: they typed or scanned the communiqués and letters into e-text form and sent them out over the Net to potentially receptive audiences around the world. Those audiences included, first and foremost, Usenet newsgroups, PeaceNet conferences, and Internet lists whose members were already concerned with Mexico's social and political life; second, humanitarian groupings concerned with human rights generally; third, networks of indigenous people and those sympathetic to them; fourth, those political regions of cyberspace that seemed likely to have members sympathetic to grass-roots revolt in general; and fifth, networks of feminists who would respond with solidarity to the rape of indigenous women by Mexican soldiers or to the EZLNA "Women's Revolutionary Law" drafted by women, for women, within and against a traditionally patriarchal society. Again and again, friendly and receptive readers spontaneously reposted the messages in new places, while sometimes translating the Spanish documents into English and other languages. In this way, the words of the Zapatistas and messages of their communities have been diffused from a few gateways through much of cyberspace.[13]

Cleaver goes on to describe how a self-organized network emerged, of different people involved in uploading, reposting, translating, and so on of Zapatista material to different locations in cyberspace; the development of electronic books on the Zapatista struggle; and then the establishment of a Zapatista Web site and archive, making the material permanently available for reference or study.[14] In short, using the Internet, and especially the Web, made it possible to circumvent the "gatekeepers" of the mass media or the publishing industry.

Indeed, today, anyone with access to the Internet and minimal HTML skills can "publish" almost any information they wish to, since publishing on the Internet is unregulated. Basically, there are no gatekeepers or censors, although some attempts are being made to prohibit the on-line distribution of hate propaganda and pornography, as well as information that can assist terrorists or criminals. Additionally, some authoritarian governments are trying to prevent their citizens from accessing the Internet out of fear that this will destabilize their regimes.[15] These efforts, however, are reminiscent of the proverbial Dutch boy attempting to plug the holes in the dike with his fingers. They will, at best, delay the distribution of information—not stop it. If we consider how, only ten years ago, "samizdat" (i.e., underground publications in Eastern and Central Europe) had to be reproduced largely on manual typewriters with carbon paper, and then smuggled abroad for redissemination, we get some idea of the distance that we have travelled.

Far more problematic is an unintentional negative aspect to the lack of regulation: namely, while there is an enormous amount of useful information on the Net, there is also a heap of rubbish in cyberspace. Anyone who has navigated the Net will know how much time can be wasted in sifting through what potentially looked interesting, but turns out to be irrelevant, trivial, or unreliable information. Of course, this is also true of the print and audiovisual media. Just as one had to learn which authors, publishers, newspapers, radio and television programs were worth reading, listening to, or watching, so one has to learn which Web sites, newsgroups, or conferences are worth visiting for the information one needs.

Two things are, however, different with the Net. The first is the speed of change. Web sites and electronic conferences are in perpetual motion: not only is new information being constantly posted but sites disappear and new ones emerge daily. The second is the magnitude of the potentially relevant information which can lead to information overload.[16]

This, of course, also provides an opportunity for commercial entrepreneurship. With such a large audience of potential consumers, information providers such as America On-Line not only give you dial-in access to the Internet, but they play an increasingly important role in organizing the information for you. As *Globe and Mail* columnist Robert Everett-Green recently pointed out, by structuring the menus that you see when you log on, these information providers are establishing a hierarchy of attention, predetermining what you should think is important.[17] They are both writing the headlines and acting as gatekeepers. For while it is true that the Net is unregulated and anyone can post anything, the likelihood that a piece of information will be read—given the vast amount of information in cyberspace—is increasingly related to the extent to which it is advertised and how much visibility it gets on the menu structure.[18]

For human rights organizations and other progressive groups, this means that reaching those you want to reach by publishing on the Internet involves more than creating a simple home page on the Net. One has to think strategically how to reach the people one wants to reach with this information, and then invest the time and effort needed to do so. While the expectation today is that information should be made available free of charge, putting information onto the Web is not cheap. To maintain and promote a well-designed and continually updated Web site takes thought, time, and resources.

Using the Web for Research

The third area in which the Internet has had an impact on how human rights organizations function is in the area of research. This is the other side of publishing—how to find the information you need. Of course, what the Web can never replace is on-the-ground fact-finding. If one wants to know whether a massacre actually occurred in a village in Kosovo, in camps in eastern Zaire, or in the jungles of Chiapas, one has to go and find out what really happened—interview refugees, witnesses, survivors; take affidavits; disinter mass graves and take photographs of the grisly remains. In short, the Internet can not replace primary research. It can, however, help enormously with secondary research.

In the past, the first thing that one did with a new project, or to prepare for a new mission, was to go to a library—either the organization's own library or a university or public one. Now, the first step is to go to the Web. The library is usually the second or the third step—to locate older or more analytical material. For this reason, doing effective research today means knowing how to find your way around the Web. As noted above, this means not only knowing how to use search engines effectively, but knowing which sites one can trust, which sites will provide reliable links to other relevant sites, and which organizations maintain directories that are gateways or portals to the information you need.

In the human rights area, there are four sites that are particularly useful in this regard. These are the directories of human rights sites maintained by Human Rights Internet (*http://www.hri.ca/coldfusion/cfidir/*) and the American Association for the Advancement of Science (*http://shr.aaas.org/dhr.htm*), and the sites of Project Diana at the University of Minnesota (*http://www1.umn.edu/humanrts/links/links.htm*) and of the High Commissioner for Human Rights (*http://www.unhchr.ch*). These are excellent points of entry for much human rights research.

In this context, one should note that not everything one needs is available free of charge on the Web. For example, while one can access many newspapers on-line free of charge on the day, week, or month that they are published, downloading material from the archives of many of these newspapers is now on a fee or subscription basis. For example, to download a single article from the archives of the *New York Times* (whether by printing or by saving the file to a disk) costs $2.50. Access to many commercial databases remains on a subscription basis and can be costly. To illustrate, Lexis-Nexis Canada charges $110/hour to access Canadian and Australian news, legal, and business information, and $230/hour to access legal materials from the United States, U.K., and Commonwealth. This does not include "premium materials" for which the cost is $297/hour.[19]

Particularly disturbing in this context is the fact that access to the United Nations Optical Disk System (ODS)—which is the multilingual archive of UN documentation, now available on-line—is only accessible to nongovernmental organizations, even those in consultative status, for an annual subscription fee. (It is available free to government missions in New York or Geneva.) The fee is $1,500/year; accredited NGOs receive a 20 percent discount. This makes it largely inaccessible to most human rights NGOs and especially those in the South.[20] Moreover, as of March 2000 the UN Department of Public Information, which manages the ODS and other UN databases, has begun to charge a similar subscription fee for access to the treaty databases, formerly available on the Web at no charge. As this is the most reliable and up-to-date source of information on which governments have signed which international treaties and with what reservations, taking this information out of the public realm in this way is a major backward step with respect to our right to information.

Conclusions

Considering the implications of the Internet for human rights work, one must acknowledge that, as radically as the Internet has changed how human rights activists gather and disseminate information, and how they communicate with each other, the Internet is just one more tool in the struggle for human rights. It is a tool that has facilitated communications worldwide, and has had a significant impact on how one does campaigning and/or research. But if one asks whether the Internet has enhanced the effectiveness of human rights NGOs and what real effect it has had on the protection of those whose rights are violated or at risk of violation—one needs to be cautious in one's response.

By and large, the information one has at present is anecdotal. Little systematic research has as yet been published, although in the past year, Human Rights Internet has been contacted by at least a dozen students or researchers investigating precisely this question. When their results are published, we will perhaps be in a better position to draw specific conclusions.

There is still, however, an enormous amount of work that needs to be done both to train ourselves and to remain on top of technological changes, but especially to ensure that colleagues in the South, and those on the front lines of the human rights struggle, have access to this technology as well. This means ensuring that they have the necessary resources to invest in the equipment needed to access the Internet; that they have the skills and expertise necessary to exploit the Internet as a medium of publishing and of research; and that repressive regimes are not able to restrict their access to the Net or interfere with the communications they send or receive.[21]

Strategically used, the Internet should be able to advance our fight against gross violations of human rights significantly. It also has enormous potential as a tool for education, which is vital to the creation of a human rights culture.

What is clear is that human rights organizations cannot afford to ignore a tool that has so fundamentally altered the ways in which we communicate or gather and disseminate information, given the central importance of information to the credibility and legitimacy of human rights NGOs. Moreover, it is clear that both governments and the private sector have made major investments in this area, and human rights NGOs cannot afford to stand on the sidelines of such developments without themselves being sidelined.

Notes

1. Suman Naresh, "Ethics and the Digital Divide," *Sources* 110 (published by UNESCO, March 1999), p. 8.

2. Neil Randall, "The World Wide Web: Interface on the Internet," in *Discover the World Wide Web with Your Sportster*, 2nd ed. (Indianapolis, Ind.: Sams.net Publishing, 1996), p. 4.

3. Network Wizards Internet Domain Survey: *www.nw.com* stated there were 43,230,000 hosts in January 1999.

4. Richard P. Claude, letter to the author, March 4, 1996.

5. *http://www.mit.edu/~mkgray/*.

6. *http://www.apc.org/english/members.html.*

7. There is an interesting e-mail dated December 24, 1993, from Debra Guzman, at that time APC's human rights coordinator, entitled Human Rights Network (HRNet). In it, Guzman explains the concept of HRNet—a new independent project she was creating—to scan a wide range of sources on computer networks and listservs and redisseminate this to human rights activists, either in the form of e-mail or by posting it in sixteen different human rights conferences.

8. "AAI and the use of the Internet and email," January 20, 1998, by Pam Clarke, Information Officer - Asia, Amnesty International, Information Resources Program, sent by e-mail.

9. Casa Allianza/Covenant House, "Welcome to rapid-response," February 13, 1998, e-mail message.

10. Arun Mehta, "How an NGO Could Benefit from the Internet," June 22, 1999, posted at *http://www.cerfnet.com/~amehta/ngo.htm.*

11. For example, the UN Development Fund for Women (UNIFEM) recently organized a world-wide teleconference on violence against women.

12. Cindy Cohen, "Who's Listening? Why Human Rights Workers Should Care About the U.S. Cryptography Battles," forthcoming in *Human Rights Tribune*, vol. 6, no. 3.

13. Harry Cleaver, "The Zapatistas and the Electronic Fabric of Struggle," circa 1995. On-line at *http://www.eco.utexas.edu/Homepages/Faculty/Cleaver/*.

14. Cleaver points to the EZLN home page: *http://www.peak.org/~justin/ezln.html.*

15. Human Rights Watch, *Silencing the Net: The Threat to Freedom of Expression On-Line* (New York: Human Rights Watch, May 10, 1996). Information on attempts to censor the net is regularly published on *http://www.eff.org/~declan/fight-censorship/*.

16. To illustrate with an anecdote, I recently searched the Web using Alta Vista (one of the most popular search engines) for "AIDS and human rights," assuming there would be a moderate amount of information. Alta Vista reported over 200,000 hits; I narrowed the search to Uganda and AIDS and still came up with more than 20,000 hits.

17. Robert Everett-Green, telephone call with the author, October 25, 1996.

18. This notwithstanding, with a modest amount of advertising, during the first month that Human Rights Internet (HRI) had its Web site up, it had over 17,000 hits. This was in 1997. Presently the site receives over 750,000 hits a month.

19. This information was faxed to HRI on July 2, 1999, in response to its request for information, as the rates are not listed on the Web.

20. Laurie S. Wiseberg, " 'Pay to Download': The UN's Optical Disk System Too Costly for NGOs," *Human Rights Tribune* 4, nos. 2–3 (1997), p. 48.

21. See Naresh, "Ethics and the Digital Divide," p. 8.

Chapter 13
The Role of the Ford Foundation

William D. Carmichael

As earlier chapters of this volume have noted, the Ford Foundation has been a major actor in the construction of the burgeoning global community of nongovernmental organizations (NGOs) in human rights and related fields. Since the mid-1970s, Ford grants have played key roles in the launching and early nurturing of several of the most prominent international human rights organizations, including Human Rights Watch, and many, if not most, such organizations are current recipients of Ford Foundation funding. In addition, through its extensive network of overseas offices, the foundation has been a critically important source of sustained support for scores of human rights NGOs in Africa, Asia, and Latin America and, during the past decade, in Russia and Central Europe.

The importance of the Ford Foundation's role in the human rights arena derives, in part, from the disturbingly fragile nature of the financial underpinnings of most human rights NGOs. With the notable exception of Amnesty International, with its substantial membership base, most international (or "northern") human rights NGOs are heavily dependent on continued funding from a worrisomely small number of foundations and affluent individual supporters. A small minority of such organizations, and a considerably larger portion of NGOs in less developed regions, rely heavily on grants from "rights-friendly" governments and intergovernmental bodies for substantial shares of their revenues. But a common characteristic of almost all human rights and rights-related NGOs is a jerry-built funding structure of questionable solidity and durability. Against that backdrop, Ford Foundation support, which has been sustained over a twenty-five-year period and will surely continue well into the new millennium, has made a critically important contribution to the development, and growing impact, of the global human rights movement.

Because of the centrality of the Ford Foundation's role as a funder of many of the organizations that are the focus of the preceding chapters, the origins and evolution of its work in the human rights field may be of particular interest to the readers of this volume. Accordingly, in the pages below, I will attempt to address, in very brief compass, each of the following questions: (1) What considerations lay behind the decision, taken by the foundation's Board of Trustees in 1975, to launch a new initiative in the field of human rights? (2) How has that undertaking evolved over the ensuing twenty-five years and what range of activities has it encompassed? (3) What can be said about the results of the foundation's very substantial investments in human rights and related fields? And (4) what are some of the principal concerns that will guide the foundation's continuing commitment to the advancement of human rights norms and practice and the strengthening of vibrant NGOs engaged in that work?

The Foundation's Decision to Work on International Human Rights Issues

From its earliest days as a major funding organization, the Ford Foundation has been publicly committed to the assistance of rights-related endeavors. Support for activities aimed at establishing "a world order of law and justice" and securing "greater allegiance to the basic principles of freedom and democracy" figured prominently among the guidelines approved by the foundation's trustees in 1949 for the greatly expanded program that the infusion of new monies from the final settlement of Henry Ford's estate permitted.[1] Since the early 1950s, under various programmatic rubrics, grants in pursuit of those aims have constituted a principal thrust of the foundation's work in the United States. But it was not until the mid-1970s that the foundation's international program and its grant making in developing countries provided funding for activities with explicit human rights objectives.

During its early years as a large foundation, the foundation's international work was strongly influenced by Cold War considerations.[2] Its decision, in the mid-1950s, to establish field offices and launch substantial programs in Asia and the Middle East stemmed from the judgment that major initiatives to spur economic development and improve the effectiveness of development-related governmental agencies were urgently needed to enable key countries in those regions to resist "the advancing tide of communist domination." The extension of the foundation's overseas work to several newly independent African nations in the early 1960s reflected similar concerns. And, paralleling the thinking embodied in the U.S. government's Alliance for Progress, the foundation's decision to open field offices and assist development efforts in several Latin American settings was a response, at least in part, to mounting concerns about Castro's Cuba and communist expansion in the Western Hemisphere.

Not surprisingly, in light of their origins and initial rationales, the foundation's programs in most overseas settings in the 1950s and 1960s were focused primarily on state institutions. Planning ministries and similar governmental bodies were seen as the foundation's most obvious partners, as were other governmental agencies engaged in development and poverty alleviation work. In the usual case, foundation assistance placed heavy emphasis on the provision of foreign "experts," complemented by overseas training for key members of the agency in question and, on occasion, by the development of relevant training programs in appropriate national institutions. In many, if not most, Asian and African settings, moreover, procedures were established under which the formal approval of a governmental "assistance coordinating" body was required prior to awarding of a Ford grant.

An obvious corollary of this partnership with host governments of various political stripes was a hesitancy or unwillingness, on the foundation's part, to enter fields of activity or propose specific grant actions that might incur the displeasure of senior host government officials. Under such arrangements, prudence dictated that the foundation assistance be restricted to technically sound and noncontroversial objectives that would readily elicit government approval and assure a continuing welcome for the foundation's program activities and staff. And under such strictures, assistance for human rights groups, which could readily, indeed accurately, be perceived as opposing certain national policies and governmental practices, was clearly off limits.

By the late 1960s, however, the situation had begun to change, particularly in Latin America. From the very beginning of its work in that region in 1961, for obvious historical reasons, the foundation's partnerships with host governments were more limited, and thus less restricting, than in the typical Asian or African setting. Although government planning agencies and development-oriented ministries in several countries (including Brazil, Chile, Colombia, and Venezuela) were recipients of Ford assistance, universities and other research institutions with looser or no government ties rapidly became the principal focus of foundation grant making in Latin America. And it is in the evolution of its support for university-based teaching and research, particularly in the social sciences, that important early harbingers of the foundation's entry into the human rights field can be identified.

Although democratically elected governments held sway in much of Latin America in 1961, a series of coups over the ensuing twelve-year period resulted in the installation of repressive military regimes in many of the countries in which the foundation was most active. And at one point or another—in Argentina in the early 1960s, in Brazil in 1969, and in Chile in 1973—the military governments "intervened" in universities, with seriously disruptive consequences for foundation-assisted programs in those institutions. Professors, many of whom had been trained and/or supported in their research activities with Ford funds, were fired and in some instances jailed or forced to seek haven in other countries. Graduate training programs, some of which had been developed with Ford funding for many years, were gutted of staff and students or otherwise compelled to close down. And the freedom of inquiry essential for effective teaching and research was curtailed in countless other ways.

The immediate foundation response to such instances of governmental intervention took two forms. The first was to fund various mechanisms that would enable academic staff members for whom leaving the country was the only viable option to find gainful employ abroad. The second, when conditions permitted, was to fund independent research institutions, most of them newly created, that would permit the displaced scholars to remain professionally active in "internal exile" in their home countries. In an earlier paper, I have discussed the use of the latter approach in responding to the

Brazilian government's university interventions in 1969.[3] And in a book analyzing the key roles that intellectuals played in engineering a successful return to democracy in Chile some seventeen years after the Pinochet coup of 1973, Jeffrey Puryear (a former Ford Foundation staff member) examines the "internal exile" strategy in considerable detail and notes that an important aim of that strategy was to help "keep critical, independent thought alive in Chile during the dictatorship, and to nurture policy expertise for a future democratic regime."[4]

The university interventions and other repressive actions of military regimes in Argentina, Brazil, Chile, and elsewhere in Latin America in the 1960s and early 1970s had at least two additional, and more far-reaching, consequences for the foundation's program activities. In a period in which the wisdom of relying solely on governmental agencies to address development needs was increasingly questioned on other counts, the university interventions underscored the need for strong nongovernmental institutions for the purpose, inter alia, of preserving freedom of inquiry and expression. The interventions also made it abundantly clear that, in the absence of effective mechanisms for restraining the repressive urges of several of the foundation's host governments, many of the otherwise laudable development initiatives that the foundation was assisting were at great risk of being thwarted.

At a gathering of the Ford Foundation's International Division staff in late 1974, these concerns were the subject of considerable debate. In a paper prepared for that gathering, foundation staff member David Heaps recited the traditional arguments for refraining from activities that might be viewed with disfavor by host governments in some overseas settings. But he also presented strong arguments in favor of foundation support for human rights research and related activities by United States and Europe–based organizations.[5] Not surprisingly, particularly in light of the divergent courses that the foundation's overseas programs were then pursuing in different parts of the world, reactions to the latter proposal were mixed. In the ensuing months, however, the Ford Foundation's president, McGeorge Bundy, and other senior staff members endorsed the principal recommendations representations of the Heaps paper, and in early 1976 the trustees' approval was sought and obtained for a special appropriation of $500,000 for "a new effort to advance human rights and intellectual freedom."[6]

The Evolution of the Ford Foundation's Human Rights Program Since 1976

Although the specific grants that were authorized and funded by the 1976 appropriation were quite limited in scope, the consequences of the board's approval of that action proved to be far greater than its limited purposes and dollar magnitude initially suggested. Most of the grants that were awarded under the appropriation supported research, conferences, and publications that were unlikely to raise the hackles of the foundation's host, or partner, governments overseas.[7] But the endorsement of grant making for international human rights purposes that the trustees' action signaled opened the door for a much more diverse and action-oriented array of actions that have indeed constituted a major element of the foundation's program over the ensuing quarter century.

Within a very few years of the approval of the modestly scaled 1976 appropriation, human rights was transposed from the distant wings to center stage in the Ford Foundation's program. In a major revision of the foundation's programmatic focus and organizational structure in 1981, "human rights and social justice" was identified as one of six major themes for future grant making and, paired with "governance and public policy," as one of the five principal units of the foundation's Program Division. In announcing those changes, the foundation's president, Franklin Thomas, stated that "fundamental civil and political liberties, and economic, social and cultural rights are at the center of the Foundation's vision of a just and humane world." Thomas also pointedly observed that "work to establish or protect these rights" should be seen as reinforcing other efforts to reduce the poverty and suffering of the disadvantaged.[8]

Complementing a vigorous program in support of rights initiatives in the United States, the foundation's grant making in the field of international human rights has extended support to a wide range of institutions extending well beyond the NGOs, both international (or "northern") and developing country–based (or "southern") that are the focus of this volume. Although the complexities of the foundation's grant-categorizing rubrics make it almost impossible to quantify the dimensions of its work in any given field, it may be conservatively estimated that the foundation has committed funds in excess of $200 million for work in the international human rights arena over the past twenty-five years. Grants to broadly focused human rights NGOs, based both in the United States or Europe and in developing countries, probably account for at least half of that sum. But much of the support that the foundation has provided under the human rights rubric has been earmarked for organizations focusing on particular target groups (e.g., women, ethnic minorities, refugees and migrants, or indigenous peoples) or issues (e.g., freedom of expression, labor rights, or reproductive rights). Under the human rights heading, sizeable sums have also been allocated to nascent public interest law groups in various developing country settings and to organizations providing legal services to individuals and groups with limited access to such services. And academic research and university-based training programs in human rights issues and related dimensions of international law have continued to claim a significant portion of the foundation's budget for international human rights work.

Over the twenty-five-year period, New York–based foundation staff, in consultation with their overseas colleagues, have gained approval for grants to a considerable array of NGOs headquartered in the United States and Europe with broadly focused rights-monitoring and advocacy missions. In the United States, Human Rights Watch, the (New York–based) Lawyers Committee for Human Rights, Physicians for Human Rights, and the International Human Rights Law Group figure prominently on that list. In Europe, the principal grantee in that category has been the Geneva-headquartered

International Commission of Jurists, but in recent years substantial funding has also been provided to the Vienna-based Helsinki Federation for Human Rights.[9]

For a number of readily discernable reasons, grants to human rights and rights-related NGOs in developing countries (and, over the past decade, in Russia and the formerly communist countries of Central Europe) have claimed very substantial shares of available budgets in some settings and very modest shares in others. Differences in the degree of political openness, the urgency of rights issues, and the strength and promise of the local NGO communities account for most of those differences, but internal factors associated with the foundation's staffing patterns and the history of its programs in particular settings have also been at play. During most of the past twenty-five years, the foundation's offices in Latin America have devoted larger percentages of their budgets to human rights and related concerns than their counterparts in Asia and Africa.[10] But in the latter continents, there are marked differences among the several countries in which the foundation works. In China, for example, where there is very little political space for such undertakings, explicitly rights-oriented activities have not been a part of the foundation's program, while in South Africa, prior to the advent of majority rule in 1994, human rights and legal services endeavors constituted the principal thrust of the foundation's program.

In part because of the insights that it may offer for an assessment of the impact of the foundation's human rights grant making (a topic to which we shall turn below), the South Africa initiative merits special attention in this brief account of the evolution of the foundation's human rights program.[11] Of some fifty South African NGOs that received Ford assistance between 1977 and 1994, a considerable portion were engaged in explicitly rights-related initiatives—the provision of legal services for victims of discriminatory legislation and repressive government practices, related "test case" litigation, and a wide array of rights education activities.[12] As noted in internal documents requesting approval for grants to those organizations, foundation support was provided with several objectives in view. One important aim was to spur the development of legal remedies that, in spite of South Africa's institutionalized discrimination and widespread rights abuses, could improve the quality of life of black South Africans in the immediate term. Another was to help build, for the longer term, a deeper understanding of the importance of the rule of law and to demonstrate to South Africans of all races that law can be effectively employed to confront discrimination and repression. And a third was to help develop, among the staff members of grantee organizations, a set of skills and a body of experience that would be of value both in spearheading the dismantlement of apartheid rule and in assuring a cadre of able, human rights–attuned leaders for post-apartheid South Africa. As noted below, from today's vantage point those objectives appear to have been realized in impressive measure, and the success of the South African undertaking has served as an important impetus for continued foundation efforts in the human rights field.

In recounting the evolution of the Ford Foundation's human rights program over the past quarter century, its support for a growing array of NGOs focusing on particular target groups and rights issues should also be highlighted. Since the early 1980s, mirroring an earlier major commitment to the advancement of the roles and status of women in the United States, grants in support of women's rights initiatives have claimed increasingly substantial shares of the funds allocated for international grant making in New York and of the budgets of most of the foundation's overseas offices. NGOs focusing on freedom of expression issues (e.g., Article 19 Research and Information Centre on Censorship, and Writers and Scholars Educational Trust) have also been recipients of Ford funding over sustained periods, as have organizations seeking to protect the rights of refugees and migrants and of indigenous people. And in recent years NGOs specializing in economic and social rights issues (e.g., housing and education) have begun to appear with increasing frequency in the annual listings of foundation grantees.

Recent Ford Foundation publications provide abundant evidence that the vigorous support for human rights NGOs and related activities that has been a central element of the foundation's program since 1976 is being steadfastly maintained. In the fall 1998 issue of the foundation's newsletter, which was devoted to a "Special Report on Human Rights," Bradford K. Smith, the vice president in charge of the Peace and Social Justice Program (in which human rights grant making is now lodged), assured his readers that, "In its reorganization in 1996, the Foundation recommitted its resources to the global fight for justice and human rights."[13] Substantiating that assertion, the newsletter profiled a small sampling of the many foundation-assisted NGOs in Africa, Asia, Central Europe, and Latin America that are at the forefront of the struggle to realize the vision set forth in the Universal Declaration of Human Rights in 1948.[14] Grant listings in the foundation's recent annual reports identify more than fifty NGOs (northern and southern) that are engaged in international human rights work with Ford Foundation support. And in mid-1999, as if to emphasize Smith's point, the foundation approved a grant to Human Rights Watch that includes a $5 million contribution to its endowment and an additional $1 million for its operating reserves.

Assessing the Impact of Ford Foundation Funding of Human Rights NGOs

Determining the impact of foundation grant making for whatever purpose is by no stretch of the imagination a science, nor is it a simple task. In attempting to assess the consequences of twenty-five years of Ford Foundation funding for NGOs in the international human rights arena, one possible approach would be to review each (or a substantial fraction) of the many hundreds of grants that the foundation has made for that purpose, examining the particular activities that each grant facilitated and the outcomes of those activities. A second possibility would be to assess changes in the effectiveness of major categories, or clusters, of grantees over the period in which they have received substantial foundation funding and then attempt to ascertain the degree to which those changes may be attributed to the foundation's support. And a third, even more speculative approach would be to identify important advances in the protection of human rights over the twenty-five-year period and then try to estimate the role that Ford grants have played in bringing about those gains.

Each of these approaches is fraught with problems. The first, case by case, methodology would require Herculean efforts of dubious cost-effectiveness—well beyond anything that the foundation has itself attempted. The second and third approaches, although more conjectural in nature, would appear to offer greater promise. They, too, of course, lie well beyond the scope of this limited survey. But they do suggest a framework for observations below.

What may be said, first of all, about the role of Ford Foundation funding in enhancing the effectiveness of three major clusters of organizations in the international human rights field—the major broadly focused United States– and Europe-based NGOs, the burgeoning community of NGOs based in developing countries and former communist states, and the more narrowly targeted, "special purpose" organizations? With regard to the first of those clusters, it is important to note that some of the most visible and productive international human rights organizations, including Human Rights Watch and the Lawyers Committee for Human Rights (both of which were founded in 1978), have been recipients of Ford funding over their entire institutional life spans.[15] Other American foundations, both large and small, have also played major roles in nurturing the rapid development of these organizations, particularly in recent years,[16] and Ford Foundation assistance now covers only modest shares of their total operating budgets (less that five percent in the case of Human Rights Watch).[17] But it is surely incontrovertible that sustained Ford funding has made a major contribution to the growing effectiveness of several major international human rights NGOs. And it may also be argued that the foundation's willingness to fund examinations of organizational and management issues and comprehensive strategic planning exercises, as it has for Human Rights Watch,[18] has played a significant role in helping such organizations respond to rapidly changing challenges and opportunities in the human rights field.

Ford funding has been a particularly crucial factor in the growth of human rights and rights-related NGOs in Africa, Asia, and Latin America and, during the past decade, in Russia and Central Europe. Because of its extensive network of overseas offices and field-based staff,[19] the foundation has had the capacity, unmatched by any other nongovernmental funder, to identify and assist scores of the most promising of such organizations in the very early stages of their development. For some of them, foundation funding has constituted (and, in some instances, still accounts for) worrisomely large portions of their total revenues. Fortunately, however, on the basis of their accomplishments with initial Ford support, many of them have succeeded in marshaling substantial additional funding from other private and governmental sources. As noted below, very few of these institutions have yet realized their full potential, but Ford funding has most certainly played a central role in facilitating their rapid emergence as increasingly vital elements of the international human rights movement.

In any examination of the consequences of the foundation's human rights program, the foundation's role in supporting NGOs focusing on the rights of particular target groups and issues requires special note. Most notably in the domain of women's rights, but also in the fields of indigenous rights and freedom of expression and in other areas as well, the foundation has aided a substantial fraction of the major institutional players. Similarly, foundation funding for organizations monitoring rights abuses in the former Yugoslavia and in Rwanda has made noteworthy contributions to the labors of the International Criminal Tribunals for those areas, and Ford funding for the Coalition for an International Criminal Court helped propel the recent creation of the latter body.

In concluding this necessarily condensed stocktaking of the consequences of Ford support for human rights NGOs, a brief revisiting of the foundation's work in South Africa may offer some additional insights. As noted above, the foundation was a major funder of many of the NGOs within that country that played key roles in challenging the policies, and indeed the legitimacy, of the apartheid regime. It also assisted a substantial portion of the efforts of international human rights NGOs to focus the world's attention on rights abuses in South Africa and mobilize support for the imposition of economic and political sanctions.[20] Although the factors accounting for the earlier-than-anticipated demise of the apartheid regime will be the subject of continuing debate, there is strong reason to believe that the labors of foundation-funded NGOs, both inside and outside the country, were significant forces in hastening the advent of majority rule. And of equal importance, in the view of this observer, foundation-assisted human rights and rights-related NGOs did indeed serve (as had been hoped) as training grounds for an impressive array of rights-attuned leaders who have assumed key governmental posts in the post-apartheid era.[21]

Ford's Continuing Role in Supporting International Human Rights Initiatives

Although the Ford Foundation's very sizable investments in international human rights initiatives over the past twenty-five years have produced impressive results, its trustees and staff are well aware that much more needs to be done to assure the continued vitality and enhance the effectiveness of the international human rights movement. Key NGOs in each of the clusters noted above require further strengthening. Advocacy strategies must be sensitively adapted to important changes in the context in which those organizations are laboring, and mechanisms that offer NGOs more influential roles in rights-related policy debates and decision-making processes must be expanded and more fully utilized. New opportunities, including those associated with the recent development of promising instruments for bringing perpetrators of particularly egregious human rights crimes to justice, must be vigorously exploited. Economic and social rights need systematic attention, and improved methodologies must be developed for measuring performance in attaining those rights. And new and expanded clienteles must be mobilized for human rights work, both to give more persuasive voice to rights concerns in policy debates and to assure stronger and more diverse financial support for the international human rights movement.

Over the next several years, the foundation's grant making will almost certainly reflect those several needs and opportunities. The end of the Cold War, the globalization of the world economy, and the preeminence of trade among the foreign policy concerns of the United States and other governments have already produced dramatic shifts in the advocacy strategies of the major international NGOs. But several of those organizations, with deservedly strong reputations for the quality of their research, documentation, and reporting work, will need continued financial support of their quests for more consequential roles in debate and policy formation on important rights issues. And in the search for workable solutions for a broad range of such issues, efforts to build coalitions between human rights NGOs and "like-minded" small and medium-sized states, such as those that played crucial roles in mobilizing support for the 1997 land mine treaty and the 1998 agreement for the establishment of an International Criminal Court,[22] will be particularly attractive candidates for Ford Foundation funding.

Unusually promising NGOs in developing countries and formerly communist states will also require continued Ford funding, not only for their rights-monitoring and advocacy work in their own national settings but also for their efforts to play more influential roles in the global human rights movement. In that regard, the development of more effective, mutually beneficial partnerships and division of labor between those organizations and United States–based and Europe-based NGOs may also merit foundation assistance. In a similar vein, "special purpose" NGOs at the forefront of work on women's rights, the rights of indigenous peoples, or other issues in need of special attention will require further institutional strengthening, and promising initiatives that incorporate such organizations in broader, "mainstream" efforts to address emerging rights issues (e.g., in the economic and social rights spheres) will claim the attention of Ford grant makers.

In the continuing struggle to make perpetrators of genocide, crimes against humanity, and war crimes accountable for their actions, the work of the International Criminal Tribunals for the former Yugoslavia and for Rwanda and the 1998 agreement for the establishment of an International Criminal Court offer new promise. Similarly, the arrest of General Augusto Pinochet, the former Chilean dictator, in the United Kingdom in October 1998 and Spain's attempt to bring him to trial have breathed new life into well-established international law norms under which crimes against humanity are offenses of "universal jurisdiction" and their perpetrators are subject to prosecution in any competent court. Attempts to make effective use of the opportunities thus presented for the development of more effective instruments of accountability and deterrence are also likely to be high-priority candidates for foundation support.

Over the past twenty-five years, with a few notable exceptions, economic and social rights have received little or no attention on the agendas of Ford-funded human rights NGOs. Recent foundation publications suggest that modest steps have been taken to correct that imbalance, which, inter alia, has been a source of divisiveness in the global human rights movement. Several foundation grantees that, up to now, have focused their labors almost exclusively on civil and political rights issues, are groping for effective strategies and tools for including economic and social rights in their agendas. Over the next several years, support for those initiatives, and for the work of other organizations concentrating on economic and social rights issues, will surely occupy an increasingly prominent place in the foundation's human rights program.

Among the most important challenges confronting human rights NGOs is the pressing need to broaden the base of committed supporters on whom they can draw both in their work in policy arenas and in their unending quest for expanded and more secure and durable funding. The urgency of that challenge derives in part from the aging of a generation of initial supporters, for many of whom dedication to the human rights cause was forged by the horrors of the Holocaust and World War II. The foundation's attentiveness to the need for expanded constituencies and broader and more secure financial underpinnings for human rights NGOs has long been manifested in various ways, including its recent contributions to the endowment campaigns of Human Rights Watch and other major grantees. In the years immediately ahead, promising initiatives to broaden constituencies and enlist new funders for human rights NGOs will be strong contenders for foundation assistance. As such efforts meet with success, Ford Foundation grants will cover diminishing shares of the budgets of the impressive array of organizations that are the focus of this volume. But in pursing the agenda outlined here, the foundation will surely remain a major contributor to growing vitality and accomplishments of the international human rights movement.

Notes

1. *Report of the* Study *for the Ford Foundation on Policy and Program* (Detroit: Ford Foundation, 1949), pp. 52, 62, and passim.

2. See, for example, "The President's Review," in *Ford Foundation Annual Report, 1953,* pp. iv–v.

3. "The Work of U.S. Foundations in Internationalizing the Rule of Law and the Protection of Human Rights," a paper prepared for a conference on "New Challenges for the Rule of Law: Lawyers, Internationalization, and the Social Construction of Legal Rules," sponsored by the American Bar Foundation and held at the University of California, Santa Barbara, in November 1997.

4. Jeffrey Puryear, *Thinking Politics—Intellectuals and Democracy in Chile, 1973–1988* (Baltimore: Johns Hopkins University Press, 1994), p. 51.

5. In recommending that course of action, however, Heaps explicitly rejected the proposal that Ford Foundation support be provided to "dissident" local organizations engaged in overt or covert opposition to oppressive national policies. The Heaps paper is on file in the foundation's archives.

6. That appropriation, which was approved in March 1976, was supplemented by an additional $1,000,000 in December of that year. In referring to those actions, the foundation's 1976 *Annual Report* noted that they were both "an extension of . . . longstanding efforts to aid scholars whose work is disrupted in their countries" and a "response to increasing acts of political repression throughout the world." *Ford Foundation Annual Report, 1976,* p. 55.

7. Recipients of those grants included the Index on Censorship, for continued research on media censorship; the London-based Minority Rights Group, for an expanded research and publications program; the Paris-based International Association for Cultural Freedom, for programs in defense of artistic and intellectual liberty; the International Commission of Jurists, for a conference in which Central and East African government officials examined ways to safeguard the rule of law in one-party states; and New York University, for the participation of American and European legal scholars in a symposium on the prospect of written guarantees for human rights in the United Kingdom. But the special appropriation also funded a grant to the University of Minnesota for a program enabling young professionals in law and related disciplines to serve as interns in major rights-monitoring and advocacy organizations. See *Ford Foundation Annual Report, 1976,* p. 55.

8. "The President's Review," in *Ford Foundation Annual Report, 1980,* pp. viii–ix.

9. Recent Ford Foundation publications have also noted a grant of $150,000 to Amnesty International (United Kingdom) for "regional seminars and a conference on human rights in Africa" (*Ford Foundation Report* 30, no. 1 [winter 1999], p. 32) and a $200,000 grant to the United States chapter of Amnesty International (Amnesty International of the USA) "to support advocacy of human rights around the world" (*1997 Ford Foundation Annual Report,* p. 90).

10. During the 1980s, in an effort to stimulate grant making in human rights, several Ford Foundation staff members with extensive experience in that field in Latin America were reassigned to key posts in Asia and Africa, where human rights work had not been a significant part of the foundation's program. The results of that strategy were mixed, but human rights has claimed increasing portions of field office budgets in several African and Asian settings since the mid-1980s.

11. The Ford Foundation's human rights work in South Africa is examined in greater detail in the paper cited in note 3 above. The observations in this paragraph are drawn from that paper.

12. Recipients of Ford Foundation grants for human rights work in South Africa during the 1977–94 period included: the Black Sash, for volunteer-staffed "advice offices" in several cities that counseled individual clients on such matters as pass law violations and housing and pension rights; the Transvaal Rural Action Committee, for assistance to black communities threatened with removal from "white" rural areas; the law faculty of the University of Natal, for an innovative "street law" program and training courses for black union leaders; and two capstone "public interest law" organizations—the Legal Resources Trust (LRT) and the University of the Witwatersrand's Centre for Applied Legal Studies (CALS).

13. *Ford Foundation Report* 29, no. 3 (fall 1998), p. 8.

14. NGOs profiled in ibid. included the Black Sash and the Community Law Centre in South Africa, the Constitutional Rights Project in Nigeria, the Indonesian Women's Association for Justice, the Helsinki Foundation for Human Rights in Poland, and the Center for Legal and Social Studies (CELS) in Argentina.

15. Since its founding (as Helsinki Watch) in 1978, Human Rights Watch has received Ford Foundation grants (including the recent contributions to its endowment and operating reserves) that total approximately $17 million.

16. As noted in recent compilations of grants for international purposes, two other United States–based philanthropic organizations with total annual outlays in excess of $100 million—the John D. and Catherine T. MacArthur Foundation, and the Open Society Institute and other entities funded by George Soros—have substantial programs in the international human rights field. Smaller foundations with strong program commitments in that field include the Arca Foundation, the Aaron Diamond Foundation, the General Services Foundation, the John Merck Fund, the Joyce Mertz-Gilmore Foundation, the Public Welfare Foundation, and the Scherman Foundation. See, for example, Elizabeth H. Rich, ed., *The Guide to Funding for International and Foreign Programs* (New York: Foundation Center, 1996), p. 325 and passim.

17. The fiscal year 2000 operating budget of Human Rights Watch is approximately $15.7 million, of which some $600,000 is covered by Ford Foundation grants.

18. As noted in the Introduction, a Ford grant to Human Rights Watch funded a study of orga-

nizational and management issues, facilitated by the Management Assistance Group, in 1993–94. Ford funding also enabled Human Rights Watch to conduct a major strategic planning exercise in 1995–96.

19. The Ford Foundation currently has offices and field-based program staff in fourteen overseas locations: Cairo, Johannesburg, Lagos, and Nairobi in Africa and the Middle East; Bangkok, Beijing, Hanoi, Jakarta, Manila, and New Delhi in Asia; Mexico City, Rio de Janeiro, and Santiago in Latin America; and Moscow.

20. Sustained funding for the Southern Africa Project of the (Washington, D.C.–based) Lawyers' Committee for Civil Rights Under Law merits particular note in this regard.

21. Among the scores of examples that could be cited, several staff members of the Ford-funded Legal Resources Trust (LRT) and the Centre for Applied Legal Studies (CALS) were deeply immersed in the drafting of South Africa's new constitution. The LRT's founder, Arthur Chaskalson, is now president of the Constitutional Court and two other members of that body were drawn from foundation-funded organizations. Another early LRT associate served as minister of justice under President Mandela, and a former CALS staff member served as Mandela's legal advisor. In addition, a former director of LRT's Durban office served on the Truth and Reconciliation Commission and the founding director of its Port Elizabeth office was named president of the Land Claims Court.

22. The labors and accomplishments of those coalitions are discussed in the introduction to the *Human Rights Watch World Report 1999*, pp. xvi–xvii. The anti–land mine treaty is officially known as the Convention on the Prohibition of the Use, Stockpiling, Production and Transfer of Anti-Personnel Mines and on Their Destruction.

Conclusion

Claude E. Welch, Jr.

NGOs and Human Rights: Promise and Performance set out to answer five questions: What are the chief goals of human rights NGOs? Who sets these goals, and how? What strategies are utilized to achieve these goals? What resources are necessary to implement these strategies successfully? How is "success" or "effectiveness" defined and determined?

It is time now to summarize and compare the responses of the various authors and ascertain the lessons learned. I do so for a simple purpose. Academics and activists need to cooperate in evaluating "success." Human rights NGOs claim their actions help resolve problems; governments assert that they are responsible for what occurs in their societies, and (particularly in authoritarian settings) question whether critical NGOs actually affect their actions. We, whether activists, scholars, or thoughtful observers, must disentangle these claims. We must determine causality. In order to suggest how the human rights community can achieve greater effectiveness, both for individual nongovernmental organizations and for the human rights movement as a whole, the strategies that work and the conditions of success must be ascertained and set forth.

A preliminary caution must first be voiced. This book does not have all the answers, and perhaps not even all the crucial questions. *NGOs and Human Rights* does not claim to be comprehensive in its coverage, and thus cannot claim universality in its conclusions. The settings in which nongovernmental organizations operate vary enormously over time and space. What Amnesty International sought to achieve in its recent campaign about the United States differed in crucial respects from its ongoing efforts to stamp out torture in Burma; the food and development aid Oxfam attempted to deliver to the war-racked southern Sudan contrasted with FIAN's lobbying and advocacy efforts to implement right-to-food policies in Western capitals; ACFODE's work with the women of Uganda to achieve a rights-protective society was carried out in ways quite different from the reports and lobbying of the Women's Rights Division of Human Rights Watch. Each organization had distinct targets, purposes, and ways of operating. Each situation demanded tailored responses—within, of course, limited resources.

This book has presented a sampling of the diverse world of human rights NGOs—

not a random sample, but a conscious choice of interesting, important organizations seeking to help ensure that governments reach the "common standard of achievement" contained in the Universal Declaration of Human Rights. Separate, lengthy monographs could be (and, in some cases, have been) written about the NGOs, countries, or issues encapsulated here in relatively brief chapters. No single treatment is comprehensive. On the whole, however, this book has offered important observations about the significant roles NGOs have played in promoting and protecting human rights, generalizations that deserve to be utilized by others.

In global terms, human rights NGOs enjoy far more recognition at the dawn of the twenty-first century than they did a half century earlier. A quiet revolution in international relations has occurred. While global prohibition regimes (in Nadelmann's terms) can be traced back earlier, the ending of World War II provided a crucial impetus for nongovernmental human rights organizations to move on stage, if not necessarily to its center. NGOs successfully lobbied at San Francisco to incorporate human rights into the fundamental purposes of the United Nations. The 1948 Bogotá declaration by the Organization of American States, the adoption of the Universal Declaration of Human Rights later that year, and the implementation of the (European) Convention for the Protection of Human Rights and Fundamental Freedoms in 1951 indicated states' willingness to open their treatment of citizens to regional or international scrutiny. From very modest beginnings, the "curious grapevine" of human rights NGOs took root, ramified, and started to bear fruit. Largely nonexistent or overlooked by governments fifty or more years ago, nongovernmental organizations now play significant, indeed central, roles in the promotion and protection of human rights. The paradigm of state sovereignty has been persistently and progressively undermined by NGOs.

Goals. This book emphasizes human rights NGOs, which have been traditionally separated from relief-, humanitarian assistance–, and development-oriented NGOs. That this distinction merits reexamination is an important lesson.

With respect to major goals, NGOs pressing for civil and political rights, and upholding freedom of individuals from major bodily harm (as through torture, slavery, or extrajudicial execution), may seem to enjoy greater media prominence and dispose of more resources than do NGOs advocating economic and social rights. This impression is misleading. Oxfam and CARE, not Amnesty International or Human Rights Watch, handle the largest budgets. On the other hand, explicit advocacy has characterized "first generation" organizations. Public recognition is central to their success. But the increasing convergence of human rights and humanitarian assistance and development NGOs in recognizing how governments shape not only political parameters, but also economic and social conditions, must be borne in mind.

The "classic" paradigm and the "conventional doctrinalists" criticized by Mutua remain alive and well. Nonetheless, the organizations working within this liberal paradigm are changing. Recognition of economic and social rights (even if cautiously phrased as "conditions"), and pressures on international financial institutions and multinational corporations, have entered NGOs' repertoires of action. Amnesty International, for example, calls in its statute (as revised in December 1997) for the promotion of "the indivisibility and interdependence of all human rights and freedoms." Although its mandate continues to stress prisoners of conscience, torture, and the death penalty, AI takes cognizance of much broader concerns. It "promotes" all rights in positive fashion, even while it vigorously opposes denial of those rights determined in Amnesty's mandate. Human Rights Watch and, even more markedly, the International Commission of Jurists, have incorporated aspects of economic and social rights into their goals.

Widening the goals for these "liberal" organizations does not run totally against the grain, but reflects the interconnected nature of all human rights. With the end of the Cold War, a global struggle that artificially separated "first" and "second generation" rights, many governments and NGOs broadened their mandates or perspectives (admittedly at different speeds and to different extents) on human rights. Continuing and in many ways widening global economic disparities underscore the importance of equitable development as a human right. The founding of FIAN International in 1986 as one of the first INGOs focusing on economic, social, and cultural rights shows these are no longer treated as second-class rights by NGOs. Human Rights Watch's "experiment" in considering economic and social conditions continues, and no doubt will be modestly expanded over time. Amnesty International, as noted, advocates promotion of all human rights. The once staid, establishment-dominated International Commission of Jurists still stresses the rule of law, but takes account of economic and social conditions and cooperates in campaigns with groups such as FIAN. In an analogous fashion, Oxfam has expanded its advocacy on behalf of civil and political rights; the urgent tasks of humanitarian relief do not automatically "trump" NGOs' criticism of government policies. Capacity building and advocacy have become more prominent for some groups concerned with disaster relief and development. The goals of the older mainline human rights and of humanitarian assistance NGOs have thus expanded—albeit hesitantly and partially—into partial convergence.

The argument that first generation rights are enforceable or justiciable while second generation rights are aspirational continues to hold sway among leaders of many human rights NGOs and numerous governments, nonetheless. This distinction parallels the long-standing contrast between promotion and protection. This is good in theory, questionable in action. Governments are supposed to guarantee rights, NGOs to monitor performance. However, in "collapsed states" NGOs have provided basic services. In increasing number, aid-giving countries have steered greater percentages of development aid through NGOs rather than through governments. A burgeoning literature now documents these transformed roles. States have not been *displaced* by non-state actors, with the singular exception of collapsed states; but, without question, they have been *supplemented*, often extensively, by them. No longer can one claim simply that governments protect human rights while NGOs promote them. Much depends on the particular right, the particular setting, the particular organizational style and leadership.

The major tasks of human rights NGOs fall in three overlapping areas: standard setting and agenda setting; protection; and promotion (including monitoring). In the time-honored paradigm of sovereign state power, governments took responsibility for the first two, while civil society was confined to the third. This neat division has eroded substantially. Human rights NGOs have become increasingly involved in fulfillment. Although boundaries among standard setting and agenda setting, protection, promotion, and fulfillment blur, the relative balance between states and NGOs has changed, and changed dramatically, starting in a hesitant fashion after 1945, and at an accelerated rate since the end of the Cold War. Let us consider these areas briefly.

NGOs have taken greater leadership initiatives in standard setting and agenda setting. This has occurred increasingly in cooperation with selected governments. International conventions continue to be drafted in state-dominated settings. But the expertise, popular support, and political savvy NGOs bring to these conferences have earned them a significant role. Several examples spring to mind: Amnesty International's role in the Convention Against Torture; Defence of Children International's impact on the text of the Convention on the Rights of the Child; the pressure for the treaty creating the International Criminal Court, in which the International Commission of Jurists and Human Rights Watch helped constitute the steering committee;[1] Human Rights Watch and many others in the coalition to ban land mines;[2] FIAN's lobbying effort to establish an optional protocol to the International Covenant on Economic, Social, and Cultural Rights. The conjoint efforts of governments and NGOs in preparing treaty language and gaining ratifications have important benefits for both. NGO participation in standard and agenda setting, nearly impossible a generation or two back, is becoming common. What was a distant and almost unthinkable goal prior to 1945 has become part of some NGOs' repertoire.

With respect to protection, formal doctrines of state sovereignty collide with the realities of the third millennium. The powers of governments have been eaten away by globalization. Multinational corporations exert substantial clout; international financial institutions exercise close to life-or-death powers over many states. The relative weakening of states' control can be observed in human rights as well. Where state collapse has occurred, as in many complex humanitarian emergencies, NGOs and international agencies have become surrogates for the collapsed governments. Development projects are often funded and implemented through NGOs, with governments on the sidelines. Providing aid to the oppressed, and solidarity with them, has long been a major goal of human rights NGOs. The erosion of state powers along the dimensions suggested here has enhanced the significance of human rights groups as well as humanitarian assistance and development NGOs.

In crucial senses, NGOs are engaged in an open-ended process. Their long-term goal—achieving a setting in which widespread or officially sponsored abuses would be unthinkable—requires the establishment of a "human rights culture" or "rights-protective society." In such a setting, presumably there would be no need for NGOs such as Amnesty International or ACFODE. Only an incurable utopian would proclaim that such a goal will be quickly (if ever) reached.

The goals of human rights NGOs remain largely in the area of promotion as contrasted with protection. Research, monitoring, and advocacy appear to be most important. The speed and ability that NGOs demonstrate in informing treaty-monitoring bodies about states' actions earn them widespread recognition. The convention-based human rights system would be almost totally ineffective if it were based solely on the reports submitted by governments. NGOs' goal of providing information about abuses remains central to the reporting systems. Advocacy has meant taking the results of research and monitoring to politically powerful participants, working in tandem with them—or, if necessary, counteracting their influence—and counteracting government actions through information, symbolic, leverage, and accountability policies.[3]

Fulfillment is the fourth goal of human rights NGOs. It is historically limited by limited resources and the power of states. Nongovernmental organizations tread less cautiously now in the domain traditionally reserved to governments, nonetheless. With collapsed states, greater willingness by donors to steer resources through NGOs rather than through "official" channels, and growing confidence on their own part, NGOs have become increasingly involved in actions directly impacting on individuals. We are witnessing an evolution possibly akin to the goal of the International Committee of the Red Cross in working with prisoners of war.

The struggle continues. Creation of a rights-protective society, to use Dicklitch's term, necessarily extends over decades (and may never be complete, as continuing abuses in democratic, highly developed countries indicate). It involves a multitude of political actors, and focuses largely on states as the primary protectors (and abusers) of human rights. For this reason, the goals of human rights NGOs are open-ended and periodically reviewed and revised, lest the groups lose their vigor or decline in effectiveness. But how are goals changed?

Setting and revising goals. NGOs have set their initial objectives through the visions of their founders, and have broadened or altered these goals through internal adaptation or through institutional fission. Let us look at several levels here: at those who initially created the NGOs; those who succeeded them as executive heads and staff; the members; and the public(s) served.

Many human rights NGOs have renowned parents. Their impacts remain years after the organizations were started. Recall the aphorism of Montesquieu: "In the birth of societies, it is the leaders of republics who create the institution; thereafter it is the institution that forms the leaders of republics."[4] For the two largest of the "classic" human rights NGOs, Amnesty International and Human Rights Watch, the mark of the founders—of Peter Benenson and Sean MacBride, and of Aryeh Neier and Robert Bernstein—can still be discerned. Almost all human rights NGOs start and remain small, and often continue to manifest the leaders' objectives. They may appeal to the already committed. Self-selection by members reinforces continuity. The influence of major funders may encourage relatively unchanged objectives rather than major alteration of them.

Institutions do adapt their goals, however. Without change, they wither and perish. Ample evidence has been given in this volume of the ways in which Human Rights Watch and (to a lesser extent) Amnesty International broadened their objectives and changed their means of operating while remaining in the liberal paradigm. As opportunities for democratization increased, the International Human Rights Law Group found new directions. Oxfam and CARE have changed dramatically in scope, more modestly in terms of objectives (particularly for CARE). FIAN, from its initial establishment by European Amnesty International activists, broadened its geographic base to many other countries. ACFODE struggled with its organizational format at least three times in its relatively brief history, a reflection in some measure of conflicting goals sought by its university-affiliated founders and its village-based subjects of action.

It appears to be rare for members of human rights organizations to establish or modify their goals. Few NGOs are structured on the lines of Amnesty International, whose dedication to maintaining members' involvement has been stressed by several authors earlier in this book. Revising AI's mandate, as Winston pointed out, involves years of effort, given the elaborate consultative process. Getting members to accept changes (as witness the dispute over the rights of gays and lesbians as a basis on which prisoners of conscience could be adopted, despite the absence of sexual orientation as an explicit basis of illegal discrimination under international law) takes time, money, and commitment; but the process also achieves greater legitimacy for the revised goal. Nonetheless, should human rights NGOs stress greater involvement by members, the experience of Amnesty International must be studied.

Even having a restricted membership does not mean individual members exercise significant influence over goal setting. The International Commission of Jurists is formally constituted of forty persons—but its survival and adoption of new goals have been mostly the results of its leaders (including Sean MacBride, Niall McDermott, and Adama Dieng). The impact of members seems more marked in terms of budget than of organizational objectives, so I shall return to this issue in the discussion of resources.

It is also rare for the subjects of NGOs' attention to take active parts in setting goals. Rhetoric and reality diverge considerably. Human rights groups—especially those based in affluent northern democracies—work on behalf of "victims." Their voices are used as evidence of effectiveness, as well as a basis for initiating action. As noted earlier, Amnesty International did not permit national sections to work on their own countries—a reasonable precaution, to be certain, in many authoritarian settings early in AI's history, and an incentive for the organization's global outlook, but arguably a disincentive for domestic involvement. Geographic, economic, cultural, historical, and other factors thus separate the major supporters of the NGOs examined in this book from the persons for whom they work.

"Victims" know they are being wronged, but may have limited leverage locally, or scant knowledge of global connections they could make. Links between domestic and international NGOs diminish these gaps, at least in theory. A clear current trend for the large, Western-based human rights groups is the establishment of formal liaisons with NGOs in developing countries, including joint research and publication. Recall the evidence from India cited in Chapter 4 comparing AI and HRW: many months of efforts went into bringing together the coalitions on child labor and caste violence; once these were established, mutual efforts could start, responsive to the priorities of the national NGOs as well as to the goals of Human Rights Watch itself. Without question, the major, Western-based INGOs recognize the importance of ties to NGOs in target countries. Coalition building and capacity building go hand in hand.

However, being based in and staffed by nationals does not automatically mean a domestic NGO is representative of its society as a whole, or perhaps even of those whose rights have been threatened. Nor have the newer, smaller human rights NGOs in developing countries felt themselves to be equal partners with their northern sisters, despite the efforts noted in the preceding paragraph. A continuing challenge for the human rights movement as a whole is to incorporate "victims" into goal setting; an equally great challenge is to develop and maintain meaningful organizational partnerships crossing the North-South divide. Though generally seen as an issue of strategy, NGOs' links with those served and with geographically separated groups must also be seen as a matter of goal setting.

Without question, funders affect the goals of human rights NGOs. What founders establish, funders maintain. NGOs are resource driven. The search for new or continuing funds is a central task—and the leaders bear the responsibility. I shall return to the resource issue in greater detail. What is clear, however, is that symbiosis exists between select foundations (such as Ford or Soros) and human rights organizations and organizers. Leaders in civil society and foundations find common ground in establishing new NGOs, providing the resources to carry out their mandates, and revising their goals and strategies in accordance with these resources.

As a general rule, the older and more successful an organization is, the more complex it becomes to revise its basic aims. The restrictive nature of Amnesty International's mandate has been commented upon several times in this volume, for example. In many respects, it is easier to establish a new NGO than to change the fundamental objectives of an existing one—a chief reason why Amnesty has served as an excellent training school for other NGOs when activists dissatisfied with its ponderous ways or restricted mandate created new organizations. Whether the tendency toward proliferation results from inertia of existing institutions that stick with their long-standing goals and strategies, from encouragement by donors, from the relative ease with which NGOs can be founded (if not necessarily maintained), or from the escalating international recognition of human rights, cannot be answered conclusively at this point. Research now underway should help clarify these points.

Successful human rights NGOs have spawned imitators. In training activists, Amnesty International towers above other human rights NGOs. One-time members or staffers founded FIAN, occupy significant positions in Human Rights Watch (although

HRW has now established such a strong reputation that it is the "NGO of choice" for a significant segment of able women and men, especially American), and encourage NGOs through ad hoc networks. Careers are possible in human rights work, through NGOs. Barriers to creation of new organizations have been reduced around the world, as part of the global rise of civil society. The models, networks, and hope for funding that exist thus mean that new NGOs can be established with relative ease.

Finally, in terms of goals, not all self-styled human rights NGOs are disinterested advocates. Their major goal may in fact be personal in nature. Dicklitch has pointed to "briefcase NGOs," hastily established to benefit from donors' largesse;[5] de Waal has criticized the "disaster industry," in which relief organizations compete in unhealthy ways for resources.[6] For some NGOs, alas, the needs and interests of the people to be served run a distant second to the personal interests of the founders and staff. In a world where an NGO can be created with little more than a letterhead, a telephone line, and seed money from a willing donor, briefcase NGOs will spring up. Even where governments have instituted strict registration requirements, inventive or desperate leaders have created shadow organizations.

Over time, however, institutional shakeout occurs. Only NGOs that are effective can hope to continue to receive support—with their success resting on the strategies they pursue.

Strategies. The strategies by which human rights NGOs pursue their goals vary. In this section, I shall look specifically at how they relate to rights-abusing and rights-protective governments, to funders, and to other NGOs.

In theory, NGOs can follow strategies that are exclusive, primary, or shared. They can seek to address an issue by themselves, as the lead partner in a coalition of NGOs (and possibly supportive governments), or as one of several participants in a network. The latter two are far more likely, evidence in this book shows. The value and importance of networks have been amply demonstrated in many of the chapters above. Few NGOs dispose of the resources necessary for an exclusive, major, long-term campaign. Amnesty International does; its standard setting efforts on torture (as Clark has demonstrated) and its national campaigns (as witness its recent sweeping focus on the United States) stand as exceptions in the world of NGO action. Advocacy networks multiply the impact of individual NGOs—and AI has in fact assumed a crucial role in many.[7] The observations of Keck and Sikkink about the importance of transnational advocacy networks accordingly receive ample confirmation in the chapters above. Large, well-funded, and prestigious northern NGOs may take a primary role in forming and leading coalitions; but even they cannot expect success on an exclusive basis. Networks allow NGOs to broaden their scope, as well as to enhance their impact. And for new, small, isolated, or national NGOs, links to established international organizations provide legitimation, publicity, audience, and the like. Networking is a basic strategy for human rights NGOs; those that do not participate risk being marginalized.

The large, northern human rights groups are taking increasing heed of the resentment they awaken among smaller, poorer southern NGOs. Recall the evidence cited earlier about two major reports Human Rights Watch prepared on India, having first spent many months helping to bring together numerous NGOs and learning their concerns. The days in which Amnesty International, Human Rights Watch, or the Lawyers' Committee for Human Rights could "parachute in" teams of researchers without extensive consultation with local NGOs have passed.

Greater emphasis is thus being laid on capacity building for NGOs. It is a joint endeavor. Funders seem willing to provide funds; the classic organizations recognize the need; recipient organizations gain in many respects. However, capacity building as a strategy remains new and relatively untested among multinational and transnational human rights NGOs. Change is (as usual) underway, but the measures of success remain somewhat cloudy.[8]

To an increasing extent, I believe as well, the large organizations examined in this book are moving from primarily research strategies ("information" and "accountability" in Keck and Sikkink's terms) toward greater advocacy. In addition, they are pressuring governments directly—including powerful ones like the United States—through links with other, sympathetic governments. Leverage politics, including the "boomerang" effect discussed by Winston, can be utilized against states of all sorts. For nominally rights-protective governments reluctant to sign or ratify a major human rights treaty, NGOs enjoy a growing repertoire of actions. For rights-abusive governments, NGOs can mobilize pressure in a wide variety of ways not necessarily dependent on support from powerful governments. Korey may be correct historically in emphasizing the advances brought through NGO cooperation with states, and in particular the United States, as suggested in the Introduction. Nonetheless, networks of NGOs and sympathetic governments are proving themselves to be more and more effective, even in the face of superpower intransigence.

NGOs are placing increasing stress upon uncovering and correcting human rights abuses attributable to multinational corporations (MNCs) and international financial institutions (IFIs). This relatively new area of activity represents a major broadening of strategy by NGOs, and merits more attention than provided in this book. I shall return to this issue later.

Electronic communications multiply NGOs' interactions. Further exploration of how human rights organizations coalesce temporarily, and how the Internet affects their effectiveness (following Wiseberg's helpful observations), would be useful. The low costs of electronic communication seem to help NGOs with a fraction of the resources of entities such as Amnesty International, Human Rights Watch, or the International Commission of Jurists to strengthen networks and provide avenues for advocacy. However, the costs of effective human rights work are not low. More broadly, what are the consequences of the dramatically different levels of resources NGOs enjoy?

Resources. In this section, I shall concentrate on financial resources, especially from four major sources: governments (unacceptable for almost all the human rights NGOs surveyed in this book), foundations, individual donors, and members. Resources are more than economic, however, so we shall give attention as well to less tangible resources, such as quality of leadership.

In sheer budgetary terms, the classic first-generation human rights NGOs are far outstripped in their budgets by their sister humanitarian assistance and development institutions. Oxfam or CARE spends in a few weeks what Amnesty International or Human Rights Watch disburses in a year (though AI or HRW spends in a month or less the entire annual budget of ACFODE, in many ways a typical human rights organization in a developing country). Contrasting levels of resources can be attributed to several factors, most notably government support and membership size.

As Scott comments, Oxfam and CARE grew out of World War II humanitarian emergencies, and continue today to provide both emergency and development aid. But these two giants differ noticeably in their major sources of revenue. CARE's historic link to the U.S. government means it can rely on large, regular grants from it; private donations constitute a far smaller portion of the budget. CARE is not critical of U.S. public efforts, and handles numerous contracts on behalf of the U.S. government. Oxfam relies far more on voluntary donations because of its desire to remain independent of any direct or indirect government pressure. It has launched effective public campaigns to expose human rights abuses and governments' roles in them. CARE utilizes what political muscle it has behind the scenes, primarily with donor states.

This contrast between Oxfam and CARE exemplifies a broader question, namely distance from government. In what respects are states allies of human rights NGOs? In what respects are they opponents? Development-oriented or humanitarian assistance–oriented NGOs differ from human rights–oriented NGOs, in large measure, due to their different relations with governments. The former generally cooperate even with rights-abusing governments in order to gain access and distribute relief. The latter oppose any significant dependence on governments, seeing in their actions the causes of human rights problems.

Aid-giving governments of the North can easily afford writing large checks for humanitarian assistance or development budgets in the form of modestly paid NGO employees, food, water, medicine, temporary shelter, and the like, especially if influential domestic farm lobbies or evangelizing religious groups are satisfied. Assistance-receiving governments of the South often resent the dependency that humanitarian assistance and development aid embody. On the other hand, such resources may help them reduce popular discontent and lubricate patron-client relations through adding resources. Development budgets may be perceived as an "angelus ex machina" by cash-strapped governments. The extent to which NGOs participate in distributing aid is thus a political issue for donors and (especially) for recipients.

Many, and perhaps most, major international human rights organizations eschew direct financial support from governments. States are the usual targets of NGO criticism. Accepting funds from them would compromise the NGOs' integrity, making them subject to (or at least suspect of) undue influence. Two events can be cited. Early its in history, the International Commission of Jurists was deeply embarrassed, and nearly forced to dissolve, when its covert funding from the CIA was revealed.[9] When Amnesty International's credibility was threatened in 1967 by accusations that its founder, Peter Benenson, had accepted British government funds to help finance AI's relief efforts in Rhodesia (Zimbabwe), Benenson was forced to resign.[10] Important lessons have been drawn from these notorious incidents. Human Rights Watch has accepted some assistance from European governments for specific projects, largely through the semi-autonomous Dutch agency NOVIB, with serious restrictions comfortable to NOVIB and HRW alike. And, with the permission of the International Executive Committee, some AI national sections have accepted government grants for narrowly defined purposes.

On the other hand, as states have rhetorically supported human rights in their foreign policy, they have also followed up with grants to NGOs. Avoiding conflicts of interest—or even the appearance of such conflict—is a significant issue. For example, the National Endowment for Democracy (NED) receives direct appropriations from the U.S. government, but tries to maintain policy autonomy through its board of directors and through contracting with entities such as the National Democratic Institute for International Affairs (NDI). Despite these steps, the NED is generally viewed as a quasi-NGO (QUANGO) or government-organized NGO (GONGO), serving as an instrument of American foreign policy. Bromley's discussion of how the International Human Rights Law Group maintains its autonomy should be recalled. Thus, though prohibitions against financial support from states exist for the classic large Western NGOs, and though these strictures are almost always enforced, some exceptions exist. As a general rule, however, I believe that more sophisticated understandings have developed. NGOs will generally tend to avoid seeking government grants, save under highly restricted and exceptional conditions; governments are also increasingly cautious in proffering assistance with explicit or even implicit strings attached.[11]

Not being able to rely on governmental largesse means, of course, dependence on other sources. Amnesty International shows the heaviest reliance on membership dues and contributions among the NGOs in this book. This strategy entails relatively high fund-raising costs—for it is manifestly cheaper to get a single donor to write an annual check for several hundred thousand dollars (as Human Rights Watch has enjoyed) than to persuade 100,000 individuals to write checks of $5 to $10 each. But there is no question that well-heeled donors provide significant portions of the budgets of almost all the NGOs examined in this book.

As Chapters 4 and 13 demonstrate, the Ford Foundation was instrumental in the development of numerous human rights NGOs in the past twenty-five years. Ford made possible many of the new initiatives Human Rights Watch undertook (although the very successful Arms Project was initiated by Rockefeller Foundation funds),[12] and the Ford Foundation's overseas offices breathed life into scores of human rights groups. The hundreds of millions of dollars George Soros plows into NGOs may, over time, have substantial impact in many countries; the Open Society Institute is a rapidly emerging player on the human rights stage, thanks to his generosity. The last word has yet to be written on the importance of foundation support for NGOs.

The financial picture is by no means rosy for human rights NGOs in many (and probably most) rights-abusing states, nonetheless. There, small, dependent NGOs confront severe budget issues. They cannot survive, save at minimal levels of activity, without outside assistance. Recall the problems and frequent reorganizations of ACFODE, where local voluntarism and contributions could provide very limited support. This evidence is suggestive, not conclusive, however. The internal operations of NGOs in general, and budget problems in particular, need far more academic attention than they have received. Scholars have concentrated their research almost exclusively on the impact of NGOs on their governments or societies, looking for examples of successful (or unsuccessful) pressure. Success, I argue, must be assessed in relative terms, that is, by examining the "inputs" of budget, leadership, preexisting networks, and the like, in order to measure the "outputs" of pressure, popular mobilization, research reports, and so on.

Individuals matter. The long shadows cast by some founders of NGOs have been alluded to in earlier chapters. Generalizations about leadership risk turning into platitudes or unprovable, self-evident statements—"Good leaders are necessary for success" or "Great individuals have founded lasting organizations." But there is not sufficient information in the chapters above to come to any stronger conclusion than that leadership is a crucial resource, part of the "success" with which this chapter concludes.

Success. Can or should we take NGOs' claims of success at face value? Were the hundreds of thousands of letters penned by Amnesty International members the crucial element resulting in the liberation of more than half the 45,000 prisoners of conscience AI adopted? Did the very public efforts of Human Rights Watch, the International Commission of Jurists, and close to three hundred other NGOs persuade states to reach agreement on the convention establishing the International Criminal Court? Has the lobbying of FIAN prepared the way for aid-giving governments to recognize access to food as a human right?

"Success" can be defined from the perspectives of many—by doer, recipient, observer, enthusiast, critic, whatever. No single definition of success can suffice. To a substantial extent, it depends on the target selected. The goal may be as circumscribed as the release of an individual prisoner of conscience (in which case hundreds of POCs and Amnesty International chapters were satisfied), or as broad as major change in an entire national culture of human rights. The greater the objective, naturally the more difficult it is to demonstrate direct connections between NGO actions and societal results. Proof of change is complex, given multicausality. The "real world" in which human rights NGOs operate is not a laboratory situation. Success is elusive to assess. This should come as no surprise. The positive impact of NGOs is difficult to measure, easy to claim.

The chapters in *NGOs and Human Rights: Promise and Performance* do not, by themselves, conclusively prove that nongovernmental organizations of the classic liberal paradigm have, by their exclusive activities, bolstered the protection of human rights. On the other hand, the authors have demonstrated that NGOs have engaged increasingly in standard setting (once the exclusive domain of states), that they have promoted human rights in an increasing number of settings and in increasing numbers themselves, that they have directly protected certain rights of millions of persons through acquiring and distributing food, medicine, and shelter, that their actions are directed in general terms toward rights-protective societies, and that they regularly join in networks that include sympathetic governments as well as NGOs.

Although most of the authors above do not cite specific evaluations of organization effectiveness, this does not mean such assessments are lacking. Donors rarely give grants without some requirements for audit or evaluation. Numerous studies of success have been carried out, particularly of development-oriented NGOs. Most of these studies, however, remain in foundation, government, or NGO files rarely consulted by scholars.

Probably the most comprehensive comparative analysis to date of NGO action was carried out for the Organization for Economic Cooperation and Development (OECD). A team of scholars focused on the efficiency and effectiveness of NGO development interventions. They examined sixty separate donor-initiated reports of 240 projects undertaken in twenty-six developing countries, and gathered information from NGOs themselves through interviews and reports on thirteen specific countries.[13] Let me summarize major observations from this study:

Despite growing interest in evaluation and growing numbers of evaluation studies, "firm and reliable evidence on the impact of NGO development projects and programmes" is still lacking; most impact assessments rely on qualitative rather than quantitative data, are undertaken very rapidly, and report on outputs measured rather than outcomes achieved or broader impact.

Donor-commissioned studies cited thirteen factors influencing project performance; in rough order of decreasing importance, they included external factors and links outside the project; competent or professional staff; involvement of the beneficiaries, responding to local need; "overall vision"; good project design and planning; institutional capacity (including adequate management, finance, and administration, and local capacity); the particular sector; knowledge of other experiences, documentation, and research, and the ability to network; sufficient funds (it is interesting to note how far down the list this occurs); ability to "stay small"; sufficient time to achieve objectives; heterogeneity of different NGO interventions; and religious, membership, or other affiliation.

Data on the impact of NGOs, the team comments, are better for economic type projects, worse for democracy or capacity-building projects, with social sector development in between.

Utilizing studies carried out by NGOs, considerable agreement existed about gaps and weaknesses, although the NGOs themselves tended both to be more critical in pinpointing weaknesses and to give greater prominence to individual leaders and leadership.

There are dangers in generalizing, since the wider contexts in which projects are placed have profound impact.

Similarly, the capabilities of the organization and the amount and duration of funds have major effects; again, there are dangers in generalizing.

Different types of development intervention require different means of evaluation.

Longitudinal, in-depth research studies are needed, a number of which should be comparative analyses of different interventions in different contexts.

Did the OECD team spend several months of intensive work, only to restate the obvious? Are their findings applicable to classic first-generation human rights NGOs? I believe additional factors must be brought into play for evaluation of success.

Earlier, I commented on NGOs' participation in standard setting, a task formally reserved for states under long-standing concepts of sovereignty. This does not mean that participating NGOs have achieved all the objectives they sought in influencing the specific wording of texts. Nonetheless, NGOs' active involvement in drafting indicates success. They have followed a trajectory of steadily increasing prominence: as already noted, they played essentially no role in the Helsinki Final Act (1975); they identified torture as a significant issue and mobilized international public opinion in favor of the Declaration on the Protection of All Persons from Being Subjected to Torture and then the Convention Against Torture and Other Forms of Cruel Inhuman or Degrading Treatment or Punishment (1975, 1984), contributing language to both; they drafted significant parts of the Convention on the Rights of the Child (1979), the Convention on the Prohibition of the Use, Stockpiling, Production and Transfer of Anti-Personnel Mines and on Their Destruction (1997), the Statute of the International Criminal Court (1998), and others. The trend is unmistakable. No longer can governments exclude NGOs from the consultative and consensus-building processes in drafting international human rights agreements—for it is increasingly NGO networks that mobilize the requisite pressure, form the relevant networks, propose the appropriate language, and lobby for rapid ratification.

Relations between NGOs and governments are shifting. In his comprehensive recent survey of international human rights NGOs, William Korey pointed to two great twentieth-century milestones in which NGOs played prominent roles: the collapse of the Soviet empire, and the disintegration of the apartheid system in South Africa.[14] Most successes over which NGOs have crowed have resulted, he argues, from deliberate linkage between them and powerful governments, in particular the United States. I think it is fair to say that superpower support is now not necessary for drafting important binding international agreements. United States opposition to the convention establishing the International Criminal Court and to the land mine treaty demonstrate this point. (U.S. ratification of both is another matter; here, NGOs are cranking up the pressure.)

The protective actions of politically oriented NGOs (as contrasted with those of NGOs focused on humanitarian assistance or development) have generally been in-direct in nature, such as reinforcing the rule of law or monitoring violations. Many prisoners of conscience adopted by Amnesty International gained freedom or better treatment, particularly in AI's early years, as a direct result of its actions. Human Rights Watch's attention to human rights monitors (along with that of many other NGOs) helps publicize and thereby protect these brave individuals; the recent declaration on human rights defenders should be recognized as an important result of vigorous lobby-ing by human rights groups. The prominence that POCs, human rights monitors, and advocates have gained resulted from NGO action; having thus become prominent, they could not be imprisoned without rapid international protests.[15]

As FIAN insists, a person who dies as a result of government-induced famine is as equally a victim of human rights abuses as one who perishes as a consequence of extra-judicial execution by agents of the state. All the more reason, accordingly, for ques-tioning the differentiation between NGOs promoting first-generation civil and political rights and NGOs concerned with second-generation economic and social rights, as well as with humanitarian assistance and development. Protection of the most basic human right, that of life itself, is essential, and is carried out by all these organizations. Oxfam and other NGOs such as Doctors Without Borders (*Médécins sans frontières*) have strongly advocated changed government policies, for example; they have not remained silent about abuses in order to gain or maintain access.

Without question, all the NGOs discussed in this book have promoted human rights. In a setting of theoretically sovereign states, this is what they can do most readily, and probably most effectively.

Most notably, NGOs have assumed responsibility in monitoring states' perfor-mance under various treaties. "Accountability politics," to use the apt term of Keck and Sikkink, is a central strategy of human rights NGOs—one that has resulted in modifica-tions of some governments' policies.[16] All the authors in this book recognize this role. NGOs have significantly supplemented states, and to a large extent supplanted them, in human rights monitoring. International treaty bodies have become heavily reliant (or nearly totally reliant, some claim) on NGO-provided information. Early framers of the United Nations envisaged states as the source of accurate, timely information. Not surprisingly, they were disappointed. Governments place their own spin on reports they submit (if they submit them at all). NGOs moved into the vacuum. Despite efforts to restrict their involvement, human rights NGOs have provided what governments do not. As Korey has observed, "What fed the new special procedures [in the United Nations for reporting on violations] was the flow of information, documentation and data from NGOs. . . . without NGOs, the entire human rights implementation system at the UN would come to a halt."[17] Success can be claimed, without question, for the objective of gathering information and feeding it into international or regional treaty bodies.

What about those areas in which success is more difficult to claim?

Marked imbalances in distribution exist in the world of human rights NGOs. They are most numerous in relatively well-off industrial democracies and in poorer developing countries characterized by relatively open political systems, but are hard to find in many rights-repressive states. The numbers of NGOs appear to be inversely correlated to the severity of human rights problems, quite the reverse of what the situations require. The more significant the abuses, so it seems, the smaller is the number of home-grown NGOs, the lesser their ambit for activity, and the more miniscule their budgets. The gaps between developed and developing countries remain marked and persistent. Historic continuity seems to prevail. The nineteenth- and early twentieth-century forerunners of current human rights NGOs were headquartered almost exclusively in powerful Western states. The explosion of NGO numbers and activities has not reversed these disparities. Influence, recognition, and resources remain concentrated in northern human rights NGOs.

However, the situation is changing. Northern NGOs increasingly partner with southern NGOs for joint research. Increasing efforts go into coalition building. Capacity building of partner NGOs is now an explicit goal of Human Rights Watch and the International Commission of Jurists, among others. An increasing number of classic human rights NGOs are explicitly partnering with local NGOs and helping them bolster their own effectiveness. Steps toward success on a truly cooperative, global foundation are thus being taken.

Economic and social rights have not received equal recognition from almost all the NGOs in this book. However, some NGOs such as FIAN International do not relegate them to the background as conditions that impact on civil and political rights, but foreground them as rights that must be monitored and advocated directly. Recent developments, including more precise guidelines for measuring the "progressive achievement" of economic and social rights, greater scope within which the Committee on Economic, Social Cultural Rights can function, and steps toward an optional protocol to the ICESCR, are encouraging. Human rights NGOs, current and as-yet unformed, will devote more time, energy, and other resources to these rights, increasingly treating them as rights rather than conditions.

What strategies for their own development should NGOs pursue? We should look at this in terms of membership base, budget sources, leadership training and renewal, and organizational mandate.

The impact of membership was not considered in most chapters above, for the simple reason that few human rights NGOs rely on large, active cadres of members to press for their goals. Amnesty International is unique among those surveyed. However, reliance on small numbers of supporters drawn from distinct social groups has inherent drawbacks. Both success and effectiveness will be bolstered, I believe, through membership efforts. This will not be easy, but it is a necessary and appropriate step toward the overarching goal of creating rights-protective societies.

NGOs' budget sources must be diversified, solidified, and expanded. Most of the organizations examined in this book are well established, with reasonably steady and relatively assured funds. Taking the NGO world as a whole, however, they are exceptions. Most human rights organizations—and especially those in developing countries—scratch out their existence from grant to grant. Funders give more readily for specific projects than for long-term institutional maintenance.

Coalition building can stretch resources by allowing NGOs to concentrate on specified areas of expertise. Accordingly, the increased number and expanded range of networks shows success with this important strategy.

Leadership is a variable that merits more attention, most notably for newer, smaller NGOs in the South. Success does not happen as a simple result of budget inputs. NGOs achieve public recognition and bring changes in public policy through their leaders. As noted previously, the heads of human rights organizations tend to be drawn from rights-conscious groups—the more educated, the urbanized middle class, those discriminated against, or those with contacts outside their home country. They often differ, sometimes markedly, from those in whose name they speak. NGO leaders must seek to build bridges of understanding, not only with the governments they influence, but with the persons or groups they represent. "Depth on the bench" is essential, for an NGO dependent on the talents of a single person may not long survive his or her leaving office. Here, evidence is mixed; not all authors gave details about the selection, backgrounds, and training of NGO leaders.

With respect to organizational mandates, NGOs must balance between restricted objectives that can be achieved (or at least approached) with limited resources, and broad objectives that appeal to larger numbers of potential supporters. Too focused or rigid a mandate, as Winston argues, may hamper even as large or effective an organization as Amnesty International; too broad or flexible a mandate, as Dicklitch suggests for ACFODE, may impede success in particular areas. The particular balance, it seems, must be decided in terms of the specific context—the nature and magnitude of rights abuses; the number of potential supporters; or the resources that realistically can be utilized. And, if an NGO does not adapt to changed circumstances, chances are that another NGO will spring up to fill the vacuum. NGOs, in short, must be adaptable to changed circumstances in order to succeed.

It is customary—and appropriate—to conclude a book of this sort with a plea for further research. *NGOs and Human Rights: Promise and Performance* has provided a wide-ranging but not totally comprehensive set of perspectives. Individual authors have suggested specific steps that should be taken; recall, in particular, how Cingranelli and Richards advocate in-depth case studies using consistent baseline data as a foundation for comparative studies. Comparisons between human rights and humanitarian assistance organizations should be pursued. The chapter by Dicklitch in this volume about Action for Development (ACFODE) should be followed by many other case studies of NGOs in developing countries. The chief needs for future research accordingly include both intensive analyses of individual NGOs or groups of NGOs, and comparative studies of groups focused on particular goals.

I would like to suggest some other desirable objectives for research:

Variables for analysis must be specified more clearly and applied more consistently—even while recognizing, as does the major OECD study summarized above, that context matters.

Human rights NGOs cannot be studied as isolated organizations. They deliberately try to impact on societies—and are themselves affected by social norms. They seek to change government policies or halt their human rights abuses—and are themselves subject to political pressures. They form parts of transnational advocacy networks, increasingly linked electronically to other NGOs. The context cannot thus be conveniently limited to single states.

Major emerging NGOs not covered in this book must be examined. I am thinking in particular of the Open Society Institute. The wealth of George Soros and his generosity toward human rights are marked. The Open Society Institute and the Soros Foundations, the latter headed by former Human Rights Watch executive director Aryeh Neier, have in a very short time made a major splash, particularly with civil and political rights in Eastern and Central Europe through a series of foundations. What are the goals, strategies, resources, and accomplishments of these new organizations? How has the Open Society Institute as a whole impacted on other human rights NGOs?

Reciprocal influences must be examined. The human rights NGOs of the South will have a direct effect in broadening the mandate of the human rights NGOs of the North, I believe, as coalition building and joint research and advocacy efforts are carried out.

NGOs' current emphasis on governments is being broadened to include multinational corporations, international financial institutions, and opposition movements. We need to determine whether the strategies and tactics developed in the struggle against rights-abusing states, and in cooperation with rights-protective states, can be successfully applied to these different types of institutions.

The last line will be the bottom line as well. Nongovernmental organizations not only show promise for improving human rights performance around the world; they have actively contributed to improvement in largely incremental steps. The world of the year 2000 differs in major respects from the world fifty years earlier, before the tendrils of the "curious grapevine" reached around the globe. NGOs have increased global awareness of human rights. Abuses cannot be concealed behind veils of sovereignty. Electronic communications link activists in all continents. The promise of NGOs is high, their performance is improving, and the stages on which they operate are increasing. Human rights merit the strongest support at the dawn of a new century and millennium.

Notes

1. The NGO Coalition for an International Criminal Court grew to include three hundred members; its steering committee was comprised of Amnesty International, the European Law

Students Association, FIDH (Fédération internationale des ligues des droits de l'homme), Human Rights Watch, the ICJ, the Lawyers Committee for Human Rights, No Peace Without Justice, Parliamentarians for Global Action, the Women's Caucus for Gender Justice in the ICC, and the World Federalist Movement. Without question, the establishment of the International Criminal Tribunals for the Former Yugoslavia and for Rwanda provided ample guidance for NGO networking, drafting legal language, and coalition building between NGOs and supportive states. Korey correctly notes the "highly significant role" played by the NGO coalition, whose lobbying "turned the tide" to overcome government narrowness. Funding from the Ford Foundation and the central involvement of Amnesty International and Human Rights Watch assisted the coalition as well. The Statute of the ICC was adopted by a vote of 121 in favor, 7 opposed (including the United States), and 21 abstaining. Quotes from William Korey, *NGOs and the Universal Declaration of Human Rights: "A Curious Grapevine"* (New York: St. Martin's, 1998), pp. 530–31.

2. The international campaign to ban antipersonnel land mines receives surprisingly little attention in Korey's lengthy study, despite the fact NGOs conceived and carried out one of the most effective international lobbying efforts ever mounted in the face of opposition from some of the world's most powerful governments (including the United States, Russia and China). Perhaps even more important, NGO representatives contributed substantially to the drafting of the Ottawa treaty. The rapidity with which this treaty was drafted, adopted and brought into force was a stunning display of NGO coalition-building—and a serious exception to Korey's overall argument that it is primarily through lobbying of powerful governments, especially the United States, that major advances in the protection of human rights have occurred. Korey's paragraphs on land mines stress Physicians for Human Rights, and, I believe, underestimate the central role of Human Rights Watch (about which Korey is, I must note, extremely laudatory) in building the global campaign. The overall coalition, the International Campaign to Ban Landmines, received the Nobel Peace Prize in 1998; the Ottawa treaty was adopted at Ottawa on September 18, 1997. For details, see Maxwell A. Cameron, Robert J. Lawson and Brian W. Tomlin, eds., *To Walk Without Fear: The Global Movement to Ban Landmines* (Toronto: Oxford University Press, 1998) and Korey, *NGOs and the Universal Declaration of Human Rights*, pp. 432–34.

3. Margaret E. Keck and Kathryn Sikkink, *Activists Beyond Borders* (Ithaca, N.Y.: Cornell University Press, 1998).

4. Quoted in Samuel P. Huntington, "Political Development and Political Decay," *World Politics* 17 (1965), p. 421; author's translation.

5. Susan Dicklitch, *The Elusive Promise of NGOs in Africa: Lessons from Uganda* (New York: St. Martin's, 1998), p. 8.

6. Alex de Waal, *Famine Crimes: Politics and the Disaster Relief Industry in Africa* (Oxford: James Currey in association with African Rights and the International African Institute, 1997).

7. Because of its size and express mandate, AI has often held back from initiating networks, lest it be accused of dominating them; but when asked to participate, it does so with great intensity, solid research, and mobilization of contacts. Korey points out that AI "may collaborate with other NGOs but doesn't itself organize collective action" (p. 527); its noninvolvement in the campaign against land mines and its limited involvement in the global effort against apartheid were discussed by Winston in Chapter 1. Consider also Human Rights Watch's cooperation with other NGOs on Rwanda, a country that otherwise the organization might have given scant attention to.

8. The OECD study, summarized in detail below, points to the difficulty in accurately assessing the success of capacity building.

9. For details, see Howard B. Tolley, Jr. *The International Commission of Jurists: Global Advocates for Human Rights* (Philadelphia: University of Pennsylvania Press, 1994), pp. 29–30.

10. Korey, *NGOs and the Universal Declaration of Human Rights*, p. 167. Internal rancor had been touched off by Benenson's accusation that British intelligence had penetrated AI's International Executive Committee.

11. Much more research needs to be carried out here. What is the impact, for example, of a modest seed grant that an American ambassador may provide from the special human rights discretionary fund to a small, indigenous NGO in a developing country? Such allocations, under $25,000, are infinitesimal fractions of the U.S. government budget, but may constitute major

parts of NGOs' budgets. Grants and their potential impact must be assessed in relative terms, not in absolute magnitude.

12. Korey, *NGOs and the Universal Declaration of Human Rights*, p. 343.

13. Sten-Erik Kruse, Timo Kyllonen, Satu Ojanpera, Roger C. Riddell, and Jean Vilajus, "Searching for Impact and Methods: NGO Evaluation Synthesis Study," A report prepared for the OECD/DAC Expert Group on Evaluation (*http://www.valt.helsink.fi/ids/ngo*, 1997), accessed February 11, 1999.

14. Korey, *NGOs and the Universal Declaration of Human Rights*, p. 8.

15. There was a downside to this prominence, as Clark and others have observed. Paradoxically, some harsh regimes learned to dispose of their targets more rapidly, through extrajudicial execution or "disappearance," rather than acknowledge imprisonment. But NGOs responded, with varying degrees of frustration and success, by devising rapid techniques of information sharing and mobilization to counter succeeding modes of repression.

16. Cindy A. Cohn, "The Early Harvest: Domestic Legal Changes Related to the Human Rights Committee and the Covenant on Civil and Political Rights," *Human Rights Quarterly* 13 (1991), pp. 295–321.

17. Korey, *NGOs and the Universal Declaration of Human Rights*, p. 9.

Contributors

Nicolas M. L. Bovay is Press and Publications Officer of the International Commission of Jurists and the author of numerous articles on international human rights law, conflict resolution, the former USSR, and other states of Eastern and Central Europe.

Mark K. Bromley is Deputy Program Director, International Human Rights Law Group and coordinator of the Law Group's work in Bosnia. His research focuses on war crimes issues and general human rights conditions for advocacy within UN system.

Widney Brown is Advocacy Director, Women's Rights Division, Human Rights Watch. She spent ten years as a counselor, advocate, and trainer with New York Women Against Rape, then worked on antiviolence and economic justice work. Brown practiced law for three years at the New York City Gay and Lesbian Anti-Violence Project before joining Human Rights Watch.

William D. Carmichael is Chair of the Advisory Committee, Human Rights Watch/Africa; member of the Executive Committee, Human Rights Watch; former Vice President, Ford Foundation; and former Dean, Cornell University Graduate School of Business and Public Administration.

David L. Cingranelli is Professor of Political Science, Binghamton University, State University of New York; coeditor, *Human Rights: Theory and Measurement* (1988), and editor, *Human Rights and Developing Countries* (1996). His research centers on measurement of human rights practices, the effect of the end of the Cold War on government respect for human rights, and American public policies, including workers' rights.

Ann Marie Clark teaches political science at Purdue University and is the author of *Diplomacy of Conscience: Amnesty International and Changing Human Rights Norms* (forthcoming) and numerous articles.

Susan Dicklitch teaches political science at Franklin and Marshall College and is the author of *The Elusive Promise of NGOs in Africa: Lessons from Uganda* (1998).

Brigitte Hamm, Researcher at the Institute for Development and Peace, Gerhard Mercator University, Duisburg (Germany), specializes in measurement of human rights.

Makau Mutua is Professor of Law, University at Buffalo, State University of New York; Codirector, Human Rights Center; former Associate Director of the Human Rights Program, Harvard Law School; coauthor of *Zaire: Repression as Policy*; and author of numerous articles and reports on human rights practices for NGOs.

Nathalie Prouvez, legal officer for Europe and the Central Asian states of the Commonwealth of Independent States (CIS), International Commission of Jurists, is responsible for monitoring UN, Council of Europe, and European Union human rights practices. She has taught at the Universities of Warwick, Lancaster, and Cambridge.

David L. Richards teaches political science at Missouri Southern State College. His research interests include government respect for human rights, political violence, and comparative political institutions.

T. Jeffrey Scott is a doctoral candidate in philosophy, State University of New York at Buffalo, and a former Peace Corps volunteer in Sierra Leone and Togo.

Claude E. Welch, Jr., SUNY Distinguished Service Professor, University at Buffalo, State University of New York, is Codirector, Human Rights Center; member, Human Rights Watch/Africa Advisory Committee; author, *Protecting Human Rights in Africa: Strategies and Roles of Non-Governmental Organizations* (1995); and coeditor, *Asian Perspectives on Human Rights* (1990) and *Human Rights and Development in Africa* (1984).

Morton E. Winston, Professor of Philosophy, the College of New Jersey, is chair of Amnesty International's Standing Committee on Organization and Development, former Chair of the Board of Directors of Amnesty International USA, Chair of AIUSA's Business and Economic Relations Steering Committee, and editor, *The Philosophy of Human Rights* (1988).

Laurie S. Wiseberg is cofounder and Executive Director, Human Rights Internet. She is the author of numerous studies of human rights NGOs and publisher of *Human Rights Tribune* and *For the Record: The United Nations Human Rights System* (annual CD-ROM).

Index

accountability politics, 42–43, 172, 275
ACFODE, 12, 17, 182–203, 270, 272, 277; accomplishments of, 192–95; assessment of goals, 190–92; effectiveness of, 175–77; establishment of, 187; funding of, 195; goals of, 183, 187–88; governance of, 188–91; lobbying by, 192–93; networking, 192, 203, 204
ACLU, 100, 151, 152
Action for Development. *See* ACFODE
African Commission on Human and Peoples' Rights, 124, 125, 131, 132
African Court on Human and Peoples' Rights, 128
African Development Bank, 124, 125
AI. *See* Amnesty International
AIUSA, 34, 37, 40, 41, 43, 90
Alianza Contra la Impunidad, 68
Alien Tort Claims Act, 43
Alston, Philip, 48, 177
American Association for the Advancement of Science, 245
American Civil Liberties Union. *See* ACLU
Americas Watch, 58, 64, 65, 68, 74. *See also* Human Rights Watch
Amin, Idi, 184, 185, 186
Amnesty International: 6, 7, 8, 9, 13, 25–71, 152, 159, 232, 233, 241, 248, 262, 263, 270, 271; accomplishments of, 29, 35, 86–89, 110; accountability politics by, 42–43, 106–7; advocacy by, 10, 18, 28, 32, 93; campaign against torture, 3, 42, 56, 87, 88, 89, 93, 264; campaign on Guatemala, 14, 55–71, 93; campaign on United States, 38, 40–42; challenges to, 45–51; comparison with Human Rights Watch, 15, 93, 102–11; decision-making within, 34; documentation by, 49, 50; and establishment of other NGOs, 35, 45, 169, 267; functions of, 87–89, 152–53; funding of, 11–12, 97, 108–9; goals of, 92, 266, 267; and Helsinki process, 94; infor-

mation politics of, 36–38; and international solidarity, 31; and land mines, 34; leadership in, 91–92; leverage politics, 39–42, 109–10; and links to other NGOs, 45; lobbying by, 27; mandate of, 14, 34, 47–48, 56, 263; membership of, 31, 32, 108, 276; networks, 107; organization of, 91; publicity by, 87; research by, 32, 228, 229, 232, 233; resources of, 10–12, 89–91; as social movement organization, 30; and South Africa, 33; strategies of, 93; standard setting involving, 5; symbolic politics of, 38–39; Urgent Action, 59, 60, 105, 241
Annan, Kofi, 25, 241
Anti-Slavery International for the Protection of Human Rights, 11
apartheid, 27, 33, 39, 44, 156
Argentina, 8, 25, 33, 58, 89, 95, 250, 251
Association of Progressive Communicators, 240
Association of Women Lawyers, 193
Aung San Suu Kyi, 39
Austria, 170

Baldwin, Roger, 152
Ball, Patrick, 226
Bangalore Declaration and Plan of Action, 122, 124
Barsh, Russel Lawrence, 216, 230
Basic Principles on the Independence of Judiciary, 128
Basic Principles on the Role of Lawyers, 129
Bebbington, Anthony, 216
Belgium, 170
Benenson, Peter, 25, 91, 100, 105, 108
Bernstein, Robert, 33, 72, 77, 95, 100, 108, 153, 265
Bernstein, Tom, 153
Black Consciousness Movement, 11
Body Shop, 241
Bollen, Kenneth, 231

Bonan-Dandan, Virginia, 177
boomerang pattern, 39, 40, 174, 269
Bosnia and Herzegovina, 42, 50, 126, 141–43,
  147
Bovay, Nicolas M.L., 15, 16
Brazil, 73, 174, 250, 251
briefcase NGOs, 268
Bromley, Mark K., 16, 271
Brown, Widney, 14–15
Buergenthal, Thomas, 94
Bundy, McGeorge, 251
Burundi, 141

CALDH. *See* Centro de Acción Legal y Derechos
  Humanos
Cambodia, 141–43, 147
Cameroon, 170
Canada, 72, 178
capacity building, 269
Cape Town Commitment, 135
CARE, 7, 17–18, 177, 207–21, 262, 270; accom-
  plishments of, 207–8; contrasts with civil and
  political rights NGOs, 208–9; founding of, 207;
  funding of, 207; goals of, 207–8
Carleton, David, 228
Carmichael, William D., 11, 19, 104
Carnegie Foundation, 97
Carter, President Jimmy, 11, 95
Casa Alianza, 241
CDDH, 128, 132
Center for Justice and Accountability, 43
Central African Empire, 95
Centre for Human Rights (University of Lim-
  burg/Maastricht), 123
Centre for the Independence of Judges and
  Lawyers. *See* CIJL
Centro de Acción Legal y Derechos Humanos, 68
Cerezo, Vinicio, 67
CERJ. *See* Consejo de Comunidades Étnicas
  "Runujel Junam"
Cernea, Michael, 206
Chapman, Audrey, 216
Charter 77, 94
Chechnya, 126
Children's Convention. *See* Convention on the
  Rights of the Child
Chile, 12, 58, 95, 250, 251
China, 47, 231, 253
Chirwa, Vera, 39
CIA, 271
CIJL, 120, 128–30
Cingranelli, David L., 18, 110, 231, 277
civil and political rights, 19, 33, 40, 47, 72, 76,
  119, 126; privileging of, 16, 77, 122, 155

Clark, Ann M., 5, 14, 88, 91, 93, 268
Cleaver, Harry, 242, 243
codes of conduct, 46, 180
Cohen, Cynthia Price, 5
Cohen, Ronald, 214
Cohen, Stanley, 10, 38, 41
Cold War, 16, 19, 39, 43, 44, 72, 87, 94, 95, 99,
  110, 158, 249, 257, 263
collapsed states, 263, 265
Colombia, 11, 17, 173, 178, 250
Colville, Mark, 65
Commission for Historical Clarification (Guate-
  mala), 59, 65
Commission on Human Rights, 88, 110, 123, 127,
  130, 131, 158, 168, 178, 179
Committee Against Torture, 158
Committee for the Convention on the Rights of
  the Child, 178
Committee of Experts on Development of Human
  Rights. *See* DH-DEV
Committee on Economic, Social and Cultural
  Rights, 123, 124, 130, 168, 177, 178
communications among NGOs. *See* NGOs, net-
  works of
CONAVIGUA. *See* Coordinadora Nacional de
  Viudas de Guatemala
Congo, *14–3*, 154, 186
Consejo de Comunidades Étnicas "Runujel
  Junam," 67
Convention Against Torture and Other Cruel,
  Inhuman, or Degrading Treatment or Punish-
  ment, 27, 42, 106
Convention on the Elimination of All Forms of
  Discrimination Against Women, 40, 41
Convention on the Prohibition, Stockpiling, Pro-
  duction and Transfer of Anti-Personnel Mines
  and on Their Destruction, 4, 257, 274
Convention on the Rights of the Child, 4, 11, 40,
  264, 274
conventional doctrinalists, 151, 154, 157, 262
Cook, Helena, 88
Coordinadora Nacional de Viudas de Guatemala,
  67
corruption, 129, 135
Costa Rica, 173
Council of Europe, 85, 126, 132, 143
Council on Sustainable Development, 4
Country Reports (U.S. Department of State), 228,
  229, 231
crimes against humanity, 257
Croatia, 145
Cuba, 47, 249
culture of human rights, 109, 145, 149, 264; in
  Guatemala, 66–68

Cuomo, Kerry Kennedy, 153
Czechoslovakia, 12, 28, 94

Dalai Lama, 25, 241
Dalit, 83, 105
DANIDA, 195
Davenport, Christian, 230
David Oliva, Saul, 62
death penalty, 29, 41, 88, 92, 93, 153, 263
Declaration of the Rights of Man and Citizen, 108
Declaration on Human Rights Defenders, 130, 131
Declaration on the Protection of All Persons from Being Subjected to Torture and Other Cruel, Inhuman or Degrading Treatment or Punishment, 3, 274
Declaration on the Protection of All Persons from Enforced Disappearances, 106
Declaration on the Right to Development, 218
DED, 195
Defence of Children International, 4, 5, 264
democracy, transition to, 127
DENIVA, 194
DeWaal, Ian, 268
DH-DEV, 132–33
Dicklitch, Susan, 17, 265, 268, 277
Dieng, Adama, 15, 120, 266
disappearance, 5, 14, 25, 29, 33, 34, 57–60, 65, 88, 153
distributive justice, 204, 215
domestic sovereignty, 86, 88
Donnelly, Jack, 94, 107
Dorsen, Norman, 153

East Timor, 126
economic and social rights, 16, 19, 33, 44, 47, 48, 72, 76, 77, 84, 119, 124, 135, 257–58, 276
ECOSOC, 177
Egypt, 17, 173
Ejército Secreto Anticomunista, 61
EKD, 120
El Salvador, 43, 74, 178
Enders, Thomas, 64
Ennals, Martin, 86, 87, 91, 102
Equatorial Guinea, 95
Ethiopia, 9, 210, 214
ethnic cleansing, 44, 45, 49
ethnic nationalism, 184
European Commission on Human Rights, 93, 169
European Committee of Social Rights. See CDDH
European Convention on Human Rights, 125, 132, 133, 262
European Court of Human Rights, 132
European Social Charter, 125, 126, 132

European Union, 37, 73, 79, 111, 175, 214
Everett-Green, Robert, 244
extrajudicial executions, 14, 25, 29, 33, 34, 65, 88, 153

Fanton, Jonathan, 77
FAO, 177
FAWE, 195
female circumcision. See FGM
FGM, 8, 35
FHRI, 196
FIAN, 16–17, 142, 167–80, 263, 264, 275, 276; campaigns by, 172–73, 176; establishment of, 169; governance of, 169–70; lobbying by, 177–79; mandate of, 170–71; networking of, 170, 173–74, 177, 179; research and intervention, 172–73; reports by, 178; urgent actions, 172, 180
FIDA, 196
Final Act of the Conference on Security and Cooperation in Europe. See Helsinki Accords
food, right to, 16
FoodFirst Information and Action Network. See FIAN
foot-binding, 8
Ford Foundation, 11, 19, 78, 81–82, 95, 97, 104, 120, 195, 248–60, 267, 271; establishment of human rights grants, 249–51; impact of, 254–56
Ford, President Gerald, 76
Forsythe, David P., 30
Frankel, Marvin, 153
Freedom from Hunger Campaign, 206
Freedom House, 229, 231, 232
freedom of expression, 256
Fund for Free Expression, 77, 95

Galaich, Glen, 231
GAM. See Grupo Apoyo Mutual
Gastil, Raymond D., 228, 231
gays and lesbians, 35, 45, 91
gender discrimination, 133, 142, 187
gender mainstreaming, 76
gender-based violence. See women, violence against
genocide, 25, 44, 45, 49, 149, 257
Gerardi, Bishop Juán, 68
German Evangelical Church. See EKD
Germany, 17, 170, 178; East, 29; Nazi, 144
Ghana, 28, 170
Girouard, Mark, 216
Global Campaign on Agrarian Reform, 174
Global Consultation on the Right to Development, 215

globalization, 7, 38, 43, 44, 46, 130, 135, 153, 175, 176, 257, 264
Goldberg, Justice Arthur, 33
Gray, Matthew, 239
Greece, 93
Greenberg, Jack, 153
Grupo Apoyo Mutual, 67
Guatemala, 12, 14, 43, 57–68, 88, 93
Guest, Iain, 88

Habitat International Coalition, 124, 174, 177, 179
Haiti, 43
Hamm, Brigitte, 16
Hammarberg, Thomas, 64
Havel, Václav, 39
Heaps, David, 251
Helsinki Accords, 11, 33, 72, 76, 94, 274
Helsinki Federation for Human Rights, 253
Helsinki Watch, 11, 33, 72, 74, 76, 93, 95, 97, 100, 108. *See also* Human Rights Watch
Henderson, Conway, 234
Henkin, Alice, 153
Henkin, Louis, 153
High Commissioner for Human Rights, 27, 77, 88, 130, 188, 240, 245
HIVOS, 195
Ho, Karl, 230
Honduras, 176
Hong Kong, 11
Howard, Rhoda E., 107
HRI. *See* Human Rights Internet
HRW. *See* Human Rights Watch
Human Development Report, 230
Human Rights Committee, 130, 168
Human Rights Internet, 9, 19, 245, 246
human rights monitors, 275
Human Rights Watch: 7, 9, 13, 26, 27, 154, 233, 248, 252, 255, 258, 262, 264, 270; accomplishments of, 110–11; accountability politics by, 106–7; advocacy by, 10, 74, 79–80, 98, 102; budget of, 95–97; comparison with Amnesty International, 15, 102–11; cooperation with other NGOs, 105–6, 276; and economic rights, 82, 98, 105–6, 155–56; establishment of, 11, 72, 95; funding of, 12, 78–79, 95–97, 104, 108–9, 252, 254; goals of, 74–77, 82, 98–101, 263; governance of, 77–79; and Internet, 80; leadership within, 100–101; leverage politics by, 109–10; media access, 37; networks, 107; organization of, 97–100; reports by, 37, 233; research by, 233; resources of, 95–97; strategies of, 101–2; structure of, 78; and U.S. government, 73; Women's Rights Division, 73–74, 80. *See also* Americas Watch; Helsinki Watch

human rights. *See* civil and political rights; economic and social rights; food, right to; rights of the child; women's rights
humanitarian assistance, 6, 17, 100, 104, 262, 275

IACHR. *See* Inter-American Commission on Human Rights
ICC. *See* International Criminal Court
ICCPR, 98, 153, 154, 168
ICESCR, 99, 106, 122, 126, 154, 168, 174, 177, 178, 180; optional protocol to, 17, 178–80, 264
ICJ, 6–8, 13, 15–16, 27, 88, 92, 119–40, 152, 154, 178, 253, 271; budget of, 120; and CILJ, 128–30; and complaint mechanism, 125–26; and cooperation with other entities, 124–26, 130–33, 276; and economic and social rights, 16, 121–26; goals of, 119–20, 263; governance of, 120; and impunity, 126–28; organization of, 120–21; and standard setting, 130–31; and support for national groups, 133–34
ICRC, 1, 265
IFAD, 177
ILO, 130, 194
IMF, 73, 175–76, 205
impunity, 43, 74, 119, 126–28, 130
India, 11, 101, 104, 105, 107, 176; HRW campaign on, 105–6, 267, 269. *See also* Dalit
indigenous peoples, 45, 133–34, 174, 175, 252, 254, 256, 257
Indonesia, 12, 176
information politics, 36–38, 171
INGOs. *See* NGOs
Inter-American Commission on Human Rights, 60, 64
International Campaign to Ban Landmines, 4, 14, 34, 75, 82, 83, 101, 264
International Center for Human Rights and Democratic Development, 193
International Commission of Jurists. *See* ICJ
International Committee of the Red Cross. *See* ICRC
International Covenant on Civil and Political Rights. *See* ICCPR
International Covenant on Economic, Social and Cultural Rights. *See* ICESCR
International Criminal Court, 15, 26, 27, 43, 72, 75, 83, 101, 127, 256, 257, 264, 274
International Criminal Tribunal for Rwanda, 75, 101, 127, 256, 257
International Criminal Tribunal for the Former Yugoslavia, 75, 101, 127, 256, 257
international financial institutions, 135, 159, 211, 262, 269, 277

International Fund for Agricultural Development. *See* IFAD
International Human Rights Law Group. *See* Law Group
International Labor Organization. *See* ILO
International League for Human Rights, 11
International League for the Rights of Man, 152
International Monetary Fund. *See* IMF
International Service for Human Rights, 131
internet, 18, 26, 44, 80, 238–47, 269
iron law of oligarchy, 109
Israel, 178
Italy, 11

Jackson-Vanik Amendment, 95
Jodice, David, 230
Joffe, Robert, 153
Jones, Sidney, 100

Keck, Margaret, 7, 29, 37, 39, 43, 87, 106, 109, 167, 173, 268, 269, 275
Kennedy, Senator Edward, 154
Kenya, 12, 178
Kirkpatrick, Jeane, 65
Konrad Adenauer Foundation, 195
Kopp, Adalberto, 216
Korea (North), 231
Korey, William, 5, 6, 11, 27, 89, 94, 95, 269, 274, 275
Kosovo, 49, 76, 80, 126
Kruse, Sten-Eric, 213, 214
Kryrgyzstan, 134

Laber, Jeri, 33
labor rights, 77
landmines campaign. *See* International Campaign to Ban Landmines
Landmines Convention (Convention on the Prohibition, Stockpiling, Production and Transfer of Anti-Personnel Mines and on Their Destruction), 4, 257, 274
Law Group, 16, 141–50, 152, 154, 252, 266, 271; access to justice programs, 146–47; accomplishments of, 148–49; advocacy model, 142–44; support for local NGOs and leaders, 145–46
Law of Abidjan, 124–25
Lawyers' Committee for Civil Rights under Law, 11, 74, 152, 154, 158, 159, 241, 252, 255
LDF. *See* NAACP Legal and Defense Fund
League for Industrial Democracy, 100
legal positivism, 86
Lenin peace prize, 92
leverage politics, 3, 39–42, 109, 171, 269
liberal values, 152

Liberia, 212
Limburg Principles, 123
Lopez, George A., 227
Lucas García, President Fernando Romeo, 61, 62, 63, 64
Lutheran World Federation, 174

Maastricht Guidelines, 123
MacArthur Foundation, 78, 97
MacBride, Sean, 92, 108, 110, 265, 266
MAI, 174
Malaysia, 11
Mandela, Nelson, 14, 156
mass media, 37
Matembe, Miria, 187, 195
Mathews, Jessica T., 26
McCann, John, 91
McCormick, James M., 234
McDermott, Niall, 266
McGrew, Anthony, 46
Médécins sans frontières, 210, 275
Mehta, Arun, 242
Mejía Victores, General Oscar, 65, 66
Mennonite Central Committee, 195
Mexico, 8, 73, 173, 178; Zapatista uprising in, 242–43
Minnesota Lawyers Human Rights Committee, 88
Mitchell, Neil J., 234
MNCs, 42, 44–46, 73, 174, 179, 262, 264, 269, 277
Mokken scale analysis, 228
Montesquieu, Baron, 265
Morocco, 12, 141, 146
Multilateral Agreement on Investment. *See* MAI
Multinational corporations. *See* MNCs
Museveni, President Yoweri, 183
Mutua, Makau, 16, 77, 98, 107, 262

NAACP Legal Defense Fund, 151
Nadelmann, Ethan, 4, 262
NAFTA, 101
Namibia, 9
Naresh, Suman, 238
Narula, Smita, 106
National Endowment for Democracy, 271
National Resistance Movement, 183
NAWOU, 193, 194, 196
Neier, Aryeh, 72, 95, 100, 108–10, 265, 277
networks, 7, 12, 13, 15, 17, 34, 170, 174, 273
NGOs: accomplishments of, 225–37, 272–76; accountability politics of, 36, 172, 265, 275; advocacy by, 10, 28, 269; assistance to victims, 10; budgets of, 276–77; capacity building, 133, 276; challenges to, 56–57; and civil and political rights, 47, 152–59; development-oriented,

NGOs (*continued*)
208–12; evaluation of, 212–17; functions of, 9–10, 43, 182, 210–12, 264–65; funding of, 252–53, 267; goals of, 3–7, 156, 182, 262–68; as information providers, 5–6, 8, 10, 26, 36, 265, 275; leadership in, 277; leverage politics of, 36, 171, 265; links among, 276; lobbying by, 6; mandates of, 155–57, 277; membership in, 153–55, 276; networks among, 7–8, 12–13, 17, 30, 173, 268–69; objectives of, 226; obstacles to, 186; proliferation of, 1; as promoters of rights, 264, 273; as providers of assistance and protection, 6, 264, 273; and relations to donors, 186; research by, 9; research on, 18, 216–17, 277–78; resources of, 10–12, 269–72; as social movements, 30; standard setting by, 3, 264, 274; strategies of, 7–10, 226, 268–69; success of, 12–13, 222–27; symbolic politics of, 36, 265. *See also* ACFODE; Amnesty International; CARE; FIAN; Human Rights Watch; ICJ; Law Group; Oxfam
Nicaragua, 63, 141, 142, 143, 147
Nigeria, 9, 141, 178, 214
Nobel Peace Prize, 33, 34, 60, 83, 89, 92, 152
norms, 42–43; evolution of, 4–5
NOVIB, 104, 120, 271
Nuremberg Tribunal, 126
NURRU, 195
Nyerere, Julius, 204

OAS, 61, 67, 85, 98, 262
OAU, 125, 128, 131
Obote, Milton, 184, 185, 186
ODHAG. *See* Oficina de Derechos Humanos del Arzobispado de Guatemala
OECD, 174, 273, 274
Oficina de Derechos Humanos del Arzobispado de Guatemala, 68
Open Society Institute, 100, 109, 271, 277
Optical Disk System, 245
Organisation Mondiale Contre la Torture, 241
Organization for Economic Cooperation and Development. *See* OECD
Organization for Security and Cooperation in Europe, 79
Organization of African Unity. *See* OAU
Organization of American States. *See* OAS
Osviovitch, Jay, 97
Ottawa Convention. *See* Landmines Convention
Oxfam, 7, 17–18, 104, 177, 195, 204–21, 262, 263, 270; accomplishments of, 206–7; contrasts with civil and political rights NGOs, 208–9; founding of, 205; funding of, 205; goals of, 206

Pagnucco, Ron, 217
Pakistan, 73
Paraguay, 178
paralegals, 134
Pasquerello, Thomas, 231
Pathfinder, 195
Peoples' Decade for Human Rights Education, 174
Peru, 178, 232
Philippines, 12, 17, 173–75, 178
PHR. *See* Physicians for Human Rights
physical integrity rights, 229
Physical Terror Scale, 231
Physicians for Human Rights, 27, 252
Pinochet, Augusto, 257
Poe, Steven C., 230, 234
Poland, 12
Political Terror Scale, 228
Population Concern, 195
Portugal, 11, 28, 125
poverty, 133
prisoners of conscience, 6, 10, 14, 25, 28, 29, 38, 39, 55, 57, 60, 88, 90, 92, 95, 102, 105, 153, 156, 263, 275
Procedural Aspects of International Law Institute, 152
Prouvez, Nathalie, 15, 16
Public Group to Assist the Implementation of the Helsinki Accords, 94

Ralph, Regan E., 74
Reagan, President Ronald, 95, 158
refugees, 45, 252
relativism, 47
Renteln, Alison Dundas, 168
Richards, David L., 18, 110, 277
Riddell, Roger, 216
Rieff, David, 107
right to development, 217, 218
right to food, 169, 180
rights of the child, 133
Ríos Montt, General Efraín, 14, 58, 63–66
Ripp, Rudolph K., 92, 93
Robinson, Mary, 77, 179
Rockefeller Foundation, 271
Roosevelt, Eleanor, 27, 86
Roth, Ken, 100, 109, 111
rule of law, 15, 16, 119, 135, 253, 275
Russia, 253
Rwanda, 49, 104, 126, 186

Safe Motherhood, 196
Sakharov, Andrei, 11, 39
Sané, Pierre, 91, 109

Saudi Arabia, 154
Scoble, Harry, 9, 43
Scott, T. Jeffrey, 17, 18, 100, 270
Senegal, 9
shame, mobilization of, 107
SIDA, 120, 195
Sierra Leone, 126, 212
Sikkink, Kathryn, 7, 29, 37, 39, 43, 87, 106, 109, 167, 173, 268, 269, 275
slavery, 7
Smillie, Ian, 210, 212, 213
Smith, Bradford K., 254
Smith, Jackie, 217
social movement organization, 29–30
Soros, George, 100, 154, 271, 277; foundations, 267
South Africa, 11, 13, 27, 33, 43, 58, 170, 274; Ford Foundation grants in, 253–54, 256
sovereignty, 264
Soviet Union. See USSR
Spain, 11
Special Rapporteur on the Independence of Judges and Lawyers, 129
Special Rapporteur on the Right to Education, 179
Sri Lanka, 178
standard setting, 3, 19, 86, 88, 130, 264, 273
Steiner, Henry, 107, 156, 157
Stohl, Michael, 228
Structural Adjustment Programs, 47
Subcommission on the Promotion and Protection of Human Rights (formerly the Subcommission on the Prevention of Discrimination and Protection of Minorities), 110, 123, 130
Swedish International Development Cooperation Agency. See SIDA
Symbolic politics, 38–39, 171

Tanzania, 80, 170
TASO, 196
Tate, C. Neal, 234
Taylor, Celia, 211
Taylor, Charles, 49, 230
Terre des Hommes, 124, 178, 179
Thailand, 11
Thakur, Ramesh, 87
Thatcher, Prime Minister Margaret, 158
Thomas, Dorothy Q., 73, 74
Thomas, Franklin, 252
Tolley, Howard E., Jr., 8, 92
torture, 5, 25, 29, 33, 60, 65, 88, 92, 93, 153
torture convention. See Convention Against Torture and Other Cruel, Inhuman, or Degrading Treatment or Punishment

transnational corporations. See MNCs
Truth and Reconciliation Commission (South Africa), 43
Tunisia, 12
Turkey, 73, 78, 176
Tvedt, Terje, 212

U Thant, 3
UDHR, 3, 25, 27, 28, 33, 47, 86, 88, 92, 93, 106, 134, 149, 153, 167, 179, 241, 254, 262
Uganda, 12, 17, 62, 73, 95, 182–97; NGO operations within, 185–87; political milieu, 183–85
Uganda Development Bank, 195
Uganda People's Defence Force, 186
Uganda Rural Development and Training Program, 194
Uganda Women's Network, 193
UN, 27, 49, 73, 111; Charter of, 3, 85; and Guatemala, 65. See also Commission on Human Rights; ICCPR; ICESCR; UDHR
UNDP, 177, 195, 212
UNESCO, 130
UNHCHR. See High Commissioner for Human Rights
UNHCR, 81, 130
UNHRA, 196
UNICEF, 194, 195
Union of International Associations, 1
United Nations High Commissioner for Refugees. See UNHCR
United States, 37, 72; and Guatemala, 62–65; human rights violations in, 38, 40, 75; right to food in, 173; treaty obligations of, 142
Universal Declaration of Human Rights. See UDHR
University of Minnesota, 245
Untouchables. See Dalit
Urban Morgan Institute on Human Rights, 123
Urgent Action, 59, 60, 87, 90, 105, 172, 241
USAID, 154
USSR, 27, 33, 44, 72, 76, 78, 127; collapse of, 274

Van Boven, Theo, 8
Venezuela, 173, 250
Vienna Conference. See World Conference on Human Rights
Vienna Declaration and Programme of Action, 48, 103
Vienna Plus Five International NGO Forum, 175, 179
Vietnam Veterans of America Foundation, 34
Villagrán Kramer, Vice President Francisco, 62, 63
voluntarism, 185, 188, 189, 190

VVAF. *See* Vietnam Veterans of America Foundation

Washington Office on Latin America, 61–62
Weaver, Sigourney, 153
Wendel-Blunt, Dierdre, 230
Williams, Jody, 34, 82
Windfuhr, Michael, 170
Winston, Morton E., 8, 13, 87, 92, 93, 107, 269, 277
Wiseberg, Laurie, 9, 19, 43, 269
women, violence against, 45, 73, 75, 186
Women, World Conference on, 240
Women's Convention. *See* Convention on the Elimination of All Forms of Discrimination Against Women
women's rights, 17, 252, 254, 256, 257; as division of Human Rights Watch, 73–74; measurement of, 230; suffrage, 8

Working Group on Enforced or Involuntary Disappearances, 64
Working Group on the Right to Development, 211
World Bank, 48, 73, 88, 176, 205, 206
World Conference on Human Rights (Vienna, 1993), 25, 48, 75, 88, 99, 121, 144, 178, 240
World Food Programme, 177
World Food Summit, 170, 179
World Vision, 195
World War II, 49, 258, 262
World Wide Web, 239, 242, 244–45

Yemen, 141, 146
Young, Iris Marion, 49

Zakaria, Fareed, 44
Zimbabwe, 170

Acknowledgments

Preparing an edited book is at least as challenging, time consuming, and pleasurable as writing a single-authored work. Different perspectives emerge; contrasting styles clash; areas of overlap appear—and all must be revised into a reasonably consistent framework. The rewards are immense, nonetheless. Only by drawing upon experts can scholarship advance. The preceding pages carry the words of several of the world's foremost specialists on human rights, much more than one person could accomplish in a similar period.

This volume represents a paragon, in my view, of how edited academic books should emerge. The official starting point came in early October 1998, when I convened a small workshop in Buffalo, thanks to financial and staff support from the Baldy Center for Law and Social Policy at the University at Buffalo, State University of New York. Initial drafts of some of the chapters were presented at that time. In the following months, the participants and several new contributors took time away from their NGO and/or academic duties to refine their ideas and write the final versions of their chapters. The book grew beyond its originally intended bounds, and some highly worthy essays had to be dropped, with deep regret on my part and those of the authors, very late in the process.

I am immensely grateful to many persons for their assistance, and in particular to Laura Mangan, Rebecca Roblee, and David Engel of the Baldy Center for their role in the workshop; to Nicole Deitelhoff for valuable research assistance and conceptualization; and to Jeff Scott for his tireless checking of obscure footnotes, thoughtful comments, and his parsing of complex syntax. I was inspired throughout the many months of preparation by University at Buffalo colleagues who have made substantial marks in the field of human rights, including Alison des Forges, Julia Hall, Makau Mutua, and Virginia Leary. *NGOs and Human Rights* was improved by the helpful comments of Felice Gaer, Rhoda Howard, Mahmood Monshipouri, and Jackie Smith on the prospectus and initial draft. The careful reading many have given to this book does not, of course, relieve me, as editor, of final responsibility for *NGOs and Human Rights*—a responsibility I gladly accept.